The German Language Today

The German Language Today describes in detail the main linguistic features of the language and the wide variety of speech forms and vocabulary existing within the German-speaking community. This clear and accessible text provides a complete introduction to basic linguistic terms and descriptions of language structures and to socio-linguistic and linguistic topics as they relate to the German language, and illustrates them widely with examples and texts.

The German Language Today describes the sounds, inflectional processes, syntactic structures, competing forms and different layers of words in the language. Topics covered include:

- The distribution of German and its dialects
- The linguistic consequences of German reunification
- Language change and the adoption of new vocabulary
- The application of modern linguistic concepts to German, incorporating the findings of the latest German linguistic research.

The book has been written with the specific needs of students in mind. It will be invaluable to students of modern German linguistics or modern German society, as well as other language courses, and will be a useful reference resource for postgraduates and teachers of German.

Charles V. J. Russ is Reader in German and Linguistics at the University of York. His other books include *Studies in Historical German Phonology* and the edited collections *The Dialects of Modern German* and *Foreign Influences on German: Past and Present*.

The German language today

A linguistic introduction

Charles V. J. Russ

London and New York

In memory of Adrian Battye (1955–93),
co-author of *The French Language Today*,
a trusted friend and colleague, greatly missed.

First published 1994
by Routledge
11 New Fetter Lane, London EC4P 4EE

Simultaneously published in the USA and Canada
by Routledge
29 West 35th Street, New York, NY 10001

© 1994 Charles V. J. Russ

Typeset in Times by Florencetype Ltd, Stoodleigh, Devon

Printed and bound in Great Britain by Clays Ltd, St. Ives plc

Printed on acid-free paper

British Library Cataloguing in Publication Data
A catalogue record for this book is available from the
British Library

Library of Congress Cataloging in Publication Data
Applied for

ISBN 0–415–10438–6 (hbk) 0–415–10439–4 (pbk)

Contents

QUGL
9097442
QUGL
6/1/95

Preface

The shift of emphasis in many courses dealing with German language from the historical and philological to the modern has not been matched with the provision of teaching material. This book is an attempt, therefore, to focus attention on the rich variety of modern language use in the German-speaking countries. It is proper that at this time after the unification of Germany attention should turn to the state of the language. In Chapter 1 a number of general issues concerning the nature of German, linguistic norms, the extent of German and its historical development are aired and in Chapter 2 the wide range of variation in German from spoken to technical and group language via dialects and archaic language is sketched out. Chapters 3 and 4 deal with the very important fact that German in Austria and Switzerland has special characteristics. Chapter 5 deals with the vexed question, albeit now historical, of the language in the former German Democratic Republic (GDR). Having established something of the nature of German and how it varies within certain defined limits, we then press on to deal with the linguistic description of German phonology (Chapter 6), orthography (Chapter 7), grammar, including morphology and syntax (Chapter 8), word formation (Chapter 9) and vocabulary (Chapter 10). The linguistic terminology is kept as simple as possible and beginners will, I hope, be able to tackle these chapters as terms are defined as they are introduced. For more advanced students there are some discussions of different points of view, treatment of controversial topics and of more recent developments in theory. It is also shown, particularly in Chapters 8, 9 and 10, that language is never constant and is always evolving. A fairly advanced knowledge of German is expected and most of the examples are unglossed, except where it seemed appropriate to give an English equivalent. Inevitably there are omissions, as regards both theory and topics discussed, but in a book such as this that is inevitable. One of the main features of this book is that illustrative texts are given in Chapters 1–5 and Chapter 7. These are provided with a minimum of explanatory notes and lend themselves to further study with or without a teacher. General readers will be able to tackle Chapters 1–5 and may then feel able to cope with the rest. The prime readership will be university students, or sixth formers, with a good knowledge of German who want to find out more about this elusive phenomenon, the German language today.

This book has benefited from many years of teaching and researching German and the linguistics of German. I am grateful to Tim Buck, Professor Walter Haas (Fribourg/Freiburg) and Professor Peter Wiesinger (Vienna), who read and commented on parts of the manuscript. My thanks are also due to Professor Martin Durrell and an anonymous reader from Routledge who read the whole manuscript and made critical and pertinent comments. I have tried to accommodate all these as best I can. The remaining faults are my own. I am also very grateful to my wife, Jenny, and sons Jamie and Thomas. They have had to bear the brunt of the stress a project like this brings with it.

Charles V.J. Russ
York

Abbreviations

acc.	accusative	MHG	Middle High German
ADJ	adjective	N(P)	noun (phrase)
ART	article	NEG	negative
dat.	dative	NHG	New High German
DEM	demonstrative	nom.	nominative
DET	determiner	nt.	neuter
ECG	East Central German	NUM	numeral
Engl.	English	obj.	object
ENHG	Early New High German	OHG	Old High German
		P(P)	preposition (phrase)
exp.	expansive	pers.	person
f./fem.	feminine	pl.	plural
gen.	genitive	prep.	preposition
INDEF	indefinite	pres.	present
INTER	interrogative	sg.	singular
Lat.	Latin	subj.	subject
LG	Low German	UG	Upper German
m./masc.	masculine	V(P)	verb (phrase)

1 Introduction

1.1 WHAT IS GERMAN?

(Ammon 1991: 19–31; Barbour and Stevenson 1990: 1–14)

This fundamental question is capable of both a simple and a complicated answer. On the simple level it can be answered by a statement such as 'the language used in Germany'. From one point of view this is undeniably true, but it is really only part of the answer. Since, however, German is used not only in Germany but also in Austria, Switzerland, Luxemburg and other countries within Europe and beyond (see 1.3), German cannot be limited to the language of one country. We might, therefore, modify our statement and say that German is the sole language used in Germany and Austria. This, while again true, excludes the important fact that it is also used in other countries, albeit with a different status. In Germany and Austria it is the sole national language, whereas in Switzerland it is used alongside French, Italian and Romansh and in Luxemburg it competes with French and Luxemburgish. Thus although there is a core area where German is used, the edges of this area are rather fuzzy.

Yet in thinking we cannot state exactly where German is used we have begged the question as to what German is and have assumed that we know what its nature is. On the one hand, written German has a standard orthography, grammar and vocabulary; on the other hand, it varies along a number of parameters (see Chapter 2). Regional differences, for instance, which have become firmed up within different national boundaries are very influential. We attempt to show this nationally determined nature of German in Chapters 3 and 4 for Austria and Switzerland. Chapter 5 discusses the case which might have developed fully if there had not been the reunification of

East and West Germany in 1990. The main descriptions of standard German (see 1.2) form the basis for Chapters 6–10.

German is also used as a spoken medium, and here standards and norms become more diffuse and difficult to pin down, although there is a recommended model of pronunciation (see 6.2). In many speech communities, what is regarded by the speakers themselves as spoken German is really a regional variety which differs considerably from written German. At its most extreme this can be illustrated by Low German (LG), Swiss German and Luxemburgish. Here the question raises itself as to whether these varieties can still be counted as German or are really separate languages. The answer to this question is not at all clear. Luxemburgish is usually regarded as a separate language, while Low German is still considered to be a dialect of German. Luxemburgish is the mother tongue of the majority of Luxemburgers, whereas Low German is the mother tongue of only part of the speakers in North Germany. Swiss German dialects, which are universally used in German Switzerland at the spoken level, would probably not be regarded by their speakers as separate languages. In all these situations, however, written German is used as an overarching variety spanning these spoken varieties. In Luxemburg this function is shared with French. However, this overarching variety is lacking, for example, in Alsace-Lorraine, Danish North Slesvig and the United States, where varieties which seem similar or related to German are used. In this book we shall include spoken regional varieties of German within our definition of German, although we obviously cannot describe them in detail (for detailed descriptions see Russ 1990). Here again we have a clear centre with a fuzziness around the edges.

If it is not clear where the borders of German lie or where the standard shades into related regional varieties, it is also not clear how far German extends back into the past. Users of written German do not have much difficulty in reading literary works produced in the past. Nineteenth-century authors such as Fontane, Grillparzer, Keller, Meyer and Storm are taught in schools and read by ordinary members of the speech community. Even eighteenth-century authors such as Goethe, Lessing, Schiller and Wieland can be understood without much difficulty, although their language differs in some respects from that of the present day. However, most prose works from the seventeenth century, for example Grimmelhausen's *Simplicissimus* (1669), are published in modernized editions for the general public. On the other hand, many seventeenth-century hymns are still sung with the original grammar and vocabulary, although the spelling has been modernized (see pp. 40f.). The period from the second half of the seventeenth century to the first quarter of the eighteenth seems to be a crucial time for the development of the modern standard. Again the boundary is fuzzy, being gradual rather than abrupt. The present-day German language is thus the result of various historical factors in its development. We cannot fully understand it unless we examine its geographical extent and its historical development. A brief historical survey of the development of German is given in 1.4.

Since our concern in this book is with the German language today we might rephrase our initial question as 'What is present-day German?' and answer it in the following ways:

1 Present-day German is the continuation, albeit with changes, of a language which has been used since the fourth and fifth centuries AD in a wide area, whose central portion lies between the Rhine in the west and the Oder in the east, the Alps in the south and the area north of the river Schlei in the north. This core area has expanded and contracted over the centuries. Its greatest extent was in the nineteenth century, when German was used in large parts of eastern Europe, millions of German speakers had arrived in the United States and Germany possessed colonies in Africa. Nowadays most speakers in eastern Europe have fled or their language has been assimilated to other languages, the German of the immigrants to North America has largely been assimilated to English and the colonies in Africa have been lost.

2 Present-day German comprises a written and a spoken variety. The former has developed over the centuries to a standardized form which, despite some variation, is understood in all the countries where it has official or semi-official status. It is also the basis for teaching German as a foreign language. The spoken variety of German is a continuum ranging from varieties which are very close to the standard to varieties which, linguistically, are sufficiently far removed from the standard that in some circumstances they can be regarded as separate languages.

3 Present-day German is also a language which is not standing still. It has considerable time-depth, having developed over the centuries, and it is still evolving. The present-day written language emerged only in the period from the second half of the seventeenth century to the first quarter of the eighteenth century. We have tried to illustrate this development in 2.4 and changes in progress in the relevant sections in Chapters 6–10.

To sum up: present-day German is a language which exists in written and spoken form, its main area of use being central Europe. The spoken form comprises a range of varieties from those near the written language to those quite far removed from it, differentiated regionally. The written form is comparatively stable and its users can understand texts from as far back in time as the eighteenth century.

1.2   WHAT 'NORMS' EXIST FOR GERMAN?

The codification, that is the recording of which forms and construc- tions in German are acceptable, is represented by the Duden volumes and other available grammars and dictionaries. By custom and long- standing usage the 'rules' of grammar and style set out in these works have become perceived as a norm which should be followed in teaching in school and when using the written language in general. In the countries where German is used there is no linguistic academy as exists in France to enforce such linguistic norms, nor is there any freedom for publishers to develop a house style as in Britain. Instead, a commercial firm, with the trade name, *Duden*, has been charged with overseeing and propagating the orthographic norm for German which was officially agreed in 1901. The name Duden goes back to Konrad Duden (1829–1911), whose *Vollständiges Orthographisches Wörterbuch der deutschen Sprache* was first published in 1880. *Duden* has grasped this opportunity very successfully and produced a num- ber of works, not only describing German but also advising and prescribing linguistic usage. All this has been further complicated by the existence of two German states from 1949 to 1990 with a parallel institution, both using the name *Duden*, one in the west in Mannheim and the other in the east in Leipzig, which have shown divergent forms to some extent (see 5.2.1). In August 1991 the *Duden Rechtschreibung*, the twentieth edition, was published, the first *Duden* for a united Germany since the thirteenth edition of 1947. In 1950 the spelling in *Duden* was recognized as being authoritative in cases of uncertainty by the *Kulturministerkonferenz* ('Conference of Education Ministers') of West Germany: 'In Zweifelsfällen wird bis auf weiteres die Schreibweise des "Duden" als richtunggebend ange- geben' ('In cases of doubt the orthography of "Duden" will be taken as authoritative'). This decision was confirmed in 1955. The *Duden* gradually expanded its range of language reference works so that it amounted to four volumes by 1959 and by the 1960s it had increased to nine, reaching the round figure of ten in 1972. An eleventh volume, *Redewendungen und sprichwörtliche Redensarten*, was published in 1992. By implication the authority of Duden as representing the orthographic norm for German has been extended, by unofficial implication, to other areas of language such as grammar and word formation, although Duden is at pains to deny this. The working and structure of the committee responsible for the language reference works (the *Dudenredaktion*) are treated by Drosdowski (1968, 1985) and the history and development of Duden feature in Russ (1980), Hatherall (1986) and Sauer (1988).

Although orthography is strictly normalized, the other levels of language allow a certain amount of variation, usually nationally determined. Pronunciation, for example, shows considerable variation, despite the setting up and propagation of a standard 'stage pronunciation' (*Bühnenaussprache*), codified by Theodor Siebs (1862–1941) and a committee of mostly North German speakers. The pronunciation recommended by Siebs was set up as a standard in 1898, not only for the stage but for public speaking in general, later being applied to broadcasting. In 1922 the title of his book was amended to *Deutsche Bühnenaussprache-Hochsprache* because of its wider application. In 1958 it became simply *Deutsche Hochsprache*. The edition of 1969, entitled *Deutsche Aussprache, Reine und gemäßigte Hochlautung*, allowed alternatives for the first time. No further edition has appeared.

The common core of inflectional and syntactic patterns together with the basic vocabulary is codified in the *Duden* volumes and set up as 'normative' not only for the united Federal Republic of Germany but also for Austria, Switzerland and some other countries. Of the eleven volumes, one of the most interesting is the grammar. Although a pre-1945 grammar existed, the first post-war edition (Grebe *et al.* 1959) was really a completely new grammar. It was normative, using terms such *weniger gebräuchlich*, *seltener*, *älter*, *mundartlich*, *umgangssprachlich*, *falsch*, *fehlerhaft*, *nicht anerkannt* to describe forms and constructions which were not acceptable to the editors. Also many of the authorities (*die großen Leitbilder*) cited were from the nineteenth and even the eighteenth century. The second edition of the *Duden Grammatik* (Grebe *et al.* 1966) was more explicit on norms, with more emphasis on description of the present-day language. The third edition of the *Duden Grammatik* (Grebe *et al.* 1973) was a grammar of the written language. It recognized an 'open' norm, for example it allowed variant forms, and supported its statements of use by empirical studies. The fourteenth edition of the *Duden Grammatik* (Drosdowski *et al.* 1984) had a new editor-in-chief and was linguistically more complex. It was intended to be descriptive as well as prescriptive, continuing the acceptance of the 'open' norm. Russ (1991) shows in more detail how the different editions of the grammar evolved in their treatment of the following: (1) the pronunciation of postvocalic /r/; (2) the mood of the verb in clauses of purpose after *damit*; (3) the type of subjunctive used after *als* (*ob*); and (4) the subjunctive with *würde*.

The vocabulary of present-day German has been codified and standardized in the two main dictionaries, the *Wörterbuch der deutschen Gegenwartssprache* (1964–76), produced by a team in East Berlin and *Duden Großes Wörterbuch* (1976–81). One-volume dictionaries such as Mackensen (1952) and Wahrig (1966) appeared and were revised regularly. In Austria this role was taken by the *Österreichisches Wörterbuch*, primarily an orthographic dictionary, which first appeared in 1951. Wiegand (1985: 190–224) provides a useful survey and copious bibliography of dictionaries since 1945. It is also at the level of vocabulary, however, where much variation exists, with different designations for one concept or thing, for example 'butcher', *Schlachter* in North Germany, *Fleischer* in East Germany, *Metzger* in South Germany and Switzerland, and *Fleischhauer* in Austria (Eichhoff 1977–8).

1.3   THE EXTENT OF GERMAN

German is used as an official language in three main countries: the united Federal German Republic, Austria and Switzerland. The situation in the Grand Duchy of Luxemburg (pop. 369,500) is complicated by the presence of French and will be mentioned separately. German is also used as a minority language in Belgium, France, The Netherlands, Denmark, Italy and eastern Europe. There are copious lexical differences between texts produced in those countries where German is an official language and which show differing political, economic and social structures. From 1949 to 1989–90 there was the additional factor of the official use of German in a separate German state, the German Democratic Republic. During that period linguists interpreted these differences either as a sign that there were four national languages or that there were four national varieties of one language. Any discussion of the problem was unfortunately intricately bound up with the political climate of the time. The pendulum swung in both German states between each view, with different linguists setting differing emphases. Some West German linguists tended to regard German in their own country as the base line, with the other varieties deviating from it. This expressed itself in the following ways. First, non-West German usage was labelled as *Besonderheiten* ('special features'), for example Rizzo-Baur (1962), Magenau (1962, 1964), Wacker (1964), Kaiser (1969–70) and Riedmann (1972). Duden produced a whole series of works under this label. Second, lexicographic practice as reflected in West German dictionaries labelled specific forms as being *österreichisch*, *schweizerisch* (or until 1990 DDR) while limiting the label *Bundesrepublik Deutschland* to words denoting West German institutions. Third, the word *Binnendeutsch* (originally a geographical term, coined by Theodor Frings, to designate the dialects in the interior of Germany, away from the sea), was used for this West German, by implication, central variety. It can be glossed 'Inner or Internal German'. Some East German linguists, but by no means all, tended to emphasize the differentation of four national varieties, for example Bock *et al.* (1973). Dieckmann (1989) traced the ups and downs of the different views. In the later years the linguistic establishment in the GDR emphasized more the common bonds between the different varieties of German (Fleischer *et al.* 1987). Fleischer (1989) wanted to balance the differentiation of German with convergent developments, for example parallel development in the language of sport. More discussion on this topic can be found in 5.2.6.

To correct this imbalance in favour of West German usage Clyne (1984: 1) applied the adjective 'pluricentric' to German, 'a language with several national varieties, each with its own norms'. Von Polenz (1988) took up this term in an endeavour to dispense with the word *Binnendeutsch*. According to Clyne (1992) German can be seen as consisting of national varieties such as Austrian Standard German, Swiss Standard German and German Standard German for the German of the united Federal German Republic. Detailed descriptions of the differences between the varieties will be exemplified in Chapters 3, 4 and 5.

The strength of German in relationship to other languages with regard to the number of speakers is difficult to gauge. Ammon (1991: 40–3) shows how different sources give different figures, without it being possible to achieve clarity on the relative number of speakers or, by extension, the position of German. This varies from sixth position with 100 million speakers in 1964 to seventh position in 1984 with 119 million speakers. In 1981 German was tenth in the ranking of the world's languages. The following list gives an overview of the distribution of German and an idea of some of the numbers of German speakers:

1 As sole official language:
    Germany 80 million (79,810,377)
    Austria 7.5 million (7,586,400)
2 As one of several official languages:
    Switzerland 6.5 million (6,567,000)
    Luxemburg 369,500
    Belgium 100,000–200,000
3 As a minority language in a particular region:
    (a) Western Europe
        France 1.2 million
        Italy 290,000
        Denmark 20,000
    (b) Eastern Europe
        Former Soviet Union 1,103,522
        Poland 1.1 million
        Hungary 220,000
        Romania 200,000
        Former Czechoslovakia 61,917
4 Outside Europe:
    United States 1,610,000
    Brazil 250,000–1,500,000
    Canada 438,680
    Namibia 20,000

The status of German in Austria and Switzerland is dealt with in Chapters 3 and 4 respectively. In the rest of this section short portraits of German in Luxemburg, Belgium, France, Italy and Denmark will be given. Strauss (1981) surveys the role of German as a minority language in western Europe. Copious bibliographical references are given in Born and Jakob (1990).

1 *Luxemburg* (Ammon 1991: 60–5; Hoffmann 1979, 1988, 1992; Newton 1987, 1990). The parliament of the Grand Duchy of Luxemburg made Luxemburgish (*Lëtzebuergesch*) an official language alongside French and German in 1984. This was the first time that this language, historically a Moselle Franconian variety, achieved official status. It is also the mother-tongue of the Luxemburgers. French and German, although co-dominant official languages which are introduced and taught in schools, are really foreign languages. Lëtzebuergesch and German are linguistically so closely related that it is easier to learn German than French. Between 1940 and 1944 Luxemburg was annexed to the Third Reich and

exposed to a policy of aggressive Germanization. After 1945 German, understandably, lost some ground to French, although the latter showed no tendency of becoming the only official language. The situations, or domains, where the three different languages, French, German and Lëtzebuergesch are used can most easily be seen from Table 1.1 which also differentiates between written and spoken usage (from Newton 1987: 155). The parentheses indicate only partial usage.

Table 1.1 The distribution of language use in Luxemburg

	Govern-ment	Adminis-tration	Courts	Police	Schools	Army	Church	News-papers/Lectures	
French	+	+	+	+	+	+	(+)	+	written
French	(+)	(+)	(+)	(+)	+	(+)	(+)	+	spoken
German	(+)			(+)	+		+	+	written
German				(+)	+		(+)	+	spoken
Luxem-burgish	(+)				(+)		(+)	(+)	written
Luxem-burgish	+	+	+	+	+	+	+	+	spoken

The following text is a Luxemburgish version of Luke 2: 1–14:

Déi nämlecht Deeg awer koum en Uerder eraus vum Keeser Augustus, fir uechter d'ganzt Räich d'Leit zu zielen [= zählen]. 'T war fir d'éischt, datt sou eng [= eine] Schätzéng koum, – dei Zäit, wou de Quirinus d'Prowënz vu Syrien ënner sech hat. All Mënsch goung sech opschreiwe loossen, jiddereen a séng [= seine] Stat. Och de Jousef koum aus Galiläa, vun der Stat Nazareth erop, an d'Davidsstat, déi Bethlehem heescht. Hie war vum David sénger Familjen. Duer goung hien [= er] sech melle mat sénger Braut, mam Maria [= mit dem, female names are always neuter], dat ewell an aneren Emstänn [= in anderen Umständen] war. Nu sin awer déi Deeg, wéi s'op Bethlehem waren, grad an déi Zäit gefall, wou d'Maria sollt nidderkommen. Sou huet en säin éischte Jong op d'Welt bruecht. Et huet e gewéckelt an eng Krëpp geluegt. Well de Wiirt hat keng Platz méi. Ma am selwechte Streech waren déi Nuecht Hiirden um Feld. Si hu gewaacht bei hirer Häärd. Hei stoung op eemol en Engel vun Eiser Herrgott vrun hinnen. Eiser Herrgott säi Liicht huet ëm se geschéngt, an't as eng freeschlech Angscht an se gefuer. Ma den Engel sot en: 'Fäärt dach nët! Kuckt, hei bréngen ech iech eng grouss Freed, fir d'Leit alleguer: Haut as iech an der Davidsstat den Erléiser gebuer. 'T as Christus, den Här! An dat hei soll iech en Zeeche sin: Dir fant e Kand, t' as gewéckelt an't läit an enger Krëpp!' An eenzock war rondrëm eng Onmass Engelen aus dem Himmel. Déi hun dem Hergott säi Luef gesongen: 'Éier Eiser Herrgott am Himmel, a Fridd op der Welt fir all déi, di Eiser Herrgott gär huet!'

(Christophory 1974: 162)

2   *Belgium* (Ammon 1991: 66–71; Barbour and Stevenson 1990: 224–30; Born and Dickgießer 1989: 39–47). German is used in a corridor along the eastern border with Germany. The area comprises six zones, in two of which, Eupen and Malmédy, German has an official status which was granted in 1963 and confirmed in 1970. Most of the area was given to Belgium in 1920 after World War I. No census figures for the number of speakers has been available since 1947, so the figure of 100,000–200,000 has to be rather uncertain. In Eupen and Malmédy there are 67,600 users of German. Here the spoken language is a German dialect, Low Franconian in the north and Moselle Franconian in the south. There are German schools and German is used in the mass media, for example the newspaper *Grenz-Echo* and radio broadcasts since 1975 from Eupen. In the other areas where French is the official language German is under pressure. The patchwork of different areas would seem to militate against the continued use of German in the long term. Magenau (1964) treats some of the characteristics of written German in Belgium.

3   *France* (Barbour and Stevenson 1990: 234–7; Born and Dickgießer 1989: 87–102; Philipp 1990). In the east of France, in Alsace-Lorraine, in the *départements* of Haut-Rhin, Bas-Rhin and Moselle there are 1.2 million users of German. Between 1871–1918 and 1940–5 the region was part of Germany and an aggressive policy of Germanization was pursued. From 1919 to 1940 the region came to France and the Germanization was vigorously reversed. Since 1945 the region has belonged to France, and French is the only official language. Alsatian dialects are spoken and understood by large sections of the population, particularly in the country and among the older generation. Code-switching between French and dialect is frequent. It is difficult to judge how far standard German is known and used. At any event it has become in practice a foreign language even though there has been voluntary teaching of German in schools

since 1952. The state has not encouraged any of the varieties of German, and French has gained ground. There is a limited amount of German material available in the shape of bilingual newspapers and dialect plays and poems. German dialect has become a badge of identity for many in the community. Magenau (1962) treats some of the characteristics of written German in Alsace.

4   *Italy* (Barbour and Stevenson 1990: 237–42; Born and Dickgießer 1989: 105–16; Rowley 1987). In Italy German is the co-official language with Italian of the autonomous region of South Tyrol. This area was until 1919 part of the Austro-Hungarian Empire and was given to Italy without any plebiscite. From 1922 to 1943 there was a policy of active Italianization. Since 1972 German and Italian have been co-official languages. German is used by 280,000 speakers (66.4 per cent of the population), Italian by 123,400 (29.3 per cent) and Ladin (another Romance language) by 18,000 (4.3 per cent). Schools have to be provided for both German and Italian pupils and officials have to know both languages, theoretically at any rate. A problem is that many Italian speakers do not know German well enough. At home German speakers use a Bavarian dialect. There is, thus, no general colloquial variety – only dialect or standard German. There is a German newspaper, *Dolomiten*. There are other German speakers, using chiefly dialect, in several valleys in northern Italy but they only represent a very small minority numerically.

5   *Denmark* (Born and Dickgießer 1989: 75–83). A plebiscite was held in the province of Slesvig in 1920 to decide where the border between Denmark and Germany should be drawn. Over 75 per cent of the population of North Slesvig, with the towns of Tøndern, Sønderborg and Aaberaa voted to belong to Denmark. This border left a small Danish minority in South Slesvig and a larger German minority in North Slesvig. The German minority live in mixed villages, nowhere is there a continual area of German settlement. They regard themselves more as a cultural and ethnic minority. German is not used in the family circle but in schools, church and in the large number of clubs of various kinds. There are eighteen private German schools and a newspaper, *Der Nordschleswiger*. Exact numbers are difficult to ascertain because any linguistic information in census returns is purely voluntary. German seems to be well established because of its status as a cultural language.

1.4   THE DEVELOPMENT OF STANDARD GERMAN

It is usual to divide the historical development of German into four periods: Old High German (OHG), Middle High German (MHG), Early New High German (ENHG) and New High German (NHG). This division into periods is for the most part arbitrary, being based on linguistic or cultural criteria; it must not be supposed that the periods are separated from each other by rigid boundaries. Schildt (1991) is a condensed survey while Wells (1985) is a more detailed work.

The road to standard New High German has been a long and tortuous one. The oldest stage of the language is called Old High German and is taken to run from 750 to 1050. An introductory text is Penzl (1986); Robinson (1992: 224–46) is a brief overview with an illustrative text. Sonderegger (1987) is an excellent work for more advanced students. The first OHG texts appear from the late eighth century. German was used in glossaries to help clerics understand Latin, then in interlinear translations to emerge finally in finished translations, such as that of Tatian's Gospel Harmony. The oldest book in German is considered to be a Latin–German glossary called *Abrogans* (*c*. 770 in Freising) after the first Latin word. Old High German (770–1050) is primarily the product of the clerical culture which existed in scriptoria such as the monasteries of Fulda in central Germany, Reichenau in southern Germany and St Gallen in Switzerland. It is more realistic to speak of several kinds of OHG than of one particular kind, since all the literary monuments from OHG times show quite a marked difference in spelling and form according to where they come from. It is normally assumed that the differences in writing reflected dialectal differences in pronunciation, each dialect region having one or more centres which produced literary works. For example, St Gallen and Reichenau were the centres of the Alemannic dialect. The most famous works written in Alemannic are: the *Reichenau Glosses* (*Reichenauer Glossen*) (*c*. 775–800), the *Benedictine Rule* (*Benediktiner Regel*) (*c*. 800), the *St Gall Vocabulary* (*Vocabularius St Galli*) (*c*. 790), and Notker's translation of the works of Boethius, Aristotle and the Psalms (*c*. 1000). Among the centres of the Bavarian dialect were Mondsee and Freising. Works written in Bavarian are: the *Wessobrunn Prayer* (*Wessobrunner Gebet*) (*c*. 770–90), the *Muspilli* (*c*. 800), a fragment of a poem about the end of the world and the *Exhortatio ad plebem christianam* (*c*. 815). The centre of the East Franconian dialect in OHG was the famous monastery at Fulda founded by Boniface and the most famous work written in East Franconian is the translation from the Latin version of the Gospel Harmony by Tatian (*c.* 830). The so-called *Isidor* (*c.* 790–800), which is a translation of the *Tractatus de fide catholica contra Judaeos* by Isidore of Seville, is a most important work. It probably came from the South Franconian region, possibly Lorraine, but its exact provenance is uncertain. Another important work claimed to have been written in the same dialect is the *Lay of Ludwig* (*Ludwigslied*) (*c.* 881–5), which cele-brates the victory of Louis III over the Norsemen in 881. Otfrid, who was a monk at Weissenburg (now Wissembourg in Alsace), wrote his *Evangelienbuch* (*c.* 863–71) in South Rhine Franconian.

Although different scribal 'dialects' existed which differed signifi-cantly, during the OHG period certain tendencies to standardization, although weak, can be seen: (1) through the Carolingian Renaissance, when under the first Emperor of the Holy Roman Empire, Charlemagne (?742–814), there are attempts to achieve the creation of good literary models and translate Christian tracts into OHG; (2) there was a certain levelling of regional lexical variation in favour of Franconian forms, e.g. *erteilen* 'to judge' over *domjan*, *tuomen* and *suonen*; (3) the term *deutsch*, from German–Latin hybrid *theod-iscus* 'of the people', came to designate the language of the German speaking peoples as opposed to the Romance speakers. These ten-dencies remained fragmentary, being dependent on clerical culture. A more detailed analysis is given in Sonderegger (1978).

Middle High German is usually regarded as extending from 1050 to 1350 and was widely used for works of literature. Within MHG there is a period from 1170 to 1250 which is known as 'classical MHG'. This is the period when the great literary courtly epics such as Hartmann von Aue's *Erec*, Gottfried von Strasbourg's *Tristan* and Wolfram von Eschenbach's *Parzifal* as well as the poetry of Walter von der Vogelweide were written. An elementary introduction to MHG is Walshe (1974), whereas Penzl (1989) is more advanced. Apart from the figure of the Holy Roman Emperor, there was no real centralized power but rather a struggle between dynasties. The courtly culture which existed in Thuringia, Swabia and Vienna shared certain values which are reflected in 'normalized' terms such as *mâze* 'moderation' and *zuht* 'good breeding'. It is controversial as to whether a standard MHG existed. The normalized forms of grammars and texts, such as the one in 1.4.1.2, are the work of nineteenth-century philologists. It is undeniable, however, that MHG writers avoided forms which were felt to be consciously dialectal. The language of the MHG poets was also not completely uniform, although poets tended to avoid rhymes which were too obviously characteristic of their particular region. The exact nature of the MHG literary language, often referred to as 'classical Middle High German', has been hotly debated.

In the period that follows, 1250–1520, there is a veritable explosion in the use of German by writers not skilled in Latin. The upsurge and growth of the independent towns meant that German was used for local laws and business dealings. For example, during the thirteenth century legal documents in many towns came to be written in German: in Strasburg in 1270, Freiburg in 1275, Augsburg in 1276, Schaffhausen in 1290 and Vienna in 1296. The language of these legal documents varied from town to town. A useful collection of these kinds of texts is Boesch (1957). Many preachers, particularly mystics, used German in their sermons. The new technical sciences, such as mining, used German for their instructional manuals. The lack of any political power centre meant that different scribal varieties arose in each main area. In non-literary texts there was thus a great deal of regional variation.

One important difference between OHG and MHG is that in MHG times the German-speaking area increased in size. Previously it had extended in the east as far as the rivers Elbe and Saale, but in the Middle Ages colonists pushed into Slavonic territories and founded villages and towns which soon grew into areas of German settlement; some groups even travelled as far as present-day Hungary and Romania. All the German territory east of the Elbe was colonized in the thirteenth century; East Prussia was invaded by the knights of the Teutonic Order for the first time in 1230 and German farmers established themselves in that territory after 1280. The settlers came from many parts of Germany and were of three main kinds: the nobles and military who built castles to subdue the land; craftsmen and artisans who worked in the towns which had grown up around the castles; and the farmers who came later when it was safe to set up farms and till the land. The main reasons for this expansion were overcrowding and the lack of land for farms in the west. Settlers from Low Germany, or in some cases from the Netherlands, settled in Mecklenburg, Pomerania and Brandenburg. As they were Low German speakers the dialect of these newly settled areas became Low German. The settlers in the area along the axis Leipzig–Dresden–Breslau came from various parts of Germany: the Rhineland, Hesse, East Franconia and Bavaria giving rise to a mixed dialect in this East Central basin. The two most influential events in the early modern period were the invention of printing and the Reformation. Printing, using movable type, was perfected in Mainz by Johannes Gutenberg (*c*. 1400–68), who produced his famous Latin Bible in 1455. Printing soon spread to many other towns such as Cologne, Strasburg, Nuremberg, Augsburg and Basle. Regional printers' language varieties arose during the sixteenth century with centres in the Upper Rhine area (Strasburg, Basle), Swabia (Augsburg), Bavaria and Austria (Munich, Vienna), the West Central German area (Mainz, Frankfurt), East Franconia (Nuremberg, Bamberg) and the East Central German (ECG) region (Leipzig, Wittenberg). Using a wide range of texts from this period, Keller (1978: 384–96) shows how these varieties differed from each other. The other decisive event to occur in the sixteenth century was the Reformation. Martin Luther (1483–1546) was instrumental in focusing attention on the written language of the East Central German area, in particular Wittenberg, where Low and High German met. His translation of the Bible and his extensive publications sounded the death knell for Low German and also for Upper German (UG) as the varieties which would shape the incipient standard. In his *Tischreden*, collected by his pupils, there is one very important statement by Luther with regard to how he sees his language:

Ich habe keine gewisse, sonderliche, eigene Sprache im Deutschen, sondern brauche der gemeinen deutschen Sprache, daß mich beide Ober- und Niederländer verstehen mögen. Ich rede nach der sächsischen Canzeley, welcher nachfolgen alle Fürsten und Könige in Deutschland; alle Reichstädte, Fürstenhöfe schreiben nach der sächsischen und unsers Fürsten Canzeley, darum ists auch die gemeinste deutsche Sprache. Kaiser Maximilian und Kurf. Friedrich, H. zu Sachsen ec. haben im römischen Reich die deutschen Sprachen also in eine gewisse Sprache gezogen.

('I haven't any certain, special language of my own but I use the common German language so that both North and South Germans can understand me. I speak according to the Saxon Chancery, which all the princes and kings in Germany follow; all Imperial Towns, princely courts write according to the Saxon Chancery of our prince, therefore that is the most common German language. Emperor Maximilian and Elector Frederick, Duke of Saxony have thus drawn together the German languages into one.')

(The German text is a nineteenth-century translation of the 'original' half-German, half-Latin text by Johannes Aurifaber (1519–75) in Luther's *Tischreden*, quoted in Keller (1978: 372).)

This ECG written language was intelligible to both North and South German. It may have differed in a number of ways from other regional written languages such as *das gemeine Deutsch* lit. 'common German' (i.e. understood by everyone), which was used in Upper Germany, or the standard form of Middle Low German which was current in North Germany and was used as a lingua franca among the towns of the Hanseatic League. The following phonological and grammatical features are usually cited as being the most important in distinguishing this East Central German type, used by Luther, from Upper German and Low German: diphthongs in the words *Zeit*, *Haus* (MHG *zît*, *hûs*) as against monophthongs in LG and Alemannic; monophthongs in words like *lieb* [liːp], *Bruder* (MHG *liep*, *bruoder*) as against diphthongs in UG; the retention of the unstressed final *-e* as against its loss, apocope, in some endings, for example dat. *zu Hause*, and the loss of the unstressed vowel, syncope, in some prefixes, for example in the past participle *gestellt*, or in the prefix *be-*, *bestellt*; the pronunciation [k] for *ch* before *s* in *sechs*, *Ochsen* as against assimilation to *ss* in LG and some small areas in UG; a long [eː] in the words *gehen*, *stehen* as against the use of a long [aː] in Alemannic; *-chen* as the main diminutive ending, *Stückchen* as against forms with *-l*, e.g. *-li*, *-le*, *-erl* in UG; attributive adjectives with a pronominal ending in the nom. sg. neuter, e.g. *mein lieb+es Kind* as against no inflection of the adjective in some LG and UG dialects; and personal pronoun forms for the first and second person sg. with the accusative ending in *-ch*, *mich*, *dich*, and the dative in *-r*, *mir*, *dir* as against one single form for the acc. and dat. in LG (Bach 1965: 249).

It was this variety of German which Martin Luther used for his works, including his translation of the Bible, and it quickly spread to most Protestant areas of German-speaking Europe. By the beginning of the seventeenth century it had ousted Low German as a written language and by the latter half of the seventeenth century it was the main basis of the written language used in Switzerland. Its progress was not so quick in the Roman Catholic south-east but by the middle of the eighteenth century it had found acceptance even there. This ECG written variety of German underwent changes in orthography, grammar and vocabulary in the seventeenth century. Luther, however, had laid the foundations for the acceptance of one variety of written German as a standard. What was important was that the East Central German area had become the focus of attention.

Although traditionally New High German is normally regarded as extending from 1650 to the present day, with Early New High

German from 1350 to 1650, according to more recent opinion it is more realistic to talk about NHG as starting during the first quarter of the eighteenth century. Several theories have been advanced to explain the rise of NHG. Konrad Burdach (1859–1936) emphasized the importance of the language of the Chancery of Prague in influencing the language of other areas and Alois Bernt (1871–1945) sought to support his claim philologically, but without success. According to Theodor Frings (1886–1968), NHG was in fact dialectologically a mixture of features from several different dialects. In the East Central German basin he sought to show that there had developed a lingua franca (called by him *die koloniale Ausgleichsprache*) which was formed from the dialects used by the settlers. The similarities between the scribal traditions of Meißen, Dresden and Prague are due to the uniformity of the ECG dialects and not, as was previously assumed, to the influence of the Imperial Chancery in Prague on the others. This *Ausgleichsprache* flowed into late medieval business language *Verkehrs- und Geschäftssprache*. In more recent times the emphasis has shifted away from the dialectal–geographical approach to a graphemic approach, studying a wide range of written sources. The main questions have been: What features have been selected by the NHG standard? Where have they been selected from? Why have they been selected? There seems not really to be a 'cradle' of NHG but rather a wide range of areas, particularly in Central and Upper Germany which have contributed certain features. Wegera (1986) is an accessible collection of the most important articles, for example by Burdach and Frings, on this subject. Van der Elst (1987) is a survey of the problems of the emergence of NHG, using illustrative text material. Hartweg and Wegera (1989: 36–48) is a useful guide through the maze of theories.

In the seventeenth century many language societies (*Sprachgesellschaften*) were founded, having as their chief aims the cultivation of the German language and its literature, its protection from Latin and French and the preservation of its purity from the influx of foreign words (Wells 1985: 279–300). The first of these societies, the *Fruchtbringende Gesellschaft*, was founded at Weimar in 1617 and it continued its activities until 1680. The *Sprachgesellschaften* had only a limited sphere of influence themselves but some of their members made lasting contributions in the search for a German standard. Martin Opitz (1597–1639), whose *Buch von der deutschen Poeterey* (1624) had an important influence on the use of German as a literary medium, was a member of the *Fruchtbringende Gesellschaft*. Another member of this society was the grammarian Justus Georg

Schottel(ius) (1612–76), who regarded the written language of the greatest and wisest men as the best German and described the same in his *Teutsche Sprachkunst* (1641) and *Ausführliche Arbeit von der Teutschen Haubt-Sprache* (1663). One facet of the development of a standard for German and the rise of *Sprachgesellschaften* was a puristic attitude towards loans. In OHG and MHG these were accepted and assimilated into the language with no problems. In Early NHG the influx of Latin words was so great that in 1571 Simon Roth produced the first *Fremdwörterbuch*, containing over 2,000 foreign words, mostly from Latin. This separation of borrowings from native vocabulary reflected a growing attitude that there is a 'pure' language. In the seventeenth century the language societies tried to ensure the purity of the language. One of the ways of bringing this about was replacing foreign words by German loan translations. Philipp von Zesen (1619–89) was instrumental in suggesting some forms, for example *Verfasser* 'author', *Urschrift* 'original', *Zweikampf* 'duel'.

In the eighteenth century the task of establishing a written standard for German was carried on by Johann Christoph Gottsched (1700–66) in his *Deutsche Sprachkunst* (1748) and by Johann Christoph Adelung (1732–1806) in his *Umständliches Lehrgebaude der deutschen Sprache* (1782) and *Vollständige Anweisung zur deutschen Orthographie* (1788). Both Gottsched and Adelung emphasized the importance of usage in establishing a standard. In their opinion the best German was the language of the educated classes of Upper Saxony, called *das Meißnische*. Adelung also produced a dictionary, *Versuch eines grammatisch-kritischen Wörterbuches der hochdeutschen Mundart* (1774–86), which was intended to be a definitive dictionary of German in the same way as the one produced by the Académie française (1635) was for French. The eighteenth century also saw the birth of a classical literary language in the works of Friedrich Gottlieb Klopstock (1724–1803), Gotthold Ephraim Lessing (1729–81), Johann Gottfried Herder (1744–1803), Johann Wolfgang von Goethe (1749–1832) and Friedrich Schiller (1759–1805).

During the nineteenth and early twentieth centuries the final steps were taken towards a standardization of German, chiefly in the realms of orthography and pronunciation. These were given great impetus by the unification of Germany in 1870–1. Linguistic prestige now shifted from the East Central German region to Berlin and North Germany. In 1880 the first edition of the *Vollständiges Orthographisches Wörterbuch der deutschen Sprache* was published by Konrad Duden (1829–1911). This was primarily intended for the German Empire, but in 1901 a conference was held in Berlin which was attended by delegates from Austria and Switzerland who proposed reforms to make the spelling proposals of 1880 and other reforms more widely acceptable. The results of the conference were incorporated into the seventh edition of the *Orthographisches Wörterbuch* in 1902. The *Duden Rechtschreibung der deutschen Sprache* (20th edn 1991) is still regarded as the ultimate authority on spelling matters in German. A standardization of pronunciation was also agreed upon at the end of the nineteenth century. In 1898 Theodor Siebs (1862–1941) published his *Deutsche Bühnenaussprache* which was the result of a conference held in the same year at Berlin attended by phoneticians, theatre managers and educationalists.

1.4.1 Illustrative texts

1.4.1.1 Old High German

To illustrate OHG we will take an extract from *Tatian*, part of the Christmas story. This is the translation from the Latin version of the Gospel Harmony by the Syrian Tatian.

Uuard thô gitân in then tagun, framquam gibot fon ðemo aluualten keisure, thaz gibrieuit vvurdi al these umbiuuerft. thaz giscrib iz êristen uuard gitan in Syriu fon ðem grauen Cyrine, inti fuorun alle, thaz biiâhin thionost iogiuuelih in sinero burgi. Fuor Ioseph fon Galileu fon thero burgi thiu hiez Nazareth in Iudeno lant inti Dauides burg, thiu uuas ginemnit Bethleem, bithiu uuanta her uuas fon huse inti fon hiuuiske Dauides, thaz her giiahi saman mit Mariun imo gimahaltero gimahhun, sô scaffaneru. Thô sie thar uuarun, vvurdun taga gifulte, thaz siu bari, inti gibar sun êristboranon inti biuuant inan mit tuochum inti gilegita inan in crippea, bithiu uuanta im ni uuas ander stat in themo gasthuse. Uuârun thô hirta in thero lantskeffi uuahhante inti bihaltane nahtuuahtâ ubar ero euuit. Quam thara gotes engil inti gistuont nâh in, inti gotes berahtnessî bischein sie, giforhtun sie im thô in mihhilero forhtu. Inti quad im thie engil: 'ni curet iu forhten, ih sagên iu mihhilan gifehon, ther ist allemo folke, bithiu uuanta giboran ist iu hiutu Heilant, ther ist Christ truhtîn in Davides burgi. Thaz sî iu zi zeichane, thaz ir findet kind mit tuochum biuuuntanaz inti gelegitaz in crippea.' Thô sliumo uuard thâr mit themo engile menegî himilisches heres got lobôntiu inti quedentiu:

'Tiurida sî thên hôhistôm gote, inti in erdu sî sibba mannun guotes uuillen.'

(Tatian, Luke 2: 8–14, from Sievers 1892: 23f.)

A NHG version of the passage is as follows:

1 Es begab sich aber zu der Zeit, daß ein Gebot von dem Kaiser Augustus ausging, daß alle Welt geschätzt würde. 2 Und diese Schätzung war die allererste und geschah zur Zeit, da Quirinius Statthalter in Syrien war. 3 Und jedermann ging, daß er sich schätzen ließe, ein jeder in seine Stadt. 4 Da machte sich auf auch Josef aus Galiläa, aus der Stadt Nazareth, in das jüdische Land zur Stadt Davids, die da heißt Bethlehem, weil er aus dem Hause und Geschlechte Davids war, 5 auf daß er sich schätzen ließe mit Maria, seinem vertrauten Weibe, die war schwanger. 6 Und als sie dort waren, kam die Zeit, daß sie gebären sollte. 7 Und sie gebar ihren ersten Sohn und wickelte ihn in Windeln und legte ihn in eine Krippe; denn sie hatten sonst keinen Raum in der Herberge. 8 Und es waren Hirten in derselben Gegend auf dem Felde bei den Hürden, die hüteten des Nachts ihre Herde. 9 Und der Engel des Herren trat zu ihnen, und die Klarheit des Herren leuchtete um sie; und sie fürchteten sich sehr. 10 Und der Engel sprach zu ihnen: 'Fürchtet euch nicht! Siehe, ich verkündige euch große Freude, die allem Volk widerfahren wird; 11 denn euch ist heute der Heiland geboren, welcher ist Christus, der Herr, in der Stadt Davids. 12 Und das habt zum Zeichen: ihr werdet finden das Kind in Windeln gewickelt und in einer Krippe liegen.' 13 Und alsbald war da bei dem Engel die Menge der himmlischen Heerscharen, die lobten Gott und sprachen: 14 'Ehre sei Gott in der Höhe und Friede auf Erden bei den Menschen seines Wohlgefallens.')

(Die Bibel nach der Übersetzung Martin Luthers, 1984: 70f.)

Notes on the passage

Most edited collections of OHG texts have a macron (¯) for the length sign instead of a circumflex (ˆ). OHG has a full set of vowels in unstressed syllables which in MHG and NHG have been reduced to *e*: *hirta, thero, burgi, forhtu*; *mihhilan, hôhistôm, truhtîn, uuârun*. There is also no capitalization of initial letters. The use of ð for *th* reflects Anglo-Saxon usage.

uuard gitan. In NHG there would be an *Es* inserted to make the sentence grammatical. In OHG, unlike NHG, statements could begin with a verb.

biiâhin thionost, lit. 'confess service', i.e. 'be counted'.

(*bithiu*) *uuanta*, causal conjunction 'for'. In NHG it has been replaced by *denn*.

hiuuiske, 'family', a word that has now died out.

euuit 'sheep', a word that has died out, related to Engl. *ewe*.

nâh in, NHG *nahe ihnen*, the third person pl. personal pronoun has added an *-en*, probably from adjectival inflection, cf. *dessen*, *deren*, *denen*.

berahtnessî 'brightness', now died out.

quad, and *quedentiu*, from the now obsolete verb *quedan* 'to speak', cf. Engl. *bequeathe*, *quoth*.

iu '(to) you' dat. pl. This has been replaced in NHG by the acc. *euch*.

mihhilan 'great', cf. Engl. dialect *muckle*.

truhtîn 'Lord', obsolete word which was originally used to designate the leader of a Germanic tribe.

sliumo 'suddenly', has now died out.

Tiurida 'glory', has now died out.

sibba 'peace', has now died out.

1.4.1.2 Middle High German

To illustrate MHG we will take an extract from *Der arme Heinrich* by Hartmann von Aue:

> Ein ritter sô gelêret was
> daz er an den buochen las
> swaz er dar an geschriben vant:
> der was Hartman genant,
> 5 dienstman was er zOuwe.
> er nam im manige schouwe
> an mislîchen buochen:
> dar an begunde er suochen
> ob er iht des vunde
> 10 dâ mite er swære stunde
> möhte senfter machen,
> und von sô gewanten sachen
> daz gotes êren töhte
> únd dâ mite er sich möhte
> 15 gelieben den liuten.

(Paul 1961: 1)

The following is a translation into NHG:

> Ein Ritter besaß solche Schulbildung,
> daß er in den Büchern lesen konnte,
> alles was er darin geschrieben fand.
> Er war Hartmann genannt
> 5   und war Lehnsmann zu Aue.
> Er nahm sich eifrig
> in verschiedenen Büchern um
> und begann darin zu suchen,
> ob er etwas derartiges fände,
> 10   womit er bedrückte Stunden
> leichter machen könnte
> und das von solchen Dingen handelte,
> daß es zu Gottes Ehre taugte,
> und womit er sich zugleich
> 15   den Menschen angenehm machen könnte.
>
> (De Boor 1963: 7)

('A knight was so learned that he read in books whatever he found written. He was called Hartmann, liegeman of Ouwe. He took many a look for himself in various books. He began to search in them (to see) whether he could find anything with which he could make an unhappy hour pleasanter and of such a nature that it might redound to God's glory and please people.')

Notes on the passage:

As in OHG there is no initial capitalization of nouns. The designation of vowel length and the use of the umlaut sign is due to editing and does not appear in the original manuscript. The main change is in the vowels of unstressed syllables, now written *e*, which represents the final vowel in NHG *bitte*. The letter combinations *uo*, *ie* were probably diphthongs, whereas *iu* was probably a long vowel like that in NHG *Bühne*. The letter *æ* probably represents a long vowel like in NHG *Bären* [ɛː]. The final consonants written *s* and *z* in *was*, *swaz* represent different sounds but it is not clear exactly how they differed. Any vowel not marked with a circumflex *â*, *ô* was pronounced short.

Line 1 *was* 'were'. The MHG consonantal alternation *s – r*, sg. *was* – pl. *wâren* has been levelled out in favour of the *r* of the pl.

Line 2 *buochen*, (dat. pl., cf. NHG *Büchern*), shows the extension of the pl. ending *-er* accompanied by umlaut to many neuter nouns.

Line 3 *swaz* 'whatever' (from OHG *so waz*), which has died out in NHG.

Line 7 *mislîchen* 'various', which has died out in NHG.

Line 9 *iht* 'anything', which has been replaced by *etwas* in NHG, although the latter did exist in MHG.

Line 13 *töhte* 'were fit for', an irregular verb in MHG which has become regular or weak in NHG *taugen*.

SELECT BIBLIOGRAPHY AND FURTHER READING

Ammon, U. (1991) *Die internationale Stellung der deutschen Sprache*, Berlin: de Gruyter.

Bach, A. (1965) *Geschichte der deutschen Sprache*, 8th edn, Heidelberg: Quelle & Meyer.

Barbour, S. and Stevenson, P. (1990) *Variation in German: A Critical Approach to German Sociolinguistics*, Cambridge: Cambridge University Press.

Die Bibel nach der Übersetzung Martin Luthers (1984), Stuttgart: Deutsche Bibelgesellschaft.

Bock, R., Harnisch, H., Langner, H. and Starke, G. (1973) 'Zur deutschen Gegenwartssprache in der DDR und in der BRD', *Zeitschrift für Phonetik, Sprachwissenschaft und Kommunikationswissenschaft*, 26: 511–32.

Boesch, B. (ed.) (1957) *Deutsche Urkunden des 13. Jahrhunderts*, Berne: Francke.

Born, J. and Dickgießer, S. (1989) *Deutschsprachige Minderheiten. Ein Überblick über den Stand der Forschung für 27 Länder*, Mannheim: Institut für deutsche Sprache im Auftrage des Auswärtigen Amtes.

Born, J. and Jakob, G. (1990) *Deutschsprachige Gruppen am Rande und außerhalb des geschlossenen deutschen Sprachgebiets*, 2nd edn, Mannheim: Institut für deutsche Sprache.

Christophory, J. (1974) *Mir schwätze lëtzebuergesch*, Luxemburg: Société Anonyme.

Clyne, M. (1984) *Language and Society in German-speaking Countries*, Cambridge: Cambridge University Press.

—— (1992) 'German as a Pluricentric Language', in M. Clyne (ed.) *Pluricentric Languages: Differing Norms in Different Nations* (Contributions to the Sociology of Language, 62), Berlin: Mouton de Gruyter, pp. 117–47.

de Boor, H. (trans.) (1963) *Der arme Heinrich. Mittelhochdeutscher Text und Übertragung* (Exempla Classica, 84), Frankfurt-on-Main: Fischer.

Dieckmann, W. (1989) 'Die Untersuchung der deutsch-deutschen Sprachentwicklung als linguistisches Problem', *Zeitschrift für germanistische Linguistik*, 17: 162–81.

Dose, M., Folz, J., Mang, D., Schrupp, C. and Trunk-Nußbaumer, M. (1990) *Duden Fremdwörterbuch* (= *DFW*), 5th edn, Mannheim: Bibliographisches Institut.

Drosdowski, G. (1968) 'Die Dudenredaktion in der 2. Hälfte des 20. Jahrhunderts', in *Geschichte und Leistung des Dudens*, Mannheim: Bibliographisches Institut, pp. 23–9.

—— (1985) 'Die Dudenredaktion', in *Sprachkultur: Jahrbuch 1984 des Instituts für deutsche Sprache* (Sprache der Gegenwart, 63), Düsseldorf: Schwann, pp. 85–92.

Drosdowski, G., Scholze-Stubenrecht, W. and Wermke, M. (1991) *Duden Die deutsche Rechtschreibung*, 20th edn, Mannheim: Bibliographisches Institut.

Drosdowski, G., Köster, R., Müller, W. and Schrupp, C. (1976–81) *Duden: Das große Wörterbuch der deutschen Sprache* (= *DGWB*), 6 vols, Mannheim: Bibliographisches Institut.

Drosdowski, G., Augst, G., Gelhaus, H., Gipper, H., Mangold, M., Sitta, H., Wellmann, H. and Winkler, C. (1984) *Duden Grammatik*, 4th edn, Mannheim: Bibliographisches Institut.

Drosdowski, G., Dose, M., Eckey, W., Folz, J., Hartmann, H., Mang, D., Mangold, M., Schrupp, C., Trunk-Nußbaumer, M., Thyen, O. and Wermke, M. (1989) *Duden Deutsches Universalwörterbuch*, 2nd edn, Mannheim: Bibliographisches Institut.

Fleischer, W. (1989) 'Zur Situation der deutschen Sprache heute', *Zeitschrift für Phonetik, Sprachwissenschaft und Kommunikationswissenschaft*, 42: 435–42.

Fleischer, W., Barz, I., Geier, R., Heinemann, H., Heinemann, W., Huth, H., Kändler, M., Koch, H., Kögler, H., Poethe, H., Porsch, P., Schröder, M., Weber, H., Wiess, I., Wittich, M. and Yos, G. (1987) *Wortschatz der deutschen Sprache in der DDR*, Leipzig: Bibliographisches Institut.

Grebe, P., Gipper, H., Mangold, M. and Winkler, C. (1959) *Duden Grammatik*, 1st edn, Mannheim: Bibliographisches Institut.

Grebe, P., Gipper, H., Mangold, M., Mentrup, W. and Winkler, C. (1966) *Duden Grammatik*, 2nd. edn, Mannheim: Bibliographisches Institut.

—— (1973) *Duden Grammatik*, 3rd edn, Mannheim: Bibliographisches Institut.

Hartweg, F. and Wegera, K.-P. (1989) *Frühneuhochdeutsch* (Germanistische Arbeitshefte, 33), Tübingen: Niemeyer.

Hatherall, G. (1986) 'The "Duden Rechtschreibung" 1880–1986', in R. K. K. Hartmann (ed.) *The History of Lexicography*, Amsterdam: Benjamins, pp. 85–97.

Hoffmann, F. (1979) *Sprachen in Luxemburg* (Deutsche Sprache in Europa und Übersee, 6), Wiesbaden: Steiner.

—— (1988) 'Luxemburg', in U. Ammon, N. Dittmar and K. J. Mattheier (eds) *Sociolinguistics: An International Handbook of the Science of Language and Society*, vol. 2, Berlin: de Gruyter, pp. 1334–40.

—— (1992) '1839–1989: Fast 150 Jahre amtlicher Zwei- und privater Einsprachigkeit in Luxemburg. Mit einem nationalsozialistischen Zwischenspiel', in W. Dahmen, G. Hoetus, J. Kramer, M. Metzeltin, C. Schmitt and O. Winkelmann (eds), *Germanisch und Romanisch in Belgien und Luxemburg. Romanistisches Kolloquium VI* (Tübinger Beiträge zur Linguistik, 363), Tübingen: Narr, pp. 149–64.

Kaiser, S. (1969–70) *Die Besonderheiten der deutschen Schriftsprache in der Schweiz* (Duden Beiträge, 30a, b), Mannheim: Dudenverlag.

Keller, R. E. (1978) *The German Language*, London: Faber & Faber.

Mackensen, L. (1952) *Neues deutsches Wörterbuch*, 1st edn, Laupheim: Pfahl.

Magenau, D. (1962) *Die Besonderheiten der deutschen Schriftsprache im Elsaß und in Lothringen* (Duden Beiträge, 7), Mannheim: Dudenverlag.

—— (1964) *Die Besonderheiten der deutschen Schriftsprache in Luxemburg und in den deutschsprachigen Teilen Belgiens* (Duden Beiträge, 15), Mannheim: Dudenverlag.

Newton, G. (1987) 'The German Language in Luxembourg', in C. V. J. Russ and C. Volkmar (eds) *Sprache und Gesellschaft in deutschsprachigen Ländern*, Munich: Goethe Institute, pp. 153–79.

—— (1990) 'Luxemburg', in C. V. J. Russ (ed.) *The Dialects of Modern German*, London: Routledge, pp. 145–49.

Paul, H. (ed.) (1961) *Der arme Heinrich von Hartmann von Aue*, 12th edn, Tübingen: L. Wolff.

Penzl, H. (1986) *Althochdeutsch* (Germanistische Lehrbuchsammlung, 7), Berne: Lang.

—— (1989) *Mittelhochdeutsch* (Germanistische Lehrbuchsammlung, 8), Berne: Lang.

Philipp, M. (1990) 'Low Alemannic', in C. V. J. Russ (ed.) *The Dialects of Modern German*, London: Routledge, pp. 313–36.

Polenz, P. von (1988) ' "Binnendeutsch" oder plurizentrische Sprachkultur?', *Zeitschrift für germanistische Linguistik*, 16: 198–218.

—— (1991) *Deutsche Sprachgeschichte: Vom Spätmittelater bis zur Gegenwart*, vol. 1, Berlin: de Gruyter.

Riedmann, G. (1972) *Die Besonderheiten der deutschen Schriftsprache in Südtirol* (Duden Beiträge, 39), Mannheim: Dudenverlag.

Rizzo-Baur, H. (1962) *Die Besonderheiten der deutschen Schriftsprache in Österreich und Südtirol* (Duden Beiträge, 5), Mannheim: Dudenverlag.

Robinson, O. W. (1992) *Old English and its Closest Relatives*, London: Routledge.

Rowley, A. R. (1987) 'Linguistic Minorities in Central Europe – the South Tyroleans and the Burgenland Croats: A Report on some Recent Comparative Research', in C. V. J. Russ and C. Volkmar (eds) *Sprache und Gesellschaft in deutschsprachigen Ländern*, Munich: Goethe Institute, pp. 122–35.

Russ, C. V. J. (1980) 'A Hundred Years of *Duden Rechtschreibung*', *New German Studies*, 8: 189–201.

—— (ed.) (1990) *The Dialects of Modern German*, London: Routledge.

—— (1991) 'The Norms of German and their Metamorphosis', in E. Kolinsky (ed.) *The Federal Republic of Germany: The End of an Era*, Oxford: Berg, pp. 323–32.

Russ, C. V. J. and Volkmar, C. (eds) (1987) *Sprache und Gesellschaft in deutschsprachigen Ländern*, Munich: Goethe Institute.

Sauer, W. W. (1988) *Der 'DUDEN'. Geschichte und Aktualität eines 'Volkswörterbuches'*, Stuttgart: Metzler.

Schildt, J. (1991) *Kurze Geschichte der deutschen Sprache*, Berlin: Volk & Wissen.

Sievers, E. (ed.) (1892) *Tatian. Lateinisch und altdeutsch mit ausführlichem Glossar*, Paderborn: Schöningh; repr. 1960.

Sonderegger, S. (1978) 'Tendenzen zu einem überregional geschriebenen Althochdeutsch', in H. Beumann and W. Schröder (eds) *Aspekte der Nationenbildung im Mittelalter*, Sigmaringen: Thorbecke, pp. 229–73.

—— (1987) *Althochdeutsche Sprache und Literatur*, 2nd. edn, Berlin: de Gruyter.

Strauss, D. (1981) 'Aspects of German as a Minority Language in Western Europe', in E. Haugen, J. D. McClure and D. S. Thomson (eds) *Minority Languages Today*, Edinburgh: Edinburgh University Press, pp. 189–200.

Van der Elst, G. (1987) *Aspekte zur Entstehung der neuhochdeutschen Schriftsprache* (Erlanger Studien, 70), Erlangen: Palm & Enke.

Wacker, H. (1964) *Die Besonderheiten der deutschen Schriftsprache in den USA* (*Duden* Beiträge, 14), Mannheim: Dudenverlag.

Wahrig, G. (1966) *Das große deutsche Wörterbuch*, 1st edn, Gütersloh: Bertelsmann.

Walshe, M. O'C. (1974) *Middle High German Reader*, Oxford: Clarendon Press.

Wegera, K.-P. (ed.) (1986) *Zur Entstehung der neuhochdeutschen Schriftsprache. Eine Dokumentation von Forschungsthesen* (Reihe Germanistische Linguistik, 64), Tübingen: Niemeyer.

Wells, C. J. (1985) *German: A Linguistic History to 1945*, Oxford: Clarendon Press.

Wiegand, H. E. (1985) 'German Dictionaries and Research on the Lexicography of German from 1945 to the Present with a Select Bibliography', *Lexicographica*, 1: 172–224.

2 Variation in German

When we talk about the German language we must not imagine it to be like a museum exhibit, set out in a glass case, never changing, or like something on a microscope slide which is exactly delimited. It is more like a chameleon, something that we know is there and yet by its movements and changes of colour it presents us with many different facets at different times and in different places.

2.1 THE NATURE OF VARIATION

Variation can be found potentially at all levels of language. However, of the different linguistic levels that can be used to describe the German language, for example orthography, phonology, morphology (inflection and derivation), syntax and vocabulary, some levels are more prone to show variation and fluctuation of usage than others. Although the spelling norm is 'fixed', there are a few variants, e.g. *Foto* or *Photo*, *Couch*, *Kautsch*. Variation occurs at the other linguistic levels: pronunciation may vary regionally and stylistically (König 1989), yet the basic phonological system of German remains fundamentally the same; inflection shows variation in endings, for example gen. sg. *des Dollars*, *des Dollar*; *ich habe/bin gestanden*; derivational morphology also shows variation in the use of the linking -*s* between the elements of compounds, for example *Werksangehörige* or *Werkangehörige*, differences in suffixes used, *unvermeidlich* or *unvermeidbar* as well as some regional variation, for example the diminutive forms -*le* (Swabian), -*li* (Swiss German), -*rl* (Bavarian), -*chen*; syntax shows uncertainty in grammatical gender *der/das Knäuel*, or in adjective inflection, for example *solche* + strong or weak adjective ending. The wide range of grammatical variation can be exemplified further from Berger and Drosdowski (1985). Although there is considerable regional variation in vocabulary, for example, *Samstag* vs *Sonnabend*, which can be seen from the maps in Eichhoff (1977–8), a very large stock of vocabulary remains common to all varieties of German, for example *Haus, Stadt, Auge, gehen, rot, schwarz*. Despite minor differences, the common core of the inflectional morphology, syntax and vocabulary of German does not vary greatly over the German-speaking area. Spelling is the most rigid of the linguistic levels, allowing only a small amount of variants. Some of these common-core features will be described in Chapters 6–10, showing how different linguistic theories have analysed them. The variation which concerns us in Chapter 2 will be that which occurs throughout all the German-speaking countries. Chapters 3–5 present variation which is largely limited to particular national linguistic communities in Austria, Switzerland and former East Germany. The more general features which will be described in this chapter will dealt with according to a selection of factors which determine their presence (Durrell 1992: 1–40; Löffler 1985: 87–175; Russ 1992). They will appear under the following headings: spoken and written German; formal and informal use of language; archaic language, and specialist, technical and group languages.

2.2   SPOKEN AND WRITTEN GERMAN

(Betten 1977, 1978; Keller 1978: 525–34 and 1981; Schank and Schwitalla 1980; Steger 1967; Steger *et al.* 1974; Wackernagel-Jolles 1971)

Language can be used in different modes. The chief distinction in this instance is between the written and the spoken mode of language use. The study of language has tended traditionally to describe the written language since of course written records exist from past times whereas spoken language is lost the moment it has been uttered. However, modern linguistics has emphasized that the spoken language is prior to the written. We learn to speak before we learn to write. In many language communities there are large groups of people who never learn to write or read and yet communicate very effectively. It is only in this century that spoken language has been 'fixed' with audio recordings, and latterly with video recordings. This has then led to the transcription of these recordings, either in a detailed phonetic script or else in a modified form of standard orthography with special signs to indicate pauses, hesitations, etc. An example of this latter type of transcription is represented by text 1 (2.2.1). In the 1960s and 1970s interest in the spoken language grew.

Archives of spoken material were set up and transcriptions of the recordings made (Texte I–IV, 1971–9). Much of the work of this nature is carried on at the Institut für deutsche Sprache in Mannheim.

The spoken language differs from the written in a number of ways:

1 The spoken language is generally not recorded for posterity in any way. With the advent of tape recording this has changed things in that now archives of spoken language can be set up. Even then there has to be a transcription of the recordings before any work of analysis can begin. There have been attempts in the past to try and reflect spoken language in written, for example in the dramas of *Sturm und Drang* and Naturalism. Many modern authors also incorporate constructions and words from the spoken language into their works, particularly in dialogue.

2 Certain constructions are preferred in the syntax of the spoken language as compared to the written although the basic construction are the same. The spoken language makes less use of complicated syntactic patterns of premodification and subordinate clauses. The spoken language allows for a frequent use of modal particles such as *doch*, *ja*, *denn*, to express the attitudes of the speakers. Pronouns can be used more frequently since it is usually obvious from the context what is being referred to. There are hesitations, false starts, switches in construction and incompleted sentences, which result from the immediacy of the spoken language. In producing written work the writer usually has time to read through, rethink and recast what is not clear.

3 In vocabulary the spoken language makes use of a wide range of everyday colloquial, sometimes vulgar, expressions. Regional variations are also more characteristic of the spoken language since it is fixed to a particular area.

4 In pronunciation universal use is made of so-called 'weak' forms of frequently used words, e.g. *ist* can appear as [ɪs, s], *und* as [ʊnt, ʊn, n̩] or one of the nasals [m̩, n̩, ŋ] depending on the preceding consonant.

The spoken language is not, however, a monolithic structure but occurs in different disguises, depending on the number and role of the participants. Conversation, for example, assumes a number of participants with different roles and much study has been done on the way the roles change. There may only be two participants, in which case we have a dialogue. Within the dialogue the roles of the participants may differ in status. For instance, they may be equal, as in a dialogue between friends, or one may be in a role of authority, for example, someone asking a question or making a transaction at a post office or social security office. There may also be the case where one person is talking, a monologue, and others listening, either present with the speaker or as a radio or television audience. Because of the difficulties of recording speech most examples tend to be of monologues or dialogues of a set kind.

2.2.1   Illustrative texts

Text 1

To illustrate some aspects of the spoken language, part of an interview with a pilot on the Rhine is given here. The transcription has been simplified somewhat. The segmentation of the flow of speech is marked with several signs: the single full-stop . is used to denote the end of a sentence or sentence structure; ,+ +, are used to denote a dependent (subordinate) clause; an oblique / is used at the beginning of a sentence to show that it contains sequences that are syntactically not connected or contain non-standard agreements; parentheses ( ) are used for insertions in the sentence. Other symbols are used as follows: +g+ stands for any articulation which is not clearly a word but may have a function within the sentence; f+ +f are used to denote a foreign or a dialect word. Neither intonation nor word stress is shown. The weak forms of the article, e.g. *n, m*, are transcribed but not symbolized in any way. The use of the standard orthography masks any detailed phonetic assimilations or elisions.

INTERVIEWER: / (Herr Schwarz) wollen Sie denn wollen Sie mir nicht erzählen ,+ wie wie + g+ die Lorelei auf den Felsen gekommen ist +, ,+ und warum sie sich das Haar kämmt +, ? .

HERR SCHWARZ: /ja) das is eine die Lorelei ist eine Sage eine Legende ,+ wie man +g+ sonst im Ausländischen sagt +, . und die Lorelei ist ein Mädchen . /dieses Mädchen wurde von einem Schiffer +g+ von einem Fischer einmal im Netz gefangen und hatte auf der Brust eine Fischschuppe . dieses Mädchen ist +g+ mit all den andern Kindern in dem Mittelalter oder in der Zeit ,+ wo f+ se + f von dem Fischer im Netz war +, aufgewachsen und hat die Jugend mit den andern Mädchen +g+ verlebt ,+ ohne daß es selbst was gemerkt hatte +, ,+ daß es eine Fabelwesen war +, . jetzt +g+ ist es aber natürlich in das Zeitalter gekommen ,+ wo so n junges Mädchen +g+ sich nach +g+ einem Jungen sehnt +, und hat sich verliebt in einen Graf von der Schönburg . /aber aus dieser Sache aus dieser Sache wurde nichts . und sie ging in ihr Elternhaus zurück . und in jedem Jahr ist im Mittelalter hier in Sankt Goar ein sogenanntes Mädchenlehen gewesen . /und diese Mädchen wurde die Mädchen ,+ die in dem Jahr achtzehn Jahre alt wurden + , öffentlich meistbietend versteigert . / das war (so gesagt) sich ein Kennenlernen . und die Burschen ,+ die in der Umgebung waren +, haben natürlich eifrig auf so n Mädchen gesteigert . / und ,+ wenn das Zuschlag erteilt wurde +, war es gewöhnlich so ,+ daß es der Liebhaber dieses Mädchens war +, . die Lorelei wurde auch einmal achtzehn Jahre alt und wurde auch öffentlich meistbietend versteigert . und der Jäger von Kurpfalz ,+ der durch die rheinischen Lande gezogen ist +, machte an diesem fraglichen Sonntag Station in Sankt Goar und ging zu diesem Mädchenlehen . er bot und bot . und schließlich wurde ihm für f+ fuffzig +f Taler die Lorelei zugeschlagen . der eigentliche Junge ,+ der dieses Mädchen haben wollte +, war sehr erbost . / aber die Lorelei tanzte mit diesem Jäger mit m Jäger von Kurpfalz den ganzen Abend die ganze Nacht und glaubt ,+ daß +g+ diese ihre große Liebe sein würde +, . aber auch aus diesem wurde nichts . / und aus dem Gram hat f+ s +f Lorelei sich später auf die Lorelei geflüchtet ihr goldenes Haar mit einem ihr blondes Haar mit einem goldenen Kamm gekämmt und Lieder in die Nacht gesungen . / und die Schiffer ,+ die den Rhein hinunterfuhren +, hörten diesen wundersamen Liedern und schauten nicht auf die Felsenriffe und liefen auf und versanken in den Fluten.

(*Texte gesprochener deutscher Standardsprache* 1,
1971: 124–5)

Several features of spoken German can be illustrated from this text. There are special phonological forms of some frequently used words, for example *is* for *ist*, *s*, *se* for *sie*, *was* for *etwas*, *so n* for *so ein*. After the prep. *mit* a contraction of the definite article is used, *m*, instead of the full form *dem*, *mit m Jäger*. The rule of word order requiring dependent infinitives and past participles to be in clause-final position after a modal is not always adhered to: *hat sich verliebt in einen Graf von Schönburg*, instead of *hat sich in einen Graf von Schönburg verliebt*. The following repetitions occur: *wie wie*; *von einem Schiffer von einem Schiffer*; *aus dieser Sache aus dieser Sache wurde nichts*; *ihr goldenes Haar mit einem ihr goldenes Haar mit einem goldenen Kamm gekämmt*. Changes of construction occur in *und diese Mädchen wurde* (also lack of agreement), then a switch to *die Mädchen* + a relative clause *wurden*. . . . In other cases items are missing and have to be inferred: *in der Zeit wo se von dem Fischer im*

Netz war (*als er sie gefangen hatte*) *und* is missing before *ihr goldenes Haar*. The lexical item *fuffzig* (*fünfzig*) is restricted to spoken language. Non-standard forms which are to be found comprise *Graf*, object (standard *Grafen*), *diese Mädchenlehen wurde*, lack of agreement between subject and verb (standard *wurden* pl.); *hörten diesen wundersamen Liedern*, where the acc. should be used, *Lieder*, or the verbal particle *zu* added. In *wenn das Zuschlag erteilt wurde* it is not clear whether *das* is simply the 'wrong' gender for *Zuschlag* or there is a mixture of construction and the speaker meant to use the neuter infinitive *das Zuschlagen*.

Text 2

Another example of spoken German is represented by a short conversation between a father and his son while they are mending a car. This shows another kind of transcription giving different information, for example about pronunciation and intonation. The intonation patterns are given by simple rising or falling lines. Those words in bold type show a strong stress. More forms show the elision of unstressed *-e* and consequent assimilations: *müssmer* for *müssen wir*, *durchgehn*, *woll'n*, but not in most cases. Again, the pronunciation of words is not shown, for instance is the vowel in *kriegst* long or short, is the immediately following consonant a plosive or a fricative? Much more information is given about the non-verbal behaviour of the participants in the conversation, what they are doing, what their mood is. Those words and phrases in parentheses are supposed and not actually articulated. Syntactically the sentences are either simple sentences or sentence fragments without verbs.

A: [flucht und stöhnt nach einem mißglückten Arbeitsgang]

B: **Hilft** doch nichts! **Hilft** doch nichts! Wir müssen **hier** runter mit'm Ding, ne

A: [stöhnt zustimmend] (Müssen hier rein, he? Wenn ich) hier reingehe . . .

B: Na, da is' doch, / wo du dann ansetzen kannst, doch nachher noch kürzer. Weiter **runter** müssmer. – Hier unten dran.

A: {Und} das muß **ganz** kurz . . . (. . .) mal die Kette dran (. . .) Wenn ich jetzt –

B: **Laß** doch mal das mit der Kette!

A: (außen dran) – so. (. . .)

B: Da müssmer doch erst mal (..........................) machen. Müßte doch noch durchgehn.

?: (. . .)

A: Jetzt (. . .)

B: Jetzt werd' ich erst mal gucken, ob ich (die nich') wieder hier drüben draufkrieg' (. . .) Halt, du mußt festhalten drüben!

A: [stöhnt] (Solcher) **Mist**!

B: Na! – **So**.

A: (. . . muß sie kommen.)

B: So, warte mal! ({Jetzt} woll'n wir) hier mal gucken. / Du mußt ein bissel vor dem Loch ansetzen, ne.

A: Ja.

B: Daß wir sie nachher 'neinklopfen.

A: [stöhnt] Mensch, ich nehm's Ding und **hau**'s gleich zusamm'! [B lacht] Dieser elende **Bin**senbau, der verdammte! [stöhnt]

B: Jetzt erst mal ansetzen, hier das Ding!

A: {Hast}'s richtig angesetzt?

B: Ja. [ungeduldig]

A: Jetzt is' das auf einmal . . .

B: **Was** is' auf einmal?

A: Hängt das in / der Luft.

B: Was denn?

A: (N'ja, warte mal . . .) Ja, so könnte's ungefähr klappen.

B: So, nun das **Ding** dran. Ich halt' jetzt das Ding mal fest. – – Du mußt tiefer!

A: Na, das is' ja das! (. . . daß ich) hier vorbeikomme . . . [stöhnt]

B: Steck doch noch mal was **drunter**, / damit du das **Ding** 'neinkriegst!

A: ({Wart}) erst mal . . .

B: Stückl **Holz** drunter! – – Du kommst doch dort mit der **Brech**stange nicht 'nein!

(Mackeldey 1987: 123ff.)

2.3 FORMAL AND INFORMAL USE OF LANGUAGE

Language can vary according to the degree of informality or formality demanded by the situation and the relationship between the language users. With regard to spoken language this means that in formal situations such as law courts or church services, a certain type of German will be used, whereas at home another type of German will be used. The type which is identified as being more appropriate to formal situations is the standard (*Hochsprache, Standardsprache*), whereas in informal situations colloquial speech (*Umgangssprache*) or dialect is used. The standard will tend to be used when one speaker is in a position of authority over the others, for example teachers and students at school and university or for contact between an employer and his employees. The students, teachers and employers will probably use colloquial speech among themselves in other situations. The standard is narrowly prescribed, whereas colloquial speech is a variety of speech which has mostly defied definition and close description. Many words and phrases are labelled in dictionaries as colloquial: *kriegen, angucken, absacken, Krach, Schwips, dreckig, was (etwas)*. There are also exclamations such as *Mensch!, toll!, prima!* A further complication in the German speech area is that there is not simply one colloquial variety but several regional varieties. Eichhoff (1977–8) consciously uses the plural form *Umgangssprachen*. There are differences which reflect all the linguistic levels of language: phonological, grammatical and lexical. The regional colloquial varieties have as their base the local dialect which in South Germany exercises a very strong influence whereas in North Germany this is not so strong. The difference between colloquial speech and dialect is rather a fluid one. In general, dialect is further removed from the standard in phonology, grammar and vocabulary and is only used for communication between the inhabitants of a particular area. It is more used in rural parts and usually lacks prestige, although recent years have seen a dialect revival with poems and pop songs in dialect.

2.3.1   Regional colloquial features

The phonological features of each area are dependent on the phonological structure of the local dialects: for example, in North Germany most words spelt with word- or stem-final -*g*, for example *Tag, Berg, sagt, Talg* are pronounced with a fricative, [x], after a back vowel and [ç] after *r*, *l* and front vowels, [tax, zaxt, bɛrç, talç]. Individual speakers fluctuate between [k] and [x, ç] in many words. This reflects the local dialects where all standard word- and stem-final *g*'s are pronounced as fricatives. Similarly in South and Central Germany the front rounded vowels short and long *ü, ö* [ʏ, yː, œ, øː] are derounded and merge with the unrounded front vowels *i, e* [ɪ, iː, ɛ, ɛː, eː]. Thus *Biene, Bühne* come to have the same stressed vowel, [iː], and the stressed vowels of *vermissen, müssen* merge in [ɪ] and those of *Söhne, Sehne* in [eː]. Speakers again fluctuate in the use of unrounded and rounded vowels. This reflects the situation in the local dialects where all the front rounded vowels have been derounded. In the case of the pronunciation of some foreign words the dialects do not play any role and there is genuine regional colloquial variation between, for instance, the pronunciation of the initial consonant in *Chemie* as [ç] in North and Central Germany and [k] in South Germany (Eichhoff 1977–8: Map 112). The stress in words such as *Tabak* and *Kaffee* also varies regionally (Eichhoff 1977–8: Maps 109, 110).

The grammatical level also shows regional colloquial variants. In the north both the simple past tense, *kam*, and the compound perfect tense, *ist gekommen*, are used in speech to designate an event in the past, whereas in the south only the perfect is used. The auxiliary used for the perfect tense of *liegen, stehen, sitzen* is *haben* in the north and *sein* in the south (Eichhoff 1977–8: Map 125). The grammatical gender of nouns varies regionally, for example *die Butter* in the north (and the standard) but *der Butter* in the south. The formation of the plural shows more umlaut forms in the south, for example *die Wägen*, than in the north, *die Wagen* (Eichhoff 1977–8: Map 119). The past participle of *hauen* is regular, weak, in the north, *gehaut*, but irregular, strong, *gehauen*, in the south (Eichhoff 1977–8: Map 124). The separation of the particle *da* from the preposition in the pronominal adverb construction, for example *da weiß ich nichts von*, is typical of the north, whereas in the south the *da* is often repeated, for example *da weiß ich nichts davon*.

At the lexical level there are a great many differences which have been the subject of much study (Eichhoff 1977–8; Kretschmer 1918). Something of the speakers' attitudes and the difficulties raised by these regional lexical differences can be seen from the following extract from Thomas Mann's *Buddenbrooks*. Mann records how Tony Buddenbrook after her second marriage to Herr Permaneder encounters various difficulties when she is transported from her native Lübeck to Munich. She writes to her parents about the difficulties she has with cooks in Munich:

> Und wenn ich 'Frikadellen' sage, so begreift sie es nicht, denn es heißt hier 'Pflanzerln'; und wenn sie 'Karfiol' sagt, so findet sich wohl nicht so leicht ein Christenmensch, der darauf verfällt, daß sie Blumenkohl meint; und wenn ich sage: 'Bratkartoffeln', so schreit sie so lange 'Wahs!' bis ich 'Geröhste Kartoffeln' sage, denn so heißt es hier.

> ('And when I say *Frikadellen* ("rissoles") she doesn't understand it, for they are called *Pflanzerln* here, and when she says *Karfiol* ("cauliflower"), it's not easy for a Christian soul to work out that she means *Blumenkohl*, and when I say *Bratkartoffeln* ("fried

potatoes"), then she shouts "Whaat!" so long until I say *Geröhste Kartoffeln* for that is what they are called here.')

(Mann 1960: 248)

2.3.2   Use of dialect

The relationship between dialect and colloquial speech is a complicated one and varies according to the geographical area concerned. The situation in Austria is described in 3.2 and the diglossic situation in Switzerland between High German and Swiss German dialects in 4.3. Löffler (1985: 147) has a map which shows the number of dialect speakers in the old West Germany and Thuringia. There is a clear difference between the north, the centre and the south of the country, with dialect use becoming more prevalent the further south one goes. Twenty-nine per cent of the people in Hamburg speak dialect, with 46 per cent in Lower Saxony and North Rhine Westphalia, increasing to 63 per cent in Hesse, 61 per cent in northern Baden-Württemberg and 71 per cent in Bavaria. Schleswig-Holstein in the north is an exception with 64 per cent. However, if we just consider the number of those who use dialect at their workplace then the range goes from 35 per cent in Schleswig-Holstein through over 50 per cent in Hesse to 61 per cent in Bavaria. There have been local investigations which have given more detail to this. Friebertshäuser and Dingeldein (1989: Map 1) show how Hesse displays a transition from a northern Low German area, where only 25 per cent of speakers use dialect, to a southern Central German area where 55 per cent of speakers use dialect. In between these areas there is a gradual rise in the percentages of dialect speakers. Within the general statement of dialect use there are differences according to situation and interlocuter. Dialect is used most with the baker or the butcher (54 per cent), decreasing in use with the postman (44 per cent), in a family situation (40 per cent) and among regulars at a pub (Stammtisch) (30 per cent). In other, more formal situations there was less use of dialect, for instance at official offices or in a bank (17 per cent) and at the doctor's (14 per cent). That the use of dialect can vary even within one dialect region is shown by an investigation carried out in Thuringia in the 1960s (Spangenberg 1986, 1990). In the eastern part of the region, in a corridor between Jena and Halle, predominantly colloquial speech is used. In the western part of the region, however, dialect use varies a great deal from extremely widespread use in Hennbergisch and Itzgründisch and south-east Thuringia, moderate but strong use in the northern slopes of the

Thuringian Forest, West Thuringia, Eichsfeld and North Thuringia to negligible use in Central Thuringia. There are also clear generational differences in that it is predominantly older speakers who use dialect. Among older groups of speakers the use of dialect is similar in men and women, whereas among younger age groups the decline of dialect is more marked among women than men. Russ (1990) provides a number of descriptions of the use of dialect in different areas; Mattheier (1990) sketches some of the trends in the use of dialect. There is the paradox that dialect use is declining but there is also an increased interest and use of dialect. In the first case it is true that the standard language is being propagated and through urbanization has been infiltrating into many different domains. This is, however, mostly true of the base dialect. The increase in dialect consciousness and use is taking place in towns among the younger generation and only in certain areas. In fact this 'dialect' use is the development of new regional non-standard varieties.

2.3.3 Illustrative texts in dialect

Text 1:

A Low German version of part of the Christmas story from Luke 2. The High German version is in 1.4.1.1.

1 In düsse Tied käm vun den Kaiser Augustus en Order rut, dat jedereen sick in de Stüerlisten inschriewen schull. 2 Düt wär ganz wat Nies – dat wörr to'n ersten Mal dörchföhrt – un domols wär Kyrenius Stattholer öwer Syrien. 3 Na, jedereen mak sick denn ock up de Reis' na sin Heimatstadt und leet sick inschriewen. 4 So güng ock Josef vun Galiläa ut de Stadt Nazareth na Judäa, na David sin Heimatstadt – de heet Bethlehem – denn he hör to David sin Sipp un Familie 5 un wull sick inschriewen laten mit Maria, de em antruut wär. Un de schull Moder warn. 6 As se dor wärn, käm de Tied dat se to liggn kamen schull. 7 Un se bröch ehren ersten Söhn to Welt un wickel em in Windeln un lä em in en Kriff; denn se harrn sünst keen Platz in de Harbarg. 8 Un nu wärn in desülwige Gegend Schäpers buten up dat Feld. De heeln nachts bi das Veehwark de Wach. Un wat passeer? Mit een Mal stünn den Herrn sin Engel vör ehr, un unsen Herrgodd sin Herrlikeit lücht öwer ehr up. Do verfehrn se sick banni. 10 Un de Engel sä to ehr: 'Man jo keen Angst! Nä, en grote Freud heff ick ju to vertelln – un all' de Lüd schüllt dat to weten kriegen – 11 denn för ju is hüt de Heiland born. De herr Christus is dat, in David sin Stadt. 12 Un dat schall

för ju dat Teeken wesn; ji ward finn'n dat Kind inwickelt in Windeln, un liggn deit dat in ein Krüff.' 13 Un knapp harr he't seggt, do swew üm den Engel en grote Swarm vun unsen Herrgod sin Hofstaat. De löwden Godd un sungen: 14 'Low un Ehr dor baben för unsen Herrgodd un Freden hier nerrn up de Eer för Minschen, de dat hartli meent un den goden Willn hebt!'

(Jessen 1962: 111)

Text 2:

A poem in Bavarian by Günter Goepfert

> Nach Bethlehem unterwegs
> Drauss tuats schneebebberln
> koid [= kalt] blost der Wind.
> Jetz gschiecht, was gescheng muaß,
> fürs himmlische Kind.
>
> Drauss tuats schneebebberln
> der Weg ist weit.
> D'Mari moant schüchtern:
> ''s is höchste Zeit!'
>
> Drauss tuats schneebebberln
> hell is de Nacht,
> Schleun di nur, Sepperl,
> und gib fein Acht!
>
> Drauss tuats schneebebberln
> halts nur fest zamm;
> 's muaß ja as Kind bald
> a Hoametl ham.

(Merkle 1978: 18)

2.4 ARCHAIC LANGUAGE

The third dimension of language variation is time: older language differs from more recent. The vocabulary of the language is especially affected. New words arise and others die out. Lexicographers recognize this by designating words that are dying out as 'obsolete' or 'obsolescent'. Obsolescent words are those whose use is becoming more restricted and only used by older speakers or in certain regions, for example *Absud* 'decoction', *Backfisch* 'flapper, teenager', *Depesche* 'telegram', *Schulmeister* 'teacher'. Obsolete words are those which are no longer used in the present-day language, but still understood by older speakers or in certain regions, for example *Base* '(female) cousin', *Binokel* 'pair of spectacles', *Nadelgeld* 'pin money', *Ordonnanz* 'order' (Ludwig 1991: 258f.). A sample of words from the letters D and E of the *Duden Großes Wörterbuch* showed 494 obsolescent or obsolete words. They were mostly nouns (205), of which 130 were of foreign origin. Of the other word classes there were 107 verbs but only 45 adjectives, 14 adverbs, 7 particles and 14 phrases. Altogether this was only a small percentage of all the words in D and E. It shows, however, how potentially difficult to understand a text from even the nineteenth century might be. The New High German period is usually taken as beginning about 1725 but of course there are many differences in the texts between then and now. Since many of the texts have become classics of German literature, readers are aware of many forms which only occur in these texts. They will understand them passively but not use them as part of their active vocabulary. The following text from Joseph Freiherr von Eichendorff's *Aus dem Leben eines Taugenichts* (1823–6) illustrates a number of archaic and obsolete forms which are nevertheless still understood today (Russ 1992: 10–13).

Indem, wie ich mich so umsehe, kömmt ein köstlicher Reisewagen ganz nahe an mich heran, der mochte wohl schon einige Zeit hinter mir drein gefahren sein, ohne daß ich es merkte, weil mein Herz so voller Klang war, denn es ging ganz langsam, und zwei vornehme Damen steckten die Köpfe aus dem Wagen und hörten mir zu. Die eine war besonders schön und jünger als die andere, aber eigentlich gefielen sie mir alle beide. Als ich nun aufhörte zu singen, ließ die ältere still halten und redete mich holdselig an: 'Ei, lustiger Gesell, Er weiß ja recht hübsche Lieder zu singen.' Ich nicht zu faul dagegen: 'Euer Gnaden aufzuwarten, wüßt' ich noch viel schönere.' Darauf fragte sie mich wieder: 'Wohin wandert Er denn schon so früh am frühen Morgen?' Da schämte ich mich, daß ich das selber nicht wußte, und sagte dreist: 'Nach Wien'; nun sprachen beide miteinander in einer fremden Sprache, die ich nicht verstand. Die jüngere schüttelte einigemal mit dem Kopfe, die andere lacht aber in einem fort und rief mir endlich zu: 'Spring Er nur hinten mit auf, wir fahren auch nach Wien.' Wer war froher als ich! Ich machte eine Reverenz und war mit einem Sprunge hinter dem Wagen, der Kutscher knallte, und wir flogen über die glänzende Straße fort, daß mir der Wind am Hute pfiff.

(von Eichendorff 1958–9, 2: 52f.)

The form *kömmt*, showing umlaut in the 3rd pers. sg. pres. of strong verbs, cf. *stoßen – stößt*, has been replaced by *kommt*, a form without umlaut. The adjective *köstlich* is now used to refer to food and wine or else, in colloquial speech, it means 'priceless'; it is used to mean 'expensive'. The verb *dreinfahren* is used here to mean 'to follow' but is now only used in the sense of 'to intervene', mostly in colloquial language. The word *holdselig* is restricted to literary usage in the meaning 'sweet, fair' and is mostly used as an adjective in contradistinction to its adverbial usage here. The form *Gesell* is no longer used and its meaning 'fellow' is obsolete or pejorative. It is only retained in the meaning 'journeyman'. The use of the 3rd pers. sg. pronoun *Er* as a polite pronoun is obsolete, as is the term of address *Euer Gnaden*. The noun *Reverenz* is used for 'bow' whereas now it is mostly used for 'reverence' in a general abstract sense. The dat. sg. final *-e* of masculine and neuter nouns, *Kopfe*, *Sprunge*, *Hute* is no longer widely used except in certain set phrases, *im Grunde*, *zu Hause*.

In other instances an archaic text may be characteristic of a particular specialist language. This is certainly so with regard to religious language. Although the liturgy and the Luther Bible have been continually revised and brought up to date, many of the famous hymns, composed between the sixteenth and nineteenth centuries, show archaic words and constructions. The following three stanzas of a popular Advent hymn is by Georg Weißel (1590–1635):

Macht hoch die Tür, die Tor macht weit;
Es kommt der Herr der Herrlichkeit,
Ein König aller Königreich,
Ein Heiland aller Welt zugleich,
Der Heil und Leben mit sich bringt;
Derhalben jauchzt, mit Freuden singt:
Gelobet sei mein Gott, mein Schöpfer reich von Rat.

O wohl dem Land, o wohl der Stadt,
So diesen König bei sich hat.
Wohl allen Herzen insgemein,
Da dieser König ziehet ein.
Er ist die rechte Freudensonn,
Bringt mit sich lauter Freud und Wonn.
Gelobet sei mein Gott, mein Tröster früh und spat.

Komm, o mein Heiland, Jesu Christ,
Meins Herzens Tür dir offen.

Ach zeuch mit deiner Gnaden ein;
Dein Freundlichkeit auch uns erschein.
Dein Heilger Geist uns führ und leit
Den Weg zur ewgen Seligkeit.
Dem Namen dein, O Herr, sei ewig Preis und Ehr.

The words *gelobet, ziehet* contain an *e* in the unstressed syllable which in modern German only occurs when the verb stem ends in *-d* or *-t*, e.g. *redet, rettet* and reflects an older stage of the language before the loss, or syncope, of this unstressed *e*, which is also used, even in modern German, for reasons of scansion in verse. The word *derhalben* would be replaced by *deshalb*. The particle *so* introduces a relative clause: *O wohl dem Land, o wohl der Stadt, So diesen König bei sich hat.* It was quite frequent in the seventeenth century but in modern German it would be replaced by the appropriate form of *der, die, das.* The imperative form *zeuch* has been replaced by *zieh* with the vowel of the infinitive. In the last line *Dem Namen dein* reflects the old possibility of having the adjective following the noun which occurred in Old and Middle High German but is now only possible in literary language, *Röslein rot*, or archaic language.

2.5 SPECIALIST, TECHNICAL AND GROUP LANGUAGES

(Feinäugle 1974; Fluck 1976, 1984; von Hahn 1980; Keller 1978: 534–42; Möhn and Pelka 1984)

The fourth type of variation that is significant for modern German is that connected with different groups of speakers. The designation *Gemeinsprache* 'common standard language' is used in this context to contrast with the specialist, technical and group languages, which are known together as *Sondersprachen*, or *Speziellsprachen*. These specialist languages can be subdivided according to their linguistic function into technical languages (*Fachsprachen*) and group languages (*Gruppensprachen*). Some of the group languages are spoken by speakers who are also members of a particular profession and can thus be called professional languages (*Standessprachen*), for example soldiers' language. There is a multiplicity of technical and group languages which has increased over the centuries. The *Duden Großes Wörterbuch* lists 184 of them, ranging from *Akustik, Anatomie, Anthropologie, Arbeitsrecht* via *Jägersprache, Kartenspiel, Kaufmannssprache, Kerntechnik* to *Zahntechnik, Zeitungswesen, Zollwesen* and *Zoologie*. Although such a large number of technical and group languages exist, they all share certain linguistic traits, differing mainly in vocabulary and means of word formation from the common standard language and also, but in a much lesser degree, in the use of some syntactic constructions. When referring to features which are common to both technical and group languages we shall use the term 'specialist language' but when referring to features which differentiate them we shall use 'technical' and 'group languages'.

2.5.1   Technical languages

All speakers of German come into contact with these technical languages at some time or other in their lives. The average speaker of modern German often meets words which are unknown to him or her or which are used in different ways from the common standard language. This frequently happens when the subject matter of a particular book or article is of a specialized nature, such as atomic physics, electronics, psychiatry, anatomy, linguistics or engineering. The reason for the lack of understanding resides in the complex nature of the subject being discussed. Even educated speakers are not experts in every field of knowledge in the present-day world, for example an industrial chemist may not understand a text on psychiatry nor a surgeon a text on electronics. The barrier to mutual understanding between the experts and lay people lies in the use of words and certain meanings of words which are peculiar to the science itself. Thus each scientific or academic specialism has its own linguistic variety. The use of certain specialized words enables the expert to feel they belong to a certain group but this, as we shall see, is not the only motive for using such terms. The main purpose of a technical language is to enable a precise designation to be given to objects, processes and concepts which form the basis of the specialization concerned. A further task is to develop new terms for the ever-increasing new specialisms and changes in knowledge that arise. Technical languages as such are not new, they have been used for such time-honoured trades and activities as carpentry, winemaking, fishing and mining, some of which have not changed very much over the centuries (Drozd and Seibicke 1973: 1–35).

Technical languages have several functions and also differ according to the participants in their use. Thus they can be descriptive, simply describing something, cf. the text on champagne-making at the end of this section: *Schaumwein (Sekt) ist moussierender Wein, der durch einen hohen Gehalt an Kohlensäure schäumt*; instructive, for example recipes: *Das weiche Fett schäumig rühren und den Zucker, Vanillezucker und die Eier nach und nach dazugeben. Das Mehl mit dem Stärkemehl und dem Backpulver vermischen und abwechselnd mit der Milch unterrühren. Den Teig in eine gut gefettete Springform füllen*; or directive, setting out rules and instructions within which people can move, for example typically instructions for games and regulations in general: *Es wird ein Spieler ausgewählt, der die Karten verteilt. Jeder Spieler erhält 7 Karten. Der Rest der Karten wird in die Mitte des Tisches gelegt und die oberste Karte wird für alle sichtbar aufgedeckt. Die Spieler nehmen ihre Karten auf, und sortieren diese nach Farbe oder numerisch. Ziel des Spiels ist es, als erster Spieler alle Karten abzulegen. Reihum kann jeder Spieler eine Karte ablegen, wenn er in Besitz einer passenden Karte ist. Paßt keine Karte, muß er vom Kartenstock eine aufnehmen.* Some times texts are mixed, containing sub-texts with different functions.

Although we have spoken of technical languages in general, we must also recognize that they are realized at different levels, depending on the role of the participants. There are: (1) the highest level, where theoretical issues are discussed by experts in the field; (2) the workshop level, where issues of production are discussed between the experts and production technicians; and (3) the level of the consumer, where the general public comes into contact with the technical product or service.

2.5.2 Linguistic characteristics of technical languages

(Beneš 1966, 1968)

It is at the level of vocabulary, however, that specialist languages distinguish themselves most from the common standard. As well as creating new words by borrowing, for example *Phonem*, *Allophon*, *Determinant*, or creating new lexical forms by word formation, for example *Oberflächenstruktur*, *Tiefenstruktur*, new meanings can be given to already existing words, for example *Knoten* 'knot' is used to refer to the node in a tree diagram, *Kompetenz* 'competence' is used for linguistic competence and *Merkmal* 'characteristic' is applied to phonological and semantic features. Other examples of new words and changes in meaning will be found in 10.2.2.1 and 10.2.4.2 and examples of new word formations in 9.7. Although the syntax of technical languages does not contain any new or different constructions from the standard language, it shows definite preferences for certain features. For instance, through the use of nominalizations the sentences are often simple sentences containing one verb: *Nach Ablauf der eingestellten Nachladezeit erfolgt die Umschaltung auf Ladeerhaltung.* Impersonal and passive constructions are also frequent. The use of the passive helps to avoid clumsy usage of *man*, for example *Das gepreßte Papier wird auf Maß geschnitten, sorgfältig von den restlichen Quellmitteln gereinigt, getrocknet und geglättet.* The use of *man* would have also required the use of *es* as well as *Papier*, for example *Man preßt das Papier, schneidet es auf Maß, reinigt es von den restlichen Quellmitteln und trocknet und glättet es.* The passive also focuses attention on the topic, *das gepreßte Papier*, rather than on the agent, *man*. There is a severe restriction in the use of verbal categories. Most verbs, for example, occur in the third person sg. or pl. There is a tendency to use simple sentences but to fill them with information. The most important part of speech is the noun and its attributes. The verbs tend to be taken from a restricted list and many have lost their full meaning and have become mere functional verbs (*Funktionsverben*), i.e. they only express meaning when used together with a noun or noun phrase. In the sentence *Die Sache wird zur Durchführung gebracht*, *bringen* is used a functional verb, for the expression *zur Durchführung gebracht* could have been rendered by the verb *durchführen*. Other functional verbs are: *geben, Auftrag geben; finden, Aufnahme finden; führen, Beweis führen; machen, Andeutung machen; leisten, Hilfe leisten; nehmen, in Einsicht nehmen; setzen, in Gang setzen; stellen, Frage stellen; treffen, Abmachung treffen.* The use of functional verbs is not limited to technical languages but occurs frequently in them. Other nominalizing constructions are used to avoid the use of verbs and thus to pack more information into simple sentences, for example the infinitive with *um . . . zu, Um Reizwirkungen zu vermeiden, zieht man Zinkpaste vor*; nominalization with *-ung, Im Bild ist die Messung eines Stabdurchmessers gezeigt* (*wie man einen Stabdurchmesser mißt*). The whole style of technical languages tends towards a formulaic use of words and constructions.

2.5.3   Text to illustrate technical language

The following passage is used to illustrate technical language. Some of the characteristics of word formation and syntax are commented on.

Schaumwein (Sekt) – Herstellung, in Deutschland erstmalig 1826. Schaumwein (Sekt) ist moussierender Wein, der durch einen hohen Gehalt an Kohlensäure schäumt. Der Oberbegriff 'Schaumwein' gilt für alle Weine, deren Kohlensäuredruck bei 20 C mindestens 3 atü (2,94 bar) beträgt. Die Kohlensäure muß durch alkoholische Gärung entstanden sein. Sekt bzw. Qualitätsschaumwein darf sich nur solcher Schaumwein nennen, der mindestens 9 Monate gelagert wurde und nach behördlicher Qualitätsprüfung eine amtliche Prüfnummer erhalten hat (Mindestalkoholgehalt 10%). In Deutschland wird Schaumwein (Sekt) aus fertigen Stillweinen durch eine zweite Vergärung gewonnen. Diese zweite Gärung kommt durch den Zusatz von Zucker und Zuchthefe (Fülldosage) zum Grundwein in Gang. Für den weiteren Produktionsgang haben sich drei verschiedene Methoden bewährt:

Rüttelverfahren (auch méthode champenoise). Gärung und Reifung finden auf der Flasche statt. Hefe und Trub werden durch Rütteln der Flaschen in eigens dazu konstruierten Rüttelpulten zum Flaschenhals transportiert und nach künstlicher Vereisung desselben entfernt.

Filterenthefung. Gärung und Reifung auf der Flasche. Danach kommt der Sekt samt Hefe und Trub auf Großbehälter und wird vor der Abfüllung über Filter geklärt.

Großraumgärverfahren. Die 2. Gärung und Reifung findet in druckfesten Großbehältern aus Edelstahl statt. Die Enthefung erfolgt gleichfalls über Filter.

Bei allen drei Verfahren wird dem fertigen Schaumwein (Sekt) vor dem Abfüllen die sogenannte Versanddosage eine Lösung aus Zucker und Wein, zur Erreichung des gewünschten Süßegrades beigesetzt. Die erste und zweite Methode sind kostenaufwendiger als das Großraumgärverfahren. Den Herstellungsverfahren wurde früher eine nicht gerechtfertigte Bedeutung beigemessen. Heute weiß man: Die Qualität wird von den verschiedenen Verfahren nicht oder unwesentlich beeinflußt. Über sie entscheidet vielmehr die Güte der Grundweine (Cuvée) und die Lagerzeit auf der Hefe. Das Rüttelverfahren ist in Deutschland nur noch vereinzelt anzutreffen, die Flaschengärung mit anschließender Filterenthefung praktizieren einige Unternehmen vor allem für Sekte mit hohem Qualitätsanspruch, das Großraumgärverfahren aber liefert den überwiegenden Mengenteil der Schaumweine und Sekte. Gesamtjahresproduktion der ca. 90 deutschen Sekthersteller 1977 ca. 240 Millionen

Flaschen. Acht Firmen halten einen Anteil von 79% an der Produktion.

(Hochrain 1978: 140–2)

Notes on the passage

Schaumwein. Wahrig (1986: 1111), defines this as: 'Kohlensäure enthaltender Wein, der beim Öffnen der Flasche stark schäumt, Sekt', and *Duden Universalwörterbuch* (1989: 1308), as 'aus Wein hergestelltes alkoholisches Getränk, das Kohlensäure enthält u. moussiert', but in this passage it is defined precisely in terms of temperature and pressure.

moussierender. From *moussieren* (French *mousser*), 'to sparkle', which is only used of drinks.

atü. The abbreviation for *Atmosphärenüberdruck* 'pressure above one *Bar* (nt.)' unit of measurement of air-pressure, Engl. *bar*, from Greek *baros* 'weight'.

Gärung. Noun formed from a verb stem by adding *-ung*. Several of these formations occur in the passage: *Vergärung*, *Reifung*, *Enthefung*, *Vereisung*.

Stillwein. In technical accounts it is necessary to distinguish between different sorts of wine: *Schaumwein*, *Stillwein* and *Grundwein*.

Fülldosage. The French loan word *dosage* is used instead of German *Dosis* (from Greek). This mixture is exactly defined in the diagram as *Versanddosage*.

Zuchthefe or *Reinzuchthefe*. This is more precise than *Hefe*.

kommt in Gang 'starts'. This illustrates the use of a functional verb *kommen* and a prepositional phrase *in Gang*.

Rüttelverfahren. This is a special 'method of shaking' the bottles which are in *Rüttelpulten*.

Trub (m.), The 'dregs' or 'draff'. A word that is only used of dregs of drinks. A related synonym is *Treber* (m.).

Filterenthefung. A variant form to those in *-ung* is the nominalized infinitive. The form *Filtrationsenthefen* is found on the diagram.

Großraumgärverfahren. This is a long compound which can be paraphrased as the 'method of fermentation which takes place in a large space'. The form *-verfahren* is a semi-suffix or suffixoid, an element of a compound which, although it has the characteristic of a suffix rather than a word, is deemed to be different from a traditional suffix (see 9.4.3) and *-ung* could be used in place of it, for example *Großraumgärung* which is in opposition to *Flaschengärung*.

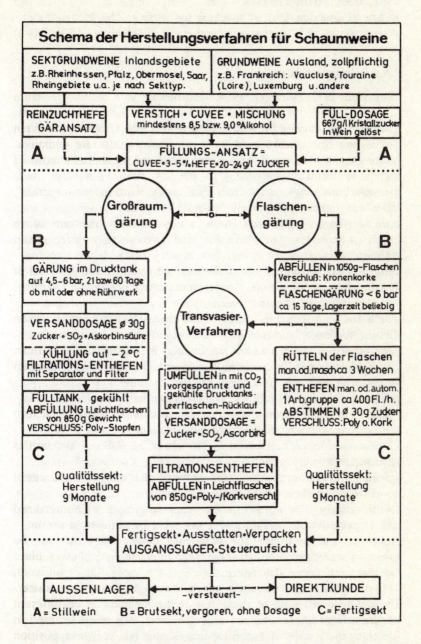

Figure 2.1 Plan of the production process used in the manufacture of sparkling wine (from *The Dictionary of German Wines*, 1978: 141)

Cuvée (nt.). Mixture of basic wines.

Rührwerk (on diagram). A machine for stirring. The semi-suffix or suffixoid *-werk* is used as a collective.

2.5.4   Group languages

(Bausinger 1972; Feinäugle 1974; Möhn 1980)

There is some overlap between technical and group languages in that the former are usually used by a particular group, for example hunting terms by hunters. Group languages also use similar linguistic means as technical languages to develop their vocabulary: for example borrowings, *posch* from Engl. *posh*; word formation *affenstark* 'very strong', *Kaputtnik* 'outsider' and new designations for ordinary things, for example hunters use *Löffel* for the 'ears of a hare', or teenagers use *Zahn* for 'girl'. Where they differ from technical languages, however, lies in very often deliberately excluding other speakers from understanding them except those who are members of the group. An extreme example of this in the past was thieves' slang (*Gaunersprache*, sometimes called *Rotwelsch*) of which there are records dating from the sixteenth century. The thieves needed a language in which they could communicate with each other but which was not understood by outsiders. This effect was achieved, not by changing the syntax, but by using ordinary words with different meanings or else creating new words, for example *Feldglocke* 'gallows', *Obermann* 'hat', *Windfang* 'coat'. Some words have become a firm part of colloquial German if not of the written standard: *blechen* 'to pay, fork out', *foppen* 'to fool', *Hochstapler* 'crook', *schummeln* 'to cheat', *schäkern* 'to tease', *schwänzen* 'to play truant', *pleite* 'bankrupt', *Kohldampf* 'hunger', *schmusen* 'to chatter, flatter', *betucht* 'well-off'. Many of these were spread through their use in student and soldiers' slang in the nineteenth century. The words of these group languages, which were of course not normally written, were collected by scholars in the late eighteenth and throughout the nineteenth century. They are now no longer in active use although some, such as *blechen* etc., have found their way into colloquial speech.

In present-day German there are not many group languages which are widely used. One of these few is the language of teenagers, particularly of those who are still at school. We will use this to illustrate the nature of group languages as it has been extensively researched in the late 1950s and early 1960s and lexicographically

described by Küpper (1970). Many of the terms are, however, obsolescent. Most of the 15,000 expressions are predictably for such
concepts as 'school reports', 'boys', 'girls', 'to cheat', 'to have to stay
down a class' and so on. One of the chararacteristics of teenage
language is its creativity and variety: for instance, Küpper has
168 expressions for 'teacher', including the following *Alleswisser*,
Arschpauker, *Bildungsschuster*, *Drummler*, *Gänseprediger*, *Klassen-
schreck*, *Stupidenrat*, *Tierquäler*, *Zwitscherpauker*. What is typical of
school teenage language is that it uses standard word forms with non-
standard meanings, for example *Zahn* 'girl'. There is an abundance of
compounds, some special formations, for example *Kummeraktie* 'report' (lit. 'worry share-certificate'), others having a normal meaning in
the standard, for example *Entwicklungshilfe* 'foreign aid' for 'cheat-
ing'. Most compounds are used for jocular effect. For instance, the
following are all designations for school: *Affenkasten*, *Bedürfnisanstalt*
(also used for 'public convenience'), *Bildungsschuppen*, *Klapsmühle*
(normally used for a mental hospital) and *Verdummungsanstalt*. The
most frequent parts of speech of the new formations are nouns, verbs
and adjectives, with nouns being the most frequent. To illustrate the
variety of possible forms the main variants for 'girl' will be examined:
Baby, *Bombe*, *Biene*, *Brumme*, *Ente*, *Hase*, *Haut*, *Puppe*, *Schnecke*,
Zahn (the last being grammatically masculine). These are all simple
nouns whose semantic motivation varies a great deal. *Baby* is an
English loan word and *Bombe* is a loan translation of English
'(sex-)bomb'. *Biene*, including the Berlin equivalent *Brumme*, *Ente*,
Hase and *Schnecke* are insect or animal names. *Puppe* is not restricted
to school slang. *Haut* and *Zahn* are of obscure origin. The productivity
of these words is shown by their ability to occur in compounds:
Bienenkorb 'girls' school', *Bienenschwarm* 'group of girls'; *Hasenstall*
'hostel for girls'; *Zahnersatz* 'substitute girl friend', *Zahnweh* 'lover's
grief'. The unstressed suffix *-i* occurs frequently with nouns in teenage
and colloquial language in general: *Heini* 'guy, chap', *Idi* 'idiot', *Raazi*
'eraser, rubber', *Süßi* 'sweety', *Schnucki* 'term of endearment for boy
or girl', *Handi* 'handwork'.

There are fewer new verbs than nouns. In some cases the same
verbal prefix is retained although different stems are used for the
same meaning: *abbohren*, *abbolzen*, *abfetzen*, *abklauen*, *abstauben*
are some of the variants of 'to cheat' (*abschreiben*). Both simple and
compound verbs are used. For instance, the following simple verbs
are used for 'to learn': *asten*, *bimsen*, *bohren*, *bolzen*, *büffeln*, *job-
ben*, *keilen*, *kümmeln*, *matchen*, *ochsen*, *pauken*, *sich schaffen*, *schan-
zen*, *stolßen*, *strebern*, *wuckeln*; and the following compounds:

anstrebern, durchackern, durchochsen, durchpauken, ehrgeizen, einochsen, einpauken, ereseln, sich hereinschaffen, sich vollpumpen. In other cases the simple or compound verb gives way to verbal phrases: *sich auf den Hintern setzen, sich auf den Hosenboden setzen, sich auf die Hosen setzen, die Nase ins Buch stecken.*

There is also a limited range of adjectives, themselves having different meanings from the standard language, used with nouns which have a different meaning in teenage language; for example *toter Zahn* 'ugly girl', *schräger Zahn* 'flighty girl'. There were 142 adjectives in Küpper (1970) designating something as 'unequalled, incomparable'. Of these *dufte, klaß, nupf, prima, schmissig, schnafte, schnuckig, toff(ig), tolfte* go back to the nineteenth century and the first quarter of the twentieth century. Others such as *gebracht, jumbig* (from *Jumbo*), *schaffe, schnell, weltisch, wupf, wummig* are not recorded before 1945 and are of obscure origin. English influence is seen in *posch* 'posh', *kingmäßig*, and perhaps *schau(ig)* 'showy'. The origin of *fädig, hip* (perhaps from *hipp, hipp, hurra*), *mickisch* is also obscure. Some of these words are not restricted to school slang but are in general use in colloquial German, for example *dufte, prima, Pauker, Zahn, büffeln, Heini, Puppe.* This is a parallel phenomenon to the spread of technical words in the standard language. There is thus a reciprocal relationship between group languages on the one hand and standard and colloquial German on the other. Each enriches the other and most speakers have access to specialist and group languages of varying kinds during their lifetime.

2.5.5 Text to illustrate group language

The following artificially constructed passage illustrates some of the features of this youth language of the 1960s. Standard German equivalents are given in brackets.

Geliebte Dorothea! Einzige Klammer! [= Freundin]
Ich schreibe Dir heute vom Stall [= zu Hause] aus, um Dir eine spitze Schaffe [= großartige Sache] mitzuteilen, obwohl mich mein brüderlicher Tastenhengst [= Bruder, der Pianist] unentwegt stört. Du kennst ihn doch: der mit dem auffallenden Pennerkissen [= langen Haarschnitt] und der stumpfen Schramme [= besonders dumme Gans] Anny als Brieze [= feste Freundin], ein typischer Fall von bescheuertem Eckzahn! [= blödem Mauerblümchen].
   Du sollst es wissen, liebe steile Haut [= flottes Mädchen], daß ich jetzt eine Zentralschaffe [= prima Stelle] im Fernsehen als

Beleuchter bekommen habe, so daß die Kohlen [= Finanzen] endlich stimmen, und ich die Miete nicht mehr scharf zu sein brauche [= schuldig bleibe]. Nun wird keiner mehr an mir herummotzen [= herummäkeln]! Morgen lasse ich mir eine Koreapeitsche [= Bürstenhaarschnitt] machen und kaufe mir kanische Rohren [= Jeans]! Die erste Rate fur den flinken Hirsch [= Motorrad] ist bezahlt. Du bekommst neue Kutten [= Kleider]. Setz' die Schlägerpfanne [= Sturzzhelm] auf! Und hinaus geht's ins Grüne in die dufte Gammeltimpe [= gemütliches Lokal], wo Gichtstengel [= Klarinette], Pfann [= Banjo] und Schießbude [= Schlagzeug] unsere Verlobungsmusik spielen! Dort werden wir ein Faß aufmachen [= froh und ausgelassen sein]; sehen, was läuft [= daß alles klargeht] und ein Rohr [= eine Flasche] nach dem anderen anbrechen. Du, süße Edelschaffe [= patentes Kind], wirst mit Deinem schauen Laufwerk [= schönen Beinen], das so viel Ankratz [= Zuspruch) hat, mit mir einen hinrocken mit Überhebe und Anschmeiße [= einen Rock-n-Roll mit Luftsprung und Tuchfühlung], daß meine Neider vom Feuerstuhle [= Motorrad) fallen! Und wenn ein Zickendraht [= Spießbürger] meine reizende Wuchtbrumme [= hübsches Mädchen] zu scharf beäugt, dann kann ich ihn fix mit einem harten Brando [= Kinnhaken] bedienen.

Abends sehen wir uns noch den letzten Heuler [= ausgezeichneten Film] an, und danach werde ich Dir bei Superscheibe [= schöne Schallplattenmusik] und Lulle [= Zigarette] den goldenen Ring aufstecken!

Du bist leider sehr dufte [= ganz große Klasse], mein bedienter Zahn! [= Mädchen mit Sex-Appeal] Küß mich, denn darauf stehe ich! [= das liebe ich]

Dein Macker [= Freund] Billy

(Krüger-Lorenzen 1960: 300)

2.5.6 Recent developments in youth language

The language of young people has proved a fruitful source of study over the years, starting with the student and school language of the nineteenth century, through the youth movements of the early twentieth to the present. Although the language of the 1950s and 1960s can be well illustrated, youth language has moved on since then. The 1980s has seen a new burst of research on the language of young people. Henne (1984, 1986) has researched this variety empirically, using questionnaires. Although the main characteristics of group languages are still present, for example development of different meanings of words, interest has also concentrated on more general characteristics of the variety. Nicknames are used, both in a positive and negative way, for example *Buletto* 'likes *Buletten* (hamburgers)', *Blitz* 'because of slowness', or 'looks like' *Gonzo, Miss Piggy*. Again, this continues a tradition of student slang. Onomatopoeic words, called *Onpos* (an abbreviation from *Onomatopöien*), particularly from comics, are used as emphatic particles to substitute for parts of sentences, *würg* (showing disapproval), *Wenn mir etwas stinkt, sage ich würg*, or as accompaniments to actions, *Batz!* (the chalk breaks as a teacher is writing on the board). Other examples, with suggested meanings, are *ächz* '(1) exertion, exhaustion, (2) rejection, (3) relief'; *bäh* 'rejection and annoyance'; *lechz* '(1) desire for something, (2) expression in a mad situation'; *seufz* 'sadness, disappointment'; *uff* 'surprise, exertion, relief'. Another aspect of youth language is the use of sayings (*Sprüche*). They occur also among other subcultures. They function as recognition signals. If a speaker responds to them in the correct way, they are part of the group and accepted. They also function as greetings, *Na Du Frosch!*, as curses, *Du Maske!*, commentaries, *Ganz cool bleiben!*, and taunts to action, *Na, wird's bald!?* The following examples are from Henne (1986: 118–25): *Ah, Ägypten* when not understanding, *Das macht einen Fix und Fox/Foxi* 'when you're tired', *Mein Hamster bohnert* 'when surprised', *Alles Roger* 'everything alright'. There are a great number of phrases that start *Ich glaub* which express either surprise or annoyance, *Ich glaub, mich beißt ein Schwein*; *'s hackert*; *mich knutscht ein Elch*; *mich leckt ein Kängeruh*; *meine Oma geht mit Elvis*.

SELECT BIBLIOGRAPHY AND FURTHER READING

Bausinger, H. (1972) *Deutsch für Deutsche*, Frankfurt: Fischer, pp. 66–76; 118–31.

Beneš, E. (1966) 'Syntaktische Besonderheiten der deutschen wissenschaftlichen Fachsprache', *Deutsch als Fremdsprache*, 3: 26–36.

—— (1968) 'Die Fachsprachen', *Deutschunterricht für Ausländer*, 18: 24–36.

Berger, D. and Drosdowski, G. (eds) (1985) *Richtiges und Gutes Deutsch*, 3rd edn, Mannheim: Bibliographisches Institut.

Betten, A. (1977) 'Erforschung gesprochener deutscher Standardsprache (Teil I)', *Deutsche Sprache*, 5: 335–61.

—— (1978) 'Erforschung gesprochener deutscher Standardsprache (Teil II)', *Deutsche Sprache*, 6: 21–44.

Drosdowski, G., Dose, M., Eckey, W., Folz, J., Hartmann, H., Mang, D., Mangold, M., Schrupp, C., Trunk-Nußbaumer, M., Thyen, O. and

Wermke, M. (1989) *Duden Deutsches Universalwörterbuch*, 2nd edn (= *DUW*). Mannheim: Bibliographisches Institut.

Drozd, L. and Seibicke, W. (1973) *Deutsche Fach- und Wissenschaftssprache. Bestandsaufnahme, Theorie, Geschichte*. Wiesbaden: Brandstetter.

Durrell, M. (1992) *Using German: A Guide to Contemporary Usage*, Cambridge University Press.

von Eichendorff, J. (1826 [1958–9]) *Aus dem Leben eines Taugenichts*, in *Gesammelte Werke*, ed. H. J. Meinerts, 2 vols, Frankfurt-on-Main: Mohn.

Eichhoff, J. (1977–78) *Wortatlas der deutschen Umgangssprachen*, Berne and Munich: Francke.

Feinäugle, N. (1974) *Fach- und Sondersprachen. Arbeitstexte für den Unterricht*, Stuttgart: Reclam.

Fluck, H.-R. (1976) *Fachsprachen*, Munich: Franke, Uni-Taschenbücher 483.

—— (1984) *Fachdeutsch in Naturwissenschaft und Technik*, Heidelberg: Groos.

Friebertshäuser, H. and Dingeldein, H. J. (1989) *Hessischer Dialektzensus: statistischer Atlas zum Sprachgebrauch* (Hessische Sprachatlanten, Kleine Reine, 3), Tübingen: Francke.

Hahn, W. von (1980) 'Fachsprachen', in H. P. Althaus, H. Henne and H. E. Wiegand (eds) *Lexikon der Germanistischen Linguistik*. 2nd edn, Tübingen: Niemeyer, pp. 390–5.

Heinemann, M. (1989) *Kleines Wörterbuch der Jugendsprache*, Leipzig: Bibliographisches Institut.

Henne, H. (1984) 'Jugend und ihre Sprache', in *Die deutsche Sprache der Gegenwart. Vorträge gehalten auf der Tagung der Joachim Jungius-Gesellschaft der Wissenschaften Hamburg am 4. und 5. November 1983 von B. Carstensen, F. Debus, H. Henne, P. von Polenz, D. Stellmacher und H. Weinrich* (Veröffentlichung der Joachim Jungius-Gesellschaft Hamburg, 51), Göttingen: Vandenhoeck & Ruprecht, pp. 59–72.

—— (1986) *Jugend und ihre Sprache. Darstellung, Materialien, Kritik*, Berlin: de Gruyter.

Hochrain, H. (ed.) (1978) *dtv-Lexikon des deutschen Weins*, Munich: dtv.

Jessen, J. (trans.) (1962) *Dat Ole un dat Nie Testament in unse Modersspraak*, Göttingen: Vandenhoeck & Ruprecht.

Keller, R. E. (1978) *The German Language*, London: Faber & Faber.

—— (1981) 'Spoken German', *Bulletin of the John Rylands Library*, 64: 117–140.

Kohler, K. J. (1977) *Einführung in die Phonetik des Deutschen*, Berlin: Schmidt.

König, W. (1989) *Atlas zur Aussprache des Schriftdeutschen in der Bundesrepublik*, 2 vols, Munich: Hueber.

Kretschmer, P. (1918) *Wortgeographie der hochdeutschen Umgangssprache*, repr. 1969, Göttingen: Vandenhoeck & Ruprecht.

Krüger-Lorenzen, K. (1960) *Das geht auf keine Kuhhaut: deutsche Redensarten und was dahinter steckt*, Düsseldorf: Econ.

Küpper, H., (1970) *Wörterbuch der deutschen Umgangssprache*, vol. VI: *Jugenddeutsch von A biz Z*, Hamburg: Claassen.

Löffler, H. (1985) *Germanistische Soziolinguistik*, Berlin: Schmidt.

Ludwig, K.-D. (1991) *Markierungen im allgemeinen einsprachigen Wörterbuch des Deutschen. Ein Beitrag zur Metalexikographie* (Lexicographica, Series Maior, 38), Tübingen: Niemeyer.

Mackeldey, R. (1987) *Alltagssprachliche Dialoge: kommunikative Funktionen und syntaktische Strukturen*, Leipzig: Verlag Enzyklopädie.

Mackensen, L. (1971) *Die deutsche Sprache in unserer Zeit*, Heidelberg: Quelle & Meyer.

Mann, T. (1960) *Buddenbrooks*, Frankfurt: Fischer.

Mattheier, K. J. (1990) 'Dialekt und Standardsprache: über das Varietätensystem des Deutschen in der Bundesrepublik', *International Journal of the Sociology of Language*, 83: 59–81.

Merkle, L. (ed.) (1978) *In dene Dag had da Jesus gsagd. Neues Testament Bairisch*, Munich: Heimeran.

Möhn, D. (1980) 'Sondersprachen', in H. P. Althaus, H. Henne and H. E. Wiegand (eds) *Lexikon der Germanistischen Linguistik*, 2nd edn, Tübingen: Niemeyer, pp. 385–90.

Möhn, D. and Pelka, R. (1984) *Fachsprachen. Eine Einführung*. (Germanistische Arbeitshefte, 30), Tübingen: Niemeyer.

Russ, C. V. J. (ed.) (1990) *The Dialects of Modern German*, London, Routledge.

—— (1992) 'Variation im Deutschen: die Perspektive der Auslandsgermanistik', *Der Deutschunterricht*, 44: 5–15.

Schank, G. and Schwitalla, J. (1980) 'Gesprochene Sprache und Gesprächsanalyse', in H. P. Althaus, H. Henne and H. E. Wiegand (eds) *Lexikon der Germanistischen Linguistik*, 2nd edn, Tübingen: Niemeyer, pp. 313–22.

Spangenberg, K. (1986) 'Untersuchungen zur Funktion, Geltung und Bewertung der Mundart in Thüringen', *Beiträge zur Erforschung der deutschen Sprache*, 6: 234–45.

—— (1990) 'Thuringian', in C. V. J. Russ (ed.) *The Dialects of Modern German*, London: Routledge, pp. 284–8.

Steger, H. (1967) 'Gesprochene Sprache: zu ihrer Typik und Terminologie', in H. Eggers, J. Erben, H. Neumann and Hugo Moser (eds) *Satz und Wort im heutigen Deutsch* (Sprache der Gegenwart, 1), Düsseldorf: Schwann, pp. 259–291.

Steger, H., Deutz, H., Schank, G. and Schütz, E. (1974) 'Redekonstellation, Redekonstellationstyp, Textexemplar, Textsorte im Rahmen eines Sprachverhaltensmodells: Begründung einer Forschungshypothese', in H. Eggers, J. Erben, O. Leys, H. Neumann and Hugo Moser (eds) *Gesprochene Sprache* (Sprache der Gegenwart, 26), Düsseldorf: Schwann, pp. 39–97.

Texte I–IV (1971–9) *Texte gesprochener deutscher Standardsprache*, 4 vols (Heutiges Deutsch, 3: Texte), Munich: Hueber & Schwann.

Wackernagel-Jolles, B. (1971) *Untersuchungen zur gesprochenen Sprache: Beobachtungen zur Verknüpfung spontanen Sprechens* (Göppinger Arbeiten zur Germanistik, 33), Göppingen: Kümmerle.

Wahrig, G. (1986) *Deutsches Wörterbuch*, ed. U. Herrmann, R. Wahrig-Burfeind, K. Rüme and N. Raum, Gütersloh: Bertelsmann.

3 German in Austria

3.1 HISTORICAL BACKGROUND

Austria has always retained an independence from the rest of the German-speaking area. The first recorded instance of the name *Ostarrîchi* for the Margraviate of 976, the central territory of the Eastern March established by Charlemagne, is in 996. It was a much smaller area than the modern state, consisting of an area stretching along the Danube eastwards from the Enns to the Wienerwald near Tulln. From 976 to 1246 it was ruled over by the Babenberg Margraves, who moved their capital eastwards from Melk to Klosterneuburg and finally to Vienna in 1156, when the territory became a Dukedom. The Babenbergs expanded their territory by inheriting Styria (*Steiermark*) in 1192. After the male Babenberg line died out their possessions were ruled by Ottokar II of Bohemia, who was defeated in 1278 at the battle of Marchfeld by Rudolf of Habsburg, who, as Rudolf I, founded the Habsburg dynasty which ruled Austria until 1918. The Habsburgs also became titular heads of the Holy Roman Empire. Territorial growth continued throughout the next centuries: in 1335 Carinthia (*Kärnten*) and Carniola (*Krain*), the latter now being part of Slovenia, were acquired; in 1363 Margarethe Maultasch handed West and South Tyrol over to the Habsburgs; between 1363 and 1523 various lordships in Vorarlberg were purchased by the Habsburgs and in 1500 the Habsburgs acquired East Tyrol and the northeastern parts of North Tyrol around Kufstein and Kitzbühel. In 1491 the Habsburgs established the hereditary right to the crowns of their northern and eastern neighbours, Bohemia and Hungary, which they obtained in 1526. The real Habsburg control of the southern and eastern parts of the Hungarian kingdom began in the eighteenth century, when in the Peace of Karlowitz in 1699 (Sremski Karlovci near Novi Sad) Austria gained Transylvania (*Siebenbürgen*), now part of Romania, Slavonia and Croatia from the Turks. This treaty established the full geographic extent of the Habsburg monarchy in eastern Europe with its accompanying multilingual and ethnic groupings. In the west of the country the Bavarian Innviertel became part of Austria in 1779 and in 1805 the Electoral Principality of Salzburg, secularized from a Prince Bishopric in 1803, was exchanged by Ferdinand of Tuscany, a Habsburg relative, for that of Würzburg. After the defeat of Austria at Austerlitz in 1805 Napoleon made fundamental changes in the map of the states which comprised German-speaking Europe. In 1805 at the treaty of Preßburg (Bratislava) Bavaria and Württemberg became kingdoms and Baden became a grand duchy. In the territorial re-arrangements that followed, Austria lost Venetia to the King of Italy, Tyrol, Vorarlberg to Bavaria and parts of present-day Baden-Württemberg (*Vorderösterreich*) to Bavaria, Württemberg and Baden. On 11 August 1804 the last Holy Roman Emperor, Francis II, assumed the title Emperor of Austria as Francis I and on 6 August 1806 he renounced his claim to the Holy Roman Empire. In the renewed war with Napoleon in 1808 Austria was first victorious but finally defeated and in the Peace of Schönbrunn lost Salzburg and parts of Upper Austria to Bavaria while East Tyrol, Carinthia, Carniola, Croatia, Istria and Dalmatia were united to form the 'Illyrian Provinces' ruled by France. After the defeat of Napoleon the Congress of Vienna in 1815 returned Lombardy and Venetia to Austria, which also received Salzburg, Tyrol back from Bavaria and the French 'Illyrian Provinces'. Austria has therefore been a separate political unit from Germany for a long time and was already a fully fledged state when in the nineteenth century a united Germany was merely a dream. Indeed, after the Austro-Prussian war of 1866 Austria distanced itself from any thought of a larger German state and in 1867 the dual monarchy of Austro-Hungary was established. This separateness shows itself, as we shall see, in many independent linguistic developments, retentions and innovations. During the last half of the nineteenth century Austria lost most of its Italian-speaking area, Lombardy (1859) and Venetia (1866), to the newly emerging independent unified Italian state. The greatest territorial losses, however, occurred after 1918, when the last Emperor, Charles I, abdicated and the First Republic of Austria was set up. In the treaty of St Germain-en-Laye (1919) this newly founded state lost all the non-German speaking parts: Istria, Trieste and Dalmatia went to Italy, while the new states of Yugoslavia, Hungary and Czechoslovakia were founded. Transylvania became part of the new state of

Romania. The most controversial loss was that of the South Tyrol to Italy, the biggest loss of a German-speaking territory. This is something which still has repercussions today. German-speaking areas lost in the east included the small areas of Wieselburg (Mason), Ödenburg (Sopron) and Güns (Köszeg) to the new Hungary, while the German-speaking area of western Hungary came to Austria and was called Burgenland. The First Republic lasted until 1933–4, when it was followed by a dictatorship. Austria, the *Ostmark* as the National Socialists called it, then became briefly part of a larger German state from 1938, the time of the *Anschluß* (annexation), until 1945. During that time it was referred as the Alp and Danube gaus (*Alpen- und Donaugaue*). After 1945 it was occupied by the Allies and the Second Republic was set up, a federal republic, consisting of nine federal states, or *Länder* (see Map 3.1). The Allies withdrew in 1955 after the signing of the *Staatsvertrag* which established Austria as a neutral state.

Since the Austro-Hungarian Empire encompassed so many different linguistic groups it is not surprising to find that there are small areas with foreign linguistic minorities in present-day Austria (Wiesinger 1990a: 440–3). There are three main groups, the Slovenes, Croats and Magyars, who are all bilingual. They comprise only about 2 per cent of the whole population. The rights of minorities were guaranteed in the *Staatsvertrag* of 1955 and the 'ethnic affiliation law' (*Volksgruppengesetz*) passed in 1976 made the legal standing of these minorities more precise. Thus for each language there is educational instruction at primary-school level; programmes are broadcast on the local radio, church services are held, printed newspapers and magazines appear and each language can also be used for official business in the region.

According to the census of 1981 there were about 18,000 Slovene speakers. They speak three very different dialects, popularly called *Windisch*, which can be divided geographically into the dialects of the Gail, Rosen and Jaun valleys in Carinthia. All three dialects differ a great deal from the Slovenian written standard language of Slovenia, part of former Yugoslavia.

The Croatian speakers number about 18,000 and live in the Burgenland, the easternmost *Bundesland*, in the south around Güssing-Oberwart, in the centre around Oberpullendorf and in the north around Eisenstadt and Neusiedl-Kittsee. This area was part of the Kingdom of Hungary until 1921. Into this depopulated area Hungarian landowners brought Croats between 1530 and 1575.

The third linguistic minority is also the smallest. These are the

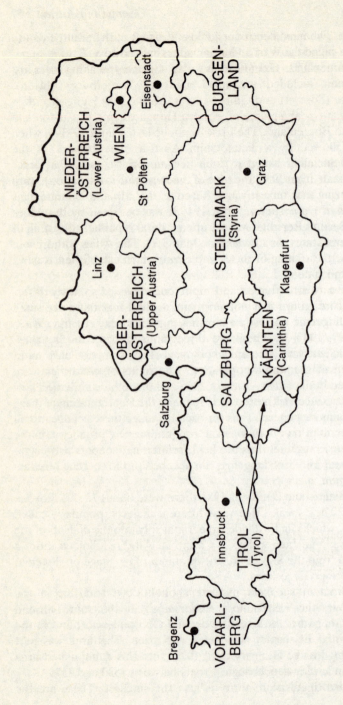

Map 3.1 Austria's federal states (Österreichs Bundesländer)

Hungarians, who number about 4,000 and also live in the Burgenland in the area called the Wart and also in Oberpullendorf and Nikitsch in central Burgenland. Gal (1979) has investigated the shifts in their bilingualism.

3.2 STATUS OF DIALECT, COLLOQUIAL SPEECH AND STANDARD LANGUAGE

The different manifestations of German in Austria are rather less clear cut than those in the diglossic Swiss situation (see 4.3). The written language is recognizably the same as that used in Germany although there are specific Austrian characteristics in vocabulary particularly but also in grammar. There is no question but that the written language is Austrian German rather than Austrian (Wiesinger 1988c). The situation as far as the spoken language is concerned is rather more complicated. Reiffenstein (1982, 1983) regards the dialect/standard situation as very fluid and to a certain extent unstable. According to him (1982: 13), one could talk about a national Austrian linguistic variety at the level of the spoken language. Moosmüller (1991) investigated the speech production and perception of academics in the public and private sector, politicians and newsreaders. She found that the best German seemed to be that of educated academics from Vienna and Salzburg. Wiesinger (1990a: 443ff.) admits a certain amount of fluidity in the spoken language but also maintains that speech varieties, especially in the east and south, can be described on a four-point scale, consisting of primary dialect (*Basisdialekt*), regional dialect (*Verkehrsdialekt*), colloquial speech and standard. He illustrates this with versions of the sentence *Heute abend kommt mein Bruder nach Hause* from the Weinviertel of Lower Austria about 20–70 km. from Vienna:

Primary dialect: Heint af d'Nocht kimmt mei[n] Bruider hoam.
Regional dialect: Heit auf d'Nocht kummt mei[n] Bruader ham.
Colloquial speech: Heit åb'nd kommt mei[n] Bruder z'Haus.
Standard speech: Heut Ab'nd kommt mein Bruder nach Haus.

The versions are in a lay transcription, phonetic versions are to be found in Wiesinger (1990a: 444). Linguistically the German dialects of Austria are part of the larger Bavarian dialect area and share many features with the latter. The only exception is the dialect of Vorarlberg, which is Alemannic like Swiss German dialects. Standard speech is also subject to regional factors in its articulation and intonation. Speakers in Austria can, for instance, usually immediately tell whether the speaker comes from Tyrol, Carinthia, Styria or Upper or Lower Austria. The standard is the language of public life. It is used in school by teachers and pupils, by the priest and the congregation in church services and in private prayer, by the mayor and chairmen of societies in speeches as well as in meetings and in public discussions.

The differentiation of present-day language use with reference to standard High German, colloquial speech and dialect in Austria especially in the east and south, has been shown by Wiesinger (1990a: 445f.) to be highly variable. Table 3.1 shows the use of the three varieties and their distribution according to situation and conversation partner. The use of dialect in shops and with officials varied along a scale from 43 per cent at the grocer's and baker's, 33 per cent at the hairdresser's, 23 per cent at the bank, 19 per cent at the doctor's, 18 per cent at a clothes shop, 10 per cent with a teacher and 9 per cent at an office in town. At the workplace the role of the interlocutor was important. With colleagues 39 per cent used dialect but with a superior at work, only 15 per cent used dialect. Not only situation and interlocutor showed a differentiation in the use of dialect in everyday communication, but also the sociolinguistic variables of class, domicile, age and sex, as Table 3.2 shows.

Table 3.1   Use of linguistic varieties according to situation and conversation partner

	Dialect (%)	Colloquial (%)	High German (%)
Everyday speech	49	49	2
Preferred speech	51	43	6
Family	60	35	5
With good friends	53	42	3
Distant acquaintances	27	46	21
Strangers	12	43	39

We can thus see that in Austria, although three-quarters of the population may be regarded as dialect speakers and although the use of dialect in the country and in small towns is stronger than in cities, it is becoming restricted more and more to conversation with close friends and family, whereas colloquial speech has generally become the everyday speech of the middle and upper classes, especially in medium and large towns. This latter variety and the standard are

Table 3.2 Use of linguistic varieties according to class, place, age and sex

	Dialect (%)	Colloquial (%)	High German (%)
Lower class	78	22	–
Middle class	50	50	–
Upper class	24	74	2
Village, small town	83	17	–
Medium and large town	32	63	5
Age 19–30	48	50	2
Age 31–60	48	50	2
Age 61–80	61	33	6
Male	55	45	–
Female	45	52	3

used with distant acquaintances and strangers and when the conversational situation becomes more formal.

3.3 CHARACTERISTICS OF AUSTRIAN GERMAN

Following Clyne's usage (1984: 5), we will call the written standard German in Austria Austrian Standard German, which differs from German Standard German, i.e. German used in the united Federal Republic of Germany, in its pronunciation, grammatical morphology and vocabulary. Each of these levels will be examined in turn and exemplified. The orthography shows only minor deviations from the standard. Most of the examples will be taken from Rizzo-Baur (1962) and Ebner (1980, 1988). Wiesinger (1988a) contains a number of relevant articles; Martin (1986) plots the literary distribution of a few words; Mentrup (1980) and Wiesinger (1988c) provide a general survey.

Although the pan-German standard of Duden is accepted in Austria, there have been moves to show independence by producing internal reference works. In 1951 the first edition of the *Österreichisches Wörterbuch* appeared, which contained a number of forms peculiar to Austrian Standard German. The thirty-fifth edition in 1979 went a good deal further. About 120 words regarded as German Standard German were asterisked. There was a great increase in colloquial and dialect words, which were often unmarked. The dictionary, anonymously edited, was deemed by many to be an example of *Sprachlenkung* (linguistic planning) and to express a separatist and egalitarian approach to language. There were a number of trenchant reviews, among which Wiesinger (1980) is perhaps the most detailed. In general the tenor of the reviews was conservative, that the dictionary had gone too far. Reiffenstein (1983: 19) detected two seemingly contradictory strands in the thirty-fifth edition: one, the separatist, overemphasizing the Austrian part of the vocabulary by listing older dialectal material, and second, a progressive linguistic planning motive in promoting colloquial items to standard status. The thirty-sixth edition of 1985 back-tracked on these developments, particularly by paying more attention to stylistic labelling, especially of colloquial forms. A survey of this controversy is to be found in Clyne (1988).

One of the criticisms of the thirty-fifth edition of the *Österreichisches Wörterbuch* was that it tended to favour Viennese forms and neglect regional variation within Austria (Wiesinger 1980: 395). Given that the dialects of Vorarlberg are Alemannic, it is not surprising that even within Austria there are regional variants at the colloquial and even standard levels. Forer and Moser (1988), investigating how far 260 items of Austrian vocabulary from Ebner (1980) were known to speakers from North and South Tyrol and Vorarlberg, found that 75 per cent of the items were known to North Tyroleans and only 55 per cent each to both South Tyroleans and speakers from the Vorarlberg. Even though many words are labelled as west Austrian, there is no homogeneous variety of that name. In several cases west Austrian provenance is not acknowledged by the *Österreichisches Wörterbuch* and other dictionaries, for example *Knollen* 'lump', *Seiher* 'sieve', *Kehrschaufel* 'spade', *Kehrwisch* 'broom', *Lutscher* 'baby's dummy', *Putzlumpen* 'cleaning cloth' and *Stopsel* 'cork, stopper' (Forer and Moser 1988: 203). Metzler (1988) found that although most informants had a passive knowledge of most of the forty east Austrian terms they were confronted with, they nevertheless preferred their own regional forms. Eichhoff (1977–8) has a number of maps which show a division of Austria into a western area and a central and eastern region; the eastern (Viennese) forms are given first: Map 18 'cleaning woman' *Bedienerin* : *Zugeherin*; Map 19 'butcher' *Fleischhauer*, *Fleischhacker* : *Metzger*; Map 22 'chimney sweep' *Rauchfangkehrer* : *Kaminkehrer*; Map 25 'hallway' *Vorraum*, *Vorzimmer* : *Hausgang*; Maps 36, 37 'afternoon snack (in the family or at work)' *Jause* : *Marende*; Map 38 'evening meal' *Nachtmahl* : *Nachtessen*.

3.3.1 Pronunciation

The spoken language of educated Austrians shows a number of deviations from the *Hochlautung* of *Siebs* and the *Duden Aussprachewörterbuch*, some of which are also current in southern Germany. Lipold (1988) and Ebner (1980) will be used for most of the following examples. Their descriptions are based on observation of speakers' behaviour. The *Österreichisches Wörterbuch* does show pronunciation, but only sporadically. The system of sounds is basically the same except that the prescribed difference between /eː/ and /ɛː/, for example *Beeren* vs *Bären*, *Ehren* vs *Ähren* is being lost, /eː/ being used for both. There are also differences in the quantity between the German standard and Austrian usage: the following stressed vowels (in bold) are short in German Standard German but long in Austrian Standard German: *Geschoß*, *ob*, *Rebhuhn*, *Walnuß*; *Politik*, *Profit*, *Notiz*, *absolut*. On the other hand, the following stressed vowels (in bold) are long in German Standard German but short in Austrian Standard German: *Geburt*, *artig*, *zart*, *Nische*, *Liter*, *Obst*, *Probst*, *Nüster*, and in unstressed syllables: *Amboß*, *spielbar*, *Altertum*, *Balkan*, *Schlendrian*. Some of these forms, particularly the foreign words, show the tendency to shortening in German Standard German. The short vowel spelt *a* has become a back rounded [ɔ] or back [ɒ] in Austrian dialect in original native words, old loans and some names. However, more recent loans, for example *Kassa*, *Taxi*, *Klasse*, and names, for example *Dagmar*, *Sandra*, show a front vowel, [a]. This front [a] is very widespread in spoken Austrian Standard German for names. Thus the border town of *Passau*, other geographical names such as *Prag*, *Amerika*, and Christian names such as *Anna*, *Alexander*, are pronounced with [ɒ] in Bavaria and [a] in Austria (Wiesinger 1990a: 452f.). Consonantal differences are less marked. The suffix *-ig* is pronounced with a final plosive, for example [*-ik*] and those words spelt with initial *Ch-*, for example *China*, *Chirurg*, *Chemie*, are also pronounced with a plosive instead of a fricative. This type of pronunciation, however, also occurs in southern Germany. The pronunciation of foreign words shows several differences from German Standard German. The final *-e* of loan words such as *Clique*, *Nuance*, *Chance* is not pronounced. There is also a tendency to stress loans on the initial syllable (this also occurs in Swiss High German), for example 'Attentat, 'Kopie, 'Marzipan, 'Uniform, 'Vatikan. Other Austrian Standard German differences in stress placement are *Mathe'matik*, *Roko'ko*, *Ta'bak* as against German Standard German *Mathema'tik*, '*Rokoko*, '*Tabak*. Lipold (1988: 47–54) has a detailed list of

Austrian Standard German pronunciations. Hornung (1988) gives the pronunciation of place-names. In the east of Austria there is a tendency to pronounce them with stress on the final syllable, for example *Land'eck* instead of *'Landeck*. Those names that end in *-au* are subject to variation, for example *Wa'chau* but *'Ramsau*.

3.3.2   Grammar

The grammar of Austrian Standard German also varies from that of German Standard German but many of the variant forms are also to be found in southern Germany. The difference is that they have an acceptable status in the written language in Austria. Rizzo-Baur (1962) and Tatzreiter (1988) have copious examples and we will draw upon them for exemplification. The differences are not fundamentally in the system but involve redistribution within the system. Thus the three grammatical genders are maintained but the membership of some nouns differs from German Standard German. The following nouns are masculine in Austrian Standard German but neuter in German Standard German: *Backbord*, *Polster*, *Gehalt*; while the following are feminine in Austrian Standard German but masculine in German Standard German: *Dreß*, *Ausschank*, *Sellerie*. Other correspondences are: neuter in Austrian Standard German but fluctuation between two genders in German Standard German: *Biskuit*, *Joghurt*, *Gulasch*, *Mündel*, *Getto*, *Chor*, *Zubehör*. In the formation of the plural the umlaut of the stem vowel is more frequent: *Erlässe*, *Pöster*, *Bögen*, *Wägen*, *Pfröpfe*. The diminutive forms in *-el* and *-erl*, pronounced [-l] and [-ɐl], for example *Sack*, *Sackel*, *Sackerl*; *Knopf*, *Knöpfel*, *Knöpferl*, form their pl. in *-n* and this ending is extended in some cases to masc. nouns *-el*, *Knödeln*. The verbal inflection shows the same variation in Austrian Standard German as in German Standard German. One feature of Austrian Standard German, however, is the merger of the 2nd and 3rd pers. sg. pres. of verbs whose stem ends in *sch*, for example *du, er duscht*, German Standard German *du duschest, er duscht*. The retention of the vowel is, however, archaic in German Standard German. The adjectival inflection is the same in Austrian Standard German. In Austrian Standard German superlative adverb forms such as *schnellst*, *billigst*, *modernst* are frequent in advertising texts, where German Standard German would use *am schnellsten* etc. Some prepositional usage differs from that of German Standard German, for example *auf Besuch kommen* instead of *zu Besuch kommen*, *auf Urlaub* *gehen* instead of *in Urlaub gehen*, and the use of *am* for *auf dem*, for example *am Land* for *auf dem Land* (this usage also occurs in Swiss High German, see 4.4.2).

3.3.3 Vocabulary

It is, however, in the vocabulary of the written German in Austria where the most striking differences between Austrian Standard German and German Standard German lie. Some forms are only used in Austria. These may be different words, for example *Paradeiser* (m.) 'tomato' or words used with a different meaning, *abgebrannt* 'penniless'. In both cases they are examples of Austrianisms (*Austriazismen*). An examination of the *Duden Großes Wörterbuch* yielded 1,357 Austrianisms, 1,199 (77 per cent) of which were nouns. There are 222 verbs (14 per cent), 89 adjectives (5.8 per cent), 35 adverbs (2.4 per cent) and twelve other words (0.8 per cent). Since most Austrianisms are nouns, this part of speech will dominate in the examples.

3.3.3.1 National Austrianisms

The most obvious Austrianisms are those which are used for specifically Austrian institutions or in official bureaucratic language. The designations for governmental and political institutions show some similarities with Germany since Austria is also a federal republic. The individual states are also called *Bundesländer* and the upper chamber of the federal parliament where they are represented is called the *Bundesrat*. The lower chamber, however, is called the *Nationalrat*, as in Switzerland, and the individual elected members are *Nationalräte/rätinnen*. The individual governments in the *Bundesländer* are lead by a *Landeshauptmann* and a team of *Landesräte*, as opposed to the German *Ministerpräsident* and his *Minister*. The designations for schools are rather complex but the types of secondary schools are officially known as *Allgemeinbildende höhere Schulen* (*AHS*) and *Berfufsbildende höhere Schulen* (*BHS*). The pupils' leaving examination is *Matura* (f.), as in Switzerland, and those who obtain it are called *Maturanten/innen*, in Switzerland *Maturanden*. The word *Abiturienten/innen* is used in some official publications, for example *Abiturientenlehrgang*. The university professor in Austria does not have a *Lehrstuhl* (m.) 'chair' but a *Lehrkanzel* (f.).

3.3.3.2 Bureaucratic language

During the nineteenth century Austria had its own vast bureaucracy which developed its own designations for official tasks and titles. Although these terms are not specific to Austria, bureaucracy is universal, they give bureaucratic officialese in the country a particular Austrian 'flavour'. The following nouns exemplify forms which are peculiar to Austrian texts: *Bollette* (f.) 'customs declaration', *Drucksorte* 'official form', *Executor* (m.) 'bailiff', *Nationale* (nt.) 'form; personal details', *Probelehrer* (m.) 'probationary teacher' (cf. *Referendar*), *Proporz* (m.) 'proportional representation', *Ruhegenuß* (m.) 'pension', *Schulbuchaktion* 'free school books' (cf. *Lehrmittelfreiheit*), *Wachebeamter* (m.) 'policeman', *Wehrdiener* (m.) 'soldier'. There are further examples in Ebner (1988: 169–74). Not only does Austrian officialese show independent forms but also gives a different meaning to ordinary words. The adjective *gewesen* is used for 'former', for example *der gewesene Spengler X* 'the former plumber X'. The first month of the year is always called *Jänner* (m.) and the second month is sometimes called *Feber* (m.), which is obsolescent, *Februar* being used as well. As in the Romance languages the word *Professor* (m.) has a broader meaning than in Germany and is used not only for a university professor but for any secondary school teacher. If anyone goes missing they are said to be *abgängig*, for example *Sechzehnjährige abgängig* 'sixteen-year-old girl missing'. An obsolescent word for the 'small-scale sale of goods' is *Verschleiß/-e* (m.) with the accompanying verb *verschleißen* and the agentive noun *Verschleißer* (m.). In Germany *verschleißen* means 'to waste, wear out'. Where in Germany there is the sign *Anliegerverkehr* 'access only for residents', in Austria *Anrainer* (m.) is used, for example *Zufahrt nur für Anrainer*. The word *Dienstgeber* (m.) 'employer' is used instead of *Arbeitgeber*, and by analogy *Dienstnehmer* (m.) 'employee' is used instead of *Arbeitnehmer*. Other examples from Wiesinger (1988b) and Ebner (1988) are: *Abfuhr* (f.) 'tax payment', *Anfall* (m.) 'beginning (of pension etc.)', *Angabe* (f.) 'down-payment', *Ausfluß* (m.) 'result of an action', *bedecken* 'to cover financially', *betreten* 'to catch in the act', *Novelle* (f.) 'amendment to a law', *Postarbeit* (f.) 'work for a deadline', *Verstoß* (m.) 'loss'. Wiesinger (1988b) also investigates the syntax of Austrian officialese which shows longer sentences than in German standard German texts and also prefers complex sentences with subordinate clauses: over 50 per cent of the sentences investigated were complex sentences. Other syntactic features were a more frequent use of passive constructions in Austrian officialese and a higher use of nouns over pronouns.

3.3.3.3 General vocabulary

At the level of general vocabulary there are also many Austrianisms in form and meaning. The following illlustrate different word forms used in Austria. The following are examples of nouns. Children do not ride on a *Karusell* (nt.) 'roundabout' but on a *Ringelspiel* (nt.). For 'types of string' the word *Spagat* (m.) is used. The stairs you may have to climb to your flat are called *Stiege(n)* not *Treppe(n)*. Clothes to be dry-cleaned are taken to the *Putzerei* (f.) in Austria not *Chemische Reinigung* (f.). Display windows in shops are known as *Auslage* (f.) and not *Schaufenster* (pl.). When the framework of a roof has been completed the workers celebrate with a *Dachgleiche* (f.), *Gleichenfeier* (f.) or *Firstfeier* (f.) in Austria but with *Richtfest* (nt.) in Germany. Examples of verbs are: *ballestern* 'to play football' (obsolescent), *benzen* 'to beg', *fadisieren* 'to be bored', *fechsen* 'to harvest' (dialectal), *gneißen* 'to notice after a long time', *hutschen* 'to swing; to go away', *jausnen* 'to eat a mid-afternoon snack (*Jause*)', *nächtigen* 'to stay overnight', *pölzen* 'to support'. Examples of adjectives and adverbs are: *ausständig* 'lacking, absent', *drappfarben* 'sand coloured', *flaumig* 'very soft', *gefinkelt* 'cunning', *händisch* 'manual', *heuer* (also used in South Germany) 'this year' (derived from it is *Heurige* (m.) for 'this year's wine' and for a restaurant serving this wine), *perzentig* (obsolescent) 'percentual', *raschest* 'as soon as possible', 'quiet', *talmi* 'false, not genuine', *unterspickt* 'flecked with fat'.

These Austrianisms are prevalent in various subject areas of the vocabulary. In the words for various professions and skills there are many differences in vocabulary between Germany and Austria and even within Austria itself. The chimney sweep is called *Rauchfangkehrer* (m.) (*Rauchfang* 'chimney', *kehren* 'to sweep'), the plumber *Spengler* (m.), the butcher *Fleischhauer* (m.) and the shop *Fleischhauerei* (f.). The potter is called *Hafner* (m.) and the purse-maker *Taschner* (m.). The cleaning lady is designated by many words but in Austria the word *Bedienerin* (f.) is most common. The main vocabulary areas where there are differences in usage between Germany and Austria is in food. The Austrian, especially Viennese, cuisine has contributed notably to world cookery with *Sachertorte*, *Wiener Schnitzel* and *Apfelstrudel* and there are many terms for things that are widespread outside Austria but whose linguistic usage is restricted to Austria itself. The general word for a pudding is *Mehlspeise/-n* (f.). There are also many differences in the words butchers use for the various cuts of meat, for example one of the most widespread is *Lungenbraten* (m.) for *Rinderfilet* (nt.) 'filet of beef' or *Wammerl* (nt.) for *Bauchfleisch vom Kalb* (nt.).

As a seasoning for beef one can have *Kren* (m.) 'horseradish' in Austria, (borrowed from Czech), whereas in Germany the term is *Meerrettich* (m.). *Palatschinken* (f.) is mostly used in the plural and has no connection with *Schinken* (m.) 'ham' but is used for pancakes filled with jam or something similar. For scrambled eggs, *Rührei* (nt.), the Austrians use *Eierspeise* (f.) and for the white of an egg *Eiklar* (nt.), the normal *Eiweiß* (nt.) being reserved for the technical medical term 'albumen'. It is also in the realm of fruit and vegetables where many striking differences lie; the following examples give some idea of these:

Some examples of Austrianisms for fruit and vegetables

Austrian	Standard New High German	Meaning
Ribisel/-n (f.)	Johannisbeere/-n (f.)	red currant
Marille/-n (f.)	Aprikose/-n (f.)	apricot
Paradeiser/- (m.)	Tomate/-n (f.)	tomato
Karfiol (m.)	Blumenkohl (m.)	cauliflower
Fisole/-n (f.)	Gartenbohne/-n (f.)	garden bean
Häuptelsalat (m.)	Kopfsalat (m.)	lettuce
Erdapfel/= (m.)	Kartoffel/-n (m.)	potato
Eierschwammerl (nt.)	Pfifferling/-e (m.)	chanterelle

For 'orange' the word *Orange* (f.) is always used and never *Apfelsine* (f.). Many culinary activities have different terms to describe them in Austria, for 'to smoke meat or fish' *selchen* is used instead of *räuchern*; *seihen* is used instead of *sieben* for 'sieving', especially of liquids; *überkühlen* is used instead of *abkühlen* for 'to cool off (a liquid)'.

3.3.3.4   *Austrianisms in meaning*

In many cases the same word exists in Germany and Austria but its meaning varies. The following nouns exemplify these Austrianisms of meaning. *Angabe* (f.) means 'a deposit payment', *aufsteigen* is used for 'going up into the next class', where *versetzen* is used in Germany. The word *Polster* (m. in Austria) is used for any sort of cushion. For a cup *Schale* (f.) is used, *Kaffeeschale*, *Teeschale*. The noun *Ordination* (f.) is used for the consulting hours of a doctor or dentist with the verb derived from it *ordinieren*: *Dr X ordiniert wieder*. For wringing clothes *schwemmen* is used and a very common verb is *sperren* for 'to lock', for *schließen*. The verb *passen* does not mean 'to fit' but 'to wait'. Examples of adjectives are: *abgebrannt* not only means 'penniless' but also 'sun-burned' and *präpotent* means 'arrogant, importunate'. The adverb *rückwärts* is often used instead of *hinten* for example on trams and buses *rückwärts einsteigen* instead of the more usual *hinten einsteigen*.

3.3.3.5 Sources of Austrianisms

Austrianisms come from foreign languages, colloquial speech and dialects. Austria has always looked east and south towards the many non-German-speaking states of the former Austro-Hungarian Empire and this has meant that it has been exposed to cultural and linguistic loans from these regions. Austrian Standard German contains a large number of loan words not only from the eastern European countries of the former Austro-Hungarian Empire but also from other languages (Ebner 1988: 163–9; Martin 1985; Rizzo-Baur 1962: 61–90; Wiesinger 1990b: 514–29). The greatest number of loans has come from Italian. The word *Kasse* (f.) appears in the Italianized form *Kassa* in Austria, a meal in the morning or late afternoon is *Marende* (f.) (West Austrian) from Italian *merenda* 'light meal, afternoon snack'. A 'customs officer' is called *Finanzer* (m.) after the Italian phrase *guardia finanziaria* which is used for 'coast guard'. The form *Parte* in *Partezettel* (m.), *Trauerparte* (f.) 'death notice' is supposed to come from Italian but it is not clear from which word, perhaps from *partenza* 'parting, in the sense of death'. Verbs have also been borrowed but have substituted the suffix *-ieren*, derived from French, for Italian *-are*, for example *skartieren* 'to throw out old documents', from Italian *scartare* 'to discard', and *sekkieren* 'to bother, torment' from Italian *seccare* 'to bother, vex'. The latter verb has a present participle in Italian *seccante* 'bothersome' which has been borrowed into Austrian Standard German as *sekkant* with the same meaning. The colloquial adjective *matsch* 'exhausted' is said to come from Italian *marcio* which, however, means 'bad, rotten'. Other examples are: *Faktura* (f.) 'bill', *Karbonade* (f.) 'chop', *Melanzini* (pl.) 'aubergines', *Pfefferone*, pl. *-i* 'peperone', *Pignoli* (pl.) 'pine kernels', *Polizze* (f.) 'insurance policy', *Stanitzel* (nt.) 'cone shaped paper bag', *Zibebe* (f.) 'sultana'.

French, which was for a long time the prestigious language of culture and diplomacy, has also left its trace on Austrian Standard

German. For 'armchair' *Fauteuil* (nt.) is used, whereas *Sessel* (m.) is used simply for 'chair'. For 'steering wheel' *Volant/-s* (m.) [volã] is used instead of *Lenkrad* (nt.). *Rechaud/-s* (m.) is used for 'gas-cooker', especially in Vienna. Some French loans have a different meaning from the one they have in Germany: *Tasse/-n* (f.), for instance, is used for 'tray', *Serviertasse* (f.), but this causes no confusion with the standard usage of *Tasse* for 'cup' since the latter is designated *Schale* (f.) in Austria. The suffixes *-ieren* and *-ist*, borrowed from French, are more widely used than in Germany, for example *röntgenisieren*, 'to X-ray', cf. *röntgen*, *plakatieren*, 'to put official posters up', *faschieren* 'to mince (meat)', *pressieren* 'to hurry' (obsolescent).

In the realm of sports vocabulary Austrian Standard German has many English loan words whereas in Germany they have been 'translated', for example *Corner/-s* (m.), *Eckball* (m.). There are nouns like *Leader* (m.) 'the club which is top of the league table', *Keeper* (m.) 'goal keeper', *Half*, *Back* (m.), *Out* (nt.), *ein Hands geben*, *Tackling* (nt.). There are also verbs: *tackeln* 'to tackle' (German Standard German *anpacken*), *skoren* 'to score' (German Standard German *ein Tor schießen*). Other English loans not connected with sport are: *Fading* (nt.) 'the disappearing of a radio signal', *Kloth* (m.) 'cotton material', *Zippverschluß* (m.) 'zip-fastener' (German Standard German *Reißverschluß*) and *Cottage* (nt.) [kot'e:ʃ] 'residential district', nowadays only referring to a fashionable district in the west of Vienna. The adjective *fesch* 'handsome, nice' is a shortened form of English *fashionable*. There is even the derived noun *Feschak* 'smart chap' (obsolescent) with a Slavonic suffix.

Slavonic languages have provided some loans in Austrian Standard German but not as many as might be expected (Martin 1984), mostly connected with food. *Powidl* (m.) 'plum jam' (German Standard German *Pflaumenmus*), comes from Czech *povidla* (pl.) 'jam', esp. plum jam'. *Schöps* (m.) 'wether' comes from Slavonic sources, although it is not clear which language, and has the compounds *Schöpsenfleisch*, *Schöpsernes* (nt.) 'mutton'. The words *Hetschepetsch* (f.) and *Hetscherl* (nt.) meaning 'hips' are also from Slavonic sources, although the form of the word is often said to result from the English pronunciation of *Hagebütte* (personal communication from Prof. P. Wiesinger, Vienna). The word *Jause* (f.) 'afternoon snack', which has been mentioned above comes from Slovene *južina* 'midday meal'. *Kren* (m.) 'horseradish' also comes from a Slavonic source. From a Balkan, though not a Slavonic, source comes *Palatschinke/-n* (f.) from Romanian/Hungarian *plăcintă* 'pudding'. Hungarian has provided: *Fogosch* (m.) 'pike-perch', *Gatehose* (f.) 'long underpants', *Mullatschag* (m.) 'wild party', *Schinakel* (nt.) 'rowing boat'.

The words we have mentioned so far have their firm place in written German in Austria. There are, however, many words which are used only in colloquial speech in Austria but sometimes find their way into written usage. Many of these are verbs: *fretten* 'to struggle with something', *picken* 'to adhere' (intransitive) and 'to stick something' (transitive). Many colloquial verbs have the suffix *-eln*: *beflegeln* 'to insult someone', *füßeln* 'to trip someone up', *äußerln* 'to take a dog for a walk'. These verbs do not have corresponding forms without *-l-*, but there is at least one pair of verbs which has a form with *l* and a form without, both with different, but related meanings, *zünden* 'to set light to' and *zündeln* 'to play with fire'. On the other hand there are verbs with forms with and without *l* where there is no difference in meaning, *abknöpfen, abknöpfeln; aufknöpfen, aufknöpfeln, zuknöpfen, zuknöpfeln*, although the forms with *l* would be more indicative of colloquial speech. Some adjectives common in colloquial usage are: *bamstig* 'posh, showy', *tak* 'gallant', *tulli* 'very good'.

Some nouns show immediately by their form that they are dialect words. The diminutive in the Bavarian dialects, to which the dialects in Austria belong, is *-el*, *-erl*, pronounced [-ɐl], which appears in many neuter nouns in colloquial use in Austria: *Schlaferl*, cf. *Schläfchen* 'nap', *Stockerl* 'stool', *Schnackerl* 'hiccups', *Stamperl* 'schnaps glass', *Busserl* 'kiss'. The dialect adjectival suffix *-ert* occurs in a number of words which are used colloquially: *letschert* 'weak, exhausted', *nackert* 'naked', *schlampert* 'sloppy', *teppert* 'stupid, silly'. Austrian dialects, like other Upper German dialects, show the loss of the vowel in the prefix *ge-*. This change is reflected in a number of words which have found their way into the written language: *Gschnas* (nt.) 'fancy dress ball', *gschert* 'stupid, rude', *Gspaß* (m.) 'fun', *Griß* (m.) 'crowd, throng'.

3.4 CONCLUSION

The status of dialects in Austria is different from in North Germany, where New High German, introduced first as a written language, has largely ousted Low German and is used, in a modified variety, in everyday speech. In Austria, as we have seen, the use of dialect is still strong. Many dialect words have become part of the colloquial usage and in some cases have found their way into the written language.

Apart from very formal situations such as law courts, in church and in education, the Austrian will tend to use some regional dialect varying to a greater or lesser degree from the written standard. Some of the more obvious differences between Austrian written German and German Standard German, result from the use in Austria of Bavarian or Upper German words, for which New High German in Germany has a different North or Central term, for example *sich verkühlen* 'to catch a cold' (Eichhoff 1977–8: Map 6). In Austria such regionalisms are perfectly acceptable in the written language, as indeed they are in South Germany. Ebner (1992: 54) points to two opposing views which exist in Austria: on the one hand, there is the emphasis on the different regions within the country and how these fit in with South Germany; on the other hand, there is the emphasis on representing Austria as an independent state with one main national variety.

3.5 ILLUSTRATIVE TEXTS

Text extracts illustrating German in Austria are taken from Behring (1971). German Standard German equivalents are given in brackets after each Austrianism.

Der Höhepunkt jeder österreichischen Mahlzeit aber ist die 'Mehlspeis' [= Süßspeise, Kuchen]. Eigentlich eine falsche Bezeichnung, denn zur Zubereitung wird zwar Mehl verwendet, was jedoch geschickt durch die Beigabe von Schlagobers [= Schlagsahne] oder ähnlichem vertuscht wird. Die besonderen Spezialitäten sind gewiß warme Mehlspeisen wie Strudel, wiederum in tausend Variationen, Aufläufe, Palatschinken [= Pfannkuchen], Schmarren [= Eierkuchen], Salzburger Nockerl [= Schaumgebäck, das heiß gegessen wird] und Fruchtknödel [= Kloß].

Ein Essen ohne Mehlspeise ist für den Österreicher fast undenkbar. Ob warm oder kalt, immer aber süß und sehr gehaltvoll, bringt sie jeden Kalorienberechner in unlösbare Konflikte.

Zur Mehlspeise trinkt man meist noch eine Schalerl [= Täßchen] Kaffee, auf diese oder jene Art zubereitet, mit oder ohne Milch, mit oder ohne Schlag [= Sahne, shortened from Schlagobers], je nachdem.

(pp. 11f.)

Tafelspitz [= gekochtes Rindfleisch], dieses köstliche Gericht, das Kaiser Franz Joseph mittags gerne zu sich nahm, wenn er keine

Gäste hatte, ist eigentlich das einfachste, zugleich auch raffinier-
teste, sicher aber berühmteste Gericht der österreichischen Küche.
Die endlose Zahl von verschiedenen Beilagen gestalten dieses
Rindfleischgericht so vielfältig, daß man es immer wieder essen
kann. Der Tafelspitz zum Beispiel wird mit geriebenem
Meerrettich, mit Apfelkren [= Apfelmerrettich], Oberskren, mit
kalter Schnittlauchsauce, heißer Dill- oder Tomatensauce,
Gemüse wie Spinat oder Fisolen [= grüne Bohnen], Petersilien-
oder Röstkartoffeln [= Bratkartoffeln] serviert.

(pp. 33f.)

SELECT BIBLIOGRAPHY AND FURTHER READING

Behring, S. (1971) *Köstliches aus der Wiener Kücher*, Munich: Südwest-
verlag.
Clyne, M. (1984) *Language and Society in the German-speaking Countries*,
Cambridge: Cambridge University Press.
—— (1988) 'A *Tendenzwende* in the Codification of Austrian German',
Multilingua, 7: 335–41.
Ebner, J. (1980) *Wie sagt man in Österreich? Wörterbuch der österreichischen
Besonderheiten* (Duden Taschenbücher, 8), 2nd revised edn, Mannheim:
Bibliographisches Institut.
—— (1988) 'Wörter und Wendungen des österreichischen Deutsch', in P.
Wiesinger (ed.) *Das österreichische Deutsch* (Schriften ₍zur deutschen
Sprache in Österreich, 12), Vienna: Böhlau, pp. 99–187.
—— (1992) 'Österreichisches Deutsch', *Der Deutschunterricht*, 44: 44–55.
Eichoff, J. (1977–8) *Wortatlas der deutschen Umgangssprachen*, 2 vols, Berne
and Munich: Francke.
Forer, R. and Moser, H. (1988) 'Beobachtungen zum westösterreichischen
Sonderwortschatz', in P. Wiesinger (ed.) *Das österreichische Deutsch*
(Schriften zur deutschen Sprache in Österreich, 12), Vienna: Böhlau, pp.
189–209.
Gal, S. (1979) *Language Shift*, New York: Academic Press.
Hornung, M. (1988) 'Die richtige Aussprache von Namen in Österreich', in
P. Wiesinger (ed.) *Das österreichische Deutsch* (Schriften zur deutschen
Sprache in Österreich, 12), Vienna: Böhlau, pp. 55–70.
Lipold, G. (1988) 'Die österreichische Variante der deutschen Standardaus-
sprache', in P. Wiesinger (ed.) *Das österreichische Deutsch* (Schriften zur
deutschen Sprache in Österreich, 12), Vienna: Böhlau, pp. 31–54.
Martin, G. D. C. (1984) 'Slavonic Influences on High German in Austria and
the German Democratic Republic', in C. V. J. Russ (ed.) *Foreign
Influences on German*, Dundee: Lochee, pp. 58–87.
—— (1985) 'Romance, Slavonic and Hungarian Elements in the High
German of Austria, Switzerland and Liechtenstein', *Strathclyde Modern
Language Studies*, 5: 21–42.
—— (1986) 'Peculiarities of Austrian High German as Reflected in Works by

Austrian Literary Authors', *Forum for Modern Language Studies*, 22: 323–41.

Mentrup, W. (1980) 'Die deutsche Sprache in Österreich', in H. P. Althaus, H. Henne and H. E. Wiegand (eds) *Lexikon der germanistischen Linguistik*, 2nd edn, Tübingen, pp. 527–31.

Metzler, K. (1988) 'Das Verhalten Vorarlbergs gegenüber Wortgut aus Ostösterreich, dargestellt an Beispielen aus dem Bezeichnungsfeld "Essen, Trinken, Mahlzeiten" ', in P. Wiesinger (ed.) *Das österreichische Deutsch* (Schriften zur deutschen Sprache in Österreich, 12), Vienna: Böhlau, pp. 211–23.

Moosmüller, S. (1991) *Hochsprache und Dialekt in Österreich. Soziophonologische Untersuchungen zu ihrer Abgrenzung in Wien, Graz, Salzburg und Innsbruck* (Sprachwissenschaftliche Reihe, 1), Vienna: Böhlau.

Österreichisches Wörterbuch (1979), 35th edn, eds E. Benedikt, M. Hornung and E. Pacolt, Vienna: Österreichischer Bundesverlag.

—— (1985), 36th edn, eds O. Back, E. Benedikt, M. Hornung and E. Pacolt, Vienna: Österreichischer Bundesverlag.

Reiffenstein, I. (1977) 'Sprachebenen und Sprachwandel im österreichischen Deutsch', in H. Kolb, H. Laüffer, K. O. Brogsitter, W. Huber, H. H. Reich and H. Schottmann (eds) *Sprachliche Interferenz – Festschrift für Werner Betz zum 65. Geburtstag*. Tübingen: Niemeyer, pp. 175–83.

—— (1982) 'Hochsprachliche Norm und regionale Varianten der Hochsprache: Deutsch in Österreich', in H. Moser and O. Putzer (eds) *Zur Situation des Deutschen in Südtirol* (Innsbrucker Beiträge zur Kulturwissenschaft, Germanistliche Reihe, 13), Innsbruck: Institut für Germanistik, pp. 9–18.

—— (1983) 'Deutsch in Österreich', in *Tendenzen, Formen und Strukturen der deutschen Standardsprache nach 1945* (Marburger Studien zur Germanistik, 3), Marburg: Elwert, pp. 15–27.

Rizzo-Baur, H. (1962) *Die Besonderheiten der deutschen Schriftsprache in Österreich und in Südtirol* (Duden Beiträge, 5), Mannheim: Dudenverlag.

Tatzreiter, H. (1988) 'Besonderheiten der Morphologie in der deutschen Sprache in Österreich', in P. Wiesinger (ed.) *Das österreichische Deutsch* (Schriften zur deutschen Sprache in Österreich, 12), Vienna: Böhlau, pp. 71–98.

Wiesinger, P. (1980) 'Zum Wortschatz im "Österreichischen Wörterbuch" (35. Aufl.)', *Österreich in Geschichte und Literatur*, 23: 367–97.

—— (1985) 'Die Entwicklung des Verhältnisses von Mundart und Standardsprache in Österreich', in W. Besch, O. Reichmann and S. Sonderegger (eds) *Sprachgeschichte: ein Handbuch zur Geschichte der deutschen Sprache und ihrer Erforschung*, vol. 2, 2, Berlin: de Gruyter, pp. 1939–49.

—— (ed.) (1988a) *Das österreichische Deutsch* (Schriften zur deutschen Sprache in Österreich, 12), Vienna: Böhlau.

—— (1988b) 'Das österreichische Amtsdeutsch', in P. K. Stein, A. Weiss and G. Hayer (eds) *Festschrift für Ingo Reiffenstein zum 60. Geburtstag*. Göppingen: Kümmerle, pp. 183–214.

—— (1988c) 'Die deutsche Sprache in Österreich: eine Einführung', in P. Wiesinger (ed.) *Das österreichische Deutsch* (Schriften zur deutschen

Sprache in Österreich, 12), Vienna: Böhlau, pp. 9–30.

—— (1988d) 'Zur Frage bundesdeutscher Spracheinflüsse in Österreich', in P. Wiesinger (ed.) *Das österreichische Deutsch* (Schriften zur deutschen Sprache in Österreich, 12), Vienna: Böhlau, pp. 225–45.

—— (1990a) 'The Central and Southern Bavarian Dialects in Bavaria and Austria', in C. V. J. Russ (ed.) *The Dialects of Modern German*, London: Routledge, pp. 438–519.

—— (1990b) 'Österreich als Sprachgrenz- und Sprachkontaktraum', in L. Kremer (ed.) *Grenzdialekte = Germanistische Linguistik*, 101–3: 501–42.

4 The German language in Switzerland

The linguistic situation in the Swiss Confederation is the result of complicated historical, geographical and social factors. The country differs fundamentally from its neighbours in three ways: first, it is a multilingual state; second, in the German part, dialects, far from being considered sub-standard, are the medium of everyday spoken interaction; and third, the written German, whether in newspapers, official documents or literary works read outside its borders, contains forms which clearly show that the writer or text is of Swiss origin. In this section we will examine these three facets of the linguistic situation in German Switzerland: multilingualism, the status of dialect and the characteristics of written German. Before doing this it is necessary to give an account of the historical background since this is in the main responsible for the present situation.

4.1 HISTORICAL BACKGROUND

The origins of Switzerland go back to the thirteenth century, when, according to tradition, on the Rütli meadow on the Urner See, south of Seelisberg, the three communities of Schwyz, Uri and the lower valley of Unterwalden swore an oath not to accept any judge from outside their communities. This oath laid the foundation stone for their subsequent independence. The fact that Switzerland began through the swearing of an oath is seen from the origin of the name *Eid-genosse*, literally 'oath companion', given to its inhabitants and the name *Eidgenossenschaft* used for their country. Over the following centuries these three original communities, which became known as cantons, were joined by others in a complicated series of leagues and alliances. By the end of the fourteenth century there were eight members of the Confederation and by the time of the Reformation

Table 4.1 Names of cantons and dates of joining the Confederation

*Nidwalden	1291	Schaffhausen	1501
*Obwalden	1291	***Appenzell-Innerrhoden	1513
Schwyz	1291	***Appenzell-Ausserrhoden	1513
Uri	1291	St Gallen	1803
Lucerne	1332	Aargau	1803
Zurich	1351	Graubünden/Grisons	1803
Glarus	1352	Tessin/Ticino	1803
Zug	1352	Thurgau	1803
Berne	1353	Vaud	1803
Fribourg/Freiburg	1481	Genf	1815
Solothurn	1481	Neuchatel	1815
**Basle-Stadt	1501	Wallis/Valais	1815
**Basle-Land	1501	Jura	1979

* The half-cantons Nidwalden and Obwalden gradually emerged in the fourteenth century from Unterwalden. ** This division dates from 1833. *** This division dates from 1697.

there were thirteen members. Table 4.1 shows when each canton joined the Confederation.

The confederates produced some of the best soldiers in Europe and themselves undertook conquests of many of the later territories which make up present-day Switzerland. In the sixteenth century an area such as Wallis/Valais was an 'allied locality' (*zugewandter Ort*) and the bailiwicks of what is now Ticino/Tessin were 'joint dependencies' (*Gemeine Herrschaften*), i.e. ruled in turn by two or more cantons. Despite the tensions and struggles of the Reformation and Counter-Reformation the Confederation held together. It was not until after the French Revolution of 1789 that there was any serious threat to its existence. In the years that followed Napoleon occupied Switzerland, dissolved the Old Confederation and set up the Helvetic Republic, which gave equal status to the allied localities and joint dependencies as well as the old cantons. After Napoleon was defeated there was no returning to the previous status of inferiority of the former allied localities and joint dependencies and their cantonal status had to be confirmed. Thus by 1815 the territorial outline of Switzerland as we know it today (see Map 4.1) was completed. The only change is that in 1979 the canton of Jura was created from the French-speaking part of the canton of Berne. One of the fundamental differences between the thirteen old cantons and the new nineteenth-century ones is that the former were all German-speaking whereas the latter, with the exception of St Gallen, Aargau and Thurgau, were non-German, or only partially German-speaking. Thus the official, or business, language of the Old Confederation was German. All correspondence, even if it was with the allied localities and joint dependencies, was carried on in German. Not until much further down the chain of communication, at the local level, was there need for any non-German language. It was only in the town of Freiburg/ Fribourg that there was any mixture of language, with French predominant. In 1481 this town became 'Von den gnaden Gottes ein ort der eidgenoschaft, darin kein ander dan tütsche sprach gebrucht wird' ('By the grace of God a town of the confederation where none other than the German language is used', quoted by Haas 1982a: 66). In 1516 the so-called 'Perpetual Alliance', lasting 250 years, which Francis I of France made with the Confederation defined full membership as co-terminous with the use of German. Freiburg/Fribourg therefore initiated a linguistic policy of Germanization which was successful as far as the official written language was concerned but was not so successful in regulating and changing private usage. The Old Confederation was thus a monolingual German unit. In the nineteenth century the new equal cantonal status of French- and Italian-speaking territories ushered in a multilingual society. With the creation of the modern Swiss constitution of 1848 and 1874, the recognition of multilingualism was enshrined in Article 116, which was changed in 1938 to include Rhaeto-Romansh: 'Das Deutsche, Französische Italienische und Rätoromanische sind die Nationalsprachen der Schweiz. Als Amtssprachen des Bundes werden das Deutsche, Französische und Italienische erklärt' ('German, French, Italian and Romansh are the national languages of Switzerland. German, French and Italian are declared the official languages of the Confederation').

4.2   THE EXTENT OF GERMAN

German is used in the largest geographical area and has the largest number of speakers but the percentages of the languages relative to each other have remained fairly constant over the last century, as can be seen from Table 4.2. The first set of figures, which shows a 6 per cent loss for German and a 3 per cent loss for French, as against a 4 per cent rise in Italian, is for the whole population, including non-Swiss. If just Swiss citizens are considered then the picture is more stable, with the biggest difference being a 2 per cent loss for French. The multilingual situation in Switzerland shows great stability despite a multiplicity of political and economic differences within the

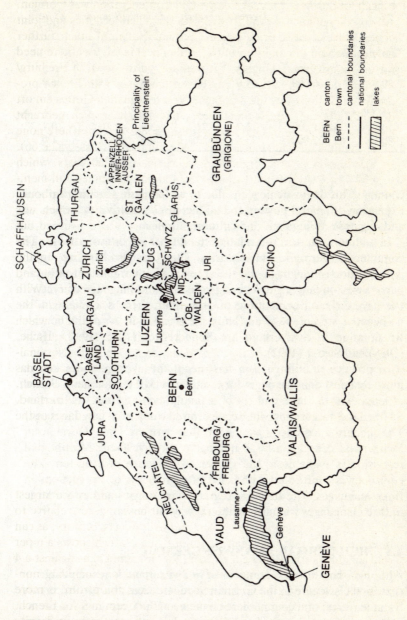

Map 4.1 Swiss cantons

BERN	canton
Bern	town
- - -	cantonal boundaries
——	national boundaries
▨	lakes

Principality of Liechtenstein

SCHAFFHAUSEN

THURGAU

APPENZELL INNER-RHODEN AUSSER

ST GALLEN

GLARUS

ZÜRICH
Zürich

ZUG

SCHWYZ

GRAUBÜNDEN (GRIGIONE)

URI

BASEL STADT

BASEL LAND

AARGAU

SOLOTHURN

LUZERN
Lucerne

OB-WALDEN

NID

TICINO

JURA

BERN
Bern

VALAIS/WALLIS

NEUCHÂTEL

FRIBOURG/ FREIBURG

VAUD

Lausanne

GENÈVE
Genève

Table 4.2   Changes in the numbers of speakers of languages in Switzerland

		German (%)	French (%)	Italian (%)	Romansh (%)	Other (%)
Total population						
1880	2,832,000	71.3	21.4	5.7	1.4	0.2
1980	6,366,000	65.0	18.4	9.8	0.8	6.0
Swiss citizens only						
1910	3,201,000	72.7	22.1	3.9	1.2	0.1
1980	5,421,000	73.5	20.1	4.5	0.9	1.0

country. This linguistic peace is due to an increasing integration and expansion of federal powers and an increased sensitive awareness of and response to linguistic and cultural pluralism.

In addition, there is the relative stability of the different language communities during recent centuries. There has also been no major politicization of language and the absence of any significant political party based on language. Although the different language communities have different perceptions of each other, there is fundamentally no negative stereotype of any language group. Surveys of the linguistic situation in Switzerland are Sonderegger (1985, 1991), Haas (1988) and Sieber (1992).

In practice multilingualism has meant the average Swiss knows more than just one language: for example, a civil servant has to know at least two, or the members of a family moving from one part of Switzerland to another will acquire proficiency in a new language. The linguistic contact has meant that written High German in Switzerland contains a large number of French loans. Multilingual television is available to the viewer at the touch of a button. The consumer is confronted with a list of ingredients or instructions in three languages. The traveller is greeted by slogans and information in three languages when using the railways or buses.

4.3   HIGH GERMAN AND SWISS GERMAN

Although the written German used in Switzerland is recognizable as that used elsewhere in the German linguistic area, apart from certain Swiss features, oral communication between the German Swiss themselves is conducted in the local dialect, which, to complicate matters, is different in Basle from Berne, which, in turn, differs from Zurich.

For these individual local varieties such as *Baseldytsch*, *Bärndütsch* and *Züritüütsch* and many others the term Swiss German (*Schwyzertütsch*) is often used but it must be made clear that this is merely a collective term for the sum of the dialects spoken in Switzerland. Illustrative texts in *Bärndütsch* and *Züritüütsch* with a commentary appear in 4.6.1. Descriptions in English of some Swiss German dialects are Keller (1961) and Russ (1990); Baur (1992) is a practical introduction based on *Züritüütsch*; Marti (1985) and Weber (1964) are grammatical descriptions of *Bärndütsch* and *Züritüütsch* respectively. The *Sprachatlas der deutschen Schweiz* (1965ff.) gives a detailed dialect-geographical survey of the variety of Swiss German dialects. Hotzenköcherle (1984), published posthumously, is a description and interpretation of the different dialect areas in Switzerland by one of the most eminent Swiss dialectologists.

This linguistic situation, whereby a standardized or High variety form is used in writing and on official occasions and an unstandardized or Low form is used in speech, is known as diglossia and occurs in other language communities. Two linguistic varieties exist whose usage is determined by the function of the utterance. Diglossia differs from bilingualism where the use of one of two varieties depends more on the interlocutor, but there are areas of overlap.

The present-day diglossic situation is as follows: the High-level variety is standard written German (*Schriftdeutsch*) and the Low-level variety is provided by the local Swiss German dialects. Figure 4.1 attempts to illustrate their distribution. Domains of usage, separate for spoken and written language, are only a selection, and are listed along the top and bottom, along a scale from formal to informal. The criss-cross area shows where the Low variety is used. The left-hand line is dotted because of the variation of usage, for instance not all advertisements are in Swiss German of course. Schwarzenbach (1969) is a detailed description of the distribution of the two varieties.

Since the eighteenth century High German has increased its use in the spoken realm, particularly as far as public speeches and lectures are concerned. Swiss German, on the other hand, has also made inroads, albeit small, into the domain of the written language. Ris (1980: 121–4) and Church (1989) sketch the development of the relationship between the two varieties in terms of dialect waves (*Mundartwellen*). The first one was from 1900 to 1920, starting from Berne, expressing itself in a renaissance of dialect literature and the preservation of the use of dialect in the cantonal parliament. The second wave, in the 1930s, included Zurich, and was an expression of anti-Nazi sentiment and of separate Swiss identity. It is often dubbed

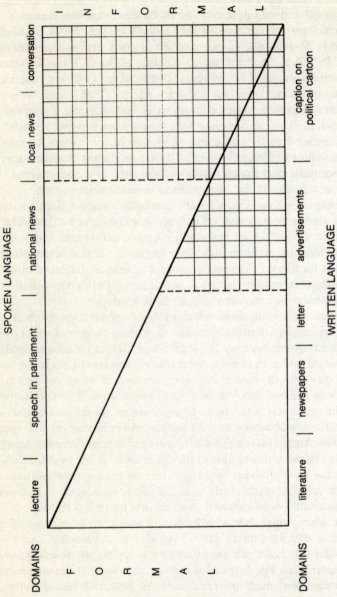

Figure 4.1 The present-day diglossic situation in Switzerland (from Russ 1987: 103)

in German the *geistige Landesverteidigung* ('intellectual defence of the nation'). The third wave started in the 1960s and has resulted in dialect songs, and more general use of dialect in spoken language. This general tendency to increased use of dialect is seen by Sieber and Sitta (1984: 37–8) as due to upward mobility of many whose knowledge of High German is not fluent, and who wish to use their native tongue, which is a Swiss German dialect. In other words, it is due to the spread of egalitarian ideas.

The increase of the electronic mass media has, of course, presented people with new choices. Is dialect or standard to be used? I should like to examine briefly two areas where changes are taking place in the relationship of High German and Swiss German dialect: television and radio, and church activities. Ris (1979: 46) reports on an increase in the use of dialect in television and radio, not only for entertainment and magazine programmes but also in political discussions. High German is used for informing the public. Lötscher (1982: 131ff.) reports that the national news and weather forecast should be High German and that the informality of the programme determines the choice of High German or dialect. Some rules, however, appear rather arbitrary: for instance, in the field of sports reporting, the radio nearly always uses dialect whereas television uses the standard, but High German is always used for live coverage. Possibly, he suggests, because the vocabulary and phrases are already known and pre-standardized. Schwarzenbach (1983: 201–10) reports that the situation has changed since his detailed investigation in 1969. He has been actively involved as a linguistic adviser in drawing up guidelines (*Richtlinien*) for the choice of High German and dialect. Several factors, such as the type of programme, its goal and character, conditions of preparation and production, pressure of time in topical programmes and the linguistic skill of writers and participants, have to be borne in mind (1983: 206–7). The situation is obviously rather fluid and it will be some time before the use of High German and dialect becomes regulated.

The next area I wish to consider is that of church activities. Swiss Protestants have their own translation of the Bible which, together with hymns and liturgy, forms a High German basis for church services. Ris (1979: 45–6) reports, however, on the use of dialect in evening services as well as for baptisms and marriages. The sermon is the main part of the service where a choice between High German and dialect can be made. Lötscher (1982: 129f.) points out that the personality of the clergyman and the character of the congregation can also play a role in the choice between the two varieties. Use of dialect is more advanced in Roman Catholic services since, after Vatican II, Latin was replaced by dialect rather than by High German. From my own observation in smaller informal Bible study groups Swiss German is the main language of expression, although it is a High German passage from the Bible that is being discussed. Another change is that portions of the Bible are now available in dialect (E. Weber 1985; Bietenhard and Bietenhard 1985). Again this is a fluid situation where in time the usage may be regulated. To sum up we may say that while a diglossic situation has existed in Switzerland probably since the eighteenth century, for a small elite since the seventeenth century, the relationship between the two varieties has undergone a number of changes and is still changing at the present.

4.4   THE CHARACTERISTICS OF HIGH GERMAN IN SWITZERLAND

The written High German used in Switzerland differs in a number of ways from German Standard German, i.e. the German used in Germany. One obvious difference in orthography is the replacement of *ß* by *ss*. This has been taking place since the 1920s and the use of *ß* is no longer taught in schools (Meyer 1989: 36f.). In this chapter we shall, therefore, follow Swiss custom and use only *ss*. Because it shows differences from German Standard German, the written German in Switzerland is termed Swiss High German (*Schweizer Hochdeutsch*). The characteristics of Swiss High German have been studied in two ways: first, by examining a large corpus of written material (Kaiser 1969 and 1970; Schilling 1970); and second, by seeing which forms are designated Swiss in German dictionaries (Fenske 1973). Meyer (1989) is a very useful source with quotations of actual usage. In Switzerland there is nothing comparable to the *Österreichisches Wörterbuch* for Austria. The reason is probably that the Swiss have always maintained their national identity by the use of dialect and were, of course, never a part of the Third Reich as Austria was. From 1937 the *Deutschschweizerischer Sprachverein* was responsible for having Swiss forms marked in the *Duden*, and since 1940 there has been a *Duden* Swiss Committee (D. Weber 1984: 59). Fenske (1973) has made a detailed survey of Helveticisms and Austrianisms in German dictionaries. She found a total of 1,768 Swiss forms, of which 401 appeared only in the Mannheim *Duden* and 414 in *Wahrig* (1968). These two dictionaries gave the best overall cover to Swiss forms: 366 forms appeared in two dictionaries, 218 in three and 87 in four. There is thus considerable uncertainty as to whether to accept Swiss forms and which forms to accept. Fifty forms appeared in five dictionaries and they seem to represent a basic list of what is considered by many to be typically Swiss forms (Fenske 1973: 13–20). Although the main emphasis in this section will be the vocabulary of Swiss High German, the grammar also differs as does pronunciation on the limited occasions when Swiss High German is used orally.

4.4.1 Pronunciation

On those restricted occasions when High German is spoken, even when this is merely the reading of a text, there is considerable variation in pronunciation. This ranges from strict adherence to the standard set up first by Siebs (see 6.2) to a heavily dialectally influenced articulation. Boesch (1957) was an attempt to provide some guidelines which would follow a middle way between these two extremes. This has been partially successful and some of the suggestions were incorporated into the nineteenth edition of Siebs. *Duden Aussprachewörterbuch*, on the other hand, has maintained that the standard should be supraregional and has not recorded any Swiss pronunciations in any of its three editions. There are differences in the pronunciation of vowels, consonants and the positioning of stress. Vowel differences mainly affect vowel length. In Swiss High German the vowels in the following words are long but short in German Standard German: *Amboss*, *Andacht* (the second vowel); *Rache*, *Hochzeit*. This results in a difference in pronunciation between *Rost* 'rust' (with a short vowel) and *Rost* 'grill' (with a long vowel). The opposite is the case for the following words, where the vowels are short in Swiss High German but long in German Standard German: *düster*, *Liter*, *Grätsche*, *pusten*, *Wuchs*. In most borrowings the vowel spelt *y* is pronounced [iː] in Swiss High German and not [yː]: *Asyl*, *Gymnasium*. The Swiss German diphthongs [iə, yə, uə], which do not occur in German Standard German, occur in place-names: *Spiez*, *Brienz*, *Flüelen*, *Üetliberg*, *Buochs*, *Muolen*. Consonantal differences are not so frequent. In Swiss High German there are more words where orthographic *v* is pronounced [f]: *Evangelium*, *Klavier*, *November*, *Provinz*, *Vagabund*, *Vikar*, *Vizepräsident*. The suffix *-ig* is, contrary to Siebs, to be pronounced with a final plosive [-ik] and not a fricative. Swiss speakers prefer to stress many French loans on the first syllable, for example 'Büro, 'Dekor, 'Karton, 'Konfitüre, 'Kondukteur. Other features include the absence of the glottal stop, the tendency for the initial stops *p*, *t*, *k* to lose their aspiration in word-initial position before vowels, the tendency for *b*, *d*, *g* to become devoiced and the pronunciation of orthographically doubled consonants, for example *pp*, *tt*, *mm*, etc. to be pronounced long.

4.4.2   Grammar

The grammatical gender of some nouns, particularly those of foreign origin, in Swiss High German differs from that used in German Standard German. The following are masculine in Swiss High German (the German Standard German gender is shown in parentheses): *Couch* (f.), *Festival* (nt.), *Salami* (m.) and *Semmel* (f.) 'bread-roll' (but mostly it occurs in the pl.). The following are neuter: *Kamin* (m.), *Tunnel* (m.), *Fondue*, (f.) and *Bikini* (m.). Many feminine French loans are neuter in Swiss High German: *Cheminée*, *Fondue*, *Raclette*, *Tenue*, *Trottinett*. The following are feminine in Swiss High German but masculine or neuter in German Standard German: *Scheitel* 'parting', *Schoss* 'part of a woman's dress', *Pfingsten* 'Whitsun' and *Foto* 'photo'. The following are neuter in Switzerland but masculine in German Standard German: *Efeu* 'ivy', *Kies* 'gravel' and *Schoss* 'sprig, shoot'. Fractions formed with the suffix *-tel*, from *Teil*, are masculine in Switzerland but neuter in German Standard German: *Drittel*, *Viertel*, *Hundertstel*. Plural forms often differ as well. The following masculine nouns differ in their pl. formation in Swiss High German from German Standard German: (1) *-e* instead of *-er* is found in *Bösewicht*; (2) the following show umlaut of the stem vowel and addition of *-e*, except when the nouns end in *-en*, *Park*, *Hag*, *Bogen*, *Kragen*, *Zapfen*; (3) some neuter nouns have the plural ending *-er* in Swiss High German in contrast to *-e* in German Standard German: *Rieder*, *Scheiter*; and (4) those dialect words ending in *-i* which occur in Swiss High German remain the same in the plural: *Buschi* 'child', *Götti* 'godfather'.

   In the morphology of verbs some old strong forms which have died out in German Standard German are still in use: *spies*, *gespiesen* (obsolescent in the literal meaning but not in figurative usage), *sott*, *gesotten*, *wob*, *gewoben* from *speisen*, *sieden*, *weben* and *gewunken* from *winken*, which is a normal and not a jocular form. Fuller 2nd pers. sg. endings are in use in the present with verbs whose stems end in *s*, *ss*, *z*, *x*, *sch*, for example *liesest*, *heissest*, *wünschest*, and in the past with strong verbs whose stems end in *d*, *t*, for example *fandest*, *botest*. There are also differences in the case that some verbs govern. The dat. is more frequent in Swiss High German and has replaced the acc. with *abpassen, anläuten, anrufen* or a prepositional phrase with *aufpassen, bestellen, einhängen, verklagen, verlangen*. Examples (from Meyer 1989): *Bitte rufen Sie mir an, um einen Termin zu vereinbaren; Wo jeder dem andern aufpasst, was er tut und was erlässt; Man verlangt mir oft die Adresse meines Coiffeurs*. The gen. object is often replaced by the dat., but this is still considered rather substandard usage: *Sie nahm sich den Gästen an*.

Differences in prepositions exist, for example instead of *innerhalb* 'within', *innert* + dat. is used: *innert wenigen Tagen*. For *jenseits* 'beyond', the preposition *ennet* + dat. is used: *ennet dem Zaun*, which can also form the first component of compound adjectives such as *ennetbirgisch*. Prepositions which exist in other German-speaking countries sometimes have a different usage in Switzerland: *ab* is used for *von* and *nach* in certain instances: *junger Mann ab (von) dem Lande*; *ab (aus) der Fremde kommen*; *zwanzig Minuten ab (nach) acht Uhr*. Another difference is the frequent use of *an* instead of *auf* – *am* (= *auf dem*) *Rücken* – and instead of *in*: *am Radio, an der Sperrstrasse*, and *an der Sonne arbeiten*.

4.4.3 Vocabulary

4.4.3.1 *National Helveticisms*

The term for a linguistic form which is typical of Swiss High German usage is *Helvetismus* (Helveticism). The most detailed study is Kaiser (1969–70) and the examples that follow are largely taken from there. Some words in use in Switzerland are designations for specifically Swiss institutions: *Eidgenosse* (m.) (weak noun) for a 'citizen of the confederation', *Eidgenossenschaft* (f.). The Swiss parliament consists of two houses, the lower house being the *Nationalrat* (m.) and the upper house being the *Ständerat* (m.). The members of these houses are also called *Nationalrat* and *Ständerat*. The parliament of each canton (*Kanton* (m.)) is called *der Grosse Rat, Kantonsrat*, or *Landrat* and a member of parliament is a *Grossrat* (m.), *Kantonsrat* or *Landrat*. In some cantons the chief of the cantonal parliament is called *Landamman* (m.), cf. *Amtmann*. When the *Nationalrat* and *Ständerat* meet together this is known as the *Bundesversammlung*. Terms for special Swiss food are: *Rösti* (f.) 'fried potatoes' and *Gnagi* (nt.) 'a bone to gnaw' which figure on the menu of many restaurants. Games peculiar to Switzerland are: *Hornussen* (nt.), a game played with a small plastic, or rubber, disk (*Hornuss* (m.)) and large bat, rather like an outsize paddle; *Jass* (m.), a card-game which is also known in South Germany; and *Schwingen*, Swiss-style wrestling. Many words connected with mountain climbing and mountainous terrain are known chiefly in Switzerland: *Fluh*, pl. ¨*/e* (f.) 'cliff face', *Klus*, pl. *-en* (f.) 'ravine', *Erdschlipf*, pl. *-e* (m.) 'avalanche (of mud)'.

4.4.3.2   Helveticisms in the general vocabulary

Far greater in number are words which, although they do not designate things peculiar to Switzerland, are nevertheless not used in German Standard German. There are differences in stylistic usage in that some words belong to official language, others to the neutral level of language, yet others are colloquial and some are dialect words. They comprise nouns, for example a 'brush to wax the floor' is *Blocher* (m.). The words for 'godfather' and 'godmother' are *Götti* (m.) and *Gotte* (f.). For 'a metal milk container' *Tanse* (f.) is used in the eastern part of Switzerland and *Brente* (f.) is used in the west, while for one made of wood *Melchter* (m.) is used. For a 'helper' *Spetter*, *Spetterin* is used, from the verb *spetten* 'to help out'. Various snacks throughout the day have special names from Swiss German which are nevertheless written. They all vacillate according to the dialect of the speaker in gender between masc. and fem.: *Znüni* (*zu neune*) 'meal in the forenoon', *Zvieri* (*zu viere*) and *Zabig* (*zu Abend*) 'meal in the afternoon'; verbs, for example *äufnen* 'to increase goods, wealth', *bodigen* 'to throw to the ground', *ferggen* 'to dispatch', *gaumen* 'to watch over something', *lismen* 'to knit', *serbeln* 'to be ailing' and *vernütigen* 'to denigrate something'; adjectives, for example *leid* used for 'bad', and *währschaft* 'genuine', which is the same form as the noun *Währschaft* (f.) 'genuineness'. More dialectal forms are *blutt* 'naked', *räss* 'sharp (of taste)', *strub* 'unkempt; difficult', *sturm* 'giddy', *träf* 'striking, apt', and *urchig* 'wild (of people)'.

4.4.3.3   Helveticisms of meaning

Speakers of German from other German-speaking countries can be misled by the different meanings given to words in Switzerland which also occur in German Standard German. *Bühne* (f.) ('stage') is used for 'hay-loft' and *Scheune* (f.) ('barn') is used for 'pigsty'. *Vortritt* (m.) is used in the sense of *Vorfahrt* 'priority'. *Tochter* (f.) has the more general meaning of 'girl': *Serviertochter* 'waitress', *Töchterschule* 'girls' school'. The 'owner of a house or a flat/ apartment' is *Hausmeister/-in*, which outside Switzerland means 'caretaker'. The word *Tracht* (f.) is used for a 'collection of clothes' and also for a 'dish carried to table'. The word *Kleid* (nt.) can be used to refer to a 'gentleman's suit' and for 'clothing' in general: *Arbeitskleid, Berufskleid*. Further examples are: *Packung* (f.) used for 'luggage, equipment', especially in military use; *Landschaft* (f.) used for the 'region belonging to the main town of a canton'; *Anzug* (m.) meaning a 'petition of proposed bill in parliament' (restricted to Basel-Stadt), and *Auffahrt* (f.) for 'Ascension Day'.

Some adjectives in Swiss High German are used in a different way from their use outside Switzerland: *beförderlich* is used for 'quick', *dürr* for 'smoked', *fest* for 'well-built, strong; fat', *streng* for something that is 'hard to bear', *wüst* 'wild, badly behaved', and *zügig* 'crowd-pulling, eye-catching'. There are also many verbs which are used with special additional meanings in Switzerland. The following chart illustrates the variety of usage:

Verb	Swiss High German	German Standard German
abdanken	'to give the funeral oration'	'to abdicate'
aufrichten	'to top out (of a building)'	'to erect'
begrüssen	'to ask someone's opinion'	'to greet'
russen	'to clean the chimney'	'to cover with soot'
vertragen	'to deliver (newspapers)'	'to endure; wear out'
wundernehmen	'to want to know'	'to surprise'.

4.4.3.4 The sources of Helveticisms

As could be expected in a multilingual country, there are many words which have been borrowed from Romance languages in Swiss High German. These receive lexical support from the word being used in French and other parts of the country. Instead of *Schaffner* 'ticket collector, guard' the word *Kondukteur* (m.) is used and for *Fahrkarte* the word *Billet* (nt.). To designate something which is second-hand the word *Occasion* is used, for example *Occasionsauto* 'second-hand car' which in German Standard German would be *Gebrauchtwagen*. The following French words are in regular use in Swiss High German: *Autocar* (m.) 'coach', *Jupe* (m.) 'lady's dress', *Salär* (nt.) 'salary, wages', *Sous-sol* (nt.) 'basement', *Velo* (nt.) 'bicycle', and *Spital* (nt.) 'hospital'. French words which end in *-ment* – *Reglement*, *Departement* – are not pronounced with a nasal vowel às in French but as [-mɛnt] and have a pl. form in *-e*, *Departemente*. Many names of shops are French, for example *Konfiserie* (f.) 'confectioner's', *Mercerie* (f.) 'haberdasher's' and *Papeterie* (f.) 'stationer's'. French influence can probably be held responsible for the fact that verbs in

-ieren or *-isieren* are more numerous in Swiss High German than in German Standard German: *parkieren* 'to park', *grillieren* 'to grill' and *schubladisieren* 'to postpone', the last form having negative connotations. The influence of Italian and Romansh is very much smaller: *Polenta* (f.) 'puree of sweet corn', *Marroni* (pl.) 'chestnuts', *Peperoni* (pl.) 'paprika', *Rustica* (m./nt.) 'holiday-house in Italian style', *Zoccoli* (f.) 'wooden sandals' and *Zucchetto* (mostly pl.) 'courgettes' come from Italian, and *Rüfe* (f.) 'avalanche' comes from Romansh *ruvina*.

Another source of Helveticisms is word formation. Affixes used in all German-speaking countries are attached to certain roots to form specific Swiss High German combinations. For instance, the suffix *-ung* is used to form several feminine nouns in Swiss High German which do not occur in German Standard German: *Gastung* 'guests' (collective), *Hirtung* 'looking after cattle', *Zeigung* 'showing the target (at a shooting match)', *Beamtung* 'making someone a *Beamte*', *Wegleitung* 'instruction', *Argumentierung* 'the action of arguing'. Forms occurring with other suffixes are: *-nis*, *Betreffnis* 'sum, due to someone', *Verkommnis* 'agreement'; *-heit/-keit*, *Sehnlichkeit* 'yearning', *Begründetheit* 'reasons'. The suffix *-schaft* is often used to form collective feminine nouns: *Dorfschaft* 'people of a village', *Klägerschaft* 'the defendant', *Talschaft* 'people in a valley'. In the realm of agentive nouns there are striking differences between Swiss and non-Swiss usage, many of which can be attributed to different stylistic levels. Several nouns with the suffix *-(l)er* belong to the official level of the written language: *Aufenthalter* 'a temporary inhabitant of a place', *Mithafter* 'someone co-responsible for a duty' and *Anstösser* 'neighbour'. Other nouns existing only in Swiss High German belong rather to the neutral level of the written language: *Einzüger* 'someone who collects dues', *Jahrgänger* 'someone belonging to a particular year group', *Kindergärtler* 'child at a kindergarten' and *Korber* 'basket maker'. Other formations are more colloquial: *Bähnler* 'railwayman', *Bergler* 'mountaineer', *Trämler* 'official on the trams'. Some are possibly short-term formations: *Fallschirmler* 'parachutist' and *Übernächtler* 'someone who stays overnight'. There are even recent formations such as *Drögeler* 'drug addict'.

Swiss High German also shows derived adjectives which do not occur in German Standard German. The most widely spread suffix is *-ig* (the non-Swiss form, if existing, is in parentheses) *nutzig* (*nützlich*), *bäumig* 'strong like a tree', *damig* (*damenhaft*), *schaffig* 'hardworking', *tanzig* (*tanzlustig*) and *daherig* (*von daher kommend*). The suffix *-bar* is used with the following adjectives, whereas non-Swiss forms show different suffixes: *fehlbar* 'guilty' (a legal term), and *wünschbar* (*wünschenswert*). The suffix *-haft* is used in *gesamthaft* where German Standard German has *gesamt*. The suffix *-lich* occurs in *hablich* 'prosperous' and *einwohnerlich* 'concerning the inhabitants'. Sometimes adjectives have umlaut in Swiss usage but none elsewhere: *sömmerlich*.

Verbal prefixes combine with different stems in Swiss High German. The prefix *ver-* is used in *verzeigen* (*anzeigen*), *vertragen* (*austragen*), and *verunmöglichen* 'to make something impossible'. The suffix *-eln* occurs frequently, often in humorous formations, for example *beineln* 'to hurry with small steps' and *schlitteln* 'to ride on a sleigh'. The prefix *er-* is used, albeit infrequently, for example *erfallen* 'to fall to one's death' and *ertrügen* 'to obtain something by deception'. There is also a tendency to use simple instead of compound verbs in Swiss High German: *blättern* instead of *durchblättern*, *decken* for *zudecken*, *denken* for *nachdenken*, *kehren* for *zurückkehren*, *meiden* for *vermeiden* and *riegeln* for *zuriegeln*. The opposite, using compound instead of simple verbs, does occur, but not nearly so frequently: *abstützen* for *stützen*, *einernten* for *ernten* and *nachfolgen* for *folgen*.

There are also examples of suffixes in Swiss High German which derive from dialect. The dialect diminutive suffix *-li*, which forms neuter nouns, is widely used for familiar objects: for example household articles, *Körbli*, *Päckli*, *Bettli*, *Brettli*; articles of clothing, particularly baby clothing, *Kleidli*, *Mänteli*, *Pullöverli*, *Hütli*, *Söckli*; food *Güggeli* (*Hähnchen*), *Rippli*, *Hörnli*, *Gipfeli*. Masculine agentive nouns can be formed with the suffix *-i*, denoting particularly people with pejorative characteristics: *Löli* 'stupid chap', *Stürmi* 'impatient person' and *Knorzi* 'miser' and 'dwarf'. The feminine suffix *-ete* is used to form actional nouns from verbs: *Frühjahrsputzete* 'spring cleaning', *Schleglete* 'fight' and *Züglete* 'removal'. The suffix *-et*, forming nouns which designate an event, is neuter but sometimes masculine. This suffix is more productive than *-ete*: *Absendet* 'prizegiving at a shooting competition', *Blühet* 'the time of blooming', *Heuet* 'hay harvest', *Jasset* 'a game of *Jass*' and *Schwinget* 'a wrestling match'.

Yet another source of Helveticisms is the continuing use of words in Swiss High German which in German Standard German have died out or are archaic. Examples of nouns are: *Mietzins* used for 'rent', *Witfrau* for 'widow' and *Liegenschaft* for 'property, piece of land'. The adjective *heimelig* is used for 'comfortable, cosy, homely', *hälftig* is the adjective from *Hälfte*. *Einhellig* is used for 'unanimous'.

Among verbs *angehen* occurs in the meaning 'to commence' and *berappen* for 'to pay'. However, it is among adverbs where this use of archaic forms is most clearly seen: *allerenden* for 'everywhere', *hinfort* 'in future', *jeweilen* 'now and then', *längstens* 'at the latest' and *vorab* 'first of all'. The correlation *so wie* is usually *so . . . als*, for example *so bald als möglich*.

4.5   CONCLUSION

What conclusions can be drawn as to how the linguistic situation in Switzerland will develop? Rupp (1983) sees little change: the written language will contain a similar number of Helveticisms; dialect will continue to be used in spoken communication, although a supra-regional koine will not emerge and the dialect wave will abate. He sees an easier relationship between standard and dialect in the realm of spoken language. What he seems to mean by this is that speakers will be less sensitive to the choice of dialect or standard in such areas as television and radio. The choice of one or the other will not be construed as having other consequences. Sieber (1992) recognizes a certain tension between Swiss German and Swiss High German but points to the fact that both are gaining ground and importance. Switzerland as well as other southern varieties of German should not let themselves be dictated to in language usage by a numerically larger united Germany.

Switzerland, like other countries, is made up of individuals with differing views, some more radical, some more conservative, as exemplified in Haas (1986) and articles in Vouga and Hodel (1990). Some speakers fear that the increased use of dialect and consequent less use of, particularly, spoken High German could lead to problems of communication with speakers from other German-speaking countries as well as the French- and Italian-speaking parts of Switzerland. This is particularly crucial if Switzerland is to play a fuller role in Europe. This increased use of dialect could lead to Switzerland becoming more of a back-water. If Swiss German became the sole language of German Switzerland then High German would indeed become a foreign language. On the other hand, the increased use of dialect is seen by others as simply an increase in the use of language in general by more and more speakers. In the past only a relatively small number of people used High German to any great extent anyway. The increased use of dialect is thus a sign of democratic progress. The fact is that the diglossic situation in Switzerland seems to be developing into a bilingual situation. One danger seen by representatives of both sides is that the increased use of dialect could lead to a more uniform Swiss German, without the great variety of the many regional forms. As an outsider one could say that this is just the way in which new supraregional varieties arise which may later become standard national languages.

Many of these different attitudes can be seen in the evaluation of the answers in a questionnaire filled in by twenty-year-old army recruits from 1985. In some cases the results were paradoxical (Schläpfer *et al.* 1991). The dialect was their mother-tongue and they felt, on the one hand, that more dialect should be used in school and in certain situations, for example informal radio programmes, sermons in church and even on solemn occasions. However, almost half also wished for a better knowledge of High German and 80 per cent thought that High German was desirable for academic lectures and news broadcasts. Whatever happens, the Swiss will want to maintain their independence. Jacob Grimm in the introduction to the *Deutsches Wörterbuch* in 1854 recognized that already when he designated their language as 'mehr als bloszer dialekt, wie es schon aus der freiheit des volks sich begreifen läszt' ('more than simply a dialect, which can be seen from the freedom of the people'). The last word I shall leave with Max Frisch, who wrote (in Kaiser 1969: 30f.), 'Als Schriftsteller halte ich nun dafür, dass unser Hochdeutsch zwar korrekt sein sollte, aber durchaus anders klingen darf als das Hochdeutsch eines Lübecker Schriftstellers' ('As an author I consider that our High German should be correct but also should sound different from the High German of a certain author from Lübeck').

4.6 ILLUSTRATIVE TEXTS

4.6.1 Texts illustrating Swiss German

4.6.1.1 *The Christmas story, Luke 2:1–16, in Bärndütsch:*

1 I dere Zyt het der Cheiser Augustus befole, me söll i sym Rych e Stüür-Schatzig dürefüere. 2 Das isch denn ds erschte Mal passiert, wo der Quirinius isch Landvogt vo Syrie gsi. 3 Da sy alli uf d Reis, für sech ga la yschetze, jede a sy Heimatort. 4 O der Josef isch vo Galiläa, us der Stadt Nazaret, nach Judäa gwanderet, i d Davidsstadt, wo Betlehem heisst. Er het drum zu de Nachfahre vom David ghört. 5 Dert het er sech welle la yschetze zäme mit der Maria, syr Brut. Die het es Chind erwartet. 6 Wo si dert sy aacho, isch d Geburt nache gsi, 7 und si het iren erschte Suhn übercho. Sie het ne gwicklet und i ne Chrüpfe gleit. Es het drum für se süsch kei

Platz gha i der Herbärg. 8 I der glyche Gäget sy Hirte uf em Fäld
gsi, wo d Nacht düre bi irne Tier Wach ghalte hei. 9 Da chunt en
Ängel vo Gott, em Herr, zue ne, und e hälle Schyn von Gott
lüuchtet um sen ume. Si sy natürlech starch erchlüpft. 10 Aber der
Ängel seit zue ne: 'Heit nid Angscht, lueget, i bringe nech e guete
Bricht, e grossi Fröid, wo ds ganze Volk aageit. 11 Hütt isch
nämlech i der Davids-Stadt öie Retter uf de Wält cho. Es isch
Chrischtus, der Herr. 12 Und a däm chöit der's merke: Dihr findet
das Chindli gwicklet und in nere Chrüpfe.' 13 Uf einisch sy umen
Ängel ume grossi Schare vom Himelsheer gsi, die hei Gott globet
und gseit: 14 'Ehr für Gott i der Höchi, und uf der Ärde Fride für d
Mönsche, won är lieb hat.' 15 D Ängel sy wider im Himel versch-
wunde, und d Hirte hei zunenand gseit: 'Mir wei doch uf
Betlehem yne di Sach ga luege, wo da passiert isch, und won nis
der Herr het z wüsse ta.' 16 Si hei pressiert und hei d Maria und der
Josef gfunde und ds Chindli i der Chrüpfe.

(Bietenhard and Bietenhard 1985: 118f.)

Before commenting on some forms in the passage, the reader might
care to examine the High German version in the Zurich translation:

1 Es begab sich aber in jenen Tagen, dass vom Kaiser Augustus ein
Befehl erging, dass der ganze Erdkreis sich einschätzen sollte. 2
Diese Schatzung war die erste und geschah, als Quirinius
Statthalter in Syrien war. 3 Und es machten sich alle auf, um sich
einschätzen zu lassen, ein jeder in seine Stadt. 4 Aber auch Joseph
ging von Galiläa aus der Stadt Nazareth hinauf nach Judäa in die
Stadt Davids, welche Behlehem heisst, weil er aus dem Hause und
Geschlechte Davids war, 5 um sich mit Maria, seiner Verlobten,
die schwanger war, einschätzen zu lassen. 6 Es begab sich aber,
während sie dort waren, da vollendeten sich die Tage, dass sie
gebären sollte. 7 Und sie gebar ihren ersten Sohn und wickelte ihn
in Windeln und legte ihn in eine Krippe, weil sie in der Herberge
keinen Platz fanden. 8 Und es waren Hirten in derselben Gegend
auf dem Felde, die hielten Nachtwache über ihre Herde. 9 Da trat
ein Engel des Herrn zu ihnen, und Lichtglanz des Herrn umleuch-
tete sie, und sie fürchteten sich sehr. 10 Und der Engel sprach zu
ihnen: 'Fürchtet euch nicht! Denn siehe, ich verkündige euch grosse
Freude, die allem Volke widerfahren wird; 11 denn euch ist heute
der Heiland geboren, welcher der Christus ist, der Herr in der Stadt
Davids. 12 Und das sei euch das Zeichen: Ihr werdet ein Kind
finden, in Windeln gewickelt und in einer Krippe liegend.' 13

Und auf einmal war bei dem Engel die Menge des himmlischen
Heeres, die lobten Gott und sprachen: 14 'Ehre sei Gott in den
Höhen und Friede auf Erden unter den Menschen, an denen Gott
Wohlgefallen hat.' 15 Und es begab sich, als die Engel von ihnen
gen Himmel gefahren waren, da sprachen die Hirten zueinander:
'Lasset uns doch nach Bethlehem hingehen und diese Sache sehen,
die geschehen ist und die der Herr uns kundgetan hat.' 16 Und sie
gingen eilends und fanden Maria und Joseph und das Kind in der
Krippe liegend.

(Kirchenrat des Kantons Zurich 1942: 77)

Notes on the passage

A large part of the vocabulary is the same in both passages, differing
in phonetic shape. The dialect has retained the MHG long *î*, *iu*, *û* as
monophthongs whereas in NHG they have become diphthongs: v. 1
Zyt, *sym*, *Rych*; *Stüür*, v. 11 *Hütt*, v. 9 *lüüchtet*, v. 3 *uf*, v. 4 *us*, v. 5
Brut. MHG *ie*, *üe*, *uo* are retained as diphthongs: v. 14 *lieb*, v. 1
dürefüere, v. 19 *lueget*, *guete*. Final *-n* is lost after unstressed *e* but
remains, or is restored if the following word begins with a vowel, *iren
erschte Suhn*, sometimes wrongly: v. 9 *um sen ume* = *um sie herum*.
This is similar to the loss and re-introduction of postvocalic *r* in
British English, *four pears* [fɔː pɛːz] as against *four apples* [fɔːr aplz],
with a 'wrong', intrusive *r* in the *idea-r-of* it. This loss of *n* affects
grammatical inflections: v. 1 infinitive *dürefüere*, past participle
befole; adjective endings v. 7 *iren erschte Suhn*; plural ending v. 4
Nachfahre. The *s* before *p*, *t* in the middle of a word becomes
pronounced [ʃ], v. 2 *isch* (with loss of final *-t*), *erschte*. The relative
pronoun is the indeclinable particle *wo*: v. 4 *wo Betlehem heisst*. The
pronominal forms, v. 12 *Dihr*, *der*, are typical of *Bärndütsch*, in
Züritüütsch they would be *iir*, *er*.

4.6.1.2 The Christmas story, Luke 2:1–14, in Züüritüütsch

This is a slightly freer version.

1 I säbere Ziit hät de Käiser Auguschtus de Befeel useggee, ali
Lüüt vo siim Riich sölid sich i Stuurliischtene iiträäge laa. 2 Die
Schatzig isch s eerscht Maal duregfüert woorde, wo de Quirinius
Landvogt vo Syrie gsi isch. 3 Da händ sich ali uf de Wääg gmacht
und sind sich gogen iiträäge laa, jeden i siini Häimetgmäind.
4 So isch au de Josef vo Galiläa, us de Stadt Nazaret, uf Judäa

ufeggange, id Davidsstadt, wo Betlehem häisst. Er hät nämli zum Huus und zur alte Familie vom David ghöört. 5 Deet hät er sich welen iiträge laa, zäme mit de Maria, siinere Verlobte, won es Chind erwaartet hät. 6 Wo s dänn deet gsi sind, da isch für sii d Ziit vo de Geburt choo. 7 Und si hät iren eerscht Soon uf d Wält praacht. Und si hät en i Windlen iigwicklet und hät en in e Fueterchrippe gläit. Si händ drum im Underschlupf kän andere Platz gfunde. 8 Und es sind i säbere Gäget Hiirten uf em Fäld gsii, wo z Nacht iri Schaafheerd ghüetet händ. 9 Und es isch en Ängel zuen ene choo, und em Herrgott siis Liecht hät um si umen ales ganz hell erlüüchtet, und si sind fürchtig verschrocke. 10 Da hät de Ängel zuen ene gsäit: 'Ir müend e kä Angscht haa! Lueged, ich han öi nämli e groossi Fröid z verchunde, won ali Lüüt aagaat. 11 Hütt isch für öi de Retter uf d Wält choo. Es isch de Chrischtus, de Herr i de Davidsstadt! 12 Und da draa chönd er s merke: Ir weerded es Chindli finde, won i Windlen iigwicklet isch und in ere Fueterchrippe liit.' 13 Und da isch um der Ängel ume uf äimaal e groossi Gschaar vom Himelsheer gsii. Die händ de Herrgott prisen und händ grueft: 14 'Ali Eer ghöört em Herrgott im Himel! Und uf der Eerde isch iez Fride, under de Mäntsche, won er geern hät!'

(E. Weber 1985: 15f.)

4.6.2 Text to illustrate Swiss High German

This is an artificially constructed text which contains a high density of lexical Helveticisms. Corresponding German Standard German forms appear in parentheses.

Der im Kanton Zürich immatrikulierte [= zum Verkehr zugelassen] Autocar [= Reisebus] verweigerte dem Velo [= Rad]fahrer den Vortritt [= die Vorfahrt] und drängte ihn über das Strassenbord [= Rand] hinaus. Der Velofahrer, ein Ausläufer [= Bote] der Konfisierie [= Konditorei] Müller, trug eine Hutte [= einen Rückentragkorb] und erlitt deshalb beim Sturz Verletzungen. Der Carführer wurde gebüsst [= musste eine Geldstrafe bezahlen]; sein Anwalt gelangte aber an die höhere Instanz. Er machte geltend, dass der Gebüsste wegen den [= NHG gen.] beidseitig [= an beiden Seiten] parkierten [= geparkten] Autos und Camions [= LKWs] sowie den Bretterbeigen [= Stapeln] vor der Sägerei Lorenz den Burschen nicht rechtzeitig habe sehen können. Ausserdem hätten Kinder, die bei der Papeterie [= Papierwarenhandlung] Meyer Trottinett [= Roller] fuhren, die Aufmerksamkeit des Chauffeurs [= Fahrers] erheischt, ebenso eine Gruppe von Wehrmännern [= Soldaten], die sich eben beim Lebhag [= bei der Hecke] rechts von der Strasse besammelte [= versammelte]. Nach Ausweis des Fahrtenschreibers sei der Car in Tat und Wahrheit [= tatsächlich] bloss mit fünfzig und nicht, wie von Zeugen behauptet, mit siebzig Stundenkilometern gefahren.

Die ausgefällte Busse [= verhängte Strafe] sei deshalb übersetzt [= übertrieben]. Da die Angelegenheit das Strassenverkehrsgesetz beschlägt [= angeht, betrifft], ist der Bezirksamman [= Beamter, der einem Bezirk [Kreis] vorsteht] zuständig, der vom Anwalt eingeladen wurde, die Angelegenheit beförderlich [= rasch] zu behandeln und nicht, wie hierzulande gang und gäbe, zu vertrödeln. Der Anwalt wandte sich auch dagegen, dass man seinen Mandanten für eine Busse [= Geldstrafe] betrieben [= eine Schuld zwangsrechtlich einziehen] habe, über deren Rechtmässigkeit man sich in guten Treuen [= im rechten Glauben] streiten könne und über die noch kein definitiver Entscheid [= Entscheidung] getroffen worden sei.

(Haas 1982: 113)

SELECT BIBLIOGRAPHY AND FURTHER READING

Baur, A. (1992) *Grüezi mitenand: praktische Sprachlehre des Schweizerdeutschen*, 10th edn, Winterthur: Gemsberg Verlag.

Bietenhard, H. and Bietenhard, R. (1985) *Ds Nöie Teschtament bärndütsch*, Berne: Berchtold Holler.

Boesch, B. (ed.) (1957) *Die Aussprache des Hochdeutschen in der Schweiz: eine Wegleitung*, Zurich: Schweizer Spiegel Verlag.

Church, C. (1989) 'German-speaking Switzerland since 1937: The *Mundartwelle* in its Historical Context', *Contemporary German Studies. Occasional Papers*, 7, University of Strathclyde, pp. 28–52.

Fenske, H. (1973) *Schweizerische und österreichische Besonderheiten in deutschen Wörterbüchern* (Institut für deutsche Sprache, Forschungsberichte, 10), Tübingen: Narr.

Haas, W. (1982a) 'Sprachgeschichte der Schweiz', in R. Schläpfer (ed.) *Die viersprachige Schweiz*, Zurich: Benziger, pp. 23–70.

—— (1982b) 'Die deutschsprachige Schweiz', in R. Schläpfer (ed.) *Die viersprachige Schweiz*, Zurich: Benziger, pp. 73–160.

—— (1982c) 'Die Besonderheiten des "Schweizer Hochdeutsch"', in R. Schläpfer (ed.) *Die viersprachige Schweiz*, Zurich: Benziger.

—— (1986) 'Der beredte Deutschschweizer oder die Hollandisierung des Hinterwälders. Über die Kritik an der Deutschschweizer Sprachsituation', in H. Löffler (ed.) *Das Deutsch der Schweizer: zur Sprach- und Literatursituation in der Schweiz* (Sprachlandschaft, 4), Aarau: Sauerländer, pp. 41–59.

—— (1988) 'Schweiz', in U. Ammon, N. Dittmar and K. J. Mattheier (eds)

Sociolinguistics: An International Handbook, Berlin: de Gruyter, 2, 2, pp. 1365–83.

Hotzenköcherle, R. (1984) *Die Sprachlandschaften der deutschen Schweiz*, eds N. Bigler and R. Schläpfer (Sprachlandschaft, 1), Aarau: Sauerländer.

Kaiser, S. (1969), *Die Besonderheiten der deutschen Schriftsprache in der Schweiz*, vol. 1: *Wortgut und Wortgebrauch* (Duden Beiträge, 30a), Mannheim: Bibliographisches Institut.

—— (1970) *Die Besonderheiten der deutschen Schriftsprache in der Schweiz*, vol. 2: *Wortbildung und Satzbildung* (Duden Beiträge, 30b), Mannheim: Bibliographisches Institut.

Keller, R. E. (1961) 'Züritüütsch, Bärndütsch', in his *German Dialects*, Manchester: Manchester University Press, pp. 30–115.

Kirchenrat des Kantons Zürich (ed.) (1942) *Die heilige Schrift des Alten und des Neuen Testaments*, Zurich: Verlag der Zwingli-Bibel.

Lötscher, A. (1982) *Schweizerdeutsch: Geschichte, Dialekte, Gebrauch*, Frauenfeld: Huber.

Marti, W. (1985) *Berndeutsche Grammatik*, Berne: Francke.

Meyer, K. (1989) *Wie sagt man in der Schweiz? Wörterbuch der schweizerischen Besonderheiten* (Duden Taschenbücher, 22), Mannheim: Bibliographisches Institut.

Ris, R. (1979) 'Dialekte und Einheitssprache in der Schweiz', in *Dialect and Standard in Highly Industrialized Societies = International Journal of the Sociology of Language*, 21: 41–61.

—— (1980) 'Probleme aus der pragmatischen Sprachgeschichte der deutschen Schweiz', in H. Sitta (ed.) *Ansätze zu einer pragmatischen Sprachgeschichte. Zürcher Kolloquium 1978* (Reihe Germanistische Linguistik, 21), Tübingen: Niemeyer, pp. 103–28.

Rupp, H. (1983) 'Deutsch in der Schweiz', in *Tendenzen, Formen und Strukturen der deutschen Standardsprache nach 1945* (Marburger Studien zur Germanistik, 3), Marburg: Elwert, pp. 29–39.

Russ, C. V. J. (1987) 'Language and Society in German Switzerland: Multilingualism, Diglossia and Variation', in C. V. J. Russ and C. Volkmar (eds) *Sprache und Gesellschaft in deutschsprachigen Ländern*, Munich: Goethe Institut, pp. 94–121.

—— (1990) 'High Alemannic', in C. V. J. Russ (ed.) *The Dialects of Modern German*, London: Routledge, pp. 364–93.

Schilling, R. (1970) *Romanische Elemente im Schweizerhochdeutschen* (Duden Beiträge, 38), Mannheim: Bibliographisches Institut.

Schläpfer, R., Gutzwiller, J. and Schmid, B. (1991) *Das Spannungsfeld zwischen Mundart und Standardsprache in der deutschen Schweiz. Spracheinstellungen junger Deutsch- und Welschschweizer: eine Auswertung der Pädagogischen Rekrutenprüfungen 1985*, Aarau: Sauerländer.

Schwarzenbach, R. (1969) *Die Stellung der Mundart in der deutschsprachigen Schweiz: Studien zum Sprachgebrauch der Gegenwart* (Beiträge zur schweizerdeutschen Mundartforschung, 17), Frauenfeld: Huber.

—— (1983) 'Schweizerdeutsch im Sprachbrauch von Radio und Fernsehen DRS – von der Analyse zur Norm', in W. Haas and A. Näf (eds) *Wortschatzprobleme im Alemannischen* (Germanistica Friburgensia, 7), Freiburg, Switzerland: Universitätsverlag, pp. 201–10.

Sieber, P. (1992) 'Hochdeutsch in der deutschen Schweiz', *Der Deutschunterricht*, 44: 28–42.

Sieber, P. and Sitta, H. (1984) 'Schweizerdeutsch zwischen Dialekt und Sprache', *Kwartalnik Neofilologiczny*, 31: 3–40.

Sonderegger, S. (1985) 'Die Entwicklung des Verhältnisses von Standardsprache und Mundarten in der deutschen Schweiz', in W. Besch, O. Reichmann and S. Sonderegger (eds) *Sprachgeschichte. Ein Handbuch zur Geschichte der deutschen Sprache*, 1, 2, Berlin: de Gruyter, pp. 1873–1939.

—— (1991) 'Die Schweiz als Sprachgrenzland: eine historisch-typologische Standortbestimmung', *Zeitschrift für Literaturwissenschaft und Linguistik*, 83: 13–39.

Sprachatlas der deutschen Schweiz (1965ff.) Begun by R. Hotzenköcherle, continued by R. Schläpfer, R. Trüb and P. Zinsli, Berne: Francke.

Vouga, J.-P. and Hodel, M. E. (eds) (1990) *Die Schweiz im Spiegel ihrer Sprachen*, Aarau: Sauerländer.

Weber, A. (1964) *Zürichdeutsche Grammatik und Wegweiser zur guten Mundart*, Zurich: Schweizer Spiegel Verlag.

Weber, D. E. (1984) *Sprach- und Mundartpflege in der deutschsprachigen Schweiz* (Studia Linguistica Alemannica, 9), Frauenfeld: Huber.

Weber, E. (1985) *S Lukas-Evangelium. Us em Griechische uf Züritüutsch übersetzt*, Zurich: Jordanverlag.

5 German in East Germany

5.1 HISTORICAL BACKGROUND

On 3 October 1990 the German people celebrated the birth of a united Germany. Since the capitulation of the Third *Reich* in May 1945 and the division of the country into four zones occupied by the Americans, British, French and Russians the country had not been united. At the Potsdam Conference in July/August 1945 the German Territories east of the Oder/Neiße rivers were given to Poland and the northeastern part of East Prussia to the USSR. From then on the different zones went different ways. In the Russian zone political parties which were anti-fascist were allowed from as early as 10 June 1945 and the following political parties came into being: KPD (Kommunistische Partei Deutschlands), SPD (Sozialdemokratische Partei Deutschlands), the CDU (Christlich-Demokratische Union Deutschlands) and the LDPD (Liberal-Demokratische Partei Deutschlands). Political activities were also allowed in the other zones and in 1946–7 elections were held for state parliaments in the new *Länder*. In 1947 the American and British zones merged to become the so-called *Bizone*, which formed the basis of the future Federal Republic. Relations between the western Allies and the Russians deteriorated and Winston Churchill spoke on 5 March 1946 of an iron curtain descending in Europe. From this time on the Russian aim of creating a communist satellite state by dividing Germany proceeded swiftly. In September 1945 land was taken from its owners in the land reform (*Bodenreform*) and agricultural collective farms and co-operatives were created. Similar measures took businesses out of private hands. In the summer of 1946 a new type of unified school (*Einheitsschule*) was created, replacing the former different schools such as grammar school (*Gymnasium*) and secondary modern school (*Mittelschule*).

On 21–2 April 1946 the two largest parties, the KPD under Walter

Ulbricht (1893–1973), who had been in exile in Moscow (1938–45), and the SPD under Otto Grotewohl (1894–1964) merged under pressure from the Russians to form the SED (Sozialistische Einheitspartei Deutschlands). The SED, with the help of the Russians, gradually strengthened their position, using mass organizations and people's congresses. In 1948 the second people's congress elected a 330-strong assembly (*Volksrat*). The trend towards a separate state continued when in May 1949 66.1 per cent of the voters agreed with the single list of candidates drawn up by the SED. The elected *Volksrat* turned itself into the *Volkskammer* and passed a constitution founding the German Democratic Republic (Deutsche Demokratische Republik) on 7 October 1949. In May 1949 the Federal Republic of Germany (Bundesrepublik Deutschland) had been promulgated by the acceptance of the Basic Law (*Grundgesetz*), with elections following in August 1949. Thus from 1949 to 1989–90 there were two separate political states in the former geographical area of the old German *Reich*, i.e. reaching as far east as the rivers Oder and Neiße. From 1949 until 1952 the GDR was divided into *Länder* like the Federal Republic of Germany, but these *Länder* were dissolved in July 1952 and replaced by fourteen *Bezirke*, an attempt to weaken past regional allegiances in favour of the new centralized state. The gap between the plans of the SED and the social and political reality in the GDR led to the unsuccessful uprising in Berlin of 17 June 1953. In the next few years the flight of so many people from the country led to the building of the wall in Berlin in August 1961 and the strengthening of the whole border between the GDR and the Federal Republic of Germany. When the SPD came to power with Willy Brandt (1913–92) as Chancellor, in the Federal Republic of Germany in 1969, with the help of the FDP (Freie Demokratische Partei), new initiatives to ameliorate the situation between the Federal Republic of Germany and the GDR were undertaken, culminating in 1972 in a treaty in which both states officially recognized the sovereignty of each other within their own agreed territorial boundaries. Although the Federal Republic of Germany and GDR were both founded in 1949, they had, however, different political, social and economic systems. Separate states, yet they shared a common language and until 1945 they possessed a common history and literature. The West German Foreign Minister in 1972, Walter Scheel, summed this linguistic bond up as follows in the treaty between the two states in 1972: 'Beide Staaten sind Teil einer Nation mit gemeinsamer Sprache, gemeinsamer Geschichte und einem engen Geflecht von Bindungen' (*Vertrag* 1972: 63) ('Both states are part of one nation with a common language, common history and a close network of ties'). The treaty was passed in the same language by the legislative chambers of both states. They used the same language and communicated with each other by means of it; however, forty years of a different political, social and economic system had obviously had an effect on the language in each state and yet not sufficiently great an effect to speak of two different languages.

Changes in the leadership had also taken place in the GDR. The architect and overseer of the wall, Erich Honecker (1912–94), took over from Walter Ulbricht as the First Secretary of the SED. In the years that followed there were moves to establish the independent development of the GDR in areas such as culture, sport and language. We can see how this affected research on language in the GDR in 5.2.6.

5.2   NORMATIVE WORKS ON GERMAN IN EAST GERMANY

In this section we will concentrate on the linguistic characteristics of German in East Germany, considering the different models which were accepted as standard and the differences in actual usage of spelling, pronunciation, grammar and lexis.

5.2.1   Spelling and the two *Dudens*

The spelling of German has been regulated by *Duden Rechtschreibung* of which two separate volumes appeared from 1951 onwards, one in West Germany (Mannheim) and one in East Germany (Leipzig). In Mannheim the fifteenth to nineteenth editions appeared from 1955 to 1986; in Leipzig the fourteenth to eighteenth editions appeared from 1951 to 1985. One early comparison of the entries under *A* in the Leipzig *Duden* volumes of the fourteenth edition 1951, fifteenth edition 1957 and the Mannheim *Duden* volumes of the fourteenth edition 1954 by Betz (1960) revealed that the differences between the *Duden Rechtschreibung* volumes, apart from the presence or absence of particular words or meanings, lay in a greater or lesser flexibility in the recognition of more colloquial forms, or in the way variants were allowed or not. The treatment of unstressed *e* was particularly diverse. The Mannheim *Duden* had only the form *abstehen* 'to stand away; to stick out', whereas the Leipzig *Duden* allowed both *abstehen* and *abstehn*, the latter form being found in colloquial usage in West Germany. The verbs ending in *-eln* and *-ern* and the nouns derived from them showed a similar discrepancy in the two volumes: the

Mannheim *Duden* had only *Abwickler* 'liquidator', *Aufrüttelung* 'shake up', whereas the Leipzig *Duden* had two forms, one with *e* and the other without, *Abwick(e)ler*, *Aufrütt(e)lung*. Both volumes, however, were inconsistent in other instances: the Leipzig *Duden* had *Anforderung*, whereas the Mannheim volume had *Anford(e)rung*. The gen. sg. masculine and neuter forms of nouns were also treated inconsistently by the two volumes, although most of the items affected were foreign or scientific words. The Mannheim *Duden* had *Aldehyds*, *Alkaloids* as the gen. sg. of *Aldehyde*, *Alkaloid*, whereas the Leipzig *Duden* had the forms *Aldehyd(e)s*, *Alkaloid(e)s*. These differences arose because both volumes were aiming at different linguistic models. The Mannheim *Duden*, which is also authoritative in Austria and Switzerland, gave more weight to the written language and formal usage, whereas the Leipzig *Duden* apparently took colloquial and spoken usage more into account. More important differences occurred where there were genuine variants, for example in pl. forms, or in the strong or weak gen. sg. forms of nouns. The Mannheim *Duden* gave only *Ahn(e)s* (the strong form) as the gen. sg. of *Ahn* 'ancestor', whereas the Leipzig *Duden* had both *Ahnes* (strong) and *Ahnen* (weak). On the other hand, the Leipzig *Duden* gave only the weak forms *Asteroiden* and *Partisanen* as the gen. sg. of *Asteroid* and *Partisan*, whereas the Mannheim *Duden* had both *-es* and *-en*. The only pl. form given for *Alk* 'auk' by the Mannheim *Duden* was *Alke* whereas the Leipzig *Duden* had both *Alke* and *Alken*. On the other hand, the Leipzig *Duden* had only *Aulen* as the pl. of *Aula* 'assembly hall, auditorium', whereas the Mannheim *Duden* had both *Aulen* and *Aulas*. The Leipzig *Duden* was more generous in allowing fluctuation in grammatical gender. The Mannheim *Duden* had only *das Anerkenntnis* 'recognizance' and *das Ar* 'are' (measurement = 100 sq. m.), whereas the Leipzig *Duden* also allowed *die Anerkenntnis* and *der Ar*. In the case of the animal 'alpaca' the Leipzig *Duden* allowed only *der* while the Mannheim *Duden* had *das*. The wool of the 'alpaca' was, however, always *das* in both volumes. These fluctuations were instances of genuine variants whose usage had not completely settled down to a norm.

If one looked up the instances where there was fluctuation in grammatical gender, strong or weak gen. sg., or between pl. forms according to *Duden Grammatik* one found that these forms showed the same fluctuation in both *Duden* volumes, for example *des Bauers* or *Bauern*; *die Knuste* or *Knüste* 'crust of bread'. Similarly verbs such as *backen* and *melken* were recorded with weak and strong past tense forms in both *Duden* volumes.

The situation has changed since Betz did his comparison and the Mannheim *Duden* of 1973 and the Leipzig *Duden* of 1972 were much more similar than the editions which Betz examined. In most cases the Mannheim volume followed the Leipzig volume in allowing more optional masculine and neuter gen. sg. forms with *-(e)s* instead of only with *-es*. The Leipzig *Duden* followed the Mannheim volume in allowing both *anhangsweise* and *anhangweise* when before *anhangsweise* was the sole Mannheim form and *anhangweise* the sole Leipzig form. The Mannheim *Duden*, on the other hand, followed the Leipzig volume in recommending only *das Alpaka* for the wool of the 'alpaca' and adding an optional *die Anerkenntnis* (for legal language) and an optional *der Ar*. One puzzling inconsistency remained in the Mannheim *Duden*: unstressed *e* before verbs ending in *-rn* could be omitted, *wandern*, but *ich wand(e)re*, however unstressed *e* before verbs ending in *-ln* could not be omitted, *wandeln, ich wandele*. The Leipzig *Duden* had both *ich wand(e)re* and *ich wand(e)le*. However, in the case of adjectives the Mannheim and Leipzig *Duden* volumes agreed in optionally omitting *e* before *-lig*, for example *langschäd(e)lig* 'dolichocephalic'. Comparison of the entries under any letter of the two most recent *Duden* volumes showed far fewer discrepancies, even of a minor kind, than when Betz made his comparison in 1960. Since these volumes were regarded as normative and prescriptive the fact that they seemed to be coming closer together was indicative of the will and desire to create one norm.

Longer-term studies of the two *Duden Rechtschreibung* volumes show how similar they became. Sauer (1988: 154f.) traces the fate of thirty-five East German formations, including some names, which appeared frequently in the 1950s and 1960s. Nine have disappeared; eight remained solely in the Leipzig *Duden*: *Friedenskämpfer, Kulturbund, Lernaktiv, MEGA* (= *Marx-Engels-Gesamtausgabe*), *Operativplan, Politökonomie, Praktizismus, Sozialdemokratismus*; seven appeared in both volumes, but marked either 'DDR' – *Traktorist, Versöhnler, volkseigen* – or 'russisch' – *Kasch* – or 'in Ostblockstaaten' – *Diversant, Politbüro, Spartakiade*; while seven appeared without any label in both volumes: *Dispatcher, Exponat, Festival, Kombine, Massenorganisation, Sowjetmensch, Westberlin/West-Berlin*. These latter examples show how the language in West Germany absorbed some Eastern formations. Two examples, *Komplexbrigade, Kursist*, only appear in the Mannheim *Duden* but were marked 'DDR'! The two final words only appear in the Mannheim *Duden, Jarowisation*, marked 'russisch' and *Abgabesoll* with no label. Sauer emphasizes the similar tendencies in both volumes and wishes for an all-German *Duden* which has now come true (see 5.2.7). The evidence gained from the common similarities and common variants was a very strong pointer to the fact that German in East and West Germany was not in danger of splitting into two languages, at least as far as the normative models provided by the *Duden Rechtschreibung* volumes which dealt with spelling and inflectional morphology were concerned.

5.2.2 Pronunciation

Linguists in East Germany also turned their attention to the norms of pronunciation. Their aim was not to produce a standard just for East Germany but to help in creating a general standard for both German states which was based on empirical descriptive studies, and was not merely prescriptive. In 1961 a separate pronouncing dictionary was produced in East Germany, *Wörterbuch der deutschen Aussprache* (*WDA*), whereas in West Germany two were produced: *Siebs*, *Deutsche Aussprache* (latest edition 1969) and the *Duden Aussprachewörterbuch*, (first edition 1974). The *WDA*, with its detailed phonetic introduction, was based on empirical studies of the pronunciation of formal reading styles used by news readers and other figures in the mass media. Being based on empirical studies it allowed many pronunciations which the West German *Siebs* volume, even in its latest edition (1969), does not countenance, or at least only in a restricted measure. The most striking example of this was the treatment of postvocalic r (for a phonetic description of these sounds see p. 128). The dental [r] or the uvular [ʀ] were both considered to be equally permissible in *WDA*, and Siebs (1969) also concurs in this. Vocalization of postvocalic *r*, however, was allowed only by Siebs (1969) in the word *der* [dɛɐ], whereas *WDA* allowed it in the following environments: after long vowels, *er*, *Uhr*, and in the unstressed prefixes *er-*, *ver-*. In both of these environments, the letter *r* was pronounced as a central vowel [ɐ]. In the final syllable *-er*, *r* fuses with the unstressed *e* to form the same central vowel [ɐ]. In the entries in the *WDA* the vocalized *r* was written in italics, as was the preceding unstressed *e*: *-ər*. The vocalization of postvocalic *r* has been recognized by West German works now (Russ 1991: 329). Similarly unstressed *-en* was allowed to be pronounced as a syllabic [n̩] or assimilated to the place of articulation of the preceding consonant, for example [geːbən, geːbn̩, geːbm̩]. To show this, the ending *-en* and the preceding stem consonant were all written in italics, for example [geː*bən*]. Although it allows many features of the spoken language to become part of the model for pronunciation, it too, like *Siebs* in all its editions, was heavily bound to the North German model and spelling. Aspiration was prescribed for the initial voiceless stops [p t k], and a labio-dental pronunciation, [v], for *w* in *Wein*; in addition long half-open [ɛ:] was recommended for the spelling of *ä* when it designated a long vowel. There was only a shift of model here in the direction of allowing optionally many assimilations which were characteristic of most spoken language: for instance, the vocalization of postvocalic *r* is very widespread in many styles of speech. Otherwise it remains firmly rooted in the North German model. This was hardly surprising since East Germany contained large Low German areas in the north which adopted standard German orthography and pronounced the words largely as they saw them written. Although in East Germany there were regions such as Thuringia and Saxony in which, similar to the Rhineland, Bavaria and Swabia, the spoken language of the educated people had regional colouring and although Walter Ulbricht and many of his followers had clear regional Upper Saxon accents, there was certainly no sign that this accent was becoming the model pronunciation in East Germany.

5.2.3   Grammatical differences

Some differences of inflection such as strong or weak inflection, differing pl. forms and fluctuations in grammatical gender have been dealt with in 5.2.1. The whole area of grammar is more difficult to describe since it is much more extensive than spelling or pronunciation. No corresponding volume to *Duden Grammatik* was produced, although grammars appeared, for example Helbig and Buscha (1974), Jung (1966) and Schmidt (1964), which describe no differences in grammar between East and West German. Even the *Wörterbuch der Sprachschwierigkeiten* (1984) shows the same kind and instances of variation within the written language which have been covered by *Duden Hauptschwierigkeiten* (1965), *Duden Zweifelsfälle der deutschen Sprache* (1972) and *Richtiges und gutes Deutsch*, *Wörterbuch der Zweifelsfälle* (1985). The developmental trends among nouns such as the loss of gen. inflections, increase of *von* instead of the gen., lack of agreement in noun phrases in apposition, increase of the two pl. formations, adding -*s* and adding umlaut and -*e*, and trends among verbs such as change from strong verb to weak and increased use of the perfect and the subjunctive with *würde*, were recorded in texts in both East and West Germany (Braun 1987; Sommerfeldt *et al.* 1988).

5.2.4 Differences in vocabulary

Linguists in both East and West Germany recognized that the main differences between the language used in their respective states were at the level of vocabulary. The morphology and syntax were the same, with the small variations that we have seen in the two *Duden Rechtschreibung* volumes. The vocabulary, however, showed not only differences in word stock but also in the meaning of words. The vast majority of differences in vocabulary resulted directly from the different political, social and economic systems of the two states. The main lexicographical work produced in East Germany was the *Wörterbuch der deutschen Gegenwartssprache* (*WDG*), which appeared in six volumes between 1966 and 1971. A detailed discussion of the whole work is (Malige-Klappenbach 1986). Although conceived as valid for the whole German speech community, from volume 4 (*M – Schinken*) (1974) the work took on an explicit ideological, Marxist–Leninist, nature. In a foreword to volume 4 we can read the following:

> In den sprachlichen Unterschieden zwischen der DDR und der BRD, die hier nur skizziert werden konnten, manifestiert sich die ökonomische, politische, inbesondere aber die ideologische Konfrontation zweier Weltsysteme. Das Wörterbuch der deutschen Gegenwartssprache wird das erste semantische Wörterbuch sein, das dieser Konfrontation auf linguistischem Gebiet Rechnung trägt.
>
> (*WDG*, 4, 1974: II, W. Neumann and R. Klappenbach)

> ('In the linguistic differences between the GDR and the Federal Republic of Germany, which can only be outlined here, the economic, political, especially the ideological confrontation of two world systems manifests itself. The dictionary of modern German will be the first semantic dictionary which takes account of this confrontation at the linguistic level.')

New words created for items and concepts particular to the GDR can be classified linguistically as neologisms (*Neuwörter*), new formations (*Neuprägungen*) and new meanings (*Neubedeutungen*). Neologisms are generally foreign words, for example *Aktiv* 'work team', *Aspirantur* 'research assistantship', whereas new formations have been created by using existing words or morphemes, for example *Arbeiterstudent*, *Arbeitsbrigade*, *Autorenkollektiv*. New meanings gave an extra meaning to an already existing word, for example *Brigade*, whose meaning was extended from referring to soldiers to workers, and *differenzieren* 'to assess the delivery of agricultural products'. Of the three processes of producing new words, new formations were the most frequent, followed by new meanings, with neologisms coming a long way behind. A sampling of words from the letters A–K of *WDG* showed that there were 250 new formations, 41 new meanings but only 12 neologisms pertaining to GDR items and concepts. A useful smaller dictionary of specifically East German words, written from a West German perspective using the same classification, is Kinne and Strube-Edelmann (1981). A popular account is Ahrends (1989).

Hellmann (1980) has a different, more detailed, classification, giving weight to meanings, which is taken up by Schlosser (1990: 13–16). Hellmann distinguishes *Lexemspezifika* which only occur in one state but for the same, or similar, object or concept, for example *Bundestag* (Federal Republic of Germany) and *Volkskammer* (GDR), and *Bedeutungsspezifika*, where the same word has a different meaning in each state. The new meanings are most striking when they refer to political concepts, for example *Friede*, *Freiheit*, *Demokratie*, *Kultur*. Connected with the *Bedeutungsspezifika* are the *Wertungsspezifika*, where the same words, with similar meanings in each state, have either positive or negative connotations: *christlich*, *idealistisch*, *Dissident* were positive in the Federal Republic of Germany and negative in the GDR, whereas *Kommunist*, *Revolution*, *Klassenkampf*, *Planwirtschaft* were negative in the Federal Republic of Germany but positive in the GDR. There are also *Häufigkeitsspezifika*, words used typically with great frequency in each state: *friedliebend*, *sozialistisch*, *Qualifizierung*, *umfassend*, *allseitig*, *Produktion*, *Massen*, *Kreis*, *wir*, *unser* in the GDR and *freiheitlich*, *Partnerschaft*, *Markt*, *Preis*, *dynamisch*, *Angebot*, *Ansicht* in the Federal Republic of Germany. Yeandle (1991), as well as giving a detailed study of the meaning of *Frieden*, a *Bedeutungsspezifikum* in the GDR, has a table showing the most frequent words in *Neues Deutschland*, the top ten of which were: *unser*, *neu*, *Arbeit*, *Partei*, *sozialistisch*, *Republik*, *Betrieb*, *Genosse*, *Volk*, *Frieden*.

To illustrate in more detail the vocabulary of German in the GDR we will refer to several different areas of social, political and economic activity. In the examples which follow the definitions are translations into English of those in German in the *WDG*.

East Germany was characterized by a total reorganization of the industrial and employment system and it was in this area that the greatest number of new coinings were to be found. Manual–industrial workers were organized into different units: the smallest unit of workers was *die Brigade*, which could be led by *ein*(*e*) *Brigade-leiter*(*in*), or *der Brigadier*, pronounced [brigadi:r] the latter term also being used for a rank in the army. Four new compounds existed with *Brigade* as the first component, *Brigadeleiter*(*in*), *Brigade-plan*, *Brigadestützpunkt*, and seventeen as the last component, (with people) *Schülerbrigade* (with machines) *Traktorenbrigade*, and (with activities) *Baubrigade*, *Erntehilfsbrigade*. Another unit was *das Kollektiv*, pl. *-e* or *-s*, 'a work or production group for the achievement of common goals'. *Kollektiv* occurred as the first component of nine compounds, for example *Kollektivaustellung*, *Kollektivjäger*, *Kollektivwirtschaft*, and as the last component of nineteen compounds: for example *Autorenkollektiv*, *Architektenkollektiv*, *Jugend-kollektiv*, *Schriftstellerkollektiv*, *Schulkollektiv*. There was also *das Aktiv*, pl. *-s*, (or seldom *-e*), 'a group of workers which strives collectively to fulfil socio-political economic and cultural tasks and strives for above average achievements'. This word also appears as the last part of five compounds: *Elternaktiv*, *Ernteaktiv*, *Gewerkschaftsaktiv*, *Lernaktiv*, *Parteiaktiv* (the first part can be a noun or a verb). A worker with 'exemplary and above-average achievements' was called *der/die Aktivist*(*in*), pl. *-en*, and this word too formed part of six compounds: *Aktivistenabzeichen*, *Aktivisten-arbeit*, *Aktivistenbewegung*, *Aktivistendissertation*, *Aktivistenehrung*, *Aktivistennadel* (worn as a lapel badge). The word *der Bestarbeiter* was also used for a worker with similar achievements. If the worker concerned had innovated a process then the word *der Neuerer*, *ein Neuerer*, which was also used in West Germany, was used but in East Germany it had become specialized and was only applied to industrial situations. Furthermore there were compounds with *Neuerer-* as the first element: *Neuererbewegung*, *Neuererbrigade*, *Neuererkollektiv*, *Neuerermethode*, *Neuerervorschlag*, *Neuererzentrum*. The larger unit in which workers function was *der Betrieb*, also used in West Germany with the same meaning, but in East Germany there were twenty-three new compounds with *Betrieb*(*s*)- as the first element. The meaning of most of them was obvious, for example *Betriebs-ferienlager*, *Betriebsfonds*, *Betriebsgewerkschaftsgruppe*, *Betriebs-plan*, *Betriebswandzeitung*. However, *Betriebsverkaufsstelle*, was a shop 'where the products of a particular factory were sold', and *der Betriebspaß* meant, not so obviously the 'general characteristics of a factory in regard to its technical and economic state'. The word *das Kombinat*, pl. *-e*, 'a large concern in which different branches of industry or stages of production were united' was used for even larger units, for example *Fischkombinat*, *Eisenhüttenkombinat*,

Textilkombinat. If there were problems to be solved or disputes to be settled in industry then such new formations as *die Konflikt-kommission* and *der Besucherrat* were among the words used for the bodies set up to deal with such matters. Agriculture too was organized in large units, *die Genossenschaft*, and the farmers who were members of these groups were called *Genossenschaftsbauern*. Since most agricultural and other kinds of land was once in private hands it had to be taken over by the state. This was known as *die Bodenreform* and the verb *kollektivieren* was used for this action of nationalizing the land. For the odd farmer or small firm which escaped collectivization the new formations *der Einzelbauer*, *der Einzelbetrieb* were used. Since education was controlled by the state there were several new terms for new situations and persons, or for states which the government wished to emphasize, for example *der Arbeiterstudent*, a student who was a manual worker before starting to study. A student who goes to the university in his own town was called *der Direktstudent*. The word *die Aspirantur* was used for a 'special course to furnish scientists for the future'. Those people who wished to pursue a university course in their free time could do so via *die Funkuniversität*.

The SED exercised a great deal of control on everyday life through its organizations. There were some cases where words which were used with a general sense in West Germany had specific party meanings in East Germany. For instance, *der Jugendfreund* also meant 'a member of the Freie Deutsche Jugend (FDJ)', while one of the meanings of *die Freundschaft* was 'the entirety of pioneer groups at a school', with the inevitable compounds: *Freundschaftsfahne*, *Freundschaftsgeschenk*, *Freundschaftspionierleiter*, *Freundschaftsrat*, *Freundschaftstreffen*, *Freundschaftsvertrag*. Candidates in an election required *eine Kandidatenkarte*. Even in rural areas life was highly organized; a village would have its *Dorfakademie*, *Dorfklub* and on *die Estrade* 'square or dais', the villagers might well put on *ein Estradenkonzert* 'a popular artistic event with a mixed programme of music, dancing and variety acts'. The village would be in *der Bezirk*, a larger administrative unit corresponding to *das Bundesland* in West Germany. The governing body of East Germany was *der Staatsrat*, whose chief executive was *der Staatsratsvorsitzende*. Laws were passed by the one legislative body, *die Volkskammer*.

A sample of new formations in *WDG*, 1, A–D, showed that almost all were nouns, sixty-six, which frequently gave rise to a large number of compounds. The only verbs recorded were *beauflagen* 'to impose on factories, collectives etc. the fulfilment of certain targets' and *chemisieren* 'to use chemical processes' and the only adjectives *agro-technisch* and *aufbauwillig*. There were no examples of new coinages in other parts of speech. This latter point is important since a comparison of the written German in Switzerland and Austria with that in West Germany shows that the differences in vocabulary were not merely reflected in different nouns but also in other parts of speech. In spite of all the differences we have shown to exist in the written language of East Germany as compared to that of West Germany, it must be said that they were smaller in number than the differences that exist in German in Austria, Switzerland and Luxemburg.

5.2.5 Linguistic borrowing

One striking difference with regard to the two German states was the extent of borrowings from other languages. While German in West Germany had been wide open to Anglo-American borrowings, East Germany had not been influenced to the same extent. Nevertheless there were examples of English loans in East Germany, *Feature*, *Sound*, *Evergreen* and Russian loans in West Germany. Interestingly enough two English loan words were frequently used in East Germany, but not so frequently in West Germany. They were *das Meeting*, pl. *-s*, and *die Kombine* 'combine harvester', pronounced [kɔmbain], pl. *-s*, which also occurred in compounds such as *Rüben-kombine*. Lehmann (1972: 112) found 638 words that in some ways were due to Russian influence. These comprised:

1 (a) loan words with a Russian root, *Kulak, sowjetisch, Subbotnik* 'extra work done for no payment';
   (b) loan words with a Greek or Latin root, *Aktiv, Diversant* 'dissident', *Kollektiv, Ökonomismus*;
   (c) abbreviations, *Kolchos* 'collective farm' (65 examples of 1a, b, c; 10 per cent)
2 partial loan words, *Elternaktiv, Fischkombinat* (53 examples; 8.5 per cent);
3 (a) formations with proper names, *Utkin-Methode, Saratower System* (49 examples; 7.5 per cent);
   (b) loan formations; *Kulturware, Wandzeitung, Held der Arbeit* (loan translation), *Einzelbauer, Neuererbewegung* (loan renditions), *Aufbausonntag* (loan creation) (353 examples; 56 per cent);
4 set phrases, sometimes quite long, *Gesetz der Verteilung nach der Arbeitsleistung* (8 examples; 1 per cent);

5 words influenced in their meaning, *Energetik* 'economics of energy', *Kader* 'up-and-coming generation' (64 examples; 10 per cent);

6 words influenced in their use, *Entwicklung* (used more frequently), or as a slogan, *Aufbau* (46 examples; 7 per cent).

Although there had been close contact between Russian and German in the GDR, there were almost no direct loans from Russian, probably because of the large difference in the phonological and grammatical structure of the two languages. There were, however, examples of loan translations among which were such constructions as Noun Phrase + Noun Phrase in the genitive, for example *Haus der Einheit*, *Aktivist der ersten Stunde*. Since the same constructions already existed in German, for example *das Ufer des Flusses*, the introduction of such examples has not changed the language radically. Siegl (1989) is able to quantify the extent of English and Russian borrowing as reflected in the Leipzig and Mannheim *Duden*. Predictably the Mannheim *Duden* has more English borrowings in absolute terms, ranging from 868 in the fourteenth edition to 1404 in the eighteenth. In percentage terms this is only a rise from 2.9 per cent to 3.89 per cent. The Leipzig *Duden* only has a rise of 340 to 952 in absolute terms but a similar percentage rise from 2.13 per cent to 3.7 per cent (Siegl 1989: 334–87). The Russian influence is smaller. Again, predictably the Leipzig *Duden* has more Russian loans, ranging from 190 (1.19 per cent) in the fourteenth edition to 293 (1.15 per cent, a slight fall) in the seventeenth edition. They reached a peak of 353 (1.33 per cent) in the sixteenth edition. The Mannheim *Duden* has only 195 Russian loans (0.65 per cent) which rise to 279 (0.77 per cent) (Siegl 1989: 68–185).

5.3 GDR GERMAN – ANOTHER LANGUAGE?

This question has, after unification and the change of the SED to the Partei des demokratischen Sozialismus (PDS), become rather academic and belongs properly to the history of German in the twentieth century (Schlosser 1990: 193). Nevertheless it merits a brief consideration here as an instructive, if controversial, example of an official attempt at linguistic change motivated by societal change. Linguists in both the Federal Republic of Germany and the GDR concerned themselves with this question. The first phase of research covered the time up to the mid 1960s when journalistic and impressionistic studies warned of an impending linguistic division between east and west

(Kinne 1977: 12–20 and 35–8). Even West German linguists such as Hugo Moser (1962) feared that a separate language would develop in the GDR. His fears were mainly based on the semantic divergence of political terms, the grammar remaining unaffected.

Es ist kein Zweifel: es besteht die Gefahr, daß die eingeleitete sprachliche Auseinanderentwicklung zu einer weiteren Sonderung innerhalb der deutschen Hochsprache führen kann; seit der Errichtung der Mauer am 13. August 1961 hat sich diese Gefahr erheblich verstärkt. Ich sage bewußt nicht Spaltung, sondern Sonderung. . . . Man fragt sich besorgt, wie lange die verbindende Kraft der deutschen Sprache ausreichen wird, um diese Sonderung zu verhindern.

(Moser 1962: 48)

('There is no doubt: the danger exists that the linguistic growing apart which has been initiated can lead to a further separation within the German standard language; this danger has become considerably stronger since the building of the Wall on the 13 August 1961. I consciously do not say "split" but separation. . . . The disquieting question is how long the binding common strength of the German language will last to prevent this separation.')

Other views were also held. The Swedish linguist Korlén (1969) sought to minimize any divergence by wanting to emphasize what united the language use of the two states. Betz (1964) sought to show that there were anyway more than two languages in Germany. There are regional, specialist and group languages and, of course, there are differences in political vocabulary. Dieckmann (1967) was extremely critical of most of the previous work and emphasized that politics and linguistics should not get mixed up. Like Betz, he saw the problem as part of the larger investigation into all the varieties of German. He also saw lack of empirical basis to many studies. This latter defect was made up for by the creation of a research institute in Bonn, under the aegis of the Institut für deutsche Sprache in Mannheim, to investigate public speech in East and West by providing a corpus of newspaper texts (Hellmann 1973) and a commentated bibliography (Hellmann 1976). The extremely useful one-volume dictionary (Kinne and Strube-Edelmann 1981) resulted from this project. In the GDR in the 1970s the linguists may have been influenced by the statement of Walter Ulbricht (extract in Kinne 1977: 23), who thought that 'Sogar die einstige Gemeinsamkeit der Sprache ist in Auflösung begriffen' ('Even the former communality of language is in the process of dissolution'), and by the change in the political climate, whereby the GDR wanted to establish itself as a socialist nation. For example Bock *et al.* (1973), sought to show that one could speak of an East German variety of German, just as the Federal Republic of Germany, Austria and Switzerland all had their varieties of German, although they felt that despite the differences that did exist it would be 'unangemessen, von zwei deutschen Sprachen zu sprechen' (1973: 532) ('inappropriate to speak of two German languages'). This became known as the *Viervariantenthese* ('four varieties thesis'). It is expressly expounded in the following extract:

> Deutsche Sprache bedeutet demnach zum gegenwärtigen Zeitpunkt den abstraktiven historisch bestimmten Sammelnamen für vier gleichberechtigte nationalsprachliche Varianten im Geltungsbereich von vier selbständigen Nationen, das Deutsche in der DDR, das Deutsche in der BRD, das österreichische und das schweizerische Deutsch.
>
> (Lerchner 1974: 265)

('The German language accordingly is meant at this present time to be the abstract, historically determined collective name for four equal national linguistic varieties in geographical areas taken up by the four independent nations, German in the GDR, German in the Federal Republic of Germany, Austrian and Swiss High German.')

In the final years of the GDR opinion seems to have reverted to concentrating more on the similarities in the German of both states. Fleischer *et al.* (1987) did not to subscribe to the *Viervariantenthese* but distinguished between 'speech community' (*Sprachgemeinschaft*), which covered the whole of the German-speaking area, and 'communication community' (*Kommunikationsgemeinschaft*), which covered the individual political states. Fleischer (1989) substitutes *Varietät* 'variety' for *Variante*. The terminological quagmire seems to have been settled somewhat by the introduction of the more neutral notion of pluricentricity for German (Clyne, 1984; von Polenz 1988). The different emphases of linguists from the Federal Republic of Germany and GDR is charted by Dieckmann (1989). Shorter accounts are Hellmann (1980) and Braun (1987). Kinne (1977) provides wide-ranging collections of texts illustrating both East and West German usage as well as opinions about the language; Schlosser (1990) covers all aspects of German in the GDR.

5.4 THE *WENDE* AND ITS LINGUISTIC IMPACT

The events that unfolded from the summer of 1989 to the official celebration of the unification of Germany on 3 October 1990, whereby the GDR ceased to exist, are well known and need not be repeated here. One consequence of these events has been the need to give a name to that part of Germany which was the GDR. This has provided a great opportunity for linguistic creative skills. In an article in the *Frankfurter Allgemeine Zeitung*, of 19 February 1992, forty-seven names were listed. Some were humorous, *Kohlonie*, *Kohlrabien*, *Transwerranien*, others pejorative *Dreck-Deponie-Reservat*; others were more predictable and neutral such as *die neuen Bundesländer*, the *Ex-DDR*, *alte DDR*, *ehemalige-DDR*, *frühere DDR*, *einstige-DDR* or *Deutschland-Ost*, *östliches Deutschland*. Time will tell which of these names will survive. Eventually there will only be a historical need for a separate name. In the new *Bundesländer* the most striking difference is that the political and economic circumstances have changed radically. There is no more SED or command economy. All those terms connected with these institutions have become historicisms. The twentieth edition of *Duden Rechtschreibung* (1991) is the first all-German *Duden* since 1947. Many of the words typical of the former GDR have been retained with the note, 'in der ehemaligen DDR', for instance *Kollektiv*, *Kombinat*, *Volkskammer*. By the next edition there will be a clear pointer as to which of the terms are the most persistent.

The most important linguistic achievement of the *Wende* was the regaining of an unmanipulated public language, exemplified by slogans such as *Wir sind das Volk!* and the capturing and use of such words as *Revolution*, *Wende*, *Opposition*, *Dialog*. The text type slogan has assumed a new importance. As with the development of the vocabulary after 1949 in the GDR there are neologisms, new formations and new meanings (see 5.2.4). Examples (from Wojtak 1990) of new words are *Ossi* 'inhabitant of east Germany' and *Wessi*, *Bundi* 'inhabitant of west Germany' and *Stadtmöblierung* 'setting up advertising hoardings, bus shelters etc.' Some new meanings have also seen the light of day, *Wendehals* 'turncoat', *Runder Tisch*. New formations can be illustrated with several compounds with *Bürger-*, *Bürgerkomitee*, *Bürgerforum*, *Bürgerinteressen*, *Bürgerbewegung*, *Bürgerprotest*, *Bürgerabwanderung*, *Bürgerexodus*, as well as words such as *Ausreisewilliger*, *Hierbleiber*, *Mauerspecht*, which will probably be forgotten one day. The English loan *Smog* has replaced the GDR euphemism *Industrienebel* and given birth to a range of complex forms: *Smogstufe, Smoggefährdungsgebiet, Smogsituation*. Good (1991) recounts further problems: for instance, in everyday communication the removal of the old ways and institutions have led to uncertainty in the use of *du* and *Sie* and forms of address such as *Genosse, Kollege* are replaced in some cases by *Herr*. Linguistic uncertainty is rife as speakers who were brought up being given one single interpretation of a word meet differing interpretations. There also has to be a learning of western terms such *Rechtsstaat, freiheitlich-demokratische Ordnung*. Speakers also have to come to terms with and digest a mass of English loans. From now on political and economic debate, no matter how diverse in terminology, will take place within one linguistic community.

5.5 ILLUSTRATIVE TEXTS

To illustrate the nature of written German in the former GDR two texts are presented ranging over a period of twenty years, with explanatory notes.

5.5.1 Text 1

Gemeinschaft freier Menschen

Mit dem Sieg der sozialistischen Produktionsverhältnisse sind in der DDR das System der Ausbeutung und mit ihm die Ursachen von Wirtschaftskrisen und Arbeitslosigkeit für immer beseitigt. Zugleich veränderte sich von Grund auf die Klassenstruktur. Es gibt keine Ausbeuterklasse mehr, die von der Arbeit anderer Klassen und Schichten leben und diese unterdrücken können. Daran vermag auch das Fortbestehen kleiner und mittlerer privat-kapitalistischer Unternehmer grundsätzlich nichts zu ändern. Alle Klassen und Schichten der sozialistischen Gesellschaft der DDR sind zu einer Gemeinschaft freier Menschen geworden. Anstelle des Klassenkampfes entwickelten sich Beziehungen kamerad-schaftlicher Zusammenarbeit und gegenseitiger Hilfe, deren Hilfe die gemeinsame Arbeit zum Wohle der Gesellschaft und des einzelnen ist.

Die soziale Basis der sozialistischen Staatsmacht der DDR bilden die Arbeiterklasse, die Klasse der Genossenschaftsbauern, die Intelligenz und die Werktätigen aller Volksschichten.

Die als führende Kraft allseitig anerkannte Klasse der sozial-istischen Gesellschaft der DDR ist die Arbeiterklasse. Sie hat sich in einem mehr als hundert Jahre währenden harten Kampf, der an

Siegen und an bitteren Niederlagen reich war, als Wahrerin der
Interessen aller Werktätigen und der Nation bewährt. Befreit von
Unterdrückung und sozialer Unsicherheit und im Besitz der Macht
und aller wichtigen Produktionsmittel lernt sie immer besser, den
Staat zum Nutzen der ganzen Gesellschaft zu lenken, die sozialis-
tische Ökonomik sowie die moderne Wissenschaft und Technik zu
meistern und den Sozialismus zum Siege zu führen. Ihr bewußter
Vortrupp, die SED, gewährleistet die wissenschaftliche Voraus-
sicht, die ideologische und organisatorische Einheitlichkeit des
Handels der Arbeiterklasse und aller anderen gesellschaftlichen
Kräfte.

(Büttner *et al.* 1964: 18)

Notes on the passage

This passage is a propaganda text extolling the virtues of the GDR
and its social and economic system.

sozialistische Produktionsverhältnisse, 'relationships between people
which arise in industrial production', a political and economic term
in opposition to *kapitalistische Produktionsverhältnisse*.

Ausbeutung 'exploitation', a negative term referring to capitalist
society, cf. *Ausbeuterklasse*.

Wirtschaftskrisen and *Arbeitslosigkeit*, negative features of capitalist
society which should not occur under socialism.

Klassenstruktur, *Klassenkampf*, further political and economic
Marxist terms.

privatkapitalistisch, the opposite of *sozialistisch*.

kamaradschaftlich, a positive term for the relations between people
under socialism.

Werktätige, cover term for all working members of society comprising: *Arbeiter*, *Genossenschaftsbauern*, a new formation 'farmers in
a collective', and *die Intelligenz* 'the intelligentsia'. The *WDG* also
includes *Angestellte*.

allseitig 'general, by everyone', a frequent word, stressing the agreement about everything in the GDR.

Produktionsmittel 'means of production', a technical political and
economic Marxist term.

5.5.2   Text 2

This text is a report which contains titles of officials and awards made to people in the GDR.

Bekenntnisse für die Kandidaten

Horst Sindermann zeichnete Werktätige und Kollektive aus Berlin (ADN). Anläßlich des 1. Mai wurden am Freitag während einer festlichen Veranstaltung im Amtssitz des Staatsrats verdienstvolle Werktätige aus allen Bereichen des gesellschaftlichen Lebens mit dem Vaterländischen Verdienstorden und dem Orden 'Banner der Arbeit' Stufe I geehrt.

Im Auftrag des Generalsekretärs des Zentralkomitees der SED und Vorsitzenden des Staatsrates, Erich Honecker, nahm der Stellvertreter des Vorsitzenden des Staatsrates Horst Sindermann, Mitglied des Politbüros des ZK der SED, diese Auszeichnungen vor. An dem Auszeichnungsakt nahmen teil: Die Mitglieder und Kandidaten des Politbüros des ZK der SED Horst Dohlus . . . sowie weitere Persönlichkeiten.

Für hervorragende wissenschaftlich-technische Leistungen wurde ebenfalls in Berlin durch Dr. Herbert Weiz, stellvertretender Vorsitzender des Ministerrates, an 84 Persönlichkeiten der Ehrentitel 'Verdienter Techniker' des Volkes beziehungsweise 'Verdienter Erfinder' verliehen.

(*Leipziger Volkszeitung*, 28–9 April 1984)

Notes on the passage

Kollektive, a loan from Russian.

Staatsrat 'council of state', central state organ, elected for five years and which functioned as a collective head of state. This latter meaning was a new meaning specific to the GDR.

Vaterländischer Verdienstorden, a decoration and linguistically a new formation. It was awarded in bronze, silver or gold by the *Vorsitzende des Staatsrats* 'the chairman of the council of state' (or, as here, his deputy) on 1 May.

'*Banner der Arbeit*', a decoration, of which there were three levels. The word is based on a Russian model.

Generalsekretär des Zentralkomitees der SED, a new formation on a Russian model, current from 1976. Before that the title was *Erster Sekretär*. This person was also the *Vorsitzende des Staatsrats*.

Politbüro, a loan from Russian.

Ministerrat 'council of ministers', the highest executive organ of the GDR, comprising forty members. This is a new formation.

'*Verdienter Techniker*' *des Volkes, '*Verdienter Erfinder*'*, two of thirty titles for which decorations were presented. Again it is a new formation on a Russian model.

SELECT BIBLIOGRAPHY AND FURTHER READING

Ahrends, M. (1989) *Allseitig gefestigt. Stichwörter zum Sprachgebrauch der DDR*, Munich: dtv.

Betz, W. (1960) 'Der zweigeteilte Duden', *Der Deutschunterricht*, 12: 82–98.

—— (1964) 'Zwei Sprachen in Deutschland?' in F. Handt (ed.) *Deutsch – gefrorene Sprache in einem gefrorenen Land?* Berlin: Literarisches Kolloquium.

Bock, R., Harnisch, H. Langner, H. and Starke, G. (1973) 'Zur deutschen Gegenwartssprache in der DDR und in der BRD', *Zeitschrift für Phonetik, Sprachwissenschaft und Kommunikationsforschung*, 26: 511–32.

Braun, P. (1987) *Tendenzen in der deutschen Gegenwartssprache. Sprachvarietäten*, 2nd. edn, Stuttgart: Kohlhammer.

Büttner, H., Doernberg, S., Graf, R., Moschütz, H.-D., Roder, K.-H., Schneider, W. and Woischwill, H. (eds) (1964) *Handbuch der DDR*, Berlin: Staatsverlag der DDR.

Clyne, M. (1984) *Language and Society in German-speaking Europe*, Cambridge: Cambridge University Press.

Dieckmann, W. (1967) 'Kritische Bemerkungen zum sprachlichen Ost-West-Problem', *Zeitschrift für deutsche Sprache*, 23: 136–65.

—— (1989) 'Die Untersuchung der deutsch-deutschen Sprachentwicklung als linguistisches Problem' *Zeitschrift für germanistische Linguistik*, 17: 162–81.

Fleischer, W. (1989) 'Zur Situation der deutschen Sprache heute', *Zeitschrift für Phonetik, Sprachwissenschaft und Kommunikationsforschung*, 42: 435–42.

Fleischer, W., Barz, I., Geier, R., Heinemann, H., Heinemann, W., Huth, H., Kändler, U., Koch, H., Kögler, H., Poethe, H., Porsch, P., Schröder, M., Weber, H., Wiese, I., Wittich, U. and Yos, G. (1987) *Wortschatz der deutschen Sprache in der DDR*, Leipzig: Bibliographisches Institut.

Good, C. H. (1991) *Language and Totalitarianism: The Case of '*East Germany*'*, inaugural lecture, University of Surrey.

Hellmann, M. W. (ed.) (1973) *Zum öffentlichen Sprachgebrauch in der Bundesrepublik Deutschland und in der DDR* (Sprache der Gegenwart, 16), Düsseldorf: Schwann.

—— (ed.) (1976) *Bibliographie zum öffentlichen Sprachgebrauch in der Bundesrepublik Deutschland und in der DDR* (Sprache der Gegenwart, 18), Düsseldorf: Schwann.

—— (1980) 'Deutsche Sprache in der Bundesrepublik Deutschland und der Deutschen Demokratischen Republik', in H. P. Althaus, W. Putschke and H. E. Wiegand (eds) *Lexikon der Germanistischen Linguistik*, 2nd edn, Tübingen: Niemeyer, pp. 519–27.

Kinne, M. (ed.) (1977) *Texte Ost – Texte West*, Frankfurt: Diesterweg.

Kinne, M. and Strube-Edelmann, B. (1981) *Kleines Wörterbuch des DDR-Wortschatzes*, Düsseldorf: Schwann.

Klappenbach, R. and Steinitz, W. (1961–77) *Wörterbuch der deutschen Gegenwartssprache*, 6 vols, Berlin: Akademie.

Korlén, G. (1969) 'Führt die Teilung Deutschlands zur Sprachspaltung?', *Deutschunterricht* 21: 5–23; repr. with a short epilogue in P. Braun (ed.) (1979) *Deutsche Gegenwartssprache*, Munich: Fink, pp. 69–92.

—— (1983) 'Deutsch in der Deutschen Demokratischen Republik. Bemerkungen zum DDR-Wortschatz', in G. Korlén, P. von Polenz, I. Reiffenstein and H. Rupp (eds) *Tendenzen, Formen und Strukturen der deutschen Standardsprache nach 1945* (Marburger Studien zur Germanistik, 3), Marburg: Elwert, pp. 61–8.

Lehmann, H. (1972) *Russisch-deutsche Lehnbeziehungen im Wortschatz offizieller Wirtschaftstexte der DDR* (Sprache der Gegenwart, 21), Düsseldorf: Schwann.

Lerchner, G. (1974) 'Zur Spezifik der deutschen Sprache in der DDR und ihrer gesellschaftlichen Determination', *Deutsch als Fremdsprache*, 11: 259–65.

Malige-Klappenbach, H. (1986) *Das 'Wörterbuch der deutschen Gegenwartsprache', Bericht, Dokumentation und Diskussion*, ed. F. J. Hausmann (Lexicographica, Series Maior, 12), Tübingen: Niemeyer.

Moser, H. (1962) *Sprachliche Folgen der politischen Teilung Deutschlands* (Wirkendes Wort, Beiheft 3), Düsseldorf: Schwann.

Polenz, P. von, (1988) ' "Binnendeutsch" oder plurizentrische Sprachkultur?', *Zeitschrift für germanistische Linguistik*, 16: 198–218.

Russ, C. V. J. (1991) 'The Norms of German and their Metamorphosis', in E. Kolinsky (ed.) *The Federal Republic of Germany: The End of an Era*, Oxford: Berg, pp. 323–32.

Sauer, W. W. (1988) *Der 'DUDEN': Geschichte und Aktualität eines 'Volkswörterbuches'*, Stuttgart: Metzler.

Schlosser, H. D. (1990) *Die deutsche Sprache in der DDR zwischen Stalinismus und Demokratie: historische, politische und kommunikative Bedingungen*, Cologne: Verlag Wissenschaft und Politik.

Siebs, T. (1969) *Deutsche Aussprache. Reine und gemäßigte Hochlautung mit Aussprachewörterbuch*, 19th edn, eds H. de Boor, H. Moser and C. Winkler, Berlin: de Gruyter.

Siegl, E. A. (1989) *Duden Ost – Duden West. Zur Sprache in Deutschland nach 1945. Ein Vergleich der Leipziger und der Mannheimer Dudenauflagen seit 1947* (Sprache der Gegenwart, 76), Düsseldorf: Schwann.

Sommerfeldt, K.-E., Fleischer, W., Huth, H., Langner, H., Meier, H., Michel, G., Porsch, P., Schröder, M., Starke, G. and Wiese, I. (1988) *Entwicklungstendenzen in der deutschen Gegenwartssprache*, Leipzig: Bibliographisches Institut.

Vertrag (1972) *Vertrag über die Grundlagen der Beziehungen zwischen der Bundesrepublik Deutschland und der Deutschen Demokratischen Republik*, Bonn: Bundesdruckerei.

Wojtak, B. (1990) 'Rede-"Wendungen" in "Wende"-Reden', *Deutsch als Fremdsprache*, 27: 47–51.

Yeandle, D. N. (1991) *Frieden im 'Neuen Deutschland': das Vokabular des 'Friedenkampfes'*, Heidelberg: Winter.

6 Phonetics and phonology

Phonetics is the science of the description and classification of sounds regardless of their function. It has three branches: articulatory, acoustic and auditory phonetics. The last one, how the ear registers sound, has not been widely developed. Acoustic phonetics consists of recording sounds and registering their pitch (frequency), amplitude (strength of articulation) and duration. The branch of phonetics which concerns us here is the articulatory branch, that is how sounds are produced or articulated. The terms of articulatory phonetics are applied to German and described in Moulton (1962), Martens and Martens (1961), MacCarthy (1975), Kohler (1977), Wängler (1983), Benware (1986) and C. Hall (1992). A useful bibliography of older works is Schindler and Thürmann (1971).

The term 'phonology' is used in at least two different senses: first to refer to the sound system of one particular language, describing the minimal distinctive sound units (phonemes); and second to refer to a particular linguistic approach, prefaced by an adjective, for example generative phonology. In this chapter we will describe the phonology of German by applying two types of phonology: first that involving phonemes, called phonemics; and second generative phonology. We will also sketch some more recent attempts to resolve some of the problems of German phonology. The treatment is not, of course, exhaustive and readers who wish to read a more detailed application of the phonological theories are referred to the further reading at the end of this chapter.

6.1 THE PRODUCTION AND CLASSIFICATION OF SPEECH SOUNDS

Sounds are produced by a stream of air which is usually expelled from the lungs in the process of breathing out. In most languages the air-stream is forced outwards and is called pulmonic egressive. Figure 6.1, the diagram of the vocal tract, should be consulted in connection with this section. The air-stream from the lungs passes outwards through the larynx, throat and vocal tract and is subject to modification by the organs of speech. The hard palate, teeth and alveolar ridge are static organs of speech, whereas the soft palate, or velum, the tongue and lips are active. Before reaching the throat or vocal tract the air-stream may be modified by the vocal cords or folds (folds of muscle at the top of the larynx). The vocal cords can assume several positions. First, they may be open but not vibrating, allowing the air-stream to pass through unhindered. This is the position for normal breathing. The speech sounds produced with this state of the vocal cords are called voiceless, for example the consonants written *p, t, k, f, ss, ß, sch, x*, etc. Second, the vocal cords may be narrowed so that the air-stream is forced through between them and they vibrate. The sounds produced in this way are called voiced: vowels and the consonants written *b, d, g, w, s* etc. Third, the space between the vocal cords, the glottis, may be briefly closed so that the air-stream is temporarily halted. The subsequent release of the air-stream by opening the glottis with no vibration of the vocal cords is called the glottal stop, for example between *e* and *a* in *Theater* or before the pronunciation of vowels at the beginning of words, *ein Apfel*.

The most important division of sounds is into vowels and consonants. In the articulation of vowels the air-stream from the lungs passes unhindered over the centre of the tongue through the mouth, whereas in the case of consonants the air-stream is either completely stopped, or narrowed so that audible friction is produced. Vowels usually form the nucleus of a syllable (see 6.6). In German vowels are always voiced.

The nasal cavity through which air from the lungs is expelled through the nose also plays an important role. The entrance to the nasal cavity can be controlled by the soft palate, or velum, which can either seal it off by making a closure with the back wall of the mouth (the pharynx), only allowing the air-stream to pass through the mouth, or it can hang loose and allow the air-stream to be expelled through both the mouth and the nose. Sounds in the production of which the air-stream is expelled only through the mouth are called oral sounds, and those in the production of which the air-stream is expelled through both the mouth and nose are called nasal sounds. In German both oral and nasal consonants exist, for instance the initial consonant in *Bein* is oral and the initial consonant in *mein* is nasal.

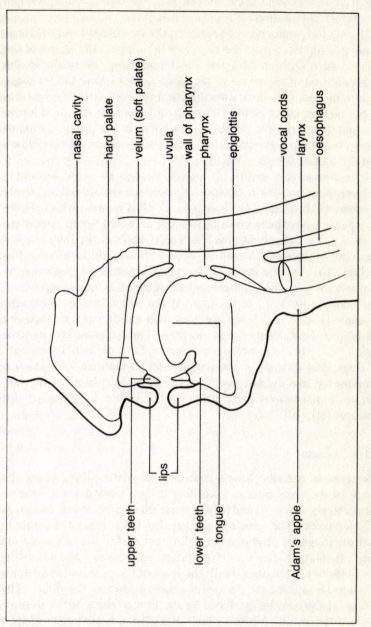

Figure 6.1 The vocal tract (From Battye and Hintze 1992: 73)

Nasal vowels exist in some French loans in German, for example *Teint* (m.) 'complexion', *Fonds* (m.) 'fund'.

During the production of vowels by the air-stream from the lungs passing unhindered over the centre of the tongue, the height of the tongue may vary, making the vocal tract large or small. In the pronunciation of the vowel of the German word *Kinn* the tongue is high in the mouth and narrows the vocal tract considerably, whereas in the pronunciation of the German word *kann* the tongue is low in the mouth and the vocal tract is very open. In the pronunciation of the vowel of the German word *Kunde* the vocal tract is very closed and the tongue is high in the mouth.

It is evident that spelling in many languages does not accurately reflect pronunciation (the relationship between sounds and spelling in German will be treated in Chapter 7). For this reason various phonetic alphabets have been invented in order to record the pronunciation of words as accurately as possible. The symbols of the International Phonetic Alphabet (IPA) will be used for the sounds described in this section. They will be enclosed in square brackets [ ]. Some of the symbols are the same as letters in the English and German alphabets, for example [p, t, k, b, d, g, a, o] but others are different, for example [ʃ, ŋ, œ, ç]. Some are used with a different pronunciation value from their alphabetic counterparts. Thus [z] is used for intervocalic voiced *s* in *reisen* which is pronounced like the initial consonant in Engl. *zeal* and not as the initial letter in German *Zeit* which is pronounced like the last two letters in Engl. *bits*. In phonetic transcription long vowels are usually written with a following [ː], for example [eː], [oː].

6.1.1   Vowels

Phoneticians describe vowels according to whether they change the shape of the vocal tract or according to the position of the tongue. Thus vowels such as [i] and [u] are classified as close vowels and [a] as an open vowel. The vowels [i] and [u] also differ from one another in that the tongue is positioned in a different part of the mouth during their articulation. The vowel [i] is produced by raising and advancing the blade of the tongue towards the front of the mouth whereas [u] is produced by raising the back of the tongue towards the velum. The vowel [a] can also be produced by the tongue being at the front or back of the mouth. Vowels whose articulation is accompanied by a relatively forward position of the tongue in the vocal tract are called front vowels. Those whose articulation is accompanied by a relatively retracted position of the tongue are called back vowels. The vowel [i] is therefore a close front vowel and [u] is a close back vowel.

In the pronunciation of [i] and [u] yet another dimension can be seen, i.e. the shape of the lips. In the articulation of [u] the lips are rounded and in the articulation of [i] the lips are spread, or neutral, and not rounded.

Before dealing with the shape of the lips in more detail, the articulation of other vowels must first be described. Between the two extremes of close [i] and [u] and open [a] there are intermediate stages. These are represented by the vowels in the German words *Bett* and *Gott*. The vowel in *Bett* is represented by the IPA symbol [ɛ] and is usually classed as a half-open front vowel. The vowel in *Gott* is represented by the IPA symbol [ɔ] and is usually classed as a half-open back vowel. The stressed vowels in German *leben* and *loben* are long half-close vowels, written [eː] and [oː]. The half-open short [ɛ] appears long only in some varieties of German: some speakers distinguish between the stressed vowels in *Beeren* and *Bären* by pronouncing the first as a long half-close vowel [eː] and the second as a long half-open vowel [ɛː]. The short vowels [i] and [u] have long counterparts in German; compare the pairs *binnen* and *Bienen*, *Bucht* and *Buch*. It has become usual to consider the short close vowels as being slightly more open with a slightly lower tongue height than the long close vowels and to write the former [ɪ] and [ʊ] and the latter [iː] and [uː].

The front vowels so far mentioned are pronounced with no lip-rounding, all the back vowels having had lip-rounding. The open vowel [a] is neutral with respect to lip-rounding. The German vowel sounds in *Bühne*, *schön* and *können* are examples of front vowels with lip-rounding. The German front rounded vowels are also distinguished according to whether they are close or open. The vowel in *Bühne* is close, the vowel in *schön* is half-close and the vowel in *können* is half-open. They are transcribed [yː], [øː] and [œ] respectively. The short counterpart of [yː] appears in *müssen* and is slightly more open, i.e. the tongue height is slightly lower. It is written [ʏ] in phonetic script. The open vowel [a] is a central vowel. During its articulation the main part of the tongue is in the centre of the vowel tract. It is a low vowel. The short vowel in *Ratte* is pronounced with the tongue slightly more advanced than for the long vowel in *raten*. They are symbolized [a] and [ɑː] respectively. Table 6.1 sets out the stressed vowels of German. There is a simplification in so far as the slight difference in tongue height between the three pairs of high vowels is ignored.

Table 6.1   Stressed vowels in German

	Front unrounded		Front rounded		Central	Back rounded
Close (high)	iː	ɪ	yː	ʏ		uː ʊ
Half-close (mid-high)	eː		øː			oː
Half-open (mid-low)	ɛ		œ		ɔ	
Open (low)	a				ɑː	

Diphthongs, i.e. vowel sounds in the production of which the position of the tongue changes during their articulation, are, for purposes of transcription, considered as having two components. They can be described in the same way as ordinary vowels. German has three diphthongs, all falling, that is having the stress on the first component. These are the sounds in the words: *mein, Haus, euch*. Phonetically they may be written [ai], [au] and [oi] respectively. The nature of the second component of the [oi] is unrounded according to Moulton (1962), MacCarthy (1975) and Kohler (1977), whereas for Siebs (1969), Benware (1986) and *Duden Aussprachewörterbuch* (1990) it is rounded, either [ø] or [ʏ]. C. Hall (1992: 105f.) transcribes it as [ɔy], but concedes that many speakers use [oi]. We will use the transcription [oi]. There is also the rising diphthong in the interjections *pfui, hui* in German.

Diphthongs must be distinguished from sequences of two vowels, for example *a* and *i* in *prosaisch, a* and *o* in *Chaos* and *u* and *u* in *Kontinuum*. In these cases the first vowel is usually long or, if short, it is close, and there is often a glottal stop or a slight pause between the two vowels.

Another type of vocalic sequence occurs in foreign words where an unstressed non-syllabic vowel precedes another vowel, which is usually, but not always, stressed. To signify that a vowel is non-syllabic the diacritic [u̯] is used. The most frequent non-syllabic vowels are [i̯, u̯], written *i* and *u*: *Studium, Italien; aktuell, rituell*. The vowels *e, y* and *o* do occur, but not so frequently: *Petroleum, Hyäne, loyal, Memoiren*. There is the tendency for the high vowels to become the palatal fricative [j] and the mid back [o] to become the bilabial fricative [w].

Hitherto the vowels we have considered have borne the main stress in the word but there are also unstressed vowels. The main vowel in unstressed syllables is the *-e* of *bitte*, written phonetically [ə], a central unrounded half-open vowel. The ending *-er* is pronounced as [ər] in very careful speech but in colloquial speech -*er* is pronounced [ɐ], a central unrounded vowel which is lower than [ə]. Other vowels do occur, for example the final vowels in *Sofa*, *Kino*, *Mutti*, *Uhu*, but mostly in foreign words or, in the case of -*i*, words denoting people. The unstressed ending -*en*, usually pronounced [-ən], is replaced in colloquial speech by a syllabic nasal symbolized [ṇ], thus *leben* may be pronounced [leːbṇ], and in some cases the syllabic nasal is assimilated to the place of articulation of the preceding plosive, [leːbm̩] *leben* in the case of a labial plosive or [dɛŋkŋ̩] *denken* in the case of a velar plosive. The ending -*el* is sometimes replaced by a syllabic [l̩], for example *Mantel* [mantl̩].

6.1.2 Consonants

In the production of consonants the air-stream from the lungs is modified by the organs of speech in the mouth. They are usually described according to the manner of articulation (how the air-stream is modified as it passes through the vocal tract), and then according to the place of articulation (where this modification takes place). The word modification has been used as a neutral term.

6.1.2.1 *Manner of articulation*

In the articulation of consonants either the air is completely blocked at some point in the mouth or the vocal tract is narrowed so much that audible friction is produced at some point. When the air-stream is completely blocked the consonants are called stops, or, in the case of egressive pulmonic stops which are the norm in German, plosives. When the air-stream is forced out with friction but there is no stoppage the sound is termed a fricative, or spirant. The initial consonants in *Pein*, *tun*, *Koch*; *Bein*, *dein*, *Gang* are plosives and the initial consonants in *fein*, *Wein*, *Safe*, *sein*, *Chemie*, *scheinen*, *ja* are fricatives as are the medial consonants in *Page*, *machen*. The plosives and fricatives are sometimes classed together as obstruents. If there is a complete sealing off of the nasal cavity by the soft palate then the resultant consonants are oral: [p t k b d g] or [f v s z ç ʃ ʒ x].

If there is a stoppage in the vocal tract which is later released and air also escapes through the nose, then the resultant sound is called a nasal plosive. The initial sounds in *Mut*, *nein*, and the final sound in *sang* are examples of nasal plosives, symbolized as [m n ŋ].

The next two types of articulation are represented in German by only one sound each. In the articulation of the initial sound in *lassen* the tongue almost touches the teeth and the air-stream flows out past the sides of the tongue. This type of articulation is called lateral. The lateral [l] in German is pronounced only in the centre and front of the mouth, whereas in English after vowels the [l] is velarized and pronounced in the back of the mouth, symbolized [ɫ], e.g. *ball*, *soul*.

The articulation of the *r*-sounds in German presents a very complex range of articulations. In initial position before a vowel as in *reisen* the *r* is pronounced in careful speech as a trill or roll (the rapid vibration of one articulator against another). In the articulation of *r* in *reisen* this either involves the tongue tip which is tapped quickly two or three times against the alveolar ridge, or the uvula which is tapped two or three times against the back of the throat. The first of these articulations is called an apical or dental roll or trill and the second is called the uvula roll or trill. These articulations are symbolized [r] and [ʀ] respectively. In colloquial informal pronunciation these rolls or trills lose their their roll or trill character and become alveolar or uvular fricatives. Sometimes they are produced with little or no friction and can be called frictionless continuants, symbolized by writing the *r* symbols upside down, for example [ɹ], [ʁ].

The [r] and [l] sounds are often referred to together as liquids. The nasals, together with the liquids, are referred to as sonorants (or resonants) as opposed to the obstruents. They can function in some instances as vowels, for example in the reduced form of the ending *-el*, *-em*, *-en* (see p. 127).

Another type of articulation, or rather a combination of already existing types, is represented by the initial sounds in *Pferd*, *Zeit*, *tschüs*. Phonetically these sounds are written [pf ts tʃ] and represent a consonant cluster of a plosive and a fricative at the same or similar point of articulation. [pf] comprises a labial plosive and a labio-dental fricative, [ts] is an alveolar plosive plus an alveolar fricative and [tʃ] an alveolar plosive plus a palato-alveolar fricative. They are known as affricates.

The initial sound in German *ja* is often classed as a palatal semi-vowel. The amount of friction, however, used to produce this sound varies a great deal; sometimes it is a frictionless continuant and has little or no friction. The term 'approximants' has also been used for sounds such as these which have no friction and in the production of which the organs of speech do nothing more than 'approximate' to an articulation. Phonetically the palatal semi-vowel is written [j].

The initial sound in German *hat* is classed as a glottal fricative, that is the glottis, the space between the vocal cords, is almost closed. It is also called a cavity fricative since most of the friction is produced in the throat cavity. The articulation of [h] is determined by the vowel that follows, and there are as many different positions of the vocal tract for [h] as there are vowels. If the glottis is closed completely a glottal stop results, symbolized [ʔ]. In English this sometimes occurs instead of the intervocalic plosive [t] in words such as *butter* or instead of the linking *r* at the end of a word when the next word begins with a vowel, for example *four apples*. In German it is found before a vowel, *ein* [ʔain], *erinnern* [ɛrʔɪnərn] (also called *harter Vokaleinsatz*) or between vowels as in *Theater* [teʔatər].

6.1.2.2 *Place of articulation*

These groups, distinguished by their manner of articulation, plosives, fricatives, nasals, laterals and trills, are also divided into several different places of articulation. These are the same for each manner of articulation, although all possible combinations do not exist. Usually it is enough to mention one place of articulation in describing the plosive, fricative or nasal. The sounds [p b f v m] are labial sounds, that is the stoppage is made by the lips or else the lips coming close together produce the friction. In the case of the plosives and nasals in German they are bilabial, that is both lips are involved in the articulation of the sound. In the case of the fricatives they are articulated not by the two articulators in the mouth which are exactly opposite to each other vertically but by two which are not exactly opposite to each other. The fricatives [f] and [v] are labio-dental and are produced by the lower lip approaching the upper teeth. The *n* in *fünf*, *Senf* is labio-dental, symbolized [ɱ]. The sounds [t d], [s z], [n] are alveolar in German, that is the stoppage or friction is made at the teeth ridge or alveoli by the tongue. Therefore [t d] are alveolar plosives, [s z] alveolar fricatives and [n] is an alveolar nasal.

At the next place of articulation there are only fricatives in German. This is the region between the alveolar ridge and the beginning of the hard palate; this is where the initial sounds in *scheinen*, *Genie*, the medial sounds in *waschen*, *Gage*, and the final sound in *Beige*, *Busch* are formed. They are termed palato-alveolar fricatives, or sometimes pre-palatal fricatives and are symbolized [ʃ], [ʒ].

The hard and soft palates, as far as German is concerned, can be taken as one place of articulation. Although the exact place of articulation of the plosive [k] is determined by the following vowel, compare the initial sounds in *Kind*, *kann*, *Kunde*, these plosives in German may be called velar or palato-velar plosives. The same variation occurs with [g] *Gift*, *gab*, *Gunst*. English has no velar fricative but German has, for example the final sound in *Buch*, *Loch*. This also varies in articulation according to the preceding vowel; *Dach* has a velar fricative after a back vowel, written phonetically [x], and *dich* has a palatal fricative after a front vowel, [ç]. German also has a velar nasal, written phonetically [ŋ], which only occurs medially and finally, *singen*, *sang*.

The lateral [l] is pronounced with the blade (or tip) of the tongue touching the alveolar ridge while the air-stream is released past the sides of the tongue. It is an alveolar sound. As already mentioned, the *r*-sounds are either alveolar or uvular.

6.1.2.3   *Other phonetic features of obstruents*

There is another fundamental distinction created by the behaviour of the vocal cords. The plosives [b d g] and the fricatives [v z ʒ] are voiced, i.e. the vocal cords are narrowed so that the air-stream is forced through between them and they vibrate, whereas the plosives [p t k] and the fricatives [f s r x] are voiceless, i.e. the vocal cords are widened and the air-stream flows through without them vibrating. The German affricates [pf ts tʃ] are voiceless.

There are three stages in the articulation of plosives: the onset (when the closure or occlusion is made), the hold (the length of the closure), and then the release (when the closure is opened). When an initial voiceless plosive is released in German a puff of air immediately follows, this being symbolized by writing [h] after the plosive, [ph th kh]. These plosives are known as aspirated plosives. In French, for instance, the initial voiceless plosives are not aspirated, but the vocal cords start to vibrate immediately after the closure is released, whereas in the case of the aspirated voiceless plosives this vibration does not start immediately. Aspiration is acoustically the absence of voicing between the release of the closure and the beginning of voicing in the following vowel. Unaspirated voiceless plosives also occur in some German dialects, particularly in the south, and in these cases the distinction between [p] and [b] is not between a voiceless and a voiced plosive, but rather between different strengths of articulation. The plosive [p] is described as being fortis, that is more force is used in its articulation, and [b] is described as being lenis, less strength being used in its articulation. The terms 'fortis' and 'lenis' are sometimes used without specifying clearly what articulatory or acoustic features they refer to and in general they are best avoided. The terms 'tense' and 'lax' have also been suggested to describe the difference in strength of articulation of consonants. We will retain the main features of voiced and voiceless.

The articulation of sounds does not merely consist of segments of words, for there are also suprasegmental phenomena such as pitch, stress and intonation which extend over whole words and also over sentences (see 6.7).

6.2 PRONUNCIATION STANDARDS FOR GERMAN

Pronunciation shows considerable variation, despite the setting up and propagation of a standard 'stage pronunciation' (*Bühnenaussprache*), codified by Theodor Siebs (1862–1941) and a committee of mostly North German speakers. The pronunciation recommended by Siebs was set up as a standard, not only for the stage but for public speaking in general, later being applied to broadcasting. It was a strict norm which allowed no alternative pronunciations. In 1922 the title of his book was amended to *Deutsche Bühnenaussprache-Hochsprache* because of its wider application; in 1958 it became simply *Deutsche Hochsprache*. The edition of 1969, entitled *Deutsche Aussprache, Reine und gemäßigte Hochlautung*, allowed alternatives for the first time. No further edition has appeared since. In 1962 the *Duden Aussprachewörterbuch* introduced the term *Hochlautung*, now called *Standardlautung*, for standard pronunciation, as an ideal norm, which was supraregional, uniform, close to the orthography and clear in enunciation. In Mangold (1984: 31) and *Duden Aussprachewörterbuch* (1990: 29) this norm is now also seen as corresponding closely to usage (*Gebrauchsnorm*). Below this norm two levels were recognized, the so-called 'moderate standard' (*gemäßigte Hochlautung*) and the 'non-standard' (*Nichthochlautung*). The East German *Wörterbuch der deutschen Aussprache*, whose first edition appeared in 1964, showed a greater tolerance of usage in allegro speech, for example the elision of unstressed [ə] in endings such as -*en*. In Austria and Switzerland national norms of pronunciation which deviate from Siebs are in use (see 3.3.1 and 4.4.1). The type of German analysed will be the prescribed standard as illustrated in *Duden Aussprachewörterbuch* (1990) and Mangold (1984). It does not reflect the different stylistic levels (*Formstufen*) of quick collo-quial speech or slow deliberate speech. It also differs from Siebs' stage pronunciation in a number of ways: (1) the vocalization of postvocalic /r/ is allowed in the ending -*er* and after long vowels and diphthongs; (2) the omission, or elision, of unstressed [ə] in the endings -*em* and -*en* is allowed, for example [groːsm̩, hatn̩] for [groːsəm, hatən], *großem*, *hatten*; (3) non-syllabic vowels are recognized, i.e. vowels that occur immediately before or after a stressed vowel, for instance *i* in *Studium* and *u* in *aktuell*; (4) a wide variety of phonetic realizations is recognized for /r/, ranging from an alveolar or uvular trill to a frictionless continuant (see p. 128).

Pronouncing dictionaries of German are *Duden Aussprachewörterbuch* (1990), Krech *et al.* (1971) and Siebs (1969). König (1989) has a collection of maps showing how even among educated speakers pronunciation varies regionally to a considerable extent.

6.3 PHONEMES AND ALLOPHONES

Theoretically the number of sounds that the organs of speech can produce is infinite, but in reality only a limited number is used in each language. The reason for this limitation is that phonetic differences are not all of the same importance. In German the difference in meaning between *Kunst* 'art' and *Gunst* 'favour' is carried solely by the difference between a voiceless velar plosive [k] and a voiced velar plosive [g] (cf. Engl. *coat* vs *goat*). Sound differences which must be made in a language in order to distinguish between the meaning of words are termed phonemic, and the sounds which make this difference are called phonemes. Thus in German and English the plosives [k] and [g] are phonemes and the difference between them, the difference of voice, is phonemic. The plosives can be written as phonemes between slant lines /k/, /g/. They form a phonemic opposition. There are many pairs of words in German which are distinguished solely by a difference of voice: *Paar* : *bar*; *Tier* : *dir*; *Kasse* : *Gasse*; *finden* : *winden*. Words such as these which differ from each other only in one phoneme are known as minimal pairs. The easiest way of establishing the phonemic system of a language is by using minimal pairs, but contrasts in a similar environment, for example before vowels, *Paß* : *Bus*, are considered to be sufficient if minimal pairs are not available. Phonetic differences which are not phonemic are termed allophonic. Phonemic and allophonic differences are set up separately for each language. The difference between [s] and [z] in German is phonemic: /s/ *reißen* : /z/ *reisen*, but in Spanish the difference is allophonic. A definition of the phoneme has proved very difficult to formulate but there are two suggestions which may be helpful. One such suggestion regards the phoneme as a family of sounds which are never in contrast with each other and which are phonetically similar. Thus in German the voiceless fricative written *ch* is palatal in *Licht* but velar in *lacht*. The articulatory difference palatal : velar does not serve to distinguish in meaning between words in German but is conditioned by the preceding vowel: the palatal fricative [ç] occurs after front vowels and liquids, for example *nüchtern. Töchter, nicht. echt, weich, Milch, durch* and the velar fricative [x] occurs after back vowels: *Bach, Loch, Bucht, Rauch.* The sounds [ç] and [x] are therefore allophones, or positional variants, of one phoneme. They are in complementary distribution, i.e. where [ç] occurs, [x] does not, and vice versa. The other suggestion regards the phoneme as an abstraction consisting of a bundle of distinctive, or phonemic, features which occur together. The phoneme /p/ in German, for instance, has certain distinctive features: it is a plosive, it contrast with fricatives, *Pein : fein*; it is labial, it contrasts with other plosives at different points of articulation, *passen : Tassen : Kassen*; it is voiceless, it contrasts with voiced plosives, *packen : Backen.* The German phoneme /p/ is thus an abstract unit consisting of three distinctive features: (1) voice; (2) point of articulation, for example labial; and (3) manner of articulation, i.e. plosive. This notion of distinctive feature is taken as of fundamental importance in generative phonology (see 6.5). The allophones of /p/ show other non-distinctive, or purely phonetic features (for example aspiration initially before a vowel) in addition to the three distinctive features. This approach regards the phoneme as an abstraction which is realized by its allophones in the speech chain. The concept of the phoneme has been applied to the description of German in Moulton (1962), Philipp (1970, 1974), Werner (1972), Kohler (1977: 156–77), Keller (1978: 553–8), Meinhold and Stock (1980: 79–170), Benware (1986: Chapter 4) and Fox (1990: Chapter 2).

6.3.1 The vowel phonemes

The maximum number of phonemes occurs in stressed position, typically in disyllabic words such as *biete* or *bitte*, comprising one stressed syllable containing a vowel followed by a consonant, followed by an unstressed vowel. Apart from the word-initial consonants, this pattern can be symbolized as VCv. There are three types of vowel-like items that occur for V: (1) short vowels, *bitte*; (2) long vowels, *biete*; and (3) diphthongs, *leite*. The short vowels also differ in quality from the long vowels, being more open, or lax, i.e. their tongue height is slightly lower than that of their long counterparts. Since the long vowels, with the sole exception of /ɛː/, are long or tense, is the phonemic feature that separates the two groups quantity or quality? Should the opposition *biete* vs *bitte* be labelled /iː/

Table 6.2   Vowel distribution before intervocalic consonants

	p	b	t	d	k	g	f	v	s	z	ʃ	ʒ	x	m	n	l	r
aː	+	+	+	+	+	+	+	+	+	+	−	+	+	+	+	+	+
a	+	+	+	+	+	+	+	−	+	−	+	−	+	+	+	+	+
oː	+	+	+	+	+	+	+	+	+	+	−	+	+	+	+	+	+
o	+	+	+	+	+	+	+	−	+	−	+	−	+	+	+	+	+
öː	+	+	+	+	+	+	+	+	+	+	−	−	−	+	+	+	+
ö	+	−	+	−	+	−	−	−	−	−	+	−	+	−	+	+	+
eː	+	+	+	+	+	+	+	+	−	+	−	+	−	+	+	+	+
ε	+	+	+	+	+	+	+	−	+	−	+	−	+	+	+	+	+
εː	−	+	+	+	+	+	+	−	+	+	−	−	+	+	+	+	+
iː	+	+	+	+	+	+	+	+	+	+	+	−	+	+	+	+	+
i	+	+	+	+	+	+	+	−	+	−	+	−	+	+	+	+	+
yː	−	+	+	+	+	+	+	−	+	+	+	−	+	+	+	+	+
y	+	−	+	−	+	+	+	−	+	−	+	−	+	+	+	+	+
uː	+	+	+	+	+	+	+	−	+	+	+	−	+	+	+	+	+
u	+	+	+	+	+	+	+	−	+	−	+	−	+	+	+	+	+

vs /i/, showing quantity as phonemic or /i/ vs /ɪ/, showing quality as phonemic? As there is already one vowel, /εː/, which, although long, is not automatically close, or tense, and, in addition, short [a] and long [ɑː] do not differ in quality in the same way, then it would seem that it is preferable, as many linguists do, to take length as being the distinctive phonemic feature, at least for the standard. The problem is compounded by the fact that /εː/ does not occur in all colloquial varieties of German. Thus one could say that length is phonemic in varieties containing /εː/, but quality is phonemic in other varieties.

In our analysis, which follows traditional lines in recognizing vowel length as being phonemic, there are seven short vowels: /i/ *bitten*, /y/ *Bütten*, /u/ *Butter*, /ε/ *Betten*, /ö/ *Götter*, /o/ *Lotto*, /a/ *Ratte* and eight long vowels: /iː/ *bieten*, /yː/ *Güte*, /uː/ *gute*, /eː/ *beten*, /εː/ *Räte*, /öː/ *löten*, /oː/ *Boten*, /aː/ *baten*. German has three diphthongs, all falling, that is having the stress on the first component: [ai] *mein*, [au] *auch* and [oi] *euch*.

The main features which serve to differentiate vowel phonemes are vowel length, lip-rounding and tongue height. Vowel length is phonemic before all intervocalic consonants except /ŋ/ and the affricate /pf/, where only short vowels occur, and /j/, /z/ and /ʒ/ where only long vowels occur. Apart from this general restriction there are also some accidental 'gaps' where certain vowels do not appear before certain consonants.

Table 6.2 shows the distribution of long and short vowels before intervocalic consonants in disyllabic words. The following lists give examples of the distribution of vowels before intervocalic consonants.

/aː/ *Stapel* 'pile', *Gabel, raten, laden, Laken* 'sheet', *lagen, Hafen, brave, Maßen, Hasen, Rage, Sprache, Samen, Bahnen, fahle* 'pale', *Haare*;

/a/ *Klappe, Krabbe, Ratte, Kladde* 'rough book', *packen, Bagger* 'excavator', *schaffen, hassen, waschen, Rache, Hammer, bannen, falle, harren* 'to wait';

/oː/ *Opa, loben, Brote, Mode, Koker* 'worker in coking plant', *Woge, Ofen, stowen* 'to steam', *Soße, Rose, Loge, malochen* 'to graft, work hard', *Koma, Sohne, Sohle, bohre*;

/o/ *stoppen, Robbe* 'seal', *Motte, Modder* 'mud', *locken, Roggen, hoffen, Rosse, Gosche* 'mouth (vulgar)', *lochen, Sommer, Sonne, bongen* 'to ring up (on a till)', *solle, dorren* 'to dry up, wither';

/öː/ *Köper* 'twill cloth', *Döbel* 'dowel', *töten, Böden, blöken* 'to bleat', *Bögen, Öfen, Möwe, Größe, lösen, Ströme, Söhne, Höhle, hören*;

/ö/ *klöppeln* 'to make fine lace', *Götter, Böcke, Böschung* 'embankment', *Löcher, können, Hölle, dörren* 'to dry';

/eː/ *Reepe* 'ropes', *geben, beten, reden, Ekel, legen, Hefe, Steven* 'stern', *Wesen, beige, nehmen, lehnen, fehlen, lehren*;

/ɛ/ *steppen, Ebbe, Wette, verheddern* 'to get muddled up', *lecken, Egge* 'harrow', *treffen, messen, dreschen, Rechen, Lämmer, rennen, Keller, sperren*;

/ɛːː/ *Säbel, Räte, gnädig, häkeln* 'to crochet', *prägen, Käfig, mäßig, Käse, schämen, gähnen, wählen, gären*;

/iː/ *piepen, lieben, bieten, Lieder, quieken* 'to squeak', *kriegen, schliefen, Diwan, gießen, bliesen, Nische, riechen, ziemen, dienen, spielen, frieren*;

/i/ *Lippe, kribbeln* 'to tickle', *bitte, Widder* 'ram', *schicken, Riggung* 'rigging', *Schiffe, wissen, wischen, wichen, Zimmer, binnen, Willen, irren*;

/yː/ *trübe, Güte, Süden, Küken, lügen, prüfen, süßen, Drüse* 'gland', *Rüsche* 'frill', *Bücher, rühmen, grünen, fühlen, führen*;

/y/ *üppig, schütten, pflücken, flügge* 'fully-fledged', *süffig, Küsse, Büsche, Brüche, dümmer, dünner, füllen, Dürre*;

/uː/ *Lupe, gruben, bluten, luden, spuken, schlugen, rufen, Muße, schmusen, wuschen, suchen, Puma, Wune* 'hole (in the ice)', *Schule, fuhren*;

/u/ *struppig, Knubbel* 'lump', *Butter, buddeln, spucken, schmuggeln, muffig, Busse, pfuschen, bruchig, Rummel, Zunge, Stulle* 'slice of bread and butter', *murren.*

6.3.2   Problems of phonemic analysis of the vowels

One of the aims of phonemic phonology is to set up an inventory of the distinctive phonological units, phonemes of a language. Disagreements have arisen among linguists who differ in their phonemic analysis in two main ways: (1) this may affect the status of a sound: is it a phoneme or an allophone? Or, (2) it may affect the analysis of complex segments such as diphthongs or affricates: are they one phoneme, which will increase the phonemic inventory, or are they simply combinations of already existing phonemes? Problems in the analysis of vowels feature in this section, those concerning consonants in 6.3.3. Apart from the discussion of quantity and quality, which has been dealt with in 6.3.1, there are disagreements concerning (1) the status of the diphthongs and (2) vowels in unstressed syllables.

Since the diphthongs seem to contain two components, are they to be regarded as unit phonemes /ai/ etc., or as clusters of a vowel plus a semi-vowel, /a/ + /j/? However, it is not clear which phoneme forms the second component. Phonetically the second component shows a wide variability of pronunciation. In the case of the diphthong in *mein* is it /i j/ or even /e/? What are the second components of the diphthongs in *auch* and *euch*? If we give weight to the phonetic unity of the sound, it is produced with a single articulatory movement then the diphthongs are clearly unit phonemes. This is the position we will adopt here.

The range of vowels in unstressed syllables differs in two points from that in stressed syllables: (1) there is no distinction between long and short vowels; and (2) the vowel [ə] only occurs in unstressed position. Through loan words there is in NHG a full range of unstressed vowels but phonetically the long vowels of stressed syllables show short, close allophones when unstressed. The following alternations illustrate this (' shows that the next vowel bears the stress): *Mo'tif > moti'vieren; 'leben > le'bendig; 'Drama > dra'matisch; 'Motor > Mo'toren; 'Muse > Mu'seum; A'syl > Asy'lant.* In the pronunciation of some speakers these shortened vowels become open and merge with the 'ordinary' short vowels [ɪ ɛ a ɔ ʊ ʏ]. According to pronouncing dictionaries, some speakers distinguish in unstressed syllables between [o] and [ɔ], *Ko'lonne* vs

Ko'llekte, as well as [e] and [ɛ], *Me'nage* vs *trai'nieren*. In general, however, these differences are determined by the number of following consonants. Before a single consonant the close vowel tends to occur, [to'tal, te'nor], but before a consonant cluster the open vowel occurs, [kɔm'pliːtsə, tɛn'dɛnts]. Open vowels also occur frequently before /r/, [tɛ'rasə]. Those linguists who regard quality and not quantity as being one of the main distinctive features of the stressed vowel system point to this continued presence of qualitative distinctions among unstressed vowels as supporting their argument. However, since nearly all the words involved are of foreign origin and vary in their pronunciation the whole basis for arguing this is rather uncertain. The most frequent unstressed vowel in word-final position in modern German is [ə], spelt *e*, *bitte*. Other vowels do occur, but mostly in foreign words, *Sofa*, *Pony*, *Auto*, *Zulu*. Since [ə] is restricted to unstressed position it is possible to regard it simply as an allophone of stressed short /ɛ/. However, contrasts such as *'Elend*, *'Moslem*, *'Totem* (with [ɛ] in unstressed position) vs *fehlend*, *Namen*, *Atem* (with [ə]) seem to show the two sounds in contrast and leave unresolved the phonemic status of [ə].

6.3.3 The consonant phonemes

In this section we are only dealing with single consonants, combinations of consonants, clusters being described in 6.4. However, the affricates [pf ts tʃ] present problems of analysis as to whether they are single phonemes, for example /pf/, /ts/, /tʃ /, or clusters, for example /p/ + /f/ etc., and their phonological status is discussed in 6.4.

The number of phonemic contrasts varies according to the position of the consonant in the word, the maximum number of contrasts being found medially between vowels. Table 6.3 shows minimal, or near minimal, pairs for initial prevocalic position, represented by C, medial intervocalic position, -C-, and syllable-final postvocalic position, -C. The non-occurrence of any phoneme is signified by the word 'lacking'.

The main difference between the three positions is that in final position voiced obstruents, i.e. plosives and fricatives, do not occur. The opposition between voiceless and voiced sounds is said to be neutralized, or it may simply be said that voiced obstruents do not occur in this position. In initial position the voiceless plosives are aspirated in North German speech and the standard pronunciation.

Table 6.3   Consonant distribution according to position in the word

Phoneme	C-	C-	-C
Voiceless labial plosive /p/	*packen*	*Lippe*	*Grab*
Voiced labial plosive /b/	*backen*	*Liebe*	lacking
Voiceless alveolar plosive /t/	*tanken*	*waten*	*Rad*
Voiced alveolar plosive /d/	*danken*	*Waden*	lacking
Voiceless palato-velar plosive /k/	*Kabel*	*Ecke*	*lag*
Voiced palato-velar plosive /g/	*Gabel*	*Egge*	lacking
Voiceless labio-dental fricative /f/	*fahren*	*Höfe*	*Schaf*
Voiced labio-dental fricative /v/	*waren*	*Löwe*	lacking
Voiceless alveolar fricative /s/	lacking	*hassen*	*Schloß*
Voiced alveolar fricative /z/	*süß*	*Hasen*	lacking
Voiceless palato-alveolar fricative /ʃ/	*schon*	*löschen*	*rasch*
Voiced palato-alveolar fricative /ʒ/	*Jalousie*	*Etage*	lacking
Voiceless palato-velar fricative /x–ç/	*Chemie*	*machen*	*Dach*
Voiced palatal fricative /j/	*jung*	*Koje*	lacking
Bilabial nasal /m/	*müssen*	*immer*	*Baum*
Alveolar nasal /n/	*nur*	*binnen*	*kann*
Velar nasal /ŋ/	lacking	*bringen*	*Ring*
Alveolar lateral /l/	*liegen*	*brüllen*	*wohl*
Alveolar or uvular fricative /r/	*Rippe*	*irren*	*sehr*
Aspirate /h/	*Hand*	lacking	lacking

6.3.4   Problems of phonemic analysis among the consonants

There are disagreements among linguists concerning, among other
things, (1) the status of [x] and [ç] and (2) the affricates. Although it
is agreed that there is a phonetic difference between the voiceless
velar fricative [x] and the voiceless palatal fricative [ç] (Kohler 1977:
86f. adds a uvular [χ]), there is disagreement about their phonemic
status. For the most part they are in complementary distribution with
[x] occurring after low and back vowels and [ç] occurring after front
vowels. In the words *tauchen* and *Tauchen* there is an apparent
contrast of /x/ with /ç/. However, this can easily be dealt with and
their allophonic status confirmed if grammatical information is
allowed in the phonological analysis, something which many phonemic phonologists were unwilling to do. They wished to use only
phonological criteria at the phonological level. In *Tauchen* where [ç]
occurred after a back vowel it was in the initial position of the
diminutive suffix. The description of the distribution of the allophones [x] and [ç] can now be framed as follows: 'The allophone [ç]
appears after front vowels and initially in words, *Chemie*, or morphemes, *-chen* and after /n l r/, the allophone [x] appears elsewhere,

i.e. after low and back vowels'. This question is still being aired. Griffen (1985: 53–72) argues that the variation in articulation lies chiefly in the vowel and need not be symbolized in the consonant. T. A. Hall (1992: 221–35) argues that both [ç] and [x] are produced by a rule of 'Dorsal fricative assimilation' which only operates within morphemes, thus in *tauchen* the [x] is within the morpheme *tauch-* while in *Tauchen*, *-chen* belongs to a different morpheme.

The analysis of the affricates presents a different problem. Are they to be considered as single phonemes /ts/ and /pf/ (monophonematic solution), which would add to the inventory of phonemes, or are they combinations of already existing consonants, /t/ + /s/ and /p/ + /f/ (biphonematic solution) like /tr/ etc.? Linguists are divided in their opinion and almost all analyses seem to use their own criteria (Werner 1972: 50–5). Several criteria seem, however, to point to the independent nature of the two parts of the affricates and thus to regarding them as clusters of two consonants. First, the ability of the individual components of the affricates to occur on their own. The affricate /ts/ contrasts with /t/ and /s/ ([s] as a realization for initial *s* only occurs in South Germany and Austria): /ts/ *zeigen*, *Teig*, *seinen*, /pf/ contrasts with /p/ and /f/, *Pfeife*, *Pein*, *fein*. Second, their ability, albeit limited, to reverse position. Of the theoretical combinations and their reversals, for example /ts st pf fp/, the sequences /ts/, /st/ and /pf/ occur as intervocalic and word-final clusters, *sitzen*, *Netz*, *beste*, *Nest*, *klopfen*, *Topf*, but not /fp/. Third, the fact that they can be divided by a morpheme boundary. Both affricates can be divided by a morpheme boundary, *rät+st*, *Ab+fall*. For these reasons it will be assumed here that the affricates [pf] and [ts] are biphonematic, being clusters of /p/ + /f/ and /t/ + /s/. This will also affect the description of consonant clusters, analysing the initial combinations of words such *pflegen* and *Zweifel* as being composed of three consonants.

6.4 PHONOTACTICS

(Benware 1986: Chapter 7; Meinhold and Stock 1980: Chapter 3; Philipp 1970, 1974: Chapter 3)

In the description of the phonemes of German we have seen how not all possible environments for vowels and consonants are filled. This is partly a matter of distribution, i.e. long vowels do not occur before intervocalic /ŋ/, voiced obstruents do not occur word-finally. A further systematic regularity which can be seen in the phonology of a language is that of the set of possible consonant clusters. While *Blick*

Table 6.4   Combinations of two consonant-initial clusters

C^2 =	m	n	l	r	v	p	t	s	ʃ	Examples
C^1 = p			+	+						*Plan, Preis*
b			+	+						*Blei, Brei*
t				+				+	+	*treu, Zeit, tschüs*
d				+						*drei*
k		+	+	+	+					*Knie, Kleie, Krähe, Qual* (/kv/ = qu)
g		+	+	+						*Gnade, gleiten, Grad*
f			+	+						*fliehen, frei*
ʃ	+	+	+	+	+	+	+			*schmal, schnell, Schlaf, Schrift, schwer, spät, stehen*

is a permissible German word, *Dlick* is not. Phonotactics describes the phonological structure of permissible words in a language. Most phonotactic descriptions deal with consonant combinations, the permissible vowel structures being handled as distribution. German words occur with either one, two or three consonants in initial position before a stressed vowel: *baten, braten, sprachen*. If we use C for consonant then the initial structure of these three words can be symbolized C, CC, CCC. This can be reduced to the formula C^1, C^2, C^3. If three consonants occur then C^1 must be [ʃ], *Splitter, spreche, streiten* and C^3 must be /l/ or /r/, whereas C^2 must be either /p/ or /t/. If C^3 is /l/ then C^2 must be /p/; in other words, /ʃtl/ is not an admissible cluster. Of the three admissible clusters /ʃtr ʃpr ʃpl/ there are not many examples of /ʃpl/, *Spleen, spleißen*. Since we have assumed a phonemic analysis of the affricates [pf ts] as a cluster of two phonemes /p/ + /f/, /t/ + /s/, then we have initial CCC clusters in *Pflaume*, /pfl/, *Pfropf*, /pfr/, and *zwei*, /tsv/. Other CCC clusters occur in initial position but only in very few words: /skl, skr/, *Sklave, Skrupel* (all loan words).

In two-consonant initial clusters (C^1, C^2), C^1 can comprise a larger number of members: /p b t d k g f ʃ/ but C^2 comprises only /l r m n v/ in native words. The permissible combinations of the two groups can be shown in Table 6.4 with '+' marking the occurrence of a particular combination.

Other possible clusters appear mostly in foreign words, /pn/ *Pneumatik*, /ps/ *Psychologie*, /ks/ *Xylophon*, /sf/ *Sphäre*, or Low German words, /vr/ *Wrack*. Through the borrowing of chiefly English, but also French words, consonant clusters with /s/ as C^1 have been introduced into German. Before /t/ and /p/ older loans have

Table 6.5 Combinations of two consonant final clusters

C² =	p	t	k	f	s	ʃ	x	m	n	l
C¹ = p		+		+	+	+				
t					+	+				
k		+			+	+				
f		+			+					
s		+	+							
ʃ		+								
x		+			+					
m	+	+			+	+				
n		+		+	+	+	+			
ŋ		+	+		+					
l	+	+	+	+	+	+		+	+	
r	+	+	+	+	+	+	+	+	+	+

substituted /ʃ/ for /s/, *Streik, Sport*, but in many recent loans both /ʃ/ and /s/ occur in variation, *Star, Stil, Spot, spontan*. Besides /st sp/, where the pronunciation of /s/ can vary with /ʃ/, there is also a group of clusters where the pronunciation of /s/ is always [s], /sk/ *Skat, Skala*, /sm/ *smart*, /sn/ *Snack*, /sl/ *Slum*. The resonants /m n l r/ always appear nearest the vowel in a consonant cluster. In prevocalic clusters they follow the obstruent whereas in postvocalic clusters they precede the obstruent, for example *Schlaf* vs *falsch*, giving a mirror image of /ʃl/ vs /lʃ/. Of the twenty-four initial CC clusters in German in Table 6.4 which contain a resonant, thirteen occur in word-final position: /lp/ *Kalb*, /rp/ *Korb*, /rt/ *Art*, /st/ *List*, /ʃt/ *Gischt*, /lk/ *Kalk*, /rk/ *Werk*, /lf/ *elf*, /rf/ *Dorf*, /mʃ/ *Ramsch*, /nʃ/ *Wunsch*, /lʃ/ *falsch*, /rʃ/ *Dorsch*. In addition there are other word-final clusters comprising resonants which do not occur in initial position nor do their mirror images, for example /lx/ *Milch*, /lt/ *mild*, /ls/ *Hals*; /ŋk/ *Bank*; /rs/ *Kurs*, /rx/ *durch*. Altogether there are forty-seven word-final CC consonant clusters in German. Table 6.5 shows their occurrence. Examples: /pt/ *bleibt*, /pf/ *Topf*, /ps/ *Krebs*, /pʃ/ *hübsch*, /ts/ *Schutz*, /tʃ/ *Matsch*; /kt/ *Takt*, /ks/ *Dachs*, /kʃ/ *tücksch*; /ft/ *Luft*, /fs/ *Treffs*, /st/ *Lust*, /sk/ *brüsk*; /ʃt / *Gischt*; /xt/ *recht*, /xs/ *mittwochs*; /mp/ *Camp*, /mt/ *Amt*, /ms/ *Sims*, /mʃ/ *Ramsch*; /nt/ *Land*, /nf/ *Senf*, /ns/ *Gans*, /nʃ/ *Wunsch*; /nx/ *Mönch*; /ŋt/ *hängt*, /ŋk/ *Bank*, /ŋs/ *langs*, /lp/ *halb*, /lt/ *Geld*, /lk/ *Kalk*, /lf/ *Golf*, /ls/ *Hals*, /lʃ/ *falsch*, /lx/ *Milch*, /lm/ *Helm*, /ln/ *Kiln*; /rp/ *Korb*, /rt/ *Bart*, /rk/ *Park*, /rf/ *Torf*, /rs/ *Kurs*, /rʃ/ *Hirsch*, /rx/ *durch*, /rm/ *Lärm*, /rn/ *Stern*, /rl/ *Kerl*.

Combinations of CCC clusters in word-final position are more

frequent than CC clusters: thirty-four end in /t/, for example *Fürst*,
Wulst, thirty in /s/, *Knirps*, *Murks*, *Rülps*, two in /ʃ/ and one in /f/,
Kampf. Groups of four consonants can occur but the final conso-
nant(s) are phonetically alveolar obstruents, mostly representing an
inflectional ending, /s/ for the gen. sg., *Markts*, /st/ for the second
person, *rülpst*, or /t/ for the third person verbal ending, *kämpft*.
There are even a small number of groups of five consonants, *kämpfst*,
Herbsts, where the final consonant is always part of the inflectional
ending. There is thus more freedom of combination among consonants after stressed vowels than before them. One constant feature is
that /r/ and /l/ are always nearest the vowel.

6.5   GENERATIVE PHONOLOGY

Generative phonology dispenses with the notion of the phoneme
altogether and uses phonological, or distinctive, features as its basic
means of distinguishing between words and characterizing sounds. It
also uses underlying forms, roughly equivalent to base allomorphs, to
which it also applies phonological rules. Through this it aims to be
able to make more widely applicable generalizations about the
phonology of the language, for example, instead of saying that intervocalic [b d g v z] become [p t k f s] in word- and syllable-final
position, a statement can be made that any obstruent which is voiced
becomes voiceless in that position. The range of distinctive features
varies but the most widely used set are derived from those used by
Chomsky and Halle (1968). Wurzel (1970) has applied them to
German and they have been slightly adapted in this description.
Benware (1986: Chapter 6) describes several generative rules. The
features are still used in recent work on phonology (Wiese 1988;
Giegerich 1989; T. A. Hall 1992). Each phonological segment in
German is thus characterized by the presence, marked by [+],
or absence, marked by [−], of certain distinctive features. Each seg-
ment should be characterized by a unique set of [+] or [−] features.
Table 6.6 sets out the distinctive features of the German consonant
system.

Some of the features are the same as, or similar to, traditional
articulatory terms for the descriptions of sounds. The features
[lateral] and [nasal] are used in their traditional way for [l] and
[m n ŋ]. The term [voice] is also used in its traditional meaning. The
feature [syllabic] characterizes vowels, and [consonantal] consonants.
[sonorant] refers to a group of consonants comprising the nasals
and liquids for which the term sonant, or resonant is also used.

Table 6.6   Distinctive features of German consonants

	p	b	t	d	k	g	f	v	s	z	ʃ	ʒ	j	ç	x	m	n	ŋ	l	r	h
Syllabic	−	−	−	−	−	−	−	−	−	−	−	−	−	−	−	−	−	−	−	−	−
Consonantal	+	+	+	+	+	+	+	+	+	+	+	+	+	+	+	+	+	+	+	+	+
Continuant	−	−	−	−	−	−	+	+	+	+	+	+	+	+	+	+	+	+	+	+	+
Sonorant	−	−	−	−	−	−	−	−	−	−	−	−	−	−	−	+	+	+	+	+	−
Nasal	−	−	−	−	−	−	−	−	−	−	−	−	−	−	−	+	+	+	−	−	−
Voice	−	+	−	+	−	+	−	+	−	+	−	+	−	−							
Anterior	+	+	+	+	−	−	+	+	+	+	−	−	−	−	−	+	+	−	+	+	−
Coronal	−	−	+	+	−	−	−	−	+	+	+	+	−	−	−	−	+	−	+	+	−
High	−	−	−	−	+	+	−	−	−	−	+	+	+	+	+	−	−	+	−	−	−
Back	−	−	−	−	+	+	−	−	−	−	−	−	−	−	+	−	−	+	−	−	+
Lateral	−	−	−	−	−	−	−	−	−	−	−	−	−	−	−	−	−	−	+	−	−

Table 6.7   Distinctive features of German vowels

	iː	ɪ	yː	ʏ	uː	ʊ	eː	ɛ	øː	œ	oː	ɔ	ɛː	aː	a
Syllabic	+	+	+	+	+	+	+	+	+	+	+	+	+	+	+
Consonantal	−	−	−	−	−	−	−	−	−	−	−	−	−	−	−
High	+	+	+	+	+	+	−	−	−	−	−	−	−	−	−
Low	−	−	−	−	−	−	−	−	−	−	−	+	+	+	+
Back	−	−	−	−	+	+	−	−	−	−	+	+	−	+	+
Rounded	−	−	+	+	+	+	−	−	+	+	+	+	−	−	−
Long	+	−	+	−	+	−	+	−	+	−	+	−	+	+	−

The feature [continuant] is used for those sounds whose articulation does not involve any occlusion of the organs of speech in the vocal tract. Other features such as [high], [back] have typically been used to describe vowels but in generative phonology have been extended to cover both vowels and consonants, [high] being used for palatal, palato-alveolar and velar sounds and [back] for velar sounds. The features [anterior] and [coronal] are more unfamiliar, the former designating labial sounds in general, the latter alveolar or dental sounds.

The vowels of German can be represented by Table 6.7, showing their distinctive features. The features [rounded] and [long] are used solely to apply to vowels. The other features have occurred in the description of the consonants although no consonants in German are characterized as [low].

6.5.1   Underlying forms and phonological rules

In the account of German consonant phonemes we saw how no voiced obstruents occurred word-finally, whereas intervocalically both voiced and voiceless sounds occurred. Thus if [bunt] is the nom. and acc., [bund+es] the gen., then the underlying form will be either of the two forms. The choice between them will be determined by whether the other one can be derived easily by a phonological rule. A general rule changing intervocalic voiced obstruents into voiceless obstruents will describe this feature of German consonant distribution. Thus to return to our example, [bund] will be the underlying form and will be changed into [bunt] by a phonological rule which states that 'a voiced obstruent becomes voiceless in word-final position'. This rules consists of three parts: (a) the structural description, stating what segment it will change; (b) the structural change, describing how the segment has been changed; and lastly (c) the environment of the change. This rule can be formalized as follows:

$$
\begin{array}{ccc}
\text{(a)} & \text{(b)} & \text{(c)} \\
\begin{bmatrix} - \text{ sonorant} \\ + \text{ voice} \end{bmatrix} \rightarrow & [- \text{ voice}] & / \ \#
\end{array}
$$

The application of such a word-final devoicing rule will derive the nom. and acc. surface form [bunt] from underlying [bund]. The alternation [t]−[d] involves the phonemes /t/ and /d/ and is traditionally called a morphophonemic alternation. Another alternation which can be described by a phonological rule is that of [x] and [ç], for example [lɔx, lœçər]. In this case the underlying form of the plural would be [lœxər] to which a phonological rule would apply, changing it from a velar fricative to a palatal fricative. It might be formulated as follows:

$$
\begin{array}{ccc}
\text{(a)} & \text{(b)} & \text{(c)} \\
\begin{bmatrix} + \text{ fricative} \\ - \text{ voice} \\ + \text{ back} \end{bmatrix} \rightarrow & [- \text{ back}] \ / & \begin{bmatrix} + \text{ vocalic} \\ - \text{ back} \end{bmatrix}
\end{array}
$$

The alternation between the underlying voiced [d] and surface [t] was an alternation between units which in a phonemic approach are phonemes. The alternation between [x] and [ç] in a phonemic approach is an alternation between allophones. Generative phonology makes no distinction between these two particular levels of representation, regarding both surface forms as being derived from the application of phonological rules to underlying forms. The underlying forms are sometimes called the deep, or systematic phonemic, level and the derived forms the surface, or systematic phonetic level. The traditional phonemic level, as used by phonemicists, is referred to as the taxonomic, or autonomous, phonemic level.

6.6 RECENT DEVELOPMENTS IN PHONOLOGY AND THEIR APPLICATION TO GERMAN

Growing out of generative phonology have come several developments of phonological theory. These are generally referred to by prefacing 'phonology' with a qualifying epithet, for example autosegmental phonology, dependency phonology, dynamic phonology, lexical phonology, natural phonology, natural generative phonology and metrical phonology. They are not quite as diverse as their names suggest and share a number of common features, notably an interest in the syllable. A survey of their methods of description and theoretical terminology is provided by Carr (1993: 157–304). We have seen how phonologists have sought to analyse German in terms of distinctive units, phonemes, or features. Growing out of an interest in the structure of words, the syllable has now assumed a new importance as a phonological unit. Up to now we have used the term syllable in an undefined way to designate that part of a word which does or does not bear stress, for example stressed and unstressed syllables. A simple syllable consists of an initial element, a nucleus and a releasing element. Thus the word *bin* can be symbolized CVC (C standing for any consonant and V for any vowel). A word such as *Streit* could be symbolized CCCVVC. The concept of the syllable as a phonological unit is based partly on the assumption that some speech sounds are more sonorous, emitting more 'noise' than others. A scale of sonority can be set up, ranging from the low vowel [a] to the voiceless plosives [p t k] as can be seen from the following:

Sonority scale
vowels: a, e, o, u, i
resonants: r, l, m, n
voiced fricatives: v, z, ʒ
voiceless fricatives: f, s, ʃ, ç, x
voiced plosives: b, d, g
voiceless plosives: p, t, k

In the structure of words those sounds that are most sonorous, the vowels, make up the peak, or highest point, the nucleus of the syllable and they are preceded or followed by sounds that are less sonorous. Thus in *Bart* the vowel is followed by a resonant and a voiceless plosive, in *Trab* the vowel is preceded by a resonant and a voiceless plosive. From the peak of the vowel the syllable descends through a resonant to a voiceless plosive. This is reflected in the phonotactics of the pre- and postvocalic consonant clusters in German (see 6.4). Using this information, a hierarchical structure of the syllable can be constructed in the form of a tree diagram (see below), comprising an onset, /tr/, the nucleus, /ɑː/ and the coda, /p/. The nucleus and the coda can further be combined to form the rhyme.

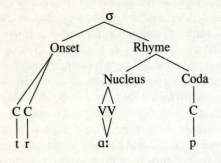

One of the goals of syllabic phonology is to set up a pattern or template for the words of a language. Traditional phonotactics does this by listing the occurring consonant clusters in a language (see 6.4); syllabic phonology does this by setting up a template for the syllable structure of words in a language, i.e. a summary in the form of a tree diagram of all the possible structures. The following diagram attempts to do that for German, based on the information in 6.4.

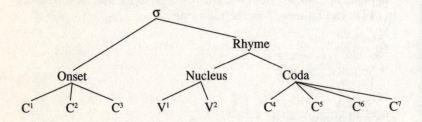

The only part of the template which is obligatory is V^1, V^2, for example *Ei*. The consonants are optional but restrictions are placed on the types of consonants occurring in the different slots in the template. C^1 is always [ʃ s], C^2 is an obstruent and C^3 a resonant, for example [ʃpl ʃpr ʃtr]. Where C^2 and C^3 occur together, then C^2 is always an obstruent and C^3 a resonant (see Table 6.4). Non-frequent clusters in foreign words will be excluded. The consonants C^4 and C^5 in word-final position are largely the mirror image of C^2, C^3, with C^4 being a resonant and C^5 an obstruent (see Table 6.5). However, there are exceptions to which we will return. In the case of C^6 and C^7, the obstruent is always an alveolar, usually an inflectional ending.

This approach to syllabic phonology is based on the sonority scale (p. 145) and the occurrence of [ʃ s] in C^1 position and [s t] in C^6, C^7 position are violations of this scale, as are C^4, C^5 clusters such as [pt ps pʃ kt] etc. (see Table 6.5). Suggestions to deal with this violation have been: (1) to count clusters such as [ʃp ʃt] as filling a single C slot; and (2) to regard [ʃ s] as being 'extrametrical' consonants which do not count as part of the syllable template but are appendices. Giegerich (1989: 69–73) discusses these alternatives and rules out the second one since [st] occurs word-internally, for example *Meister, Hamster*. He would like to accept the first suggestion, which regards [ʃp ʃt] as complex segments and not sequences. This means that phonetically they are two sounds but phonologically they function as only one unit, occupying one C slot. As is probably now becoming clear, the old question of whether the affricates in German are one phonological unit or two (see 6.3.4 for earlier discussion) is still very much alive. Giegerich comes to the conclusion that 'Affricates are phonetically complex elements that behave phonologically like single units' (1989: 69). Other recent studies that take this line are Griffen (1985: 123–48), T. A. Hall (1992: 15f.) and Wiese (1988: 60ff.).

Another phenomenon which receives attention from syllabic phonology is vowel length or quantity. The parallelism between long vowels and diphthongs is maintained by symbolizing both of them VV at the CV level, for example *Baum* and *nahm* are both CVVC. However, at the phonetic segmental level the long vowel is only realized by one segment as is illustrated in the diagram on p. 148.

This is the exact reverse of the treatment of the affricates (T. A. Hall 1992: 18–23). Giegerich (1989: 25) follows a similar course, but uses different symbolism. Wiese (1988: 62–78) has a slightly different scheme, viewing diphthongs as comprising VC, the C being a resonant, at the CV level. He distinguishes between quantity at the syllabic level and length at the phonetic level. All agree, however, that length and tenseness combine at the underlying level to characterize long vowels. The status of length and quantity, one of the

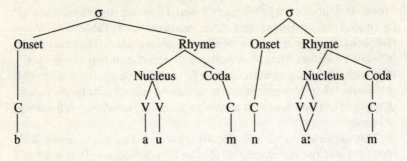

classic phonological areas of controversy (see 6.3.1) continues to be the subject of debate.

6.7   SUPRASEGMENTAL FEATURES

The previous sections have dealt with the segmental sounds of German, i.e those sounds that can be arrived at by the segmentation of the speech chain into C and V units. Other phenomena which cover more than single C and V units are called suprasegmental elements, for example stress and intonation. Other features such as tempo and rhythm will not be dealt with.

6.7.1   Stress

(C. Hall 1992: 109–16; Kohler 1977: 191–6; MacCarthy 1975: 8–16)

It is a feature of languages like German that among the vowels in disyllabic words one of the vowels is more prominent than the other, for example *Friede*, *Auto*, *Sponti*, *Pizza*. This prominence may express itself in more force of articulation, loudness, higher pitch and length. Such syllables are said to be stressed, or accented. Not all words, however, are stressed. Definite and indefinite articles, prepositions and many such functional words never bear the stress. Some unstressed function words undergo phonetic reduction (see 2.2). The role of word stress in German is a complex one. In general it is predictable and rules for its occurrence can be given. In a few cases, however, it is distinctive, for example with the verbal prefixes *durch*, *über*, *um*, *unter*, which are stressed when they are separable and unstressed when they are inseparable. The following examples illustrate this stress contrast, which correlates with a semantic contrast: '*durchbrechen* 'to break something in two' vs *durch'brechen* 'to break through something'; '*überfahren* 'to ferry someone over (a river etc.)' vs *über'fahren* 'to run someone over'; '*umreißen* 'to pull something over' vs *um'reißen* 'to sketch out'. In most cases, however, the placement of stress is predictable. In making statements of stress-placement rules a certain amount of morphological information is needed and also one needs to know whether we are describing native or foreign words.

In words of more than one syllable potentially any syllable can bear the stress: '*Königin, Pro'fessor, Gene'ral*; '*Alter, Al'tar*. The placement of the stress can also shift, sg. *Pro'fessor* becomes pl. *Profes'soren*. To describe the regularities of stress it is best to distinguish between stems, or underived forms, and affixes. Thus the placement of the stress in underived forms is typically on the penultimate syllable, *Pro'fessor*, '*Alter*; this would also include forms such as *Fo'relle, Ho'lunder, Wa'cholder, le'bendig* which are usually regarded as exceptions to a rule which states that stem vowels in native words are stressed. This regularity, which we can call the penultimate syllable stress rule, has the advantage that it accounts for the stress shift of *Pro'fessor* to *Profes'soren*, and '*Japan* to *Ja'paner*. In fact the unstressed suffixes of German can be divided into two groups: one which keeps the stress placement of the original form, '*König,* '*Königin,* and a second group which makes the stress conform to the penultimate syllable stress rule, which usually involves a stress shift, '*Japan* to *Ja'paner*. Most native suffixes belong to the first group: for example *-chen,* '*Wägelchen*; *-heit, -igkeit, Ge'legenheit,* '*Müdigkeit*; *-ig,* '*kugelig*; *-lich,* '*leserlich*; *-nis,* '*Hindernis*; *-tum, Be'amtentum*; *-ung, Ver'wirklichung*. In most cases there could be no shift anyway since the unstressed vowel *e* occurs before the suffix. The suffixes *-isch*, and *-(i)aner* belong to the second group. Another group of suffixes always bear the stress. The following are examples of some common foreign suffixes: *-al, glo'bal*; *-ar/-är, Aktio'när, famili'är*; *-ant/-ent Fabri'kant, Stu'dent, rele'vant*; *-ell, paral'lel*; *-est, Pro'test*; *-ie, Che'mie*; *-ion, Nati'on*; *-ist, Lin'guist*; *-iv, Kollek'tiv, ak'tiv*; *-ös/-os, skanda'lös*; *-tät, Pari'tät*; *-ukt, Pro'dukt*; *-ur, Abi'tur*. The suffix *-ei*, originally a foreign suffix, is always stressed but it occurs with native stems, for example *Schweine'rei*. Foreign suffixes containing two vowels are stressed on the first vowel since the second one is usually the unstressed *e*: *-age, Bla'mage*; *-ieren, bug'sieren*. Examples of final unstressed vowels other than *e* are *-ismus, Real'ismus*, *-itis, Bron'chitis*. The suffix *-ik* is an exception. Being foreign, it should bear the stress, as it does in *Mu'sik*, *Fab'rik*, but the penultimate vowel is stressed in *Gram'matik*, *Pho'netik*.

6.7.2 Intonation

(Fox 1984; C. Hall 1992: 116–37; Kohler 1977: 196–207; MacCarthy 1975: 17–28)

For many years the study of German intonation was sadly neglected. Schindler and Thürmann (1971) contains a much smaller number of items on suprasegmentals than segmental sounds. An early work in English is Barker (1925); the area was taken up in Germany by von Essen (1964); Isačenko and Schädlich (1970) provide an idiosyncratic description; Fox (1984) is the most accessible account in English; Meier (1984) is a general bibliography but contains a number of items on German.

Utterances are not spoken all on one pitch level but rise and fall to give the impression of tunes. Unlike music, there are no fixed scales of notes but considerable variety of pitch. The symbolization of intonation is difficult and different schemes are in use. All of them, however, show the rise, fall or level pitch of the voice. We will follow von Essen (1964: 16) and Fox (1984: 7), who use '—' for stressed syllables and '.' for unstressed syllables.

The changes in pitch are usually located in the syllable which has the most stress in the utterance. This syllable forms the nucleus of the tone, or intonation, group. The minimum group is a simple sentence: *Heute ist Montag*. Complex sentences may contain more than one tone group ('‖' marks the boundary of a tone group): *Wir wollten nach Stuttgart, ‖ aber wir hatten nicht genügend Zeit*. Within each tone group there is a nucleus, the stressed syllable, which shows the most pitch changes and sometimes one or more stress groups, comprising a stressed syllable and unstressed vowels. In our examples the nucleus would be *Mon-*, *Stutt-* and *Zeit*. The syllables between the nucleus and the first stressed syllable of the tone group are known collectively as the head, and any unstressed syllables before the head are known as the pre-head. The only obligatory part of the tone group is the nucleus. Likewise any syllables after the nucleus are known as the tail. Our examples can thus be divided as in the diagram opposite.

The crucial changes in pitch affect the nucleus. Following C. Hall (1992), we can classify the intonation patterns of German on the pattern of the nucleus into five patterns. The patterns are also typical

1		Heute ist		Mon-		tag	¯.¯.
(no pre-head)	ǀ	head	ǀ	nucleus	ǀ	tail	

2	Wir	ǀ	wollten nach	ǀ	Stutt-		gart fahren . ¯ . . ¯.
	pre-head	ǀ	head	ǀ	nucleus	ǀ	tail

3		aber wir hatten nicht genügend	Zeit	..−¯..¯.−
(no pre-head)	ǀ	head	ǀ nucleus ǀ	(no tail)

of certain types of sentence. Since there is an overlap in the sentence types that occur with the falling pattern and the rising–falling pattern, it seems best to deal with them together. For the same reasons the rising and falling–rising patterns will be grouped together.

Type 1 contains a nucleus with a falling pattern:

1 *Er hat jetzt genug geschlafen.* ..¯.−.−.
2 *Schreiben Sie bitte bald!*   −..−.−
3 *Wann fährst du nach Hause?* .−..−·

Type 1a contains a nucleus with a rising–falling pattern:

1 *Er hat gewonnen!*   ...¯.
2 *Trink doch deine Milch!* −.−._
3 *Wie alt bist du?*   .−−.
4 *Wunderbar!*   −·.

Both these patterns are used typically for statements (1), commands (2) and questions containing *wh*-question words such *wann*, *was*, *wer*, *wie*, *wo* (3). Type 1a is also used for exclamations (4).

Type 2 contains a nucleus with a rising pattern:

1 *Spielst du mit?*   _.−
2 *Was schreibst du jetzt?* _−.¯

Type 2a contains a nucleus with a falling–rising pattern:

1 *Bist du jetzt müde?*   ..¯−.
2 *Übrigens,* ǁ (*wir wollen euch nächste Woche besuchen*). −.¯.
3 *Achtung!* −·

Both these patterns are used typically for questions which can be answered by *yes* or *no* (1), questions containing *wh*-question words such *wann*, *was*, *wer*, *wie*, *wo* to make them more polite and friendly or to confirm their content (2). Type 2a is also used for non-final, or dependent, tone groups (2) and friendly warnings (3).

Type 3 contains a nucleus with a level pattern:

1 *Wenn wir Zeit hätten, (würden wir jetzt verreisen).* −.−·
2 *Möchtest du Bier oder Wein?* −.−−·−
3 *Ich möchte Äpfel, Birnen, Bananen und Pflaumen.* .−.−..−.−.
4 *(guten) Abend; Danke.* −·−·;−·

This pattern is used typically for non-final, or dependent, tone groups (1), the first part of so-called alternative questions (2), for lists, except for the last item (3) and for ritual greetings and non-committal expressions (4).

There is no agreement on the number of distinctive intonation patterns in German. Kohler distinguishes six tones (1977: 198f.) whereas MacCarthy (1975: 18–23) has two basic tunes, one of which is subdivided into a tune that ends on a high level pitch while the other rises to a high pitch. Writing about intonation can only give some pointers to listen to. The real exploration of this topic, as with phonology in general, comes from the spoken word itself.

SELECT BIBLIOGRAPHY AND FURTHER READING

Barker, M. (1925) *A Handbook of German Intonation for University Students*, Cambridge: Heffers.

Battye, A. C. and Hintze, M. A. (1992) *The French Language Today*, London: Routledge.

Benware, W. A. (1986) *Phonetics and Phonology of Modern German*, Washington, D.C.: Georgetown University Press.

de Boor, H., Moser, H. and Winkler, C. (eds) (1969), *Siebs: Deutsche Aussprache. Reine und gemäßigte Hochlautung mit Aussprachewörterbuch*, Berlin: de Gruyter.

Carr, P. (1993) *Phonology*, London: Macmillan.

Chomsky, N. and Halle, M. (1968) *The Sound Pattern of English*, New York: Harper & Row.

Duden Aussprachewörterbuch (1990) ed. M. Mangold, Mannheim: Bibliographisches Institut.

Essen, O. von (1964) *Grundzüge der hochdeutschen Satzintonation*, Düsseldorf: Henn.

Fox, A. C. (1984) *German Intonation: An Outline*, Oxford: Clarendon Press.

—— (1990) *The Structure of German*, Oxford: Clarendon Press.

Giegerich, H. J. (1989) *Syllable Structure and Lexical Derivation in German*, Bloomington: Indiana University Linguistics Club.

Griffen, T. D. (1985) *Aspects of Dynamic Phonology*, Amsterdam: John Benjamins.

Hall, C. (1992) *Modern German Pronunciation*, Manchester: Manchester University Press.

Hall, T. A. (1992) *Syllable Structure and Syllable-Related Processes in German* (Linguistische Arbeiten, 276), Tübingen: Niemeyer.

Isačenko, A. and Schädlich, H.-J. (1970) *A Model of Standard German Intonation*, The Hague: Mouton.

Kohler, K. J. (1977) *Einführung in die Phonetik des Deutschen*, Berlin: Schmidt.

König, W. (1989) *Atlas zur Aussprache des Schriftdeutschen in der Bundesrepublik*, 2 vols, Ismaning: Hueber.

Krech, H., Krech, E.-M., Kurka, E., Stelzig, H., Stock, E., Stötzer, U. and Teske, R. (1971) *Wörterbuch der deutschen Aussprache*, 3rd. edn, Leipzig: Bibliographisches Institut.

MacCarthy, P. (1975) *The Pronunciation of German*, Oxford: Oxford University Press.

Mangold, M. (1984) 'Der Laut', in *Duden Grammatik*, 4th edn, Mannheim: Bibliographisches Institut, pp. 21–58.

Martens, C. and Martens, P. (1961) *Phonetik der deutschen Sprache*, Munich: Hueber.

Meier, R. (1984) *Bibliographie zur Intonation* (Bibliographische Arbeitsmaterialien, 5), Tübingen: Niemeyer.

Meinhold, G. and Stock, E. (1980) *Phonologie der deutschen Gegenwartssprache*, Leipzig: Bibliographisches Institut.

Moulton, W. G. (1962) *The Sounds of English and German*, Chicago: University of Chicago Press.

Philipp, M. (1970) *Phonologie de l'allemand*, Paris: Presses Universitaires de France; German edn, Stuttgart: Kohlhammer, 1974.

—— (1974) *Phonologie des Deutschen*, Stuttgart,: Kolhammer.

Rausch, R. and Rausch, I. (1988) *Deutsche Phonetik für Ausländer*, Leipzig: Verlag Enzyklopädie.

Schindler, F. and Thürmann, E. (1971) *Bibliographie zur Phonetik und Phonologie des Deutschen* (Bibliographische Arbeitsmaterialien, 1), Tübingen: Niemeyer.

Siebs, T. (1969) *Deutsche Aussprache. Reine und gemäßigte Hochlautung mit Aussprachewörterbuch*, 19th edn, eds H. de Boor, H. Moser and C. Winkler, Berlin: de Gruyter.

Wängler, H.-H. (1983) *Grundriß einer Phonetik des Deutschen*, 2nd edn, Elwert: Marburg.

Werner, O. (1972) *Phonemik des Deutschen*, Stuttgart: Metzler.

Wiese, R. (1988) *Silbische und lexikalische Phonologie: Studien zum Chinesischen und Deutschen* (Linguistische Arbeiten, 211), Tübingen: Niemeyer.

7 German spelling and its reform

English has long been renowned for the difficulties of its spelling system but German also provides many difficulties for those learning to read and write. German, like English, is written with an alphabetic writing system, each sound receiving a separate orthographic symbol. This makes it different from languages like Japanese, where each syllable is given a separate symbol, or Chinese, where each morpheme or word is given a separate sign.

The ideal situation in alphabetic writing systems is one symbol for each sound, or rather for each phoneme (a significant speech sound). Alphabets are said to be more or less 'phonemic' according to the degree in which they match up to this principle. Although this phonemic principle is desirable, it is not the only principle which may be appealed to in justifying the symbols of a writing system. Others that have been advanced and will be illustrated here are the phonemic principle, the morphophonemic principle, lexical principles and the grammatical principle.

7.1 THE PHONEMIC PRINCIPLE

The phonemic principle of one symbol or letter for one sound or phoneme shows many inconsistencies in German. In fact there are only three phonemes which are represented by just one letter: /j/, *ja*, *Boje* 'buoy'; /h/ *Hahn*; and /z/ which is written *s*, *sein*, *Sinn*, *lesen*. The latter two signs, *h* and *s*, are also used for other phonemes, as will be shown later. We will ignore for the moment the fact that letters occur as both small and capital letters since this is not reflected in pronunciation, for example *j*, *J*, *h*, *H*, *s*, *S*. The principle of one letter for one phoneme can be broken in several ways:

(a)   A phoneme may be represented by a cluster of two or more letters, for example /ʃ/ is spelt *sch*, as in *schon*, *waschen*, *Wunsch*, except before *t* and *p*; /x–ç/ is represented by the digraph (a cluster of two letters) *ch*, as in *ich*, *nach*, *Woche*, and /ŋ/ is spelt with the digraph *ng*, as in *lang*, *länger*.

(b) A phoneme may be spelt by several different letters which are in complementary distribution, i.e. one is used in one position in the word or before a certain letter and the other is used in a different position or before a different letter. The phoneme /ʃ/ is spelt *sch* in all positions except before *p* and *t* at the beginning of words, when it is written *s*, for example *schon*, *schreiben*, *schlimm*, *schnell*, *schwamm* but *stehen*, *sparen*. The phoneme /ʒ/, mostly found in French words, is spelt *j* before *a* or *o*, as in *Jalousie* 'blind', *Jargon*, *Journal*, but *g* before *i* and *e*, as in *Giro*, *Genie*, *arrangieren*, and medially after a stressed vowel and before unstressed *-e*, as in *Etage*, *Blamage*. The stops /p t k, b d g/, the nasals /m n/ and the liquids /l r/ are spelt double medially after a short vowel before unstressed *-e*, as in *Rippe*, *Sitte*, *Robbe* 'seal', *Kladde* 'rough book', *Roggen*, *schwimmen*, *sinnen*, *füllen*, *irren*. This also happens to the plosive /k/ but instead of the expected *kk*, which only appears when a word is divided to continue on the next line, the 'double sign' is *ck*, *Brücke*. The fricative /f/ is also involved in this rule, *Schiffe*, but other signs are used for this phoneme which will be discussed in (c). The voiceless plosives /p t k/ also have these double letters after short vowels in monosyllables, *schlapp*, *glatt*, *Blick*, but *bb*, *dd* and *gg* do not appear in this position. Double /m n/ also appear in monosyllables after short vowels, *Kamm*, *kann*, but some words, notably prepositions, are written with one *n*, as in *in*, *an*, *von* (but cf. *bin*). The liquids /l r/ are written double after short vowels in monosyllables, *soll*, *Narr*. The fricative /s/ also takes part in this rule, *wissen*, but has the additional complication that *ss* never appears finally, *ß* being written (apart from in Switzerland, where *ß* is not usually used), *gewiß*. (This letter comes from the old long typographic *s* and *z* being written together.) It is the only survival from the Gothic script. The letter *ß* is not only used finally instead of *ss* but also medially after long vowels and diphthongs, *Buße* 'repentance', *reißen*, *gießen*, and before inflectional endings, *ihr wiß-t*, *er muß-te*. The use of *ß* is one of the most controversial features of modern German spelling and it has been suggested that it should be replaced entirely by *ss* (see pp. 168, 171f.). Also under the heading of predictability of letters could come the use of *q* before *u* in the cluster *qu* for *k*, as in *Quelle*, *Qualität*, *Quittung* (the *u* is pronounced as a voiced [v]). There seems to have been no demand to change this cluster, whereas Dutch, for instance has *kw* in some common loan words, *kwaliteit, kwitantie* 'bill'.

(c) A phoneme may be spelt by several different letters but the distribution of the letters is largely random. For instance, some of the letters used for the phonemes /f/ and /v/ overlap/. The letter *w* is used for initial and medial /v/, *Wein, wo, Möwe*, but *v* occurs in foreign words, *Vase, vage, brave* (inflected form). After /l, r/ only *v* occurs, *Malve, Pulver, Salve*. The sign *v* is also used initially for /f/ in some words, *Vater, Vogel*, but *f* is used as well, *Fall, Fohlen*. For medial /f/ *ff* occurs after short vowels, *Schiffe*, and *f* after long vowels and diphthongs, *liefen, Schleife*, and follows the normal doubling rule. In the one word *Frevel* 'outrage', *v* is used for medial /f/. Before initial /l r/ *f* is used, *fließen, fressen*, with the one exception of the one word *Vließ* (nt.) 'fleece'. In Greek loan words the phoneme /f/ is written *ph, Physik, Orthographie, Apostroph*. The overlap in the use of the letter *v* for both /f/ and /v/ leads often to uncertainty in the pronunciation of *v* in non-initial position. In names such as *David, Eva, Sievers* or *Nerven* the *v* is sometimes pronounced as /f/ and sometimes as /v/.

The introduction of foreign words is one of the root causes of one single phoneme being spelt randomly by more than one letter. The chief offenders in this are learned words from Greek containing *ph, th* and *rh, physisch, theoretisch, rhythmisch*. The digraph *ph* is used for /f/, as we have seen, *th* for /t/ and *rh* for /r/. It has been suggested that in common foreign words *ph, th, rh* should be replaced by *f, t, r*, i.e. *fysisch, teoretisch, rytmisch* (see 7.4). A step in this direction has been allowing the variants, *Photo, Foto*; *Telephon, Telefon*. The phoneme /k/ initially is usually rendered by *k*, as in *kann, Kind*, but in foreign words it is rendered by *c*, as in *Café, Curry, Code, kh*, as in *Khaki*, and *ch*, as in *Charakter*. In South Germany *ch* before *i* or *e* renders /k/, *Chemie, Chirurg, China*, but in North German and the standard pronunciation the *ch* in these words is pronounced like the *ch* in *ich*, [ç]. The digraph *ch* is also used in some French loan words for the phoneme /ʃ/ *Chef, Champignon, Chance*.

The spelling of vowels from Greek does not present many difficulties except that for the long /yː/ the letter *y* is used, for example *Mythos, physisch*, whereas in German words *ü*, as in *über*, or *üh*, as in *Bühne*, are used. Loans from French and English show many different vowel signs for vowel phonemes. The digraph *ou* often occurs in French loans for /uː/, *Cousine, Routine*, but in English loans it is used for the diphthong [au], *Couch*, as is *ow*, as in *down*. The digraph *eu* is used for /ø:/ in the endings *-eur*, *-euse* for agentive nouns from verbs in *-ieren*, as in *frisieren*, *Friseur*, *Friseuse*, *massieren*, *Masseur*, *Masseuse*, although there is the variant form *-ör*, *-öse*. For an unstressed /i/ at the end of English words *y* is used, *Rowdy*, *Party*, *Pony*, *Teddy*. French nasal vowels are rendered by exactly the same spelling as in French: *Fonds*, *Teint*, *Chance*, *Bonbon*, but are pronounced in a different way. For more details of the spelling of foreign words see *Duden Aussprachewörterbuch* (Mangold 1990: 60–96).

(d)   Another but not so usual way for the orthography of a language to offend against the principle of one phoneme being rendered by one letter is if one letter is used for a cluster of phonemes, i.e. the exact opposite of (a). This is not frequent but the use of the letter *x* for /ks/, *Hexe*, exemplifies it, as does the use of the sequence [ks], generally spelt *cks*, as in *drucksen* 'to hum and haw', or *chs*, as in *wachsen*. The use of *z* initially for /ts/ is another, more important, example, *Zeit*, *Zins*, *Zug*. This, of course, assumes that we are regarding /ts/ as comprising two phonemes. This also occurs medially after long vowels and diphthongs, *duzen*, *siezen*, *Brezel*, *reizen*, but it is written *tz* after short vowels, *sitzen*, *Ketzer*, and *zz* in Italian loans, *Pizza*. In the words *Rätsel*, *Lotse* /ts/ is spelt *ts* after a long vowel. Finally after short vowels /ts/ is spelt *tz*, as in *Sitz*, *Schmutz* and after diphthongs and long vowels *z*, as in *Reiz*, *Flöz* 'stratum (in mining)'.

One of the most troublesome areas in German spelling is the designation of vowel length. The short vowels in German are written with one symbol each: /i/ *wissen*, /u/ *Busse*, /ü/ *müssen*, /ö/ *Schlösser*, /o/ *gossen*, /e/ *essen*, *Fässer* (the relationship between *e* and *ä* is dealt with in 7.2), /a/ *Gasse*, and in words of two syllables the doubling of the medial consonant shows that the preceding vowel is short. The quantity of long vowels, however, is shown in several ways: (1) in disyllabic words one letter may be followed by a single consonant, *geben*, *raten*; (2) the vowel letter may be doubled, *Saal*, *Boot*; or (3) it may be followed by *h*, as in *Stahl*, *lahm*, or in the case of /i:/ by *e*, as in *sieben*, *Lied*. These ways of designating long vowels are not used equally for all long vowels. Table 7.1 shows how they are distributed. The distribution of length signs is not entirely random. The letter *e* only appears after *i*, and only *o*, *e* and *a* can be doubled. The letters *i* and *y* are mostly used in foreign words: *Mine*, *Tiger*, *Maschine*; *Mythos*, *physisch*, *zynisch*. The length sign *h* is used before *l*, *m*, *n*, *r*, as in *kahl*, *nahm*, *Lohn*, *wahr*, and only exceptionally before other consonants, *Fehde* 'feud', *Naht*, and in the inflected forms of verbs whose stems end in the letter *h*, for example *nähen*, *du nähst*, *er näht*.

The signs *ü* and *i* do not appear in monosyllables in word-final position alone but always followed by *h*, as in *früh*, or, in the case of *i*, by *e*, as in *sie*. Although the doubled vowels do not usually appear in open syllables, the important exceptions are plural forms *Aale*, *Haare*, *Paare*, *Staaten*; *Beeren*, *Beeten*; *Boote*, *Moose*, and words such as *Waage*, *Seele*, *verheeren*. In these examples the doubling of the letters to show vowel length is unnecessary since the occurrence of a vowel letter before a single medial consonant shows that the latter is long. Similarly the length sign *h* is used unnecessarily in the following examples since the vowel is long by position: *lehnen*, *stehlen*, *nehmen*, *lehren*. Before medial and final /x/, spelt *ch*, the spelling does not show whether the preceding vowel is short or long: *Rache* (short), *Sprache* (long); *Koch* (short), *hoch* (long). Long vowels are also designated with one letter in closed syllables if the vowel alternates with a long vowel in an open syllable in inflected forms: *Tag*, *Tages*; *legt*, *gelegt*, *legen*. Before consonant clusters there is no way of telling from the orthography whether a vowel is short or long since it will always be written with a single letter: *Herd* (long), *Herz* (short); *düster* (long), *Küste* (short).

Table 7.1 Designation of long vowels

Phoneme	Spelling	Examples
/iː/	i, ih, ie, ieh	Bibel, ihn, sieben, sieht
/uː/	u, uh	Stube, Stuhl
/yː/	ü, üh, y	lügen, früh, physisch
/oː/	o, oo, oh	loben, Boot, Sohn
/øː/	ö, öh	hören, Höhle
/eː/	e, ee, eh	geben, See, Lehrer
/ɛː/	ä, äh	Käse, Nähte
/aː/	a, aa, ah	baden, Saal, Sahne

7.2 THE MORPHOPHONEMIC PRINCIPLE

In an inflected language like German with many words or stems appearing in several inflected forms, often with different pronunciation, the spelling of the different inflected forms may reflect the difference of pronunciation or else it can maintain the unity of the word or stem by always writing it the same. This is the case when the differences are automatically conditioned by the phonetic environment. In final position in German only voiceless obstruents occur, and thus in any stem with a medial voiced obstruent, this will automatically be changed to a voiceless obstruent when it appears in word-final position, for example /taːges/ gen. but /taːk/ nom./acc. Such an automatic alternation is called morphophonemic. In normalized MHG texts this alternation, and similar ones, affecting *b* and *p*, *d* and *t*, was shown directly in spelling: MHG *tages, tac; wîbes, wîp; todes, tot*. This is fully consistent with the principle of one letter for each phoneme wherever it occurs. However, in NHG this principle has been overruled by the principle of maintaining the unity of words and stems (*Schemakonstanz*). Thus we have in NHG *Tages, Weibes, Todes* and the nom./acc. forms *Tag, Weib, Tod*. This uniform writing of words and stems is the implementation of the morphophonemic principle. This also occurs in English words, for example *nation, national*, where the first vowel *a* is pronounced differently in each word. The uninflected words *ab, ob*, and *irgend, ihr seid* have their final consonant written *b* and *d* although they have no medial forms with *b* or *d*. This morphophonemic principle affects *s*, as in *lesen* (voiced), *las* (voiceless), and *v*, as in *brave*, (voiced), *brav* (voiceless). It is also used in word formation, *tödlich, todmüde* and *Todfeind* are derived form *Tod, Todes*. Double consonants used after vowels to show that the vowels are short are retained in inflected forms as shown here:

pp: kippen, er kippt(e), kipp!
tt: wir schnitten, er schnitt; glatter, glatt
ck: blicken, er blickt; die Blicke, der Blick
ff: wir pfiffen, er pfiff
ss/ß: wissen, gewiß, gewußt
mm: glimmen, es glimmt, glomm
nn: rinnen, er rinnt, er rann
ll: sollen, er soll, ihr sollt
rr: irren, er irrt, irr!

This does not affect medial double consonants before unstressed syllables. In these latter cases the double consonant is replaced by a single one in word-final position: *nn, Königinnen, Königin; ss, Hindernisse, Hindernis; Atlasse, Atlas*. This also applies to the following words: *der As, Asse*, 'ace', *der Gros, Grosse* 'a gross' and *der Bus, Busse*, although in this last case this may be due to the longer form *Omnibus, Omnibusse*.

The relationship between the letters *ä* and *e*, which are both used for the short phoneme /ɛ/, is also governed largely by morphology. If the word containing /ɛ/ has an inflected form or related word containing *a* then it is written *ä*. This can be in inflection: sg. *Gast*, pl. *Gäste*; comparison of adjectives, *schwach*, *schwächer*, *am schwächsten*; second and third person sg. pres. of strong verbs: *fallen*, *du fällst*, *er fällt*; subjunctive of strong verbs, and some irregular verbs, *fand*, *fände*, *brachte*, *brächte* (but note the subjunctive of verbs like *nennen* which are written with *e*, *nennte*, and not with *ä*!); and in word formation: *arm*, *ärmlich*; *Faß*, *Fäßchen*; *krank*, *kränklich*; *kalt*, *Kälte*; *Kraft*, *kräftig*. In some cases homonyms are distinguished by writing *e* and *ä* (see 7.3.1).

There are three main diphthongs in modern German, /ai/, /au/ and /oi/ (or /oy/). In interjections /ui/ also occurs, *pfui!* The diphthong /au/ is spelt *au* in German words, *glauben*, *faul*, *laut*, but in some foreign words it is also spelt *ou*, as in *Couch*, *foul* and *ow*, as in *Clown*, *Rowdy*. The diphthong /ai/ is spelt *ei*, but also *ai* in some words, *Kaiser*, *Haifisch*, *Mai*, *Kai*, *Mais*. Some names are spelt with *ey*, as in *Speyer*, and *ay*, as in *Karl May*, *Bayern*. An orthographic distinction is made between *bayerisch* 'belonging to Bavaria' and *bairisch* 'belonging to the Bavarian dialect'. In the foreign words *Linotype* and *Nylon* the diphthong /ai/ is spelt *y*. The stems of some words with *ei* end in *h*, which is kept in the inflected forms, for example *leihen*, *er leiht*, *Verleih*. Also affected by the morphophonemic principle is the spelling of the diphthong /oi/. This is spelt *äu* if it results from mutation of *au*, as in *gläubig* from *glauben*, pl. *Häuser* sg. *Haus*, *du läufst*, *er läuft* from *laufen*. Otherwise it is spelt *eu* in German words, *Freund*, *Freude*. A few words are still spelt with *äu* although their connection with a related word with *au* is tenuous or now non-existent: *Knäuel*, *Säule*, *läutern* (originally related to *lauter*), *räudig*, *räuspern*, *sträuben*. In foreign words and names it is also spelt *oi*, as in *Boiler*, *Konvoi*, *Loipe* 'cross-country ski run' (from Norwegian) and in the exclamation *ahoi!* and *toi*, *toi*, *toi!* 'touch wood' and *oy*, *Boy*, *Boykott*.

7.3   LEXICAL PRINCIPLES

Several different orthographic principles are covered under this heading. The clearest example in this category is the homonymy principle, that of writing words differently that are pronounced the same, for example *malen* 'to paint' and *mahlen* 'to grind'. Other phenomena show an affinity with syntax: for instance, the use of capital and lower-case letters (*Groß- und Kleinschreibung*) distinguishes lexical items but according to their word class, for example nouns are capitalized.

The writing of items as one word or two separate words (*Zusammen-
und Getrenntschreibung*) deals again with individual lexical items, but
in this case is not restricted to a single word class, but it affects the
syntax of the sentence.

7.3.1   The homonymy principle

One of the advantages of the written language is that different letters
can be used for the same sound thus distinguishing words which are
pronounced the same, homonyms. The list below shows how the
different signs for vowel length are used in this way (for the use of
capital and lower-case letters in this way, see 7.3.2):

wider	against	*wieder*	again
das Lid	eye-lid	*das Lied*	song
die Mine	mine, refill	*die Miene*	air, countenance
der Stil	style	*der Stiel*	stick
das Mal	time, occasion	*das Mahl*	meal
malen	to paint	*mahlen*	to grind
der Fön	hair-dryer	*der Föhn*	warm Alpine wind
die Dole	drain, culvert	*die Dohle*	jackdaw
die Sole	saltwater	*die Sohle*	sole
das Meer	sea	*mehr*	more
leeren	empty	*lehren*	teach

The usual digraph for /ai/ is *ei* but *ai* is used to distinguish between
homonyms:

das Laib	loaf	*der Leib*	body
die Saite	string of an instrument	*die Seite*	side
die Waise	orphan	*die Weise*	way, manner
schwaigen	to make cheese	*schweigen*	to be silent

The letters *ä* and *e* are also used to distinguish homonyms:

die Blässe	paleness	*die Blesse*	blaze, white spot
die Äsche	grayling (fish)	*die Esche*	ash (tree)
die Färse	heifer	*die Ferse*	heel
die Lärche	larch	*die Lerche*	lark
die Stärke	strength	*die Sterke**	heifer
rächen	to avenge	*rechen*	to rake
schlämmen	to dredge	*schlemmen*	to carouse

* North German

Among the consonant signs there are fewer examples of their use to differentiate between homonyms. The sign *ß* is used in *daß* 'that' (conjunction) to distinguish it from *das* 'the, that' (article, demonstrative or relative pronoun). In word-final position *d* and *t* are used to distinguish *ihr seid* from *seit* 'since'. The use of the letters *f* and *v* in initial position help to distinguish *fiel* 'fell' and *viel* 'much'.

7.3.2   The use of capital and lower-case letters (*Groß- und Kleinschreibung*)

One of the unique characteristics of German is the use of capital letters for all nouns, not just proper names. Thus in the sentence *Es gibt in der deutschen Sprache große und kleine Buchstaben, aber keine großen und kleinen Laute in der Aussprache* (Augst 1984: 60) the words *Sprache*, *Buchstaben*, *Laute*, *Aussprache* have initial capital letters and are nouns. However, the word *Es* also begins with a capital letter but is not a noun. The capital letter is, of course, explained by the word being at the beginning of a sentence. This is an exception to the purely lexical use of capital letters and brings in a syntactic criterion. Another exception is illustrated by the words *Ihnen*, *Sie* for 'you (polite)' as against *ihnen*, *sie* 'they'. In this instance we have the complementary use of another principle, the homonymy principle, to distinguish between two separate meanings and functions. The rules for the use of capital and lower-case letters have become rather complicated. *Duden 1: Rechtschreibung* (Drosdowski *et al.* 1991) contains twenty-two rules, the more detailed Mentrup (1968) contains eighty-two rules and long lists of exceptions, while Ewald and Nerius (1988) contains forty-eight rules. In all the investigations of the frequency of types of spelling mistakes, the difficulties with capital and lower-case letters figure prominently. Over a quarter of spelling mistakes, disregarding punctuation, are in this realm. This is further confirmed by the letters written to the *Duden*. In a sample of letters from 1988, 140 out of 420 enquiries about orthographic topics, excluding punctuation, featured use of capital or lower-case letters. As we shall see, different factions interested in reforming German spelling have taken up cudgels in this area. In the 1970s there was a strong movement to restrict capitalization to sentence-initial position, names and the polite pronouns *Ihnen*, *Sie*. This was called the *gemäßigte Kleinschreibung* and is used for the whole of Drewitz and Reuter (1974). The periodical *Zeitschrift für germanistische Linguistik* appeared from 1973 to 1976 entirely in *gemäßigte Kleinschreibung*.

The use of capitals has been attacked on the linguistic grounds that it does not reflect any difference in pronunciation but membership of a grammatical word class. Even in this case it is often not at all clear, especially in the case of the nominalization of other parts of speech, when a word is considered to have become a noun. As we have seen, the present rules are very complicated. This has led critics of the use of capitals to argue that the learning of these complicated rules takes up so much time for both pupils and teachers that its abolition would provide more time and effort for more important matters. Similarly in business, the abolition of capitals would enable typists to do their work more quickly, leaving time and effort for other things. This has been proved by the few firms who have tried to introduce the extended use of lower-case letters. Critics of the abolitionists say that to restrict the use of capital letters would mean a break with the past. Would people still be able to read the German classics? They also maintain that it is a myth that the restriction of capital letters would make it easier for children to master spelling. As some children are gifted in mathematics or art or languages and find other subjects difficult, so some children are gifted in spelling and some are not. The problem would not be solved by abolishing capitals except at the beginning of sentences, proper names and pronouns of address. They also maintain that texts where capitals are used to designate nouns are easier to read, one can see at a glance which are the nouns. Most of these reasons are difficult to evaluate but they also try to give linguistic reasons: for instance, they have tried to find sentences where the use of capital letters affects the meaning of the sentence. One example which is often quoted is *Er hat in Berlin liebe genossen* (*kleinschreibung*). For the critics this sentence is ambiguous and its two meanings can be resolved by using capitals for the appropriate words: *Er hat in Berlin Liebe genossen* 'He enjoyed love in Berlin' and *Er hat in Berlin liebe Genossen* 'He has dear comrades in Berlin'. However, one could argue that in the spoken language intonation and word stress would clearly differentiate between the two meanings, with the stress on *Liebe* or *Genossen*. The polemic between the two camps has been quite fierce at times and spelling reform is still a subject which is difficult to discuss objectively. For the development of different suggestions, see 7.4.

7.3.3   The writing of items as one orthographic word or two separate words (*Zusammen- und Getrenntschreibung*)

An orthographic word is a sequence of letters between two spaces. It can be a simple form, *Land*, a form with a suffix or prefix, *ländlich*, *untreu*, or a compound, comprising two words which can occur on their own, *Haustür*, *Fensterscheibe*, *eislaufen*, *radfahren*. Compounds are very often, but not invariably, written as one orthographic word. The verb *radfahren* is one orthographic word but *Auto fahren* is two. In some instances the writing of a form as one orthographic word or two can reflect a difference in meaning, for example *gutschreiben* 'to credit' vs *gut schreiben* 'to write well'. This is perhaps an even trickier area than capitalization since it can apply to words of most word classes. Although it only occurred as 7.75 per cent of spelling mistakes, disregarding punctuation, it occurred in 103 enquiries on orthography, excluding punctuation, that reached the *Duden* in 1988. Again, the rules for writing items as one word or two separate words have become rather complicated. *Duden Rechtschreibung* (Drosdowski *et al.* 1991) contains a mere eight rules, whereas the more detailed Mentrup (1968) contains eighty-five rules and long lists of exceptions; Herberg and Baudusch (1989) is more detailed and contains 111 rules. Some idea of the complexity of the situation can be gauged by looking at the list below. This gives the contrasting forms of some lexical items comprising one vs two orthographic words for a variety of different parts of speech or word classes:

> noun + verb: *Auto fahren* vs *radfahren*
> adj./participle + verb: *breit schlagen* vs *breitschlagen*
> verb + verb: *hängen bleiben* vs *hängenbleiben*
> adverb + verb: *da bleiben* vs *dableiben*
> preposition + verb: *mit arbeiten* vs *mitarbeiten*
> noun + adjective: *der Stab war wie ein kleiner Finger dick* vs *ein fingerdicker Stab*
> adjective + adjective: *bitter kalt* vs *bitterkalt*
> adverb + adjective: *eben soviel* vs *ebensoviel*
> adjective + participle: *nahe stehend* vs *nahestehend*
> adverb/pronoun + participle: *darauf folgend* vs *darauffolgend*
> adverb + adverb: *wie viel* vs *wieviel*

7.4 THE NORMALIZATION OF GERMAN ORTHOGRAPHY AND SUGGESTIONS FOR REFORM

In 1901 a spelling conference took place at which a normative system of spelling for the whole of German-speaking Europe was agreed upon. This was a modified form of the system used in Prussian and Bavarian schools as exemplified in Konrad Duden's *Vollständiges Orthographisches Wörterbuch der deutschen Sprache* (1st edn 1880). The main changes agreed in 1901 were to substitute *t* for *th* initially before vowels, *Thal* became *Tal* (*Thron* remained, however); *z* was substituted for *c* before *i*, *Elektrizität* for *Elektricität*; *aa* was reduced to *a* in some words, *Waare, baar* became *Ware, bar*. In 1902 the new spelling system was used officially by the German Empire and Austria. In Switzerland it had been accepted since 1892. The seventh edition of Konrad Duden's *Orthographisches Wörterbuch* contained the subtitle *Nach den für Deutschland, Österreich und die Schweiz gültigen amtlichen Regeln*. In his foreword Konrad Duden (1829–1911), whose surname has become used as a tradename for the books published by the Dudenverlag, said that he regarded his dictionary as only being an intermediate stage (*Zwischenziel*) and hinted that more spelling reforms might be needed but that no one need worry about when they would come about. The successor of the *Orthographisches Wörterbuch* is the *Duden Rechtschreibung*, which was published in a separate edition in Leipzig between 1951 and 1985. The spelling system set out in both volumes was no different from that of the seventh edition of 1902, except that roman type is now used instead of Gothic type. In 1991 the twentieth edition was published for a united Germany.

The 1901 orthographic system had its critics from the beginning and movements for spelling reform have continued ever since. Mostly these were lone voices but pressure groups such as the Swiss Bund für vereinfachte rechtschreibung, founded in 1924, and similar societies in Germany and Austria, always kept interest in spelling reform alive. However, any moves could only come from all the countries concerned taking common steps. After 1933 this proved impossible and thus it was not till after 1945 that common discussions of spelling reform could get underway again. Enthusiasm was great and interested parties from the Federal Republic of Germany (including, however, such East German scholars as Theodor Frings, Ruth Klappenbach and Wolfgang Steinitz), Austria and Switzerland formed the Arbeitsgemeinschaft für Sprachpflege, which discussed ways of reforming the spelling of German. On 16 May 1954 they produced their suggestions, *Empfehlungen zur Erneuerung der deutschen Rechtschreibung*, at a conference in Stuttgart, whence the name *Stuttgarter Empfehlungen*. The recommendations were accepted unanimously by all members of the working party and were submitted to the authorities in the Federal Republic of Germany, Austria and Switzerland (*Stuttgarter Empfehlungen* 1955). They contained the following eight points plus an appendix about the designation of vowel length:

1 Lower-case letters should be used for the initial letter of all words, except at the beginning of sentences, proper names, for pronouns of address, certain abbreviations and designations of God. This is called for the first time *gemäßigte Kleinschreibung*.

2 There should be a uniformity in consonant clusters. This would mean replacing *tz* by *z*, *spitzen* – *spizen*, *ß* would become *ss*. In the case of the creation of consonant clusters with three members the same, the three would be reduced to two, for example *Schiffahrt*, but if the word was divided at the end of a line, the third consonant would re-appear, for example *Schiff-fahrt*.

3 Orthographic variants are to be dispensed with and only one form allowed.

4 The assimilation of foreign words to the German spelling system should go further than at present, replacing *ph*, *th*, *rh* by *f*, *t*, *r* and short unstressed *y* by *i*. The sequence *ti*, if pronounced [tsi], should be spelt *zi*, for example *Sensazion* instead of *Sensation*. The replacement of *c* by *z* and *k*, *eu* by *ö* and other substitutions in loan words should continue.

5 There should be more writing of lexical items as two separate words rather than one. To illustrate this the committee simply give a list of examples.

6 In word division at the end of lines the cluster *st* should also be divided, for example *Kas-ten* (traditionally this does not happen, *Ka-sten*). On the other hand, *ck* should be treated like *sch*, *ch*, and not divided: *lo-cken*, *wa-schen*, *ma-chen*. In addition foreign words are to be divided like German words, for example *Pä-da-go-gik* instead of the word being divided *Päd-ago-gik*.

7 Punctuation should be simplified by less use of commas, particularly before *und* and *oder* and before infinitive constructions.

8 Names are unaffected by these suggestions.

The designation of vowel length was also examined and it was suggested that the length marker *h* could be dispensed with after vowels other than *e*, with the exceptions of the pronouns *ihm*, *ihn*. They also suggest that *ie* should be replaced by *i* except before *ss*.

The result of the publication of these recommendations was that in 1956 the Minister of the Interior and the Permanent Conference of Education Ministers of the *Länder* of the Federal Republic of Germany set up the Arbeitskreis für Rechtschreibregelung, which in turn set up three committees, the first to look into the use of capital and lower-case letters and the designation of vowel quantity, the second to deal with punctuation, foreign words (*Fremdwörter*) and variant forms, and the third to deal with problems of syllable division and which words should be written together as one word or as two separate words. The members were all from the Federal Republic of Germany, being academics, representatives of publishing houses, journalists and trade-unionists. In October 1958 the working party produced their recommendations which have become known as the *Wiesbadener Empfehlungen*. The text was published as *Empfehlungen* (1959) and is reprinted in Drewitz and Reuter (1974: 139–64). They made six major recommendations, all of which were also to be found in the *Stuttgarter Empfehlungen*:

1 The use of lower-case letters was to be extended to all words except in the following cases: at the beginning of sentences, in proper names, polite pronouns of address, for example *Sie*, *Ihr*, *Ihnen*, and for certain specialist, usually scientific, abbreviations, for example H_2O.
2 The comma was not to be used for marking grammatical or syntactic divisions unless the writer felt it to be appropriate (this is probably the weakest of the recommendations).
3 Syllable divisions should follow speech and not sense divisions.
4 No variant spellings should be allowed.
5 The spelling of foreign words should be made to fit the German spelling system as far as possible.
6 Only genuine compounds should be written together as one word. If in doubt the words should be written separately.

Other points such as the simplification of consonant clusters, for example *tz* to *z*, and designation of vowel length were not accepted. The *Wiesbadener Empfehlungen* thus dealt primarily with spelling matters not affecting the phoneme–letter relationships; in other words, it affected least the visible form of words (*Schriftbild*). These conclusions, which did not imply any action on the part of the government, were accepted by the working party with fourteen votes for and three against. During the following years it was decided to test opinion in Austria and Switzerland. However, voting among the members of the Austrian Commission on Spelling (Österreichische Kommission für Rechtschreibung), which was set up in 1960, resulted in a tie, 10 : 10, and in 1963 the Swiss Conference on Spelling Reform (Schweizerische Konferenz für die Rechtschreibereform), meeting in Zurich, rejected the recommendations with only one vote in favour. The GDR was apparently in favour of reform on the basis of the recommendations but there seems to have been no official statement of their interest and willingness. With lack of support in Austria and Switzerland for their recommendations the working party in the Federal Republic of Germany did not themselves press their recommendations further.

This defeat for spelling reform only proved a temporary setback, and pressure to introduce the *Wiesbadener Empfehlungen* steadily mounted in the years that followed. In July 1972 the Conference of Germanists at *Pädagogische Hochschulen* in North-Rhine-Westphalia passed a resolution that *gemäßigte Kleinschreibung* should be used in the primary school (*Grundschule*). This resolution was supported by section I of the Conference of Germanists in Trier in October 1973. On 6 October 1973 in Frankfurt-on-Main an important conference, *vernünftiger schreiben*, was held, which was organized by the PEN-Zentrum of the Federal Republic of Germany, the Association of German Writers (Verband deutscher Schriftsteller) and the Trade Union for Education and Science (Gewerkschaft für Erziehung und Wissenschaft). At the end of the congress a resolution was passed by 156 votes to three in favour of introducing *gemäßigte Kleinschreibung* and other recommendations of 1958. In addition, the participants wanted to substitute *ss* for *ß* and the use of the form *das* for both the article and pronoun *das* and the conjunction *daß*. This was something which had not been suggested in 1958 but had been put forward by the other conferences in 1972 and 1973. The letter *ß* is, of course, hardly used in Switzerland and not when words are printed in capitals, for example DER GROSSE DUDEN. Representatives from Austria and Switzerland were present and spoke up in favour of the outlined reforms. Representatives from the GDR were invited but did not attend. A sign of the interest in the reform is that the proceedings of the congress were published, using *gemaßigte Kleinschreibung* naturally (see Drewitz and Reuter 1974).

Interest in reform was still maintained by scholars and lay people in the different German-speaking countries who founded the *internationaler arbeitskreis für deutsche rechtschreibung* in 1973 with its headquarters in Tuttlingen. The pace quickened up after Dieter

Nerius became head of the research group *Orthographie* in the GDR Academy of Sciences and a Kommission für Rechtschreibfragen was established by the Institut für deutsche Sprache in Mannheim, headed by Wolfgang Mentrup. Starting in 1978 with a conference in Vienna scholars representing all the German-speaking countries worked together in the late 1970s and throughout the 1980s to produce sets of rules for different areas of German orthography: use of capital and lower-case letters, syllabification of words at the end of lines, punctuation, words written separately or together, the use of *s/ss/ß* and foreign words (Kommission für Rechtschreibfragen 1985). In Vienna in 1986 these areas were officially recognized as being those where the rules of spelling had become too complicated since 1901. In February 1987 the commission was officially asked by the Permanent Conference of Education Ministers of the *Länder* of the Federal Republic of Germany to prepare suggestions for reforming the German spelling system for all the areas except the use of capital and lower-case letters. This omission, or rather postponement, since a reform suggestion is envisaged at a later date, is because the commission and the Gesellschaft für deutsche Sprache agreed to differ on their suggestions in Vienna in 1986. In October 1988 the commission was able to submit their suggestions to the Permanent Conference of Education Ministers for the five areas (Kommission für Rechtschreibfragen 1989):

1 Punctuation. The use of commas was regulated by making them compulsory after exclamation and question marks, for example *'Kommst du morgen?', sagte er*; and *'Komm bitte morgen!', sagte er*. Commas may be omitted in main clauses before *und* and *oder*, for example *Der Vater liest und die Mutter hört Radio*, and before infinitive constructions, unless the sense demands it, for example *Ich hoffe sehr dich morgen wieder zu sehen*, but *Ich hoffte, gestern in die Stadt gehen zu können*. Both these suggestions were to be found already in the *Stuttgarter Empfehlungen*.

2 Division of words at the end of a line. The cluster *st* could be divided and foreign words syllabified like German words. Again, both suggestions were contained in the *Stuttgarter Empfehlungen*.

3 Writing lexical items as one word or two (*Zusammen- und Getrenntschreibung*). The norm should be to write these as separate words, thus *kennen lernen, liegen lassen, sitzen bleiben*. This takes the general idea from the *Stuttgarter Empfehlungen* but makes it explicit.

4   Phoneme–letter relationship. This area affected the 'look' of individual words and groups of words. There were three main areas affected: the doubling of vowels, except for *ee*, should be dropped, for example (1) *Haar* > *Har*, *Boot* > *Bot*; (2) *ai* > *ei* in nine words *Meis* < *Mais*; and (3) *ä* > *e* in a small number of words, for example *demmern* < *dämmern*. Where there is a need to distinguish between homonyms the opposition *ai* : *ei* and *ä* : *e* remained. The following, rather nonsensical, sentence, which is given according to the new rules, illustrates the proposed changes: *Der Keiser streubt sich gegen die Statsgeschäfte und fängt liber im Mor Ale.* According to the present orthography it is *Der Kaiser sträubt sich gegen die Staatsgeschäfte und fängt lieber im Moore Aale* ('The Emperor shows reluctance for affairs of state and would rather catch eels in the marsh'!). These suggestions did not feature in the *Stuttgarter Empfehlungen*.

5   Foreign words, including the question of variant forms. Both foreign and nativized forms, such as *chic*, *schick*, would be allowed to co-exist for about ten years, after which one would be omitted. It may be either the foreign or the nativized form. This was more generous than the *Stuttgarter Empfehlungen*, which recommended the abolition of variants.

The Permanent Conference of Education Ministers reacted swiftly, but negatively, rejecting the recommendations in 1990. Predictably (4), which changed the 'look' of words, seemed to have caused most upset among journalists and the public.

Nothing daunted, the scholars submitted further recommendations in 1992 (Internationaler Arbeitskreis für Orthographie 1992) for six areas, including capital and lower-case letters. The suggestions for the different areas are:

(A)   Phoneme–letter relationship. The suggestions of 1988 have been dropped, except for the substitution of *ä* for *e* in several words, for example *überschwänglich*. The main guiding principle has been uniform shape for morphemes (*Schemakonstanz*). This leads to the following changes: *nummerieren*, cf. *Nummer*; *platzieren*, cf. *Platz*, *Ass*, cf. *Asse*; and *fitt*, cf. *fitter*. Sequences of three consonants are allowed, *Schifffahrt*, and *h* introduced before *-heit*, as in *Rohheit*. The alternation of *ss* and *ß* is regulated to allow *ß* only after long vowels and diphthongs, *weiß*, *gießen*. The sequence *ss* thus gains ground, being allowed to occur word- and morpheme-finally after a short vowel: *wisst*, *müsst*; *Kuss*, *Fluss*. The distinction between *das* (neuter article and relative prounoun) and *daß* (conjunction) is eliminated in favour of *das* for both functions.

(B)   Writing lexical items as one word or two (*Zusammen- und Getrenntschreibung*). As in 1988 the norm is to write items as separate words, for example *kennen lernen*, even if there is difference in meaning, for example *sitzen bleiben*.

(C)   The use of the hyphen is recommended for compounds where one part is a proper name or an abbreviation, for example *Foto-Müller*, *MRW-Sender*. This was not tackled in 1988.

(D)   The use of capital and lower-case letters (*Groß- und Kleinschreibung*). This was an area where recommendations were not put forward in 1988 because of disagreements within the group. This time the way forward has been to submit three alternatives: (D1) the status quo; (D2) modified use of capital letters, containing rules for use of both capital and lower-cases letters; and (D3) writing nouns with lower-case letters except for, (1) the first word of a heading, title or address, (2) the beginning of sentences, (3) proper names, and pronouns of address, for example *Sie*, *Ihr*, and titles such as *Eure Magnifizenz*.

(E)   In punctuation the use of the comma is simplified as in the 1988 recommendations.

(F)   The syllabification of words again follows the recommendations of 1988, allowing the division of *st* and recommending the German syllabification of foreign words.

Whether these recommendations will find favour with politicians is uncertain. It may be that other more pressing problems will delay any discussion and decision. However, after the unification of Germany it would seem appropriate if a modest reform, as exemplified by these recommendations, could take place before the twenty-first century. Many of them have been suggested for about forty years!

7.5 ILLUSTRATIVE TEXTS IN *GEMÄßIGTE KLEINSCHREIBUNG*

Here are some illustrations of *gemäßigte Kleinschreibung*. Readers are left to judge for themselves whether they think it has advantages over the traditional state of affairs.

1   Die schrift ist ein mittel der sprachdarstellung, die rechtschreibung ist die normierte form dieses mittels. Die sprache kann ohne schrift bestehen, die schrift oder die rechtschreibung ohne sprache ist undenkbar. Es ist unbestritten, daß die rechtschreibung im dienste der sprache steht, die sie optisch fixiert. Kann die rechtschreibung ihre aufgabe im dienste der sprache nicht mehr erfüllen, so muß sie den veränderten sprachverhältnissen angepaßt werden.

(Drewitz and Reuter 1974: 129)

2   Unser vorschlag: Setzen Sie sich in Ihrem bereich für die kleinschreibung ein! Schreiben Sie alles klein, was Sie in eigener verantwortung schreiben. Befürworten Sie die verwendung der neuen ortografie in Ihrer firma, in Ihrem verein, in Ihrer gemeinde, in Ihrer zeitung oder in anderen publikationen.

Als lehrer sind Sie mitverantwortlich für das verhältnis, das die heutige und die kommende generation zur rechtschreibung haben.

(leaflet from *Bund für vereinfachte
rechtschreibung*, Zurich 1976)

3   In einem von akademikern bewohnten haus in Düsseldorf steht schon seit jahr und tag an der innenseite der kellertür eine aufforderung zum abschließen der tür mit einigen orthographischen fehlern, ohne korrekturen. Hintergründe oder beweggründe solchen verhaltens zeigen die soziale einschätzung der richtigkeit der rechtschreibung. Man möchte von sozialkritischer komik und lächerlichkeit sprechen. Es ist nicht gelogen, ein lehrer, der später schulrat wurde, hat seine erste liebesgeschichte spontan abgebrochen, als er von seiner freundin einen brief mit ein paar orthographischen fehlern bekam. Wie viele briefe oder eingaben werden aus angst von rechtschreibfehlern überhaupt nicht erst geschrieben! Und das telefon kann nicht immer ersatzdienste leisten.

(Drewitz and Reuter 1974: 18)

SELECT BIBLIOGRAPHY AND FURTHER READING

Augst, G. (1977) 'Rechtschreibung – Schlechtschreibung', in G. Augst, *Sprachnorm und Sprachwandel: vier Projekte zu diachroner Sprachbetrachtung* (Studienbücher zur Linguistik und Literaturwissenschaft, 7), Wiesbaden: Athenaion, pp. 179–225.

—— (1984) 'Der Buchstabe', in *Duden 4: Grammatik*, Mannheim: Bibliographisches Institut, pp. 59–87.

Drewitz, I. and Reuter, E. (1974) *vernünftiger schreiben. reform der rechtschreibung*, Frankfurt: Fischer.

Drosdowski, G., Scholze-Stubenrecht, W. and Wermke, M. (1991) *Duden 1: Die deutsche Rechtschreibung*, 20th edn, Mannheim: Dudenverlag.

Empfehlungen des Arbeitskreises für Rechtschreibregelung (1959) Authentischer Text (Duden-Beiträge 2), Mannheim: Bibliographisches Institut: also in I. Drewitz and E. Reuter *vernünftiger schreiben. reform der rechtschreibung*, Frankfurt: Fischer, 1974, pp. 139–64.

Ewald, P. and Nerius, D. (1988) *Die Groß- und Kleinschreibung im Deutschen: die geltende Regelung Problemfälle und Schwierigkeiten*, Leipzig: Bibliographisches Institut.

Herberg, D. and Baudusch, R. (1989) *Getrennt oder zusammen? Ratgeber zu einem schwierigen Rechtschreibkapitel*, Leipzig: Bibliographisches Institut.

Internationaler Arbeitskreis für Orthographie (1992) *Deutsche Rechtschreibung. Vorschläge zu ihrer Neuregelung*, Tübingen: Narr.

Kommission für Rechtschreibfragen (1985) *Die Rechtschreibung des Deutschen und ihre Neuregelung* (Sprache der Gegenwart, 66), Düsseldorf: Schwann.

—— (1989) *Zur Neuregelung der deutschen Rechtschreibung* (Sprache der Gegenwart, 77), Düsseldorf: Schwann.

Mangold, M. (ed.) (1990) *Duden 6: Aussprachwörterbuch*, 3rd edn, Mannheim: Dudenverlag.

Mentrup, W. (1968) *Die Regeln der deutschen Rechtschreibung: an zahlreichen Beispielen erläutert* (Duden Taschenbücher, 3), Mannheim: Bibliographisches Institut.

Nerius, D. (ed.) (1987) *Deutsche Orthographie*, Leipzig: Bibliographisches Institut.

Riehme, J. (1988) *Gleich gesprochen – verschieden geschrieben. Zum Verwechseln ähnliche Wörter und ihre richtige Schreibung*, Leipzig: Bibliographisches Institut.

Stuttgarter Empfehlungen (1955) 'Empfehlungen zur Erneuerung der deutschen Rechtschreibung', *Der Deutschunterricht*, 3: 125–8; repr. in B. Garbe (ed.) *Die deutsche rechtschreibung und ihre reform 1722–1974* (Reihe Germanistische Linguistik, 10), Tübingen: Niemeyer, 1978, pp. 137–41.

Weisgerber, L. (1964) *Die Verantwortung für die Schrift. Sechzig Jahre Bemühungen um eine Rechtschreibreform* (Duden-Beiträge, 18), Mannheim: Bibliographisches Institut.

Zabel, H. (ed.) (1987) *Fremdwortorthographie: Beiträge zu historischen und aktuellen Fragestellungen* (Reihe Germanistische Linguistik, 79), Tübingen: Niemeyer.

8 German grammar

8.1 THE NATURE OF GRAMMAR

Many people probably regard grammar as rather a dirty word. It is equated in learning one's mother tongue with such exercises as dividing sentences into phrases and clauses, then parsing each word, i.e. assigning them to a part of speech, or in the case of learning a foreign language by rote learning of innumerable exceptions. It has even been abandoned by many in favour of learning language in a 'natural' way, i.e. the way one acquires one's native language.

We will regard the main task of the grammar of a language as giving us a description of every sentence in the language which is grammatical and the constructions needed to produce it. By 'grammatical' we mean correct, acceptable to native speakers. In consideration of what is correct we must, however, clearly distinguish descriptive and prescriptive grammar. The former is an approach to grammar which seeks simply to describe actual usage, both spoken and written, the latter seeks to prescribe usage, i.e. to tell users of the language what they should say/write. Examples of prescriptive rules of grammar in German: 'Do not use *würde* in a *wenn*-clause', and 'The word *trotzdem* should only be used as an adverb and not as a subordinating conjunction meaning "although".' Our notion of a correct or grammatical sentence will be one that is acceptable to native speakers rather than that prescribed as correct by grammarians. Ungrammatical sentences and constructions will be marked with '*'.

Describing the grammatical constructions in a language involves the following. (1) It should divide sentences up into their constituent parts, and demonstrating thereby that there are basic sentence patterns composed of strings of positions, or slots, rather than strings of words and then showing that these positions can be filled in a variety of ways. Thus it will show for German that there is a subject slot which may be filled by a noun, pronoun, phrase, clause, etc.: *Peter ist alt*; *er kommt*; *der nächste Winter kommt bestimmt*; *daß er nicht da ist, wundert mich*. (2) It should show that there are levels within the sentence, so that the relation of constituents to the sentence is not one of equality but of hierarchy. (3) It should provide labels to assign the words of a language to a word class, for example noun, verb, etc., so that general statements about sentences can be made. Transformational generative grammar demonstrates how simple sentences are changed by transformations and how sentences may be joined together to produce other sentences of potentially infinite complexity. Ideally the description should, by relating back to basic patterns, show those sentences which are related and those which are not. We shall not be dealing with this approach in detail since much of the discussion is rather technical and the theory has changed significantly since its introduction in 1957 by Noam Chomsky. It has now become known as Government and Binding Theory (*Rektion-Bindungs-Theorie*). An outline of the latest proposals in general can be found in Radford (1988) and Haegemann (1991), while Grewendorf (1988) applies the theory to German. Of the grammatical works that we shall cite most, *Duden Grammatik* (1984), Eisenberg (1986), Engel (1988), Flämig (1991), Heidolph *et al.* (1981), and Hentschel and Weydt (1990) contain a variety of different theoretical viewpoints, while Durrell (1991) and Helbig and Buscha (1991) are intended for foreign learners and are more practical in their approach.

8.2 DIVISIONS AND UNITS OF GRAMMAR

(Bergenholtz and Mugdan 1979: 48–102; Fox 1990: 80–120; Heidolph *et al.* 1981: 458–87)

Traditionally grammar is divided into morphology and syntax, the former dealing with the structure of words and the latter with the structure of sentences. Morphology itself can be divided into inflection and derivation. The usual distinction made between inflection and derivation is that inflection deals with the different forms of a word or phrase according to its syntactic uses, for example *der Junge* nom. sg., *den Jungen* acc. sg., *des Jungen* gen. sg., *die Jungen* nom. pl., whereas word formation, also called derivational or lexical morphology, deals with new words which usually belong to different word classes from the words from which they were formed. For instance, *sprechen*, *spricht*, *sprach* are all inflected forms from the lexical unit, or lexeme, *sprech-*, whereas *Sprache*, *Spruch* are different words and not merely inflected forms of *sprechen*. We will symbolize lexemes by writing them with capital letters, for example SPRECH. Word formation is described in Chapter 9. Here we will focus on inflection and syntax. The borderline between these two is not always easy to draw since not all words inflect in all instances. A fundamental division does exist, however, between those word classes in German whose members inflect, for example nouns, adjectives, verbs, pronouns, etc., and those whose members do not, for example prepositions, conjunctions. Syntax, on the other hand, deals not with the internal structure of words but how they can be built up into larger units such as phrases which in turn form larger units called sentences.

Traditionally the basic unit of inflectional morphology was the word, but modern linguists have suggested that the basic unit should be the morpheme. In the words *Tat+en* 'deeds' and (*sie*) *sag+en* 'say', the parts separated by '+' are morphemes: the smallest meaningful units into which an utterance can be divided. There have been many problems with dividing words into morphemes and in defining the term itself. It has been shown that morphemes very often have little or no meaning. What 'meaning' do the morphemes *-er* and *-e* have in the strong and weak inflection of adjectives, for example *ein schlecht+er Tag*, *der richtig+e Augenblick*? Their occurrence is automatically determined by the type of article or other word used in front of them. Other problems arise with regard to the segmentation of words into morphemes. Words such as *Boote*, *Kinder*, *macht* can easily be divided into the morphemes *Boot+e*; *Kind+er*; *mach+t*. What about words such as *trank*, *fuhr*; *Gärten*, *Mütter*? Various possibilities of dividing these and other forms have been suggested: *tr . . . nk* and *a*; *trink* and a 'replacive' morpheme, for example '*i* is replaced by *a*'; and *trank* plus a zero variant of the past tense morpheme. All this was motivated by the desire to keep the parallelism in the formation of the past tense between *trank* and regular verbs such as *machte*, the latter being clearly divisible into *mach-* and *-te*. It seems more satisfactory to maintain *trank* as an indivisible unit, a morph, which comprises the two morphemes *trink-* and past tense. However, this is to extend the use of the term morpheme from an actual unit of speech to cover grammatical category, or more precisely, the member of a grammatical category, something rather more abstract. Processes such as replacing *i* by *a* in the past tense pose no problem if the word is taken as the basic unit of morphology. (This is not to ignore the fact that words can in many cases be divided into morphemes.) We can then avoid the need for segmentation in many instances by listing the word forms of a lexeme as a paradigm comprising the lexeme + grammatical categories, *trank* = TRINK + past + sg. + 3rd pers. In our description we shall adopt this approach and treat inflected forms as the realization of lexemes and grammatical categories. Where necessary, we will, however, divide forms up into morphemes, using the latter term for actual items of language.

The internal structure of those words amenable to easy segmentation will be treated in terms of stems and endings, for example *Taten*, *Boote* will be said to consist of a stem, *Tat*, *Boot* and an ending, *-en*, *-e*. The stems *Tat*, *Boot* are free stems, i.e. they can occur on their own without any ending, but many stems in German are bound, i.e. they only appear with an ending: *helf-*, *helfen*, *helft* but not *help*. This is particularly true of foreign words, for example *Flex+ion*, *Flex+iv*, *flex+ibel* but no *Flex*! Endings are invariably bound forms, *-e*, *-t*, *-st*, *-en*, etc. Some stems and endings do not have simply one form but have several variants. For instance, the stem of the word *lesen* has two variants: in *les+en* the stem is pronounced [leːz-] and in *les+t* it is pronounced [leːs-]. Unlike word forms which express different grammatical categories, the variants of the morphemes, the stems and endings, are determined by adjacent sounds. Thus in our example the voiced alveolar fricative [z] occurs before a vowel and the voiceless alveolar fricative [s] occurs before a voiceless alveolar plosive [t]. The spelling disguises this difference in the form of the stem. The adverb *jetzt* has the form *jetz-* when it occurs in the adjective *jetz-ig*. The distribution of the pronominal adverbs, for example *da*, *dar* and *wo*, *wor* in *damit*, *darin*, *wovon*, *worauf*, is determined entirely by whether the second morpheme in the construction begins with a vowel. Endings can also have varying forms. In German the distribution of the endings *-et* and *-t* for the 3rd pers. sg. and 2nd pers. pl. of regular verbs is determined by the final consonant of the stem. When the stem of the verb ends in *d* or *t*, *reden*, *redet*; *retten*, *rettet*, or comprises a cluster of obstruent plus nasal, *atmen*, *atmet*; *regnen*, *regnet*; *zeichnen*, *zeichnet*, *-et* occurs, otherwise the ending is *-t*. The term allomorph is used for these different shapes of morphemes which are in complementary distribution with each other through phonological conditioning.

8.3 PARTS OF SPEECH

(Bergenholtz and Mugdan 1979: 126–41; *Duden Grammatik* 1984: 88–91; Engel 1988: 17–20; Fox 1990: 145–63; Heidolph *et al.* 1981:

487–96; Helbig and Buscha 1991: 19–21; Hentschel and Weydt 1990: 13–20)

One basic assumption in describing the grammar of a language is that it consists not simply of individual words but classes of words which behave in similar ways. These classes are necessary in order to make general statements about the formation of units such as phrases, clauses and sentences. These word classes (*Wortklassen*, *Wortarten*) are traditionally known as parts of speech. We want to examine the basis for setting up word classes in German and suggest how these might be characterized. As far as possible we will retain the traditional labels. Every grammatical theory works with word classes, even if they define and label them in different ways.

The number of word classes in German fluctuates from grammar to grammar. There is general agreement about the main word classes such as noun, verb, adjective, pronoun and adverb. The smaller classes of uninflected particles range, however, from three – preposition, conjunction and interjection (*Duden Grammatik* 1984: 88) – to eight (Engel 1988: 21). This gives Duden eight word classes in all and Engel fourteen. Even the main classes contain sub-classes such that nouns include count nouns and mass nouns, verbs include transitive or intransitive verbs, modal verbs, etc., pronouns include personal, possessive, indefinite and negative pronouns. Bergenholtz and Schaeder (1977: 73–5), using syntactic criteria, elevate many of these sub-classes to independent word classes arriving at a grand total of fifty-one!

Three kinds of criteria are used to divide words into word classes: semantic, syntactic and morphological. Semantic criteria can be illustrated by defining nouns as being words for 'people or things' and verbs as designating 'actions'. Linguists have tended to be rather sceptical of semantic criteria for word classes. Verbs such as *schlafen*, *existieren* do not really designate actions. Nouns such as *Gerechtigkeit*, *Liebe*, *Frieden* are not the names of people or things. In practice, semantic criteria have tended to be applied only to such word classes as nouns and verbs. Other classes, such as adverbs, are said to modify verbs, *sie rudert schnell, er schreibt gut*. This definition is using a syntactic criterion of saying that another word class is modified by the adverb. Syntactic criteria can also be illustrated by saying that a preposition governs a noun, or a conjunction is used at the beginning of a clause. In all these instances of syntactic definition the existence and labelling of other word classes is presupposed. Kufner (1962: 51f.) illustrates the importance of syntactic criteria by quoting a nonsense poem, *Gruselett* by Christian Morgenstern (1871–1914). Although the passage contains nonsense words (in bold), they can easily and unambiguously be assigned to word classes on the basis of syntactic position.

Der **Flügelflagel gaustert**
durchs **Wiruwaruwolz**
die rote **Fingur plaustert**
und grausig **gutzt** der **Golz**.

Morphological criteria are whether a word is inflected or not or has a particular prefix or affix, for example nouns inflect for number, verbs for tense, nouns often have the suffix *-heit. -ung*, etc.

The most comprehensive way of looking at word classes is to try and use all three types of criteria, bearing in mind that the syntactic and morphological are more useful. The first and most obvious division of German words is into those that inflect and those that remain uninflected. Forms that can inflect include *Stuhl* (noun), *süß* (adjective), *trinken* (verb), *ein*, *der* (articles), *mein*, *dein* (possessive adjectives), *er*, *dieser* (pronouns), etc., while uninflected forms include *bald* (adverb), *bei* (preposition), *bevor* (conjunction), *aha!* (interjection).

An added problem to setting up word classes is that not all the members of a word class are characterized by all the possible defining features of that class. This can be illustrated by examining several characteristics of forms that function as nouns and seeing which conform to certain features and which do not. In Table 8.1 various word-class features are represented by numbers, 1 = can function with an article, 2 = can inflect for the possessive case, 3 = can inflect for pl., 4 = can function as a subject or object, 5 = has a derivational suffix, 6 = inflects in the oblique cases in the sg. (acc., gen. and dat.) and 7 = the inflection is influenced by definite and indefinite articles, possessive adjectives, etc. The most useful criteria for defining nouns are that they function as subject or object and that they take an article (both syntactic criteria), followed by the ability to form a plural. Interestingly enough, the so-called adjectival nouns, *Studierende* and *Arme* score highly on all the criteria whereas the more intuitively obvious nouns score somewhere in the middle. Thus word classes have central and peripheral members and are not homogeneous. Such word classes are, however, essential for making general statements about sentence structure.

Table 8.1   Characteristics of nouns

Noun	1	2	3	4	5	6	7	Score
Studierende	+	+	+	+	+	+	+	7/7
Arme	+	+	+	+	−	+	+	6/7
Sträfling	+	+	+	+	+	−	−	5/7
Mensch	+	+	+	+	−	+	−	5/7
Zeichnung	+	−	+	+	+	−	−	4/7
Haus	+	+	+	+	−	−	−	4/7
Maus	+	−	+	+	−	−	−	3/7
Erziehung	+	−	−	+	+	−	−	3/7
Fünf	+	−	+	+	−	−	−	3/7
Milch	+	−	−	+	−	−	−	2/7
Anna, Hans	−	+	−	+	−	−	−	2/7
Total	10	6	8	11	4	3	2	

8.4   SENTENCE STRUCTURE

(*Duden Grammatik* 1984: 566–84; Eisenberg 1986: 33–69; Fox 1990: 202–34; Latour 1985: 27–47; Welke 1988: 21–52)

Sentences do not simply consist of a string of separate words but are hierarchically ordered. Thus in the sentence *Die Rosen blühen im Garten* (cf. *Duden Grammatik* 1984: 606) there are five words, but if we had to divide it into two then we might make the division between *Rosen* and *blühen*. In other words *die* belongs more closely to *Rosen* and forms a unit with it, while *blühen* and *im Garten* belong more closely together. Our intuitive cut is confirmed by the fact that we can substitute a pronoun for *die Rosen*, for example *Sie blühen*, or we can question the two words, *Was blühen? – Die Rosen*, or we can split *die Rosen* from *blühen*, obtaining a so-called cleft sentence: *Es sind die Rosen, die blühen*. All this shows that we are dealing with one unit, which we may call a constituent. The rest of the sentence *blühen im Garten* is also a constituent, shown by the fact that we can substitute *wachsen* for it, *Die Rosen wachsen*. The constituent *blühen im Garten* can itself be further divided into the constituents *blühen* and *im Garten*. This can be shown by the fact that we can move *blühen* to the front to create a question, *Blühen die Rosen im Garten?*, and that we can question the constituent *im Garten*, *Wo blühen die Rosen? – Im Garten*. These constituents themselves can be divided into further units, the words themselves: *die*, *Rosen*, *blühen*, *im*, *Garten*. To distinguish intermediate units such *die Rosen*, *blühen im Garten*, *im Garten* from the individual words which cannot be further divided, except into stems and endings, the former are called immediate constituents and the latter ultimate constituents. A more traditional word for immediate constituents is phrase and since the basic word in this phrase is a noun we can call it a noun phrase (NP). NPs can consist of nouns alone, *Rosen sind schön*, or a complex structure such as *die sehr schönen Rosen*. As the basic word of *blühen im Garten* is a verb then this constituent is a verb phrase (VP). The constituent *im Garten* (*in dem Garten*) contains an NP *dem Garten* but the whole is not an NP because we cannot apply the tests we have used on *die Rosen*. The other constituent is a preposition which determines the case of the article so we can call *im Garten* a prepositional phrase (PP).

One way of showing the hierarchical structure of sentences and the relationship of the different constituents to each other is by means of a tree diagram. Thus the structure of another sentence *Der Gärtner bindet die Blumen* (*Duden Grammatik* 1984: 607) can be shown by the following diagram:

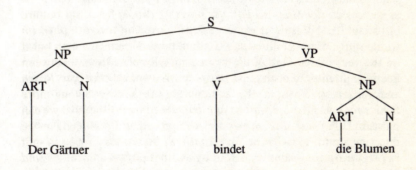

The branches of the tree diagram join at nodes which can be labelled: *der Gärtner* = noun phrase (NP), *bindet die Blumen* = verb phrase (VP), which itself consists of the verb *bindet* and the NP *die Blumen*. These tree diagrams represent the phrase structure of the sentence. Every sentence in a language can be represented by a phrase-structure tree diagram. In order to draw such a diagram one needs to know what the constituents of the sentence are and how they are to be labelled. Typically these are terms such as NPs, VPs or noun, verb, article, adjective. The terms at each node are said to dominate those of the constituent immediately below, thus S dominates the NP *der Gärtner*, and VP dominates the node V *bindet* and the NP *die Blumen*. We have used categorial labels such as NP, VP, etc., but where do functional labels such as subject and object fit in? We could add them to our diagram but they are really superfluous since by position the NP which is directly dominated by the node S is the subject and the NP which is directly dominated by the verb is the object. This approach is favoured by transformational generative grammar. Other approaches, for example *Duden Grammatik* (1984), prefer a functional approach, using the labels such as subject, object, predicate directly in their syntactic diagrams.

One linguistic theory which has taken the verb as the main component of the sentence and described sentences in terms of which constituents pattern with the verb is valency theory (*Valenztheorie*). Linguists, starting with the Frenchman Lucien Tesnière (1893–1954), have evolved a method of describing the syntactic categories of verbs by concentrating on the items that have to accompany a verb, drawing on the term 'valency' from the discipline of chemistry. Apart from so-called impersonal verbs which only occur in the 3rd pers. sg., *es schneit*, most verbs have to be accompanied by an NP which functions as its subject: *der Mann schläft, der Junge ißt den Apfel*. The structure of the subject NP is dealt with in 8.5. However, in the verb phrase a whole range of possibilities and combinations of elements depending on the verb exists. One of the main principles of valency theory has been the attempt to distinguish between what are called *Ergänzungen* and *Angaben*. Thus in the sentences (1a) *Sie wartete auf ihre Schwester* and (1b) *Sie wartete auf dem Bahnsteig*, the prepositional phrases (PPs) *auf ihre Schwester* and *auf dem Bahnsteig* have a different status in each case. In (1b) it may be replaced by an adverb (a pro-form), for example *dort*, or by another phrase, *eine Stunde*, or it may be omitted altogether. It is not essential to the grammaticality of the sentence. The PP in (1b) is an *Angabe*. Tesnière called them *circonstants*, which Fox (1990: 217) glosses 'circumstantial element' and Durrell (1991: 349) calls 'adverbial'. In (1a), on the other hand, the NP cannot be omitted. **Sie wartete auf* is ungrammatical. It may be pronominalized, *auf sie*, or another different NP used, *Sie wartete auf die Post*. In this sentence the choice of the verb + NP demands the preposition *auf*. This close relationship between verb and prep. is usually noted by entering the latter in the dictionary entry for the appropriate verb. This type of PP is termed an *Ergänzung*, Tesnière's *actant*, which Fox glosses 'participating elements' and Durrell calls 'complements'. The important characteristic of the *Angaben* is that they are specific and usually obligatory to certain verbs. Thus there is a class of verbs like *warten* which take the prep. *auf*: for example *achten auf, sich beziehen auf, sich freuen auf*, etc. Other verbs combine with other prepositions in the same way: *denken an, lachen über, leiden unter, rechnen mit, stimmen gegen, zweifeln an*. The terminology is rather unclear but we will refer to *Ergänzungen* as 'complements' and *Angaben* as 'adjuncts'. Engel has eleven such complements of the verb (1988: 187–98) of which the five listed below are the most important:

1 Subject: *Dieser Mann ist mein Nachbar*. Usually this is a noun or pronoun in the nom.
2 Acc. object: *Meine Schwester schreibt einen Brief.*
3 Gen. object: *Wir gedenken der Unglücklichen.*
4 Dat. object: *Zigaretten schaden der Gesundheit.*
5 Prepositional object: *Wir rechnen mit deinem Kommen.* The following prepositions can occur as complements of verbs: *an* + acc./+ dat., *auf* +acc./+ dat., *aus, bei, durch, für, gegen, in*, + acc./+dat., *mit, nach, über* + acc., *um, unter* + acc./+ dat., *von, vor, zu*. The other six are adverbial and clausal complements.

Valency theory can also portray the structure of sentences in tree forms, but their trees show relationships of dependence and are not meant to show the linear structure of the sentence. The valency or dependency tree for *Die Rosen blühen im Garten* is shown below:

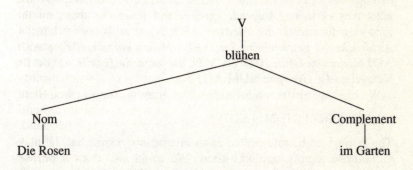

We will try and combine something of both approaches, regarding the two main constituents of the sentence as NP and VP. The traditional term 'clause' will be avoided. It is not really needed, for a traditional clause is simply a verb phrase; however, we shall still use it to refer to subordinate clauses, those VPs introduced by a subordinating conjunction, for example *weil*, *wenn*, etc. In this chapter we will discuss the internal structure of NP and VP and the morphosyntactic categories which are realized by their internal constituents. In the discussion of the VP we will make use of the notion of basic sentence pattern (*Satzbauplan*) determined by the adjuncts and complements of the verb.

8.5   THE INTERNAL STRUCTURE OF THE NP

(*Duden Grammatik* 1984: 569–75, 590–4; Durrell 1991: 41–123; Engel 1988: 603–48; Heidolph *et al*. 1981: 254–77; Helbig and Buscha 1991: 596–606; Hentschel and Weydt 1990: 315–27)

In this section we shall look at some of the word classes and their distribution within the noun phrase and the morphosyntactic categories, for example gender, number, cases, which are realized by different inflectional endings and processes. The NP itself consists of a head and other optional modifying elements. The head is a noun and every NP contains a noun (some important exceptions will be mentioned later). Thus *der Mensch*, *zwei Wörter*, *Ausdrücke*, *gesprochene Sätze*, *ein einzelnes Wort*, *die vier Laute*, *die folgende Tabelle*, *zwei große Gruppen* are all examples of NPs. (These examples are from *Duden Grammatik* (1984: 21ff.).) These strings of words all contain a noun preceded by some other, or in one case no other, elements. Using traditional terminology we can call these elements definite, *der*, *die*, or indefinite articles, *ein*, numerals *zwei*, *vier* and adjectives *einzelnes*, *folgende*, *große*, and represent them by the following formulae: *der Mensch* ART N, *zwei Wörter* NUM N, *Ausdrücke* N, *gesprochene Sätze* ADJ N, *ein einzelnes Wort* ART ADJ N, *die vier Laute* ART NUM N, *die folgende Tabelle* ART ADJ N, *zwei große Gruppen* NUM ADJ N.

We can thus abstract a formula which accounts for all these NPs:

NP → (ART) (NUM) (ADJ) N.

The arrow is to be interpreted as an instruction 'rewrite as'. Items in parentheses signify optional items. We could also draw a phrase-marker tree to show the structure of the NP as in the diagram opposite.

Although our examples do not give us an actual instance of this full string we can simply add an ART to give *die zwei große Gruppen* which is a perfectly grammatical German NP. Some linguists now want to show that all the intermediate constituents between the

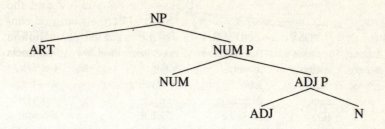

highest, or maximal, NP and the lowest, or minimal, N are in fact types of noun-like or nominal constructions. Constituents such as *zwei große Gruppen* or *gesprochene Sprache* occur on their own and, like so-called 'maximal' NPs, i.e those with a full structure of articles and adjectives, can be questioned, pronominalized or used in a cleft sentence.

Another alternative is when the NP consists solely of a pronoun or a proper name. In these instances modifiers do not normally occur: *Er hat auch die Register erstellt, Paul Grebe . . . betreute (die Duden-Grammatik)*. Thus the NP in German consists either of a pronoun, or a proper name or a noun plus modifiers. This can be shown by the following diagram, where each of the possibilities is mutually exclusive.

	→	1	Pronoun
NP	→	2	Proper name
		3	NP → (ART) (NUM) (ADJ) N.

We shall now examine each class of words which occur at each place of structure in the NP. The class labelled ART comprises a variety of words apart from the forms such as the definite article, *der* etc., and indefinite article, *ein* etc., which we have already met and are illustrated by the forms in bold in the following examples, taken from *Duden Grammatik* (1984): e.g. **ihren** *ungewöhnlichen Erfolg*; **mein** *besonderer Dank*; **wie viele und was für** *Laute*; *an* **diesen wenigen** *Beispielen*; **keine** *Wörter*; *aus* **deren** *Kombination*; **alle anderen** *. . . Kombinationen*. These words represent possessive adjectives, *mein*, *deren*, interrogative adjectives, *wie viele*, *was für*, the negative adjective, *keine*, and a quantity adjective, *alle*. The variety of forms and functions leads us to consider using another cover term for all these words. They can be called determiners, abbreviated DET (*das Determinativ*, pl. *-e*). Thus we can show their relationship to the node DET in Figure 8.1:

DET

ART	POSS	DEM	INDEF	NEG	INTER
Articles	Possessives	Demonstratives	Indefinites	Negatives	Interrogatives
der etc.	mein,	dieser,	aller,	kein etc.	welcher,
ein etc.	dein,	jener,	ein wenig,		was für,
zero	sein,	derjenige,	einiger,		wie viele
	ihr,	derselbe	etlicher,		wessen
	dessen,	solcher	irgendein,		
	unser,		jeder,		
	euer,		lauter,		
	ihr,		mancher,		
	Ihr		mehrer,		
			beide,		
			vieler		
			weniger		

Figure 8.1   The constituents of the determiner

Although they normally occur mutually exclusively in the DET position in the NP, there is a limited amount of co-occurrence between the different sets, for example *ein* can co-occur with *solcher* and *jeder*, *mehrerer* and *vieler* with *solcher*, *jeder* with *solcher*, *dieser* with *ein* and *vieler*, *der* with *ein* and *vieler*. In view of phrases such as *solch eine Freude* and *manch ein Beamter* it might be worthwhile setting up a further group, called pre-determiners, comprising the uninflected forms *solch* and *manch*. These forms are members of a closed set since they can be listed exhaustively.

The cardinal numerals are also a closed set, and unlike the determiners they do not inflect for case or gender. There are remnants of inflection in postnominal position in the gen. case when the case is not shown in an article or adjective, for example *die Aussagen zweier Zeugen*, or in the dat. in the phrase *zu zweien*. The ordinal numerals inflect like ordinary adjectives. The adjectives themselves which occur in the nearest position to the noun are an open class but comprise different sub-classes.

8.5.1   Morphosyntactic categories of the noun

The head and its modifiers in the NP inflect in German according to a number of different categories: gender, number and case. The head of the NP, the noun, determines which grammatical gender the inflections of the modifiers take. In German each noun is assigned to one of three grammatical genders: masculine, feminine and neuter. Grammatical gender is thus an inherent category of the noun, that is why it is usually marked in a dictionary entry. The second morpho-syntactic category is number, which is not inherent in the noun but is semantic, its choice depending on extralinguistic context, i.e. whether we are talking about more of an item or not. In German number is realized by two terms, singular and plural. Third the NP may inflect for the category of case, according to whether it functions as a subject, direct or indirect object or whether it is governed by a preposition. We will review each of these categories in turn. The realization of the categories by the members of the NP is extremely complex. Durrell (1979) sketches out some of the problems involved.

8.5.1.1 Grammatical gender

(*Duden Grammatik* 1984: 199–212; Durrell 1991: 1–9; Eisenberg 1986: 159–67; Engel 1988: 501–3; Flämig 1991: 450–6; Heidolph *et al.*, 1981: 571–6; Helbig and Buscha 1991: 269–76; Hentschel and Weydt 1990: 145–51)

In German nouns grammatical gender is expressed by different means among the members of the NP. The determiners have differ-ent inflections for gender and these in turn govern what the endings of the adjectives are. These endings are also used to express the categories of case and number and thus there are no unique endings for gender. Thus *der Mensch* is not simply masculine, *die Schrift* not simply feminine, *das Wort* not simply neuter, but nom. sg. as well. The noun itself, the head of the NP, although determining the gender of the determiners and adjectives, rarely shows by its form that it is of a certain grammatical gender, *Maus* is feminine and *Haus* is neuter; *Pfad* is masculine and *Rad* is neuter. In the case of complex derived nouns with specific suffixes, then, these in many instances give a clear signal as to the gender of the noun as in the following examples:

Masculine suffixes: *-ich*: *Teppich*, *Fittich*; *-ig*: *König*, *Honig*; *-ling*: *Schmetterling*, *Sträfling*; *-s*: *Schnaps*, *Knicks*.
2 Feminine suffixes: *-ei*: *Bücherei*, *Plauderei*; *-in*: *Königin*, *Freundin*; *-heit*: *Blindheit*, *Einheit*; *-schaft*: *Landschaft*, *Freundschaft*; *-ung*: *Bildung*, *Vergebung*.

3 Neuter suffixes: *-chen*: *Wägelchen*, *Mädchen*; *-icht*: *Dickicht*,
　Spülicht; *-tum*: *Eigentum*, *Christentum*.

Even among this group of suffixes there are some exceptions, for
example *die Reling* (from Engl. *railing*), *der Kehricht*, *der Irrtum*,
der Reichtum. Foreign suffixes are more numerous and in many
instances also show the gender of the noun clearly, for example
masculine *-ant*: *Musikant*; *-ismus*: *Realismus*; *-ist*: *Optimist*; feminine *-ade*: *Marmelade*; *-age*: *Garage*; *-anz*: *Distanz*; *-ie*: *Kolonie*;
-ik: *Phonetik*; *-(at)ion*: *Kalkulation*; neuter *-ing*: *Clearing*; *-(i)um*:
Gremium; *-ment*: *Dokument*. (There is a full list in *Duden
Grammatik* (1984: 206–8).) Thus the longer and more morphologically complex a noun is in German, the easier it is to ascertain its
gender. However, there are a number of suffixes which do not
clearly show the gender of a noun. The common ending *-e* occurs
with nouns of all three genders: masculine *der Gute*, *der Erbe*,
feminine *die Güte*, neuter *das Gute*, *das Erbe*. The nominal suffix
-nis occurs mostly with neuter nouns, *das Hindernis*, *Verhältnis* but
Erlaubnis, *Ersparnis*, *Finsternis*, *Kenntnis* and *Wildnis* are feminine.
Compounds in *-mut* include the masculine *Hochmut* but feminine
Sanftmut. The most problematic endings are *-el* and *-er*, which
occur with nouns of all three genders, for example *der Artikel*, *die
Partikel*, *das Siegel*; *der Bäcker* (all agentive nouns in *-er* are masculine), *der Ginster*, *die Butter*, *die Mutter*, *das Pflaster*, *das Muster*.
There are some, albeit weak, pointers to a link between meaning
and grammatical gender. Durrell (1991: 1–4) and *Duden
Grammatik* (1984: 200–5) give examples such as days of the week,
months and seasons being masculine whereas names of trees are
feminine and metals neuter.

8.5.1.2　Number and case

(*Duden Grammatik* 1984: 238–52; Durrell 1991: 9–19; Eisenberg
1986: 144–51; Engel 1988: 505–11; Flämig 1991: 456–72; Heidolph *et
al.*, 1981: 576–91; Helbig and Buscha 1991: 137–44; Hentschel and
Weydt 1990: 239–46)

The category of number in German comprises the two terms singular
and plural. In contrast to English the formation of the plural in
German nouns is rather difficult. There are eight possible ways of
forming the plural as is shown here:

Plural formation in German (1)

1 by adding the suffix -*e* to the sg. stem: *Tag, Tag-e*;
2 by adding the suffix -*e* to the umlauted form of the sg. stem: *Gast, Gäst-e*;
3 by adding the suffix -*er* to the sg. stem and umlauting the vowel of the sg. stem wherever possible: *Bild, Bild-er, Brett, Brett-er, Blatt, Blätt-er, Huhn, Hühn-er*;
4 by adding the suffix -*en* to the sg. stem: *Tat, Tat-en*;
5 by adding the suffix -*n* to the sg. stem: *Gabe, Gabe-n*;
6 by adding the suffix -*s* to the sg. stem: *Auto, Auto-s*;
7 by using the same form as the sg.: *Haken* (there is a change of article in the case of masculine and neuter nouns);
8 the sg. stem is umlauted but no suffix is added: *Garten, Gärten*.

The number of endings can be simplified if phonologically conditioned allomorphs are recognized. The endings -*en* and -*n* are in complementary distribution: -*en* only occurs after nouns whose stems end in a consonant, for example *Fahrt, Pflicht, Universität, Freundschaft, Wohnung*, whereas -*n* occurs if the noun stem ends in a vowel, for example *Reise, Blume, Katze, Bäckerei, Etage*. Thus endings 4 and 5 can be grouped together. The nouns that show no pl. ending or simply umlaut the sg. stem (groups 7 and 8) usually end in -*el*, -*er*, or -*en*: *Onkel, Maler, Haken, Mängel, Väter, Bögen*, so the occurrence of the ending -*e* in *Tage, Gäste* is phonologically predictable. The recognition of these allomorphic variations reduces the number of actual pl. formations to five, as is shown below:

Plural formation in German (2)

1 by adding the suffix -*e* to the sg. stem, unless it ends in -*el*, -*er*, or -*en*: *Arm, Arm-e, Balken*;
2 by adding the suffix -*e* to the sg. stem, unless it ends in -*el*, -*er*, or -*en*, and umlauting the sg. stem: *Arzt, Ärzt-e, Faden, Fäden*;
3 by adding the suffix -*er* to the sg. stem and umlauting the vowel of the sg. stem wherever possible: *Bild, Bild-er, Brett, Brett-er, Blatt, Blätt-er, Huhn, Hühn-er*;
4 by adding the suffix -*en* or -*n* to the sg. stem: *Frau, Frau-en, Flut, Flut-en, Lippe, Lippe-n, Linie, Linie-n*;
5 by adding the suffix -*s* to the sg. stem: *Kino, Kino-s, Wrack, Wrack-s, Baby, Baby-s*.

Although the inventory of pl. endings has been somewhat simplified in our analysis, the difficulty of predicting pl. forms still remains.

The phonetic shape of the word is no absolute guide. The sg. forms *Saal*, *Aal* show the same phonetic environment for the vowel but one takes umlaut in the pl., *Säle*, while the other does not, *Aale*. Gender is also considered to play a role in predicting pl. forms. Augst (1979: 224) found that feminine nouns typically take the ending -(*e*)n, while masculine and neuter nouns take -*e*. Together with the rule accounting for the absence of -*e* in nouns in -*el*, -*er*, or -*en* and a rule which says that nouns in -*e* will take -*n* in the pl., 75 per cent of noun pl. forms can be predicted. However, for foreign learners the umlaut of the stem vowel plays an important part in the acquisition of the pl. system and since -*er* occurs mostly with neuter nouns, it can be regarded as the typical neuter pl. ending, since it occurs in very frequently used words. A real problem remains with the masculine nouns, particularly monosyllabic forms. The ending -*e* is certainly the regular ending, but what about umlaut of the stem vowel? In Augst (1975: 39–45) 287 out of 696 masculine nouns with umlaut-susceptible stem vowels actually show umlaut (41 per cent), whereas 409 do not show umlaut (59 per cent). Russ (1989) attempted to investigate this question by using a set of nonsense words, but the result was inconclusive: 172 words (26.46 per cent) showed umlaut and -*e*, while 160 words (24.62 per cent) showed no umlaut and -*e*. Mugdan (1977: 97) found that -*en* was the most frequently used ending, occurring in 52 per cent of his corpus, the next most frequent ending was -*e* without umlaut, 22.6 per cent, followed much further behind by the absence of ending with those nouns ending in -*el*, -*er*, and -*en*. The umlaut forms were not considered.

The category of case is usually combined with that of number or gender. The only really separate case form is the -*n* of the dat. pl., *Häusern*, *Tagen*. The sg. masc. and nt. ending is -(*e*)s for the gen, and -*e* for the dat. Those nouns, traditionally called weak, which take -(*e*)n in the non-nominative cases, for example *der Mensch*, *den Menschen*, *des Menschen*, *dem Menschen*, could be said to have case endings although they are not distinct from each other. It is the determiners and modifiers of the nouns which really show distinctions of case as the example of the definite article shows:

		Sg.		Pl.
	m.	f.	nt.	
Nom.	der	die	das	die
Acc.	den	die	das	die
Gen.	des	der	des	der
Dat.	dem	der	dem	den

8.5.2 Current changes in the NP

(Admoni 1973, 1990: 252–57; Braun 1987: 104–24; Glück and Sauer 1990: 54–65; Sommerfeldt *et al.* 1988: 193–207 and 224–9)

These affect a number of areas. Since the nineteenth century the size and complexity of sentences have decreased. There seems to be a causal link between an increase in the percentage of NPs in sentences and a decrease in the percentage of subordinate clauses. This has had the effect of making the NP bear much more meaning. What was formerly expressed by subordinate clauses and infinitival constructions is now borne by nominal forms. Thus the complex sentence *Nachdem der Bürgermeister dem Professor die Urkunde überreicht hatte, begann das Festessen* with a main and a subordinate clause can be made into one single sentence through nominalizing the subordinate clause, for example *Nach der Überreichung der Urkunde an den Professor durch den Bürgermeister begann das Festessen*. The size of the NP has remained constant since the nineteenth century, but the percentage it makes up of the sentence as a whole has risen. The modifiers of the noun remain fairly constant except in two instances: (1) the possessive gen. which comes after the noun shows a tendency to be replaced with a prepositional construction with *von* + dat., *das Rad des Freundes* > *das Rad vom Freund*; (2) the gen. obj. NP is being replaced in many cases by a prepositional construction.

In the noun itself there is a trend towards the indeclinable word, what Admoni (1970: 11f.) has called *Monoflexion*. Of the two remaining masculine and neuter case endings, dat. sg. *-e* and gen. *-es*, the dat. has all but disappeared apart from in set phrases, for example *im Grunde*, and the gen. shows clear signs of going the same way through the introduction of loan words such as *Dollar*, *Lotto*, *Marketing* (Rowley 1988). In the plural the *-s* suffix seems to be on the increase. It is favoured by Low German and nautical terms, *Decks*, *Tiefs*, loan words, *Beagles*, *Clusters*, *Pizzas*, nouns in *-i*, *Knackis* 'convicts', *Pullis*, abbreviations, *CDs*, *LKWs*, *PCs*, and sentence words, *Lebehochs*.

The use of the preposed expanded adjectival attribute, for example *ein über Deutschland nach dem Südosten ziehendes Tief*, has decreased by about a third in the present century (Weber 1971: 77–148).

8.6   THE INTERNAL STRUCTURE OF THE VP

(*Duden Grammatik* 1984: 576–84; Durrell 1991: 347–82; Eisenberg 1986: 276–99; Engel 1988: 443–93; Flämig 1991: 105–14 and 199–210; Heidolph *et al.*, 1981: 331–457; Helbig and Buscha 1991: 536–63; Hentschel and Weydt 1990: 327–56)

Apart from the situation where the verb occurs on its own, there are a large number of constituents which can make up the VP. On the basis of the combination of different kinds of complements including all the possible optional elements linguists have set up sentence patterns (*Satzbaupläne*) for German. These basic sentence patterns are usually described in both functional and categorial terms. Thus not only functional terms such as 'object' and 'subject' are used but also categorial terms such as 'prepositional phrase'. These sentence patterns must be clearly distinguished from 'sentence types', such as 'statement' and 'interrogative', which refer to the meaning of the sentence. In our description we will combine *Duden Grammatik* (1984: 635ff.), which has thirty-seven patterns, with Engel (1988: 198–218), who has forty-nine. There are twenty-two patterns, set out in Table 8.2, which are common to both. The original numbering is retained for ease of reference. The omissions result from the fact that Duden has several different patterns for different types of dat. constructions and Engel differentiates various kinds of impersonal constructions. Heringer (1988: 329), in a more informal description, cites the following as the most frequent sentence patterns in German: (1) NP nom. + verb + NP acc.; (2) NP nom. + verb + prep. NP; (3) NP nom. + verb + NP dat. + NP acc.; (4) NP nom. + verb; (5) NP nom. + verb NP dat.; and (6) NP nom. + verb + NP acc. + prep. NP. The value of these sentence patterns could lie in their exemplificatory character, but which are the most widely used? *Duden Grammatik* (1984: 634) has some useful figures on this. Of the basic sentence patterns listed in Table 8.2 only four have values of over 10 per cent in Thomas Mann's *Buddenbrooks*: (2) subj. + pred. + acc., 29.8 per cent; (7) subj. + pred. + space adverbial, 17 per cent; (1) subj. + pred., 12.9 per cent; and (9) subj. + pred. + adj., 10.2 per cent. A comparable study of the leading article in a quality newspaper yielded the following results: (2) subj. + pred. + acc., 26.1 per cent; (5) subj. + pred. + prep. obj., 12.8 per cent; (1) subj. + pred., 11.7 per cent; and (9) subj. + pred. + adj., 11.5 per cent. One notable change in frequency was that pattern (7) subj. + pred. + space adverbial, which was second in *Buddenbrooks*, came fifth with

8.1 per cent. The other change was that pattern (5) subj. + pred. + prep. obj. jumped from fifth position in *Buddenbrooks* with 6.5 per cent to 12.8 per cent and second position, reflecting the increased use of prepositions instead of cases with verbs. (1) subj. + pred. + acc. has maintained its position as the main pattern.

8.6.1 Types of verb

(*Duden Grammatik* 1984: 92–107 and 115–43; Durrell 1991: 221–63 and 327–46; Eisenberg 1986: 70–104; Engel 1988: 393–411; Flämig 1991: 362–85; Heidolph *et al.*, 1981: 497–500; Helbig and Buscha 1991: 34–137; Hentschel and Weydt 1990: 64–80)

Verbs can be divided up into classes on the basis of morphological, semantic and syntactic criteria.

Morphologically verbs have been traditionally classified on the basis of how they have formed their past tense. Those verbs which signify the change to past tense and past participle by changing their stem vowel, for example *finden > fand > gefunden*, have been called strong verbs whereas those verbs which do not change their stem vowel but add a dental suffix, *-t-*, to which person and number endings are appended, for example *machen > machte > gemacht*, have been called weak verbs. Since the weak verbs are the more numerous, Augst (1975: 235) says they amount to 95.3 per cent of basic verbs, and any borrowed verbs or new formations inflect according to the weak pattern (see 10.3.1.7), they are also called 'regular' verbs. The strong verbs are a closed set which has shrunk throughout the history of German, from 349 in Old High German to 169 in New High German (Augst 1977: 160f.). There are other much smaller groups of verbs which also show peculiarities in forming the past tense. There are:

1 the verbs *brennen, kennen, nennen, rennen, senden, wenden* which show the addition of a dental suffix and vowel change, for example *brennen > brannte* (the verbs *senden, wenden* in some instances do not show the vowel change);
2 verbs such as *denken, bringen* and the obsolescent *dünken* which show not only the addition of a dental suffix and vowel change, but also a change of stem-final consonant, for example *denken > dachte, bringen > brachte* and *dünken > deuchte*;
3 verbs such as *mahlen, gären, backen* which have a mixture of strong and weak forms in fluctuation;

Table 8.2 Sentence patterns common to Duden and Engel

	Duden		Engel
1	subj. + pred.	2	subj. *Der Mandelbaum blüht.*
2	subj. + pred. + acc.	3	subj. + acc. *Der Gärtner bindet die Blumen*
20	acc. + acc.	4	acc. + acc. *Sie hat mich Polnisch gelehrt*
12	subj. + pred. + acc. + gen.	6	acc. + gen. *Man beschuldigt ihn der Unterschlagung*
11	subj. + pred. + acc. + dat.	7	acc. + dat. *Walther schenkt seiner Mutter Blumen*
13	subj. + pred. + prep.	10	acc. + prep. *Sie hat mich mit meinem Nachbarn verwechselt*
14	subj. + pred. + acc. + place	14	acc. + dir. *Ich hänge das Bild an die Wand*
19	subj. + pred. + acc. + app. acc.	16	acc. + noun *Klaus nennt mich einen Lügner*
4	subj. + pred. + gen.	18	gen. *Ich harre seiner*
3	subj. + pred. + dat.	19	dat. *Der Sohn dankt dem Vater*
21	subj. + pred. + dat. + prep.	20	dat. + prep. *Ich gratuliere dir zu diesem Erfolg*
22	subj. + pred. + adj.	22	dat + adj. *Es geht mir schlecht*
5	subj. + pred. + prep.	24	prep. *Er dachte über die Insel nach*
23	subj. + pred. + prep. + prep.	25	prep. + prep. *Er sprach zu den Kindern über seine Reise*
17	subj. + pred. + adj. + prep.	27	prep. + adj. *Er handelte niederträchtig an ihm*
6	subj. + pred. + noun in nom.	32	noun *Karl ist mein Freund*
9	subj. + pred. + adj.	33	adj. *Du sollst gesund bleiben*
24	subj. + pred. + adj. + dat.	41	dat. + adj. *Ich bin diesem Mann fremd*
7	subj. + pred. + place	29	situation *Das Buch liegt auf dem Tisch*
8	subj. + pred. + time	31	expansive *Sie hat um zwei Kilo abgenommen*
15	subj. + pred. + acc. + time	15	acc. exp. *Er zog das Gespräch in die Länge*
16	subj. + pred. + acc. + adj.	17	acc. + adj. *Die Mutter machte die Suppe warm*

4 the verbs *sein*, *haben*, *werden*, which exhibit a number of highly irregular forms.

In addition, the modal verbs *dürfen*, *können*, *mögen*, *müssen*, *sollen*, *wollen* and *wissen* are usually reckoned a separate sub-group of anomalous verbs. They have no *-t* ending in the 3rd pers. sg. pres. which makes the 1st and 3rd pers. sg. pres. the same: *ich*, *er/sie/es darf*; *kann*, *mag*, *muß*, *soll*, *will*, *weiß*. In addition, all of them except *sollen* have a different vowel in the pl. pres. from the sg.: *darf*, *dürfen*; *kann*, *können*; *mag*, *mögen*; *muß*, *müssen*; *will*, *wollen*; *weiß*, *wissen*. In forming the past tense they also show several different combinations. The verbs *sollen*, *wollen*, simply use the dental suffix like a weak verb with no change of vowel, while *dürfen*, *können*, *müssen* are like those of group 1 since they show the addition of dental suffix and a vowel change, albeit not from *a* to *e*. The non-modal preterite-present verb *wissen* would fit into group 1, for example *wissen* > *wußte* since it shows a change of stem vowel in addition to the addition of a dental suffix. The verb *mögen* would fit into sub-group 2 since it shows not only the addition of a dental suffix and a vowel change, but also a change of stem-final consonant, for example *mögen* > *mochte*. In the formation of the past tense, therefore, it is rather misleading to make the modals a group on their own. All these verbs are simply irregular in their inflection. The term irregular is sometimes confusingly applied to the strong verbs as well, for example *Duden Grammatik* (1984: 133ff.), when in earlier editions it was reserved for the sub-groups 1–4. A more consistent usage would be weak, strong and irregular (Durrell 1991: 224; Engel 1988: 393f.). If one wanted to dispense with the terms strong and weak altogether, then we could perhaps use the terms, regular, for example *machen*, irregular, for example *finden*, and anomalous, for example the sub-groups 1–4. The uncertainty of usage in describing verbs such as *finden*, *reiten*, *kriechen*, *fahren* as irregular or strong reflects their historical origin and development. In OHG and MHG these verbs could be subdivided systematically into vowel-gradation classes (*Ablautreihen*). With sound changes and analogical changes these classes have been distorted and changed so much that only relics of the original patterns remain. Linguists have refused to write them off as an amorphous set of verbs but have attempted to describe synchronically the patterns of vowel change in the infinitive, 3rd pers. sg. pres., the past tense and the past participle. Halle (1953) started with the four basic vowels of the past tense: [u(:)], *trug*, *fuhr*, *schund*, [o(:)], *bog*, *fror*, *floß*, [i(:)], *lief*, *hieß*, *fing*, and [a] and [a:], *schwamm*, *kam*. From these basic vowels Halle sets up rules to derive the other forms of the verbs. Out of his 117 verbs he has seven classes, ranging in membership from thirty-six to one. Ulvestad (1956) also attempted to classify these verbs and ends up with forty-eight classes, ranging in membership from twenty, for verbs like *bleiben*, to one. Generative treatments of German irregular verbs have followed similar lines. Ross (1967) divides irregular verbs into seven classes according to their stem variants but he also takes into consideration verbs like *brennen–brannte*. As well as stem variants Ross uses categories like [Stamm = PP], i.e. the stem vowel of the pres. is the same as that of the past participle, [Prät = PP], the stem vowel of the past tense (preterite) is the same as that of the past participle, and third, [Pres Umlaut], the stem vowel of the pres. is umlauted in the 3rd. pers. sg. All these categories have + or − values. He then presents phonological rules, which generate for each class those forms that are predictable, for example in forms such as *gesungen* and *begonnen*, *u* is taken as the basic stem vowel which is lowered to *o* except before nasal plus underlying consonant /ng/. Wurzel (1970: 63–79) takes a similar approach, which, however, seems clearer in that he assumes morphological categories such as [+/− PP = Stamm], the stem vowel is/is not the same as that of the past participle, and [+/− PP = Prät], the vowel of the stem vowel of the past participle is/is not the same as that of the past tense (preterite), as primary. This enables him to set up three classes which are then divided into subclasses on the basis of the combination of stem vowel variants. Class 1 has six sub-classes and has the primary category [+ PP = Stamm], for example *lesen*, *gelesen*; class 2 has seven sub-classes with the primary category [+ PP = Stamm], for example *flog*, *geflogen*; class 3 has the primary category [− PP = Stamm], [− PP = Prät], for example *werfen*, *warf*, *geworfen*. In other words, the stem vowels of the pres., past tense and past participle are all different. If one wants to attempt a classification of the irregular verbs then two types of characteristics can be used: first, the more abstract category of whether the vowel in the infinitive is the same or different from the vowel in the past tense and/or the past participle; and second, which combination of vowels forms the actual vowel-gradation pattern. In modern German there are three patterns of the first kind: for example (1) the vowel of the pres. is not the same as the vowel of the past tense, which is, however, the same as that of participle (V1 V2 V2), where V = vowel and the numeral denotes sameness or difference; (2) the vowels of the present, the past tense and the past participle are all different (V1 V2 V3); and (3) the vowel of the pres. and the past participle are the

Table 8.3 Patterns of strong verb classes

Group			Pattern			Example	Number of verbs
V1	V2	V2	ei	i	i	*bleiben, beißen*	38
V1	V2	V2	ie	o	o	*biegen, gießen*	22
V1	V2	V2	e	o	o	*fechten, schwellen*	6
V1	V2	V2	e [eː]	o [oː]	o [oː]	*weben*	5
V1	V2	V2	e [ɛː]	o [oː]	o [oː]	*gären, (er)wägen*	2
V1	V2	V2	au	o [oː]	o [oː]	*saugen, schnauben*	2
V1	V2	V2	ü	o [oː]	o [oː]	*lügen, trügen*	2
V1	V2	V2	i	o	o	*glimmen, klimmen*	2

same but both are different from the vowel of the past tense (V1 V2 V1). Within these three main groups there are sub-groups, shown in Table 8.3, according to the realizations of the particular vowels.

The following verbs represent one pattern each: *schwören, erlöschen, saufen, (er)schallen, schinden.*

V1	V2	V3	i	a	u	*binden*	18
V1	V2	V3	e	a	o	*helfen, sterben*	9
V1	V2	V3	i	a	o	*beginnen*	6
V1	V2	V3	e	a [aː]	o	*brechen, treffen*	5
V1	V2	V3	e [eː]	a [aː]	o [oː]	*befehlen, empfehlen, stehlen*	3

The following verbs represent one pattern each: *bitten, gebären, gehen, hängen, liegen, nehmen, sitzen, werden.*

V1	V2	V1	e [eː]	a [aː]	e [eː]	*geben, lesen*	6
V1	V2	V1	a [aː]	u [uː]	a [aː]	*fahren, graben*	5
V1	V2	V1	a [aː]	i [iː]	a [aː]	*blasen, schlafen*	4
V1	V2	V1	e	a [aː]	e	*essen, vergessen*	4
V1	V2	V1	a	i [i]	a	*fallen, halten, lassen*	3

The following verbs represent one pattern each: *fangen, hauen, heißen, laufen, kommen, rufen, stoßen.*

Another morphological criterion is the internal shape of verbs, some of which consist only of a stem to which endings are added, for example *find+en, mach+en*. These are known as simple verbs. Or the verb consists of a prefix, which can be stressed or unstressed, a verb stem and an ending: *ab+fahr+en; ab+mach+en; be+fahr+en; be+leg+en*. The prefixes in the first two verbs are stressed and separable, but unstressed and inseparable in the last two verbs. This criterion cuts across the division between irregular

Table 8.4   Syntactic classes of verbs

Verb	Past participle	Infinitive without zu	with zu
sein	ist gegangen		ist zu sehen
haben	hat gesagt		hat zu sagen
werden	wird gemacht	wird kommen	
können etc.		kann kommen	
hören etc.		hört ihn kommen	
lassen		läßt ihn kommen	

and regular, affecting verbs of both types and is not relevant for their inflection.

Semantically verbs can be divided into groups on the basis of shared categories of meaning, for example verbs of movement, verbs of perception. For some examples see the list on page 245.

The most important division of verbs is, however, that according to syntactic criteria, although morphological and semantic criteria have also played a role. Most main, full or lexical, verbs always occur on their own in a sentence, whereas a few occur with other word forms of the verb, the infinitive and the past participle. When used with the infinitive some verbs take the infinitive marker *zu*. Table 8.4 gives a sample of some of these verbs.

Syntactically and semantically these verbs have differing functions: *sein*, *haben* and *werden* are used to form tenses, for example the perfect *ich bin gekommen*, *ich habe gegessen*, the future, *ich werde morgen kommen*. The latter verb is also used with the past participle to form the passive voice, *das Fenster wird geschlossen*. They are traditionally known as auxiliary verbs. The other verbs occur only with an infinitive. The verbs like *können* are *dürfen*, *mögen*, *müssen*, *sollen*, *wollen*. They are traditionally known as modal verbs or modal auxiliaries. The verbs like *hören* are verbs of perception, for example *fühlen*, *spüren*, *sehen*. The verb *lassen* is a causative verb.

How many syntactic sub-classes of verbs are there here? Syntactically *sein* and *haben* are distinguished from the others in that they only occur with the past participle. The verb *werden* occurs with both the past participle and the infinitive, whereas the other verbs only occur with the infinitive. The group of verbs like *können* also show some special morphological features: (1) they lack an ending in the first and third person sg., pres., for example *ich kann*, *er kann* (cf. *ich mahne*, *er mahnt*); and (2) with the exception of *sollen*, they show a different vowel in the sg. from the pl. in the pres., *darf*, *dürfen*; *kann*, *können*; *mag*, *mögen*; *muß*, *müssen*; *will*, *wollen*; (3) they use a form of past participle which is the same as that of the infinitive in the perfect when modifying a full verb, for example *ich habe schreiben müssen*. They also share certain semantic categories of probability, possibility, permission, compulsion and volition. It is chiefly because of their morphological and semantic characteristics that they are traditionally set apart as a class of modal verbs. Their membership is not fixed, however, and some verbs are on their way to becoming modals. Most notable of these is *brauchen* or *nicht brauchen*, which is used without *zu* in its function as a modal. It lacks, of course, morphological features 1 and 2 although it does show feature 3. Conversely the verb *wissen* shows all the three morphological categories but semantically is regarded as not falling into the range of the modals. The verb form *möchte* belongs as a separate verb among the modals because of its different meaning from *mögen* (Eisenberg 1986: 96). The line between the full verbs and the auxiliaries and modals is fluid. As we have seen, the criterion of taking an infinitive without *zu* can vastly increase the number. Engel (1988: 406f.) has several more classes. As well as the auxiliary verbs *haben*, *sein*, *werden*, *gehören*, *erhalten/bekommen/kriegen* and modal verbs *brauchen*, *dürfen*, *können*, *mögen*, *müssen*, *sollen*, *wollen*, he has twenty modality verbs (*Modalitätsverben*), *anheben*, *anstehen*, *belieben*, *drohen*, *gedenken*, *geruhen*, *sich (ge)trauen*, *haben*, *pflegen*, *scheinen*, *sein*, *stehen*, *umhin können*, *sich unterstehen*, *sich vermessen*, *vermögen*, *versprechen*, *verstehen*, *wissen*, six verbs that take a subordinate clause (*Nebensatzverben*), *bedeuten*, *finden*, *sich fragen*, *es heißt*, *sich sagen*, *wähnen*, sixteen infinitive verbs (*Infinitivverben*), *bedeuten*, *fahren*, *fühlen*, *es gibt*, *gehen*, *gelten*, *haben*, *heißen*, *helfen*, *hören*, *kommen*, *lassen*, *lehren*, *schicken*, *spüren*, and the two participle verbs *kommen* and *stehen*. Eisenberg (1986: 71), on the other hand, has a threefold division of non-main verbs into auxiliaries, *sein*, *haben*, *werden*, copula verbs, those that occur before a predicative adjective or a noun in the nom., for example *sie wird Lehrerin*, which comprise *sein*, *bleiben*, *werden*, and seven modal verbs comprising *dürfen*, *können*, *möchten*, *mögen*, *müssen*, *sollen*, *wollen*. *Duden Grammatik* (1984: 94f.) recognizes auxiliaries, which form tenses and the passive, the modals: *dürfen*, *können*, *mögen*, *müssen*, *sollen*, *wollen*, but not *möchte* as a separate verb, although it is accepted that *brauchen* is on its way to becoming a modal. The existence of verbs that occasionally modify other verbs, for example *pflegen*, *scheinen*, *vermögen*, *drohen* (which correspond to Engel's modality verbs) is hinted at. There is therefore agreement among linguists about a core of auxiliary and modal verbs even if at the edges there is some fuzziness as to which might belong and which might not. This uncertainty reflects the fact that this area of syntax is undergoing changes.

8.6.2   Morphosyntactic categories of the verb

Verbs occur in different inflected forms depending on who is participating in the action, how many participants there are, when the action is taking place, whether it was real or imagined and whether the participant(s) were actively taking part or allowing themselves to be acted upon. These descriptions represent the different morphosyntactic categories, person, number, tense, mood and voice, which are represented by inflectional changes in the verb form itself or in an auxiliary verb. Person and number are always expressed by changes to the verb form itself, *sage, sagst, sagt, sagen*; *fahre, fähst, fährt, fahren*, whereas the categories of tense and mood are sometimes expressed by changes to the verb itself, for example *sagte, ging, fuhr*, and sometimes by changes to an auxiliary verb, the full verb being in the form of the infinitive or past participle, *ich werde gehen, ich würde sagen, ich habe gesagt, ich wäre gefahren*. The category of voice is expressed in the passive only by the use of the different forms of an auxiliary, *werden*, plus the past participle, *das Lied wird gesungen*. The structure aux. + verb is called analytic, or compound, whereas the use of inflectional forms of the main verb stem itself is called synthetic. Thus the present and simple past tense use only synthetic forms, the perfect, pluperfect and passive use only analytic forms and the subjunctive uses both synthetic and analytic forms. Historically the synthetic forms are older and the analytic forms more recent.

8.6.2.1   *Person and number*

The verb in German has three persons, 1st, 2nd and 3rd, and two numbers, sg. and pl. The categories of person and number are expressed by the use of a combination of personal pronouns, or NPs and inflectional changes, for example not only the typical adding of suffixes but also including the changing of stem vowels. The choice of personal pronoun/NP determines the inflectional ending which must agree with it in person and number. Thus *du*, 2nd pers. sg., always occurs with the ending *-st*, *ihr*, 2nd pers. pl., with *-t*. As with number and case the person/number endings are combined, that is they express both categories together. There is no way of deciding which part signals 'person' and which 'number'. Together this gives us the traditional paradigm of six endings and pronouns for the present tense as shown in the following chart:

		Sg.			Pl.	
1	*ich*	verb stem	*-e*	*wir*	verb stem	*-en*
2	*du*	verb stem	*-(e)st*	*ihr*	verb stem	*-(e)t*
3	*er, sie, es*	verb stem	*-(e)t*	*sie, Sie*	verb stem	*-en*

Although there are grammatically six person/number distinctions made, there are only four distinct endings since the 3rd pers. sg. and 2nd pers. pl. have the same ending, as do the 1st and 3rd pers. pl. The pronouns are all important, the endings repeating the information are to a certain extent redundant.

The forms of the ending themselves are subject to some variation. The ending *-(e)t* represents the allomorphic variation between *-et*, when the stem of the verb ends in *d* or *t*, *reden*, *redet*; *retten*, *rettet*, or comprises a cluster of obstruent plus nasal, *atmen*, *atmet*; *regnen*, *regnet*; *zeichnen*, *zeichnet*, otherwise the ending *-t* occurs. This does not apply when the stem vowel of the verb changes, for example *finden*, *findet*, but *treten*, *tritt*; *raten*, *rät*. In speech the ending *-e* is often elided, *ich mach'*, *wir mach'n*.

The endings of the past tense of regular verbs are the same as those for the present, with the sole exception of the 3rd pers. sg., which ends in *-e*. Again there are only four distinct endings for six person/ number distinctions. Since the past tense stem ends in *-t* the full endings *-est*, *-et* occur for the 2nd pers. sg. and pl., as shown here:

		Sg.			Pl.	
1	*ich*	verb stem + *t*	*-e*	*wir*	verb stem	*-en*
2	*du*	verb stem + *t*	*-est*	*ihr*	verb stem	*-et*
3	*er, sie, es*	verb stem + *t*	*-e*	*sie, Sie*	verb stem	*-en*

The irregular verbs have the same endings for the past tense pl. and the short ending *-st* for the 2nd pers. sg., unless the stem ends in *d* or *t*, for example *sangst*, *gabst*, but *ludest*, *rittest*. There is no overt ending for the 1st and 3rd pers. sg.: *sang*, *gab*, *lud*, *ritt*.

8.6.2.2 *Tense*

(*Duden Grammatik* 1984: 143–55; Durrell 1991: 278–91; Eisenberg 1986: 111–21; Flämig 1991: 386–401; Heidolph *et al.*, 1981: 507–20; Helbig and Buscha 1991: 137–60; Hentschel and Weydt 1990: 86–106)

Traditionally six tenses are recognized in German: the present, the past tense, or preterite, which are synthetic formations, and the analytic formations, or compound tenses: perfect, pluperfect, and the future and the future perfect. The latter two are referred to in German grammars as Futur I and Futur II: *sie werden schreiben*; *sie werden geschrieben haben*. Not all of them are used equally. *Duden Grammatik* (1984: 143ff.) shows how in the written language 90 per cent of tense forms are made up of the present (52 per cent) and the past tense (38 per cent), the other tenses following a long way behind: perfect 5.5 per cent, pluperfect 3.2 per cent, future 1.5 per cent and future perfect 0.03 per cent.

The formation of the tenses presents some problems, especially among the group of irregular and anomalous verbs. Perhaps more systematic is the need to choose between *haben* and *sein* as the auxiliary in the perfect and pluperfect. The choice depends on the syntactic and semantic characteristics of the verb concerned. All transitive verbs, reflexive verbs and modals take *haben*: *Sie hat ihre Mutter besucht*, *Sie hat sich beeilt*, *Sie hat in die Stadt gemußt*. With intransitive verbs there is the added complication that the meaning of the verbs influences the choice of auxiliary. Those verbs that desig- nate a continuing state, so-called durative verbs, take *haben*, as in *Sie hat geschlafen*, whereas those intransitive verbs that designate the completion of an action, so-called perfective verbs, and those desig- nating motion or change of state take *sein*: *Sie ist eingeschlafen*, *Sie ist gefahren*. In a few instances there is opposition between duration and motion with the same verb which is marked by the use of *haben* and *sein*: *Sie hat zwei Stunden geschwommen* vs *Sie ist ans andere Ufer geschwommen*.

The relationship of grammatical tense and time has always been the subject of great discussion. As with other grammatical categories such as gender, the relation between the grammatical and the natural phenomenon is not exact. The meanings of the tenses are rather complicated and they should not be equated with time categories. For instance the present tense is often used for other periods of time, for example the future *In einer Woche geht das Semester zu Ende*, the past *1918 endet der erste Weltkrieg*. The perfect tense can be used to refer to future time, for example *Bis Montag habe ich den Aufsatz fertig geschrieben*. Tense is not solely signalled by inflection of the verb or the use of auxiliaries; adverbs of time may also be used to refer to periods of time: present adverbials include *jetzt*, *nun*, *in diesem Augenblick*, *heute*, *dieses Jahr*, future adverbials include *bald*, *morgen*, *in einer Woche*, and past adverbials include *gestern*, *letztes*

Jahr, vor einiger Zeit, damals. The category of tense is thus realized by the sentence as a whole. To deal with the difficulty of meshing tense with time linguists have introduced the concept of relative and absolute time. An utterance can thus be viewed from different points of view. There is the moment of speaking (*Sprechzeit*), the moment the event happened (*Aktzeit*) and the moment the speaker considers something to happen or have happened (*Betrachtzeit*). According to Hentschel and Weydt (1990: 89), these distinctions which have been taken up by Helbig and Buscha (1991) and Eisenberg (1986) were originally made by the logician Hans Reichenbach (1891–1953). Of these three, the third leaves several possibilities open, whereas the first is unambiguous and the second is usually clearly discerned. In *er hat den Brief (gerade) geschrieben* the moment of speaking and the moment of the event as well as the moment the speaker considers the event to have happened are simultaneous. This is when we can talk of an absolute tense. On the other hand, in *Er hatte den Brief (schon damals) geschrieben* the moment of speaking is now but the event referred to lies in the past as does the time the speaker considered the event to have happened. Here we can speak of relative tense. Similarly *Er wird den Brief bis morgen geschrieben haben* has been uttered in the present but the event referred to and considered to have happened lies in the future and is another example of the use of a relative tense. Helbig and Buscha (1991: 158–60) use the terms absolute and relative in a slightly different way. The term relative is used by them when the choice of tense is determined by the context and by other events, *Nachdem er in Leipzig angekommen war, besuchte er uns*. The pluperfect *angekommen war* is determined by the choice of *nachdem*.

The traditional six tenses in German have not been accepted by all linguists. *Duden Grammatik* (1984: 144) accepts the labels and redefines their meaning and use. Helbig (1972: 36ff.) points to linguists who want to increase the number of tenses to twelve. This comes about chiefly by giving tense variants the status of independent tenses. Engel (1988: 494–6) does not believe in any system of tenses since the analysis of the tenses is so fraught with difficulty. As with many things, a more adequate answer lies in between the extremes. Of the six traditional tenses the future seems different from the rest. Since future tense forms always refer to something which has not yet happened there is a certain amount of uncertainty which is akin to the meaning of some of the modal verbs. Fox (1990: 183), following a linguistic parallel in the analysis of English, rejects a future tense for German. The use of *werden* here is simply parallel to that of modal verbs such as *sollen, wollen*, etc. He further proposes to designate the present the non-past, since it fulfils more functions than simply being used to designate what is happening here and now. The distinction between the non-past (present) and the perfect is not between present and past, since both refer to the present, but aspectual, between perfect, a state has been reached, and non-perfect, a state has not been reached, the action is continuing. This is a similar distinction to that made by Fourquet (1969) between 'incomplete' (*unvollzogen*) and 'complete' (*vollzogen*). The difference between the simple and compound tenses is, therefore, one of aspect rather than tense. This now gives a symmetrical pattern of distinctions as shown below:

	Non-perfect	Perfect
Non-past	sie kommen	sie sind gekommen
Past	sie kamen	sie waren gekommen

The relationship between the tenses is, however, not as clearcut as the chart above shows. Particularly the relationship between the simple non-perfect past and the non-past perfect is not always distinct. In speech there is a clear regional division between the north and central part of Germany, where the simple non-perfect past is chiefly used, and the south of Germany, where the compound non-past perfect is used. *Duden Grammatik* (1984: 150f.) admits the interchangeability between the two when referring to things in the past, for example *Kolumbus hat Amerika entdeckt* or *Kolumbus entdeckte Amerika*, but this cannot happen when making general statements, *Wenn der Pfeil die Sehne des Bogens verlassen hat, so fliegt er seine Bahn*, or referring to the future, *Wirklich gesiegt haben wir nur, wenn die Eingeborenen den Sinn der Schutzgebiete einsehen*.

8.6.2.3   Mood

(*Duden Grammatik* 1984: 155–76; Durrell 1991: 306–26; Eisenberg 1986: 121–31; Engel 1988: 418–26; Flämig 1991: 401–16; Heidolph *et al.*, 1981: 520–39; Helbig and Buscha 1991: 188–207; Hentschel and Weydt 1990: 106–16)

This is one of the more complicated topics in German grammar. Is mood a grammatical category, or is it a sentence category? Mood marks sentences according to the attitude of the speaker/hearer as to whether what is being said is factual, certain, uncertain or doubtful. Traditionally three moods are recognized, indicative, subjunctive and imperative. The use of the indicative implies that something is 'real',

Er schrieb den Aufsatz, while the use of the subjunctive often implies that something may not be real, *Er sagte, er schreibe den Aufsatz*, or *Wenn er den Aufsatz schriebe, könnte er jetzt ausgehen*. The imperative is used to give commands and is sometimes seen as a sentence type. The interplay between imperative and indicative can be seen from the fact that a command can be given using a declarative or interrogative sentence in the indicative, *Du kommst hierher! Willst du hierherkommen?* as opposed to *Komm hierher!* The indicative is the unmarked, usual, mood for the verb and the imperative occurs chiefly in the 2nd pers. sg. and pl. and 1st pers. pl., whereas it is the subjunctive which poses problems for native speakers and foreign learners and has been the subject of numerous linguistic studies.

The attitude of speaker/hearers towards events can be expressed by a number of different means: (1) by so-called modal particles, *wohl, vielleicht*, as in *Der Hund ist wohl weg, Der Arzt ist vielleicht tüchtig!*; (2) by modal verbs, *Das mag wahr sein*; or (3) by inflection of the verb, *Wenn er käme, wüßten wir alles genau, Sie behauptet, eine andere habe es getan*. This whole area of meaning is called modality but we will only be looking at how it is reflected in forms of the verb.

The subjunctive consists of both synthetic and analytic forms. The synthetic inflections are formed in the following ways. The endings *-e, -est, -e; -en, -et, -en* are added to the stem of the infinitive to form the present subjunctive of regular, strong, modal and irregular verbs (the 3rd pers. sg. is given as an example): *mache, fahre, könne, wisse, habe*. The verb *sein* uses the stem *sei* but has no ending in the 1st and 3rd pers. sg. The same set of endings are added to the past stem to form the past subjunctive of the irrregular verbs, modals and auxiliaries, with mutation of the stem vowel where possible, with the exception of *sollen* and *wollen*: *führe, könnte, wüßte, hätte, wäre*. The verb *brauchen* shows its affinity with the modal verbs by having a mutated subjunctive, *bräuchte* etc. (This is not yet fully accepted by *Duden Grammatik* (1984: 207, fn. 1).) The regular verbs could also be said to add the same set of endings to their past stem but since they do not undergo any mutation of the stem vowel the resulting forms are the same as those of the indicative: *machte, sagte, buchte, raufte*. The resulting paradigms are given below. The forms in parentheses are the same as those of the indicative.

Pres. subjunctive

	Irregular verb	Regular verb	Modal
1	(fahr-e)	(mach-e)	dürf-e
2	fahr-est	mach-est	dürf-est
3	fahr-e	mach-e	dürf-e
1	(fahr-en)	(mach-en)	(dürf-en)
2	fahr-et	mach-et	dürf-et
3	(fahr-en)	(mach-en)	(dürf-en

Past subjunctive

	Irrregular verb	Regular verb	Modal
1	führ-e	(macht-e)	dürft-e
2	führ-est	(macht-est)	dürf-est
3	führ-e	(macht-e)	dürft-e
1	führ-en	(macht-en)	dürft-en
2	führ-et	(macht-et)	dürf-et
3	führ-en	(macht-en)	dürft-en

Jäger (1971: 119) found that over 90 per cent of all subjunctive forms occurred in the 3rd pers. sg. It is thus questionable as to whether many of the other forms which are always listed in the subjunctive paradigm do actually occur. In most cases when we refer to the subjunctive we shall be referring to 3rd pers. sg. forms unless stated otherwise.

The analytic construction for the past subjunctive is to use *würde, würdest, würde; würden, würdet, würden*, the past subjunctive forms of *werden*, plus the infinitive. These forms have become a separate auxiliary to express the subjunctive. The rules for their use are complex and have changed over the years. Prescriptive grammarians are not fond of them and often rail against their use. This analytic construction has become increasingly used to replace the synthetic subjunctive. Jäger (1971: 207) reports 21.3 per cent of *würde* forms in conditional sentences. The first edition of the *Duden Grammatik* (1959: 124f.) took a moderate line, saying that although some might reject its use, preferring older and more euphonious simple forms, it is nevertheless becoming more frequent and any grammar must recognize this development. Similar comments are to be found in the second edition (1966: 119), with more understanding in the third edition (1973: 114ff.). The fourth edition (1984: 171f.) sets out more specific recommendations. The analytic form *würde* plus the infinitive should be used if the synthetic subjunctive forms are unusual or unclear (*nicht eindeutig*). The unusual forms are those such as *verdürbe, beföhle* which are not frequent and considered elevated or affected. Since in the case of the regular verbs there is no distinction between indicative and subjunctive in the past tense, this situation means that the subjunctive can only be clearly shown by using *würde* plus the infinitive. The auxiliary *würde* is also used for euphonic reasons to replace the future of the main verb *werden*, i.e. not *getragen werden werde* but *getragen würde*.

Up to now we have simply labelled the subjunctive forms present or past subjunctive because they form their inflected forms from the present or past stem. These labels may be kept if it is understood that no tense distinction is implied by them. Their use, as we shall see, does not correspond to the traditional distinction between present and past tense that occurs in the indicative. This can be inferred from the use of the past subjunctive in indirect speech when the present form of the verb is the same as the indicative, *Er sagt, er habe jetzt keine Zeit und die Herren müßten warten*. The present subjunctive form is *habe* and the past subjunctive form *müßten*, the present indicative and subjunctive form is *müssen*. To avoid the misunderstanding that might be involved in using labels such as present and past subjunctive the terms *Konjunktiv I* and *Konjunktiv II* are used in German for the present and past subjunctive respectively. Thus *habe* is *Konjunktiv I* and *müßten* is *Konjunktiv II*. These terms are to be found already in the first edition of *Duden Grammatik* (1959: 120) but their first use may go back to Fourquet (1952), who uses *subjonctif I* and *subjonctif II*, although the recognition of the lack of importance of tense goes back to the 1920s and 1930s. The usual English terms are past and present subjunctive (Durrell 1991: 307) but there have been attempts to use other terms. Kufner (1962: 84) suggests *special subjunctive* for the present subjunctive, since it is not so frequently used, and *general subjunctive* for the past subjunctive. We shall simply use the terms 'subjunctive I' and 'subjunctive II'.

If the subjunctive forms are not distinguished by tense, is there any distinction between them and how is it to be described? Both subjunctive forms share a common category of referring to non-real situations or events. Table 8.5, adapted from Engel (1988: 426), shows where their functions are in complementary distribution and where they might contrast. Examples (from Jäger 1971): (1) indirect speech: *Man sagt, etwa, man könne sich vorstellen, daß die Vorgänge in der Natur gesetzmäßig bestimmt seien* (1971: 78); *Sie meinte, Tiere, die arbeiteten und also Feierabend hätten, wären eine Blasphemie* (1971: 138); (2) unreal comparison: *Heute kommt mir ja vor, als sei das etwas übertrieben gewesen* (1971: 410); *Hanna tat als schliefe sie*

(1971: 408); (3) adhortative: *Man nehme einen kräftigen Oxydator, zum Beispiel Fluor* (1971: 416); (4) wish: *Ich wäre lieber in irgendein Hotel gefahren* (1971: 398); (5) concessive: *Wie dem auch sei, ich muß mich jetzt der . . . Bewegungstherapie . . . unterziehen* (1971: 418); (6) conditional: *Wenn man von einem Symptom unmittelbar auf eine Krankheit schließen könnte, wäre die Medizin sehr einfach* (1971: 388); (7) politeness: *Hätten Sie vielleicht noch ein Exemplar?* (Engel 1988: 424). Types 5 and 7 are restricted to a few formulaic phrases. Type 3 is also not frequent; Jäger (1971: 238f.) has only forty-nine examples (27.4 per cent) of subjunctive I occurring ouside indirect speech and conditional sentences. It is difficult to gauge the frequency of type 4 since Jäger (1971: 205f.) has no separate category but lists them under the heading of incomplete conditional sentences. Under this category he has fifty-two examples (2.1 per cent) of subjunctive II occurring outside indirect speech. The main bastion of subjunctive II is, however, in conditional sentences, type 6. Engel (1988: 426) calls them hypothetical. Of the subjunctive forms in total, Jäger (1971: 28f.) found 2,481 (39.4 per cent) were subjunctive II occurring ouside indirect speech, of which 2,254 (90.7 per cent) occurred in conditional sentences (Jäger 1971: 189). All the types dealt with so far have had either subjunctive I or II, but the first two types are the more interesting area since they show both forms being used. In type 2, unreal comparisons, which are mostly introduced by *als* (*ob*) and similar particles, subjunctive II is more frequent according to Jäger (1971: 226), with 177 occurrences (69.1 per cent) as opposed to seventy-nine occurrences of subjunctive I (30.9 per cent). How far does this difference in distribution correspond to a difference in meaning? *Duden Grammatik* (1st edn, 1959: 554) regards subjunctive II as the usual form but subjunctive I is used if the probability of the statement is being stressed or if the subjunctive I form is unclear, i.e. in the case of regular verbs. *Duden Grammatik* (2nd edn, 1966: 596) makes a similar statement about the use of subjunctive I if the Subjunctive II form is unclear. In addition it is stated that subjunctive I is used to express the fact that the statement is 'only supposed, i.e. without guarantee', which seems to contradict what is said in the previous edition. In *Duden Grammatik* (3rd edn, 1973: 107) and Jäger (1971: 229f.) there is said to be no difference in meaning between the two. This is repeated by *Duden Grammatik* (1984: 163). Here we have a good example of genuine variation with no obvious differentiation of function between the competing forms. Historically the use of subjunctive I has been gaining ground since the eighteenth century (Jäger 1969: 87).

Table 8.5 Distribution of subjunctive forms

Function	Subjunctive I	Subjunctive II	Würde possible?	Konjunktiv I and Konjunktiv II exchangeable?
1 Indirect speech	+	+	+	+
2 Unreal comparison	+	+	+	+
3 Adhortative	+	−	−	−
4 Wish	−	+	+	−
5 Concessive	+	−	−	−
6 Conditional	−	+	+	−
7 Politeness	−	+	+	−

The use of the two subjunctive forms in indirect speech is more difficult to describe. Jäger (1971: 28f.) has almost twice as many subjunctive I forms as subjunctive II forms in indirect speech: 2,123 as opposed to 1,312. In addition he found 544 indicative forms. In some cases the subjunctive II forms are the result of the so-called 'replacement rule' by which a subjunctive II form is used if the subjunctive I form is the same as the indicative: Engel (1988: 419) *Es hieß, ich gebe die Leitung ab → Es hieß, ich gäbe die Leitung ab* or *Man sagt, wir haben es gewußt → Man sagt, wir hätten es gewußt*. This is not always followed, however: *Warum sagt sie's nicht, daß ich ihr Leben zerstört habe* (Jäger 1971: 334). Some subjunctive II forms occurred in direct speech in conditional sentences or unreal conditions and remained unchanged when they were put into indirect speech, *Erst als ich aufgelegt hatte, wurde mir klar, daß er der erste war, mit dem ich gern noch länger telefoniert hätte* (Jäger 1971: 368). A difference of meaning between the two subjunctive forms is said to exist in that subjunctive II is said to show more scepticism. The statement using subjunctive I, *Er sagt, er sei krank*, simply reports the fact, but the use of subjunctive II, *Er sagt, er wäre krank*, shows that the speaker does not believe it. This view is put forward by Flämig (1959: 56f.), Helbig and Buscha (1974: 165) and appears in earlier editions of *Duden Grammatik* (1st edn, 1959: 556; 2nd edn, 1966: 585; 3rd edn, 1973: 110). Jäger (1970: 24; 1971: 172) also accepts it and discusses these cases in detail. He seems to allow some use of subjunctive II to express distancing on the part of the speaker. This is not accepted now (*Duden Grammatik* 1984: 171, fn.; Lockwood 1987: 270; Durrell 1991: 313). The difficulty here is that a linguistic variant has been taken up by prescriptive grammarians and a distinction, possibly an artificial one, made and taught. This could then, in turn, influence linguistic usage.

A different approach to the subjunctive in indirect speech is taken by Eisenberg (1986: 121–31). He maintains that there is no grammatical category termed indirect speech and that the presence or absence of the subjunctive depends on the verb concerned. Thus the subjunctive is possible in a *daß* clause with certain verbs, for example *Karl meint/hört/hofft/glaubt, daß Egon bleiben wolle*, but not with others: the sentences **Karl versteht/vergißt/entschuldigt/weiß, daß Egon bleiben wolle* are ungrammatical; the construction should be, *daß Egon bleiben will*. Those verbs that take the subjunctive are termed non-factive verbs, while those that do not are termed factive verbs. The meaning of the verbs determines the presence or absence of the subjunctive. However, verbs of saying can take either the indicative or the subjunctive. The verb *berichten* is a factive verb, i.e. it should always take the subjunctive: thus both *Bild berichtet, daß der Graf verhaftet worden sei* as well as *Bild berichtet, daß der Graf verhaftet worden ist* are grammatical. Eisenberg accounts for this by maintaining that *berichten* and verbs like it have a non-factive variant. The subjunctive in such constructions is thus determined by the choice of verb. If a factive verb is chosen then the indicative will always occur, but if a non-factive verb or a verb with a non-factive variant is chosen then the subjunctive or the indicative occurs. The verbs *behaupten, beschuldigen, erklären, lügen, unterstellen, vorwerfen* are examples of non-factive verbs, and *berichten, hervorheben, mitteilen, sagen, unterstreichen* are examples of factive verbs with a non-factive variant. The advantages of Eisenberg's analysis are first that it makes a more general statement about the occurrence of the subjunctive since the verbs of saying are only a sub-set of non-factive verbs which take the subjunctive, and second it ignores the concept of indirect speech which has no clear status and is often difficult to define, replacing it by the term factivity.

8.6.2.4   Voice

(*Duden Grammatik* 1984: 176–89; Durrell 1991: 292–305; Eisenberg 1986: 132–43; Engel 1988: 453–62; Flämig 1991: 416–29; Heidolph *et al.*, 1981: 540–60; Helbig and Buscha 1991: 161–88; Hentschel and Weydt 1990: 116–26)

The category of voice is again one which only applies to verbs. There are two terms in this category for German, active and passive.

In forming the passive the NP which is the subject, or actor, of the active sentence becomes the agent of the passive sentence, whereas the object NP of the active sentence becomes the syntactic subject of the passive sentence. In the active sentence *Der Vater begrüßt seinen Sohn*, the object *seinen Sohn* becomes the subject of the passive sentence while the subject of the active sentence becomes the agent of the passive sentence, *Sein Sohn wird vom Vater begrüßt*. Apart from the interchange between subject and object there is also: (1) the use of the prep. *von* to denote the agent phrase; (2) the use of the auxiliary verb *werden* plus the past participle of the verb. The verb *werden* is used elsewhere as an auxilary to form the future where it takes an infinitive. As a copula verb meaning 'to become' it shows some overlap with the passive construction. This can be shown by the examples below. The passive has the same variety of tenses as the active does.

Functions of the verb *werden*

	Passive	Copula verb
Present	er wird gelobt	er wird müde
Past	er wurde gelobt	er wurde müde
Future	er wird gelobt werden	er wird müde werden
Perfect	er ist gelobt worden	er ist müde geworden
Pluperfect	er war gelobt worden	er war müde geworden
Future perfect	er wird gelobt werden	er wird gelobt worden sein

In the perfect, pluperfect and future perfect there is a clear morphological distinction between the two constructions in that the past participle of *werden* always occurs without the prefix *ge-* in the passive. In the case of the present, past and future the difference between the passive construction and copula verb is not always clear, *er wird behindert*. The type of passive formed with the auxiliary *werden* is known as the actional passive (*Vorgangspassiv*) and is in opposition to the passive formed with the auxiliary *sein*, called the statal passive (*Zustandspassiv*), *Die Tür wird geschlossen* vs *Die Tür ist geschlossen*. The actional passive focuses on the process of becoming shut whereas the statal passive focuses on the result, the state, of being shut. Of the two passive constructions the actional passive is more frequent, occurring in a ratio of 3:1 to the statal passive. Brinker (1971: 107) has 73.8 per cent of passive forms with *werden* and 26.2 per cent with *sein*. The statal passive will be dealt with later.

Modern linguists and traditional grammarians have been united in regarding the active sentences as being basic and the passive ones derived from them. Helbig and Buscha (1991: 166ff.) have some examples with the minimum of formalization. We will alter their abbreviations slightly to be more consistent with the terminology we have employed in this section. From a string $NP'_1 \, V \, NP''_2$, where the subscripts denote the cases, 1 = nom., 2 = acc., and the indices serve to identify the different NPs, the following passive string is derived: NP''_1 *werd* PP V *von* NP'_2. *Der Lehrer lobt den Schüler* → *Der Schüler wird vom Lehrer gelobt*. These syntactic changes involve the permutation of elements, in this instance the NPs, and the insertion of lexical items, for example auxiliary *werd-*, prep. *von* and the elements that make up the past participle, the prefix *ge-* and the ending *-t* or, in the case of the irregular verbs, *-en*. This type of syntactic process is known as a transformation and was introduced into linguistic theory by Noam Chomsky. For more about the motivation behind transformational syntax and the development of the theory see Radford (1988), Haegemann (1991) and Grewendorf (1988). The passive has always been a good example for transformational analysis since it involves so many syntactic processes (see Bierwisch 1963; Huber and Kummer 1974; Höhle 1978).

We have seen how an acc. obj. becomes a nom. subj. in the passive transformation. However, when the obj. NP is in the dat. or gen. then there is no case shift, the NP remaining in the case it had in the active sentence. *Der Lehrer hilft dem Schüler* → *Dem Schüler wird vom Lehrer geholfen* and *Der Lehrer gedachte des Toten* → *Des Toten wurde vom Lehrer gedacht*. Huber and Kummer (1974: 221–34) have different transformational rules to account for this. One thing that all these three sentences have in common is that the agent NP *vom Lehrer* can be deleted: *Der Schüler wird gelobt, Dem Schüler wird geholfen, Des Toten wurde gedacht*.

8.6.3 Word order

(Bierwisch 1963: 30–49; *Duden Grammatik* 1984: 715–29; Durrell 1991: 453–84; Eisenberg 1986: 300–8; Engel 1988: 303–55; Flämig 1991: 219–49; Heidolph *et al*., 1981: 702–64; Helbig and Buscha 1991: 564–84; Hentschel and Weydt 1990: 382–96)

As we have seen, the verb plays an important role in the syntactic structure of German, determining the shape and structure of sentences. In determining rules for word order in German the position of the verb is taken as paramount. If we classify sentences and clauses in

German according to the position of the verb we see that there are the following possibilities:

1 Verb in initial position: (a) *Bist du fertig?*, (b) *Komm sofort hierher!*, (c) *Treten Vokale als Nichsilbenträger auf, dann nennt man sie unsilbisch*. The first example is a question, the second an imperative and the third a conditional sentence. An alternative form for the conditional is to start with *wenn*, in which case the verb will be last in the subordinate clause, *Wenn Vokale als Nichsilbenträger auftreten, . . .*

2 Verb in second position, preceded by a variety of different constituents in initial position: (a) the subject NP: *Der Mensch spricht in Wörtern*; (b) adverbs and adverbial phrases: *In der Tat hat die Menschheit lange gebraucht . . . , Allerdings entsprechen sich die Anzahl der Laute . . .* ; (c) object complements: *Diesen Phonemwechsel zwischen /b/ und /p/ nennt man Morphophonem*, *Diesem Mann kann geholfen werden!*, *Für Speisen und Trinken wurde gesorgt*.

3 Verb in final position, typically in subordinate clauses: *Wörter, die sich nur durch ein einziges Phonem unterscheiden, heißen Minimalpaare*, *Es kommt vor, daß in bestimmten Wörtern ein Phonem durch ein anderes ersetzt werden kann, ohne daß sich die Bedeutung ändert*.

These three positions of the verb can be schematized as VSO, SVO, SOV, where S = subject and O = object. However, since the preverb position in SVO is often taken by other constituents than the subject it is better to use a more general notation such as VXY, XVY and XYV, where X and Y are any non-verb constituents.

For the many other functions of words, including emphasis and the phenomenon of the sentence frame (*Satzrahmen*), the reader is referred to the sections of the works cited above as there is no space to include them here.

8.6.4 Changes in the VP

(Admoni 1990: 262–5; Braun 1987: 125–49; Glück and Sauer 1990: 45–50 and 65–75; Sommerfeldt *et al*. 1988: 234–40)

The continued assimilation of irregular verbs to regular is an ongoing change although they belong to the most frequent verbs in the language and new compounds are being formed. There are also several changes taking place in the tense system. Several tenses are becoming less frequent. The simple past tense is giving ground to the compound perfect and the pluperfect is being replaced by the perfect. Thus prescriptive rules such as *nachdem* always needing the pluperfect do not correspond to usage. The future, if we regard it as a tense, is also becoming less frequently used and the future perfect is being replaced by the perfect, very often accompanied by a particle such as *doch* or *wohl*. On the other hand, we can witness the genesis of a new 'double' perfect tense, *Das habe ich vergessen gehabt*, with the meaning of a completed action in the past. This does not seem to be restricted to any particular area although it occurs frequently in the south. Another development is the emergence of a progressive form *ich bin am Schreiben* 'I am writing' which *Duden Grammatik* designates as 'regional' (*landschaftlich*). Only time will tell if these two forms will become part of the mainstream of German. The subjunctive is becoming optional and being replaced more and more by the indicative. There is also a clear trend from synthetic to analytic shown by the replacement of subjunctive forms such as *stünde* by *stehen würde*; the development of main verbs to auxiliaries, for example in the passive, *bekommen*, *gehören*, *erhalten*, *kriegen*; the genesis and spread of the so-called 'function' verbs (see p. 44). There are changes of the position of the verb in subordinate clauses beginning with *weil*. Normally the verb should come in final position in such clauses: *Eine solche Zerlegung wäre aber nicht sinnvoll, weil /be:/ und /t/ hier keine Bedeutung haben*; however, there is increasing evidence that the normal second position for the verb is occurring in such clauses (Gaumann 1983).

SELECT BIBLIOGRAPHY AND FURTHER READING

Admoni, W. G. (1970) *Der deutsche Sprachbau*, Munich: Beck.
—— (1973) *Die Entwicklungstendenzen des deutschen Satzbaus von heute* (Linguistische Reihe, 12), Munich: Hueber.
—— (1990) *Historische Syntax des Deutschen*, Tübingen: Niemeyer.
Augst, G. (1975) 'Zum Pluralsystem', in his *Untersuchungen zum Morpheminventar der deutschen Gegenwartssprache* (Forschungsberichte des Instituts für deutsche Sprache, 25), Tübingen: Niemeyer, pp. 5–70.
—— (1977) 'Wie stark sind die starken Verben?' in his: *Sprachnorm und Sprachwandel*, Frankfurt: Athenaion, pp. 125–77.
—— (1979) 'Neuere Forschung zur Substantivflexion', *Zeitschrift für germanistische Linguistik*, 7: 220–44.
Bergenholtz, H. and Mugdan, J. (1979) *Einführung in die Morphologie*, Stuttgart: Kohlhammer.

Bergenholtz, H. and Schaeder, B. (1977) *Die Wortarten im Deutschen*, Stuttgart: Klett.

Bierwisch, M. (1963) *Grammatik des deutschen Verbs* (Studia Grammatica, 2), Berlin: Akademie.

Braun, P. (1987) *Tendenzen in der deutschen Gegenwartssprache*, 2nd edn, Stuttgart: Kohlhammer.

Brinker, K. (1971) *Das Passiv im heutigen Deutsch* (Heutiges Deutsch, 1, 2), Munich: Hueber.

Duden 4: Grammatik (1984), eds G. Drosdowski, G. Augst, H. Gelhaus, H. Gipper, M. Mangold, H. Sitta, H. Wellmann and C. Winkler, 4th edn, Mannheim: Bibliographisches Institut.

Durrell, M. (1979) 'Some Problems in the Morphology of the German Noun Phrase', *Transactions of the Philological Society*, pp. 66–88.

—— (1991) *Hammer's German Grammar and Usage*, rev. edn, London: Edward Arnold.

Eisenberg, P. (1986) *Grundriß der deutschen Grammatik*, Stuttgart: Metzler.

Engel, U. (1988), *Deutsche Grammatik*, Heidelberg: Groos.

Flämig, W. (1959) *Zum Konjunktiv in der deutschen sprache der Gegewart: Inhalte und Gebrauchsweisen*, Berlin Akademie.

—— (1991) *Grammatik des Deutschen*, Berlin: Akademie.

Fourquet, J. (1952) *Grammaire de l'allemand*. Paris: Hachette.

—— (1969) 'Das Werden des neuhochdeutschen Verbsystems', in U. Engel, P. Grebe and H. Rupp (eds) *Festschrift Für Hugo Moser*, Düsseldorf: Verlag Enzyklopädie

Fox, A. (1990) *The Structure of German*, Oxford: Clarendon Press.

Gaumann, U. (1983) *'Weil die machen jetzt bald zu': Angabe- und Junktivsatz in der deutschen Gegenwartssprache* (Göppinger Arbeiten zur Germanistik, 381), Göppingen: Kümmerle.

Glück, H. and Sauer, W. W. (1990) *Gegenwartsdeutsch*, Stuttgart: Metzler.

Grewendorf, G. (1988) *Aspekte der deutschen Syntax: eine Rektions-Bindungs-Analyse* (Studien zur deutschen Grammatik, 33), Tübingen: Narr.

Haegemann, L. (1991) *Introduction to Government and Binding Theory*, Oxford: Basil Blackwell.

Halle, M. (1953) 'The German Conjugation', *Word*, 9: 45–53.

Heidolph, K. E., Flämig, W. and Motsch, W. (1981) *Grundzüge einer deutschen Grammatik*, Berlin: Akademie.

Helbig, G. (1972) *Probleme der deutschen Grammatik für Ausländer*, Leipzig: Verlag Enzyklopädie.

Helbig, G. and Buscha, J. (1974, 1991) *Deutsche Grammatik; ein Handbuch für den Ausländerunterricht*, 2nd, 13th edn, Leipzig: Verlag Enzyklopädie.

Hentschel, E. and Weydt, H. (1990) *Handbuch der deutschen Grammatik*, Berlin: de Gruyter.

Heringer, H. J. (1988) *Lesen lehren lernen: eine rezeptive Grammatik des Deutschen*, Tübingen: Niemeyer.

Höhle, T. (1978) *Lexikalistische Syntax: die Aktiv-Passiv-Relation und andere Infinitkonstruktionen im Deutschen* (Linguistische Arbeiten, 67), Tübingen: Niemeyer.

Huber, W. and Kummer W. (1974) *Transformationielle Grammatik des Deutschen, I*, Munich: Fink.

Jäger. S. (1969) 'Beharrungstendenzen in der Schriftsprache', in U. Engel and P. Grebe (eds) *Neue Beiträge zur deutschen Grammatik: Hugo Moser zum 60. Geburtstag gewidmet* (Duden-Beiträge, 37), Mannheim: Dudenverlag, pp. 78–93.

—— (1970) *Empfehlungen zum Gebrauch des Konjunktivs* (Sprache der Gegenwart, 10), Düsseldorf: Schwann.

—— (1971) *Der Konjunktiv in der deutschen Sprache der Gegenwart* (Heutiges Deutsch, 1, 1), Munich: Hueber.

Kufner, H. L. (1962) *The Grammatical Structures of English and German*, Chicago: University of Chicago Press.

Latour, B. (1985) *Verbvalenz: eine Einführung in die dependentielle Satzanalyse des Deutschen*, Munich: Hueber.

Lockwood, W. B. (1987) *German Today: The Advanced Learners' Guide*, Oxford: Clarendon Press.

Mugdan, J. (1977) *Flexionsmorphologie und Psycholinguistik*, Tübingen: Narr.

Radford, A. (1988) *Transformational Grammar: A First Course*, Cambridge: Cambridge University Press.

Ross, J. R. (1967) 'Der Ablaut bei den deutschen starken Verben', *Studia Grammatica*, 6: 47–118.

Rowley, A. R. (1988) 'Zum Genitiv des ganz besonderen Typ', *Muttersprache*, 98: 58–68.

Russ, C. V. J. (1989) 'Die Pluralbildung im Deutschen', *Zeitschrift für germanistische Linguistik*, 17: 52–67.

Sommerfeldt, K.-E., Fleischer, W., Huth, H., Langner, H., Meier, H., Michel, G., Porsch, P., Schröder, M., Starke, G. and Wiese, I. (1988) *Entwicklungstendenzen in der deutschen Gegenwartssprach*, Leipzig: Bibliographisches Institut.

Ulvestad, B. (1956) 'The Strong Verb Conjugation in German', *Word*, 12: 91–105.

Weber, H. (1971) *Das erweiterte Adjektiv- und Partizipialattribut im Deutschen* (Linguistiche Reihe, 4), Munich: Hueber.

Welke, K. M. (1988) *Einführung in die Valenz- und Kasustheorie*, Leipzig: Bibliographisches Institut.

Wurzel, W. U. (1970) 'Das Ablautsystem', *Studien zur deutschen Lautstruktur* (Studia Grammatica, 7), pp. 69–79.

9 Word formation

In discussing word formation we shall draw on general works such as Bauer (1988) and Bergenholtz and Mugdan (1979) as well as specific works on German, for example Henzen (1965), Erben (1983), Wellmann (1984) Olsen (1986), Naumann (1986) and Fleischer and Barz (1992). Lipka and Günther (1981) is a collection of seminal articles. For German we are fortunate in having the detailed corpus-based studies of Kühnhold and Wellmann (1973) on the verb, Wellmann (1975) on the noun, Kühnhold *et al.* (1978) on the adjective and Ortner *et al.* (1991) and Pümpel-Mader *et al.* (1992) on compounding. Useful shorter accounts can be found in books on the structure of modern German, for example Fox (1990), Keller (1978).

9.1 THE UNITS OF WORD FORMATION

(Bauer 1988: 7–25; Bergenholtz and Mugdan 1979: 12–29 and 116–25; Fleischer and Barz 1992: 21–44)

The word, although the basic unit of word formation, contains smaller, minimal units, morphemes. The term word is used to refer both to simple words, for example *Haus*, *Baum*, which are not further analysable, and complex words, *Haustür*, *Zeichnung*, *Sterblichkeit*, which can be divided into smaller units. The former cannot be analysed into any smaller units whereas the latter may be divided into smaller units, or morphemes. We can recognize the morphological structure of complex words by comparing them with simple ones. The occurrence of *Haus* and *Tür* as separate, independent units shows that *Haustür* is a complex word comprising two morphemes. In the case of *Zeichnung* and *Sterblichkeit* the morphemes into which they can be segmented, do not occur on their own but always in combination with other morphemes, *Zeichn-* in *zeichnen*, *-ung* in *Rundung*, *sterb-* in *sterben*, *-lich* in *reichlich* and *-keit* in *Seligkeit*. Those morphemes that can occur independently, such as *Haus* and *Tür*, are called free morphemes, whereas those that can only occur together with another morpheme, *Zeichn-*, *-ung*, *sterb-*, *-lich* and *-keit*, are called bound morphemes. Morphemes can be further divided into stems and affixes. Stems, or roots, are what is left when the affixes have been removed. We will use the term stem. They can be either bound, *Sterb-*, *Zeichn-*, or free, *Haus*, *Tür*. The combinations of two or more free stem morphemes is known as a compound, *Schlafzimmer*, *Braunkohle*, *Weinglas*. The combination of a bound or free stem and a bound morpheme is a derived form, *Schöpfung*, *Kindheit*. The term affix covers prefixes, used before stems, *schlafen*, *verschlafen*, and suffixes, used after stems, *träge*, *Trägheit*. Stems and affixes can both be called morphemes. However, since stems normally carry the lexical meaning of the whole word, they can be called lexical morphemes. Affixes, which signify inflectional categories or derivational functions, can simply be called morphemes. In our description of German word formation we will be more precise and use the traditional terms suffix and prefix when referring to non-lexical morphemes.

The term word itself covers several different usages. We may speak of *Haus*, *Hauses*, *Häuser* as being word forms of the same lexical word, or lexeme, HAUS. We can distinguish between the two usages of word and word form by writing the former in capitals and the latter in conventional spelling. Thus *Haus*, *Hause*, *Häuser* are inflectional word forms of the lexeme HAUS. Every lexeme will have several inflectional word forms. In some exceptional instances only one word form for a lexeme may exist, for example *die Milch*. These are mostly non-countable nouns. Otherwise most lexemes have at least two word forms – *Junge*, *Jungen*; *Tat*, *Taten*; *Kino*, *Kinos* – and sometimes more – *Kraft*, *Kräfte*, *Kräften*; *Mutter*, *Mütter*, *Müttern* (three word forms); *Tag*, *Tages*, *Tage*, *Tagen*; *Gast*, *Gastes*, *Gäste*, *Gästen* (four word forms). Verbs have even more: *mache*, *machst*, *macht*, *machen*; *machte*, *machtest*, *machten*, *machtet*, *gemacht* (nine word forms). The forms *häuslich*, *hausen*, *Häuschen*, on the other hand, are usually considered to be new separate lexical items, words. They also themselves have different word forms: *häuslich*, *häuslicher*, *häusliche*, *häusliches*, *häuslichen*, *häuslichem*; *hausen*, *hause*, *haust*, *hauste*, *hausten*, *gehaust*. The word *Häuschen*, like all diminutives, has two word forms, *Häuschen*, *Häuschens*.

9.2 INFLECTION VS DERIVATION

(Bauer 1988: 73–87; Bergenholtz and Mugdan 1979: 142–4; Fox 1990: 120–3)

Within morphology there is a division between inflection and derivation, word formation. Inflection deals with the different forms of a word according to its syntactic status. Derivation, or word formation, also called lexical morphology, on the other hand, deals with new words which usually belong to different parts of speech from the words from which they were formed. Several criteria are cited to support this distinction, although none of them is unproblematic. First, derivational affixes change the word class of their base or stem. The forms *häuslich*, *hausen*, *Häuschen*, on the other hand, are considered to be separate lexical items. This can be shown from the fact that a dictionary gives them each a separate entry, whereas *Haus*, *Hauses*, *Häuser* occur under the single entry *Haus*. An exception to this is the word *Häuschen*, which does not change its word class. Since it has a separate meaning from *Haus*, it is regarded as a separate word. Other exceptions to this criterion that a new derived word will belong to a different part of speech are presented by the feminine suffix -*in*, as in *Kollege*, *Kollegin*, the collective prefix *Ge-*, as *Berg*, *Gebirge*, the negative adjectival prefix *un-*, as in *sicher*, *unsicher*, *treu*, *untreu*, as well as numerous verbal prefixes which do not create words belonging to different parts of speech, although they are words with a clearly different meaning, *fahren*, *abfahren*, *ausfahren*, *verfahren*. Second, inflectional affixes tend to have a more straightforward and regular meaning whereas the meaning of derivational affixes is more diffuse. The interpretation of this criterion depends on the notion of meaning we employ. Even with fairly uncomplicated categories it can be seen that inflectional affixes tend to designate categories such as 'singular', 'plural', 'person', 'accusative', etc. Derivational affixes, on the other hand, are more difficult to pin down. The suffix -*ig*, for example, in one analysis, is listed as having twenty-five different meanings! (Kühnhold *et al.* 1978: 108f.). For example the three most frequent are: (1) 'to have' or 'to be full of', *dreifenstrig*, *dunkelhaarig*, *saftig*, *staubig*; (2) 'to be like', *milchig*, *breiig*, *wurstig*, *spiralig*; (3) 'something/somebody does something', *bröckelig*, *dösig*, *schläfrig*, *zittrig*. Third, inflectional affixes tend to be regular and derivational affixes tend to be semi-productive. The second person sg. pres. ending -*st* is inflectional since it occurs with all kinds of verbs: regular verbs, *machst*, strong verbs *schreibst*, modal verbs *kannst*, *sollst*, and even with the anomalous verbs 'to have', *hast*, and 'to be', *bist*. Derivational affixes occur with a limited number of stems. As an illustration let us consider the process of deriving agentive nouns, for example nouns for people who do things, *Schwimmer* from *schwimmen*. In two-thirds of the cases the formations add the suffix *-er* to a verbal stem, *Empfänger*, *Bäcker*, *Maler*, but there are also the suffixes *-ent*, as in *der Lieferant*, *Produzent*, *-ende*, as in *der Studierende*, *Vorsitzende*, *-ling*, as in *der Eindringling*, *Ankömmling*, *-bold*, as in *der Raufbold*, *Scherzbold*, *-ator*, as in *der Kompilator*, *Organisator*, *-eur*, as in *der Monteur*, *-ist*, as in *der Komponist* (Wellmann 1975: 339–57). However, some inflectional affixes are less regular than *-st*. The third person sg. pres. ending *-t*, for example, does not occur with modal verbs, for example *er/sie/es kann*, *darf*, *soll*, etc. Noun pl. endings are notoriously irregular in German and do not occur with uncountable nouns, for example *Milch*, *Blei*, *Gold*. Fourth, following on from the tendency for inflectional affixes to be regular and derivational affixes to be semi-productive is the fact that the former tend to be much smaller in number than the latter. Even though there are five plural morphemes for German nouns, *-(e)n*, *-er* (plus umlaut of the stem vowel where possible), *-e*, *-e* (plus umlaut of the stem vowel in certain lexemes) and *-s*, there are twenty-nine derivational affixes for nouns in German (twenty-six suffixes and three prefixes) (Wellmann 1975: 97). Fifth, the inflectional affixes are a closed set. Only with difficulty do new inflectional suffixes arise, for example *-s*, through borrowing. The derivational affixes, on the other hand, are more an open class, new ones being easily borrowed or created. This criterion, of course, presupposes a diachronic analysis. Sixth, derivational affixes tend to occur nearer the stem than inflectional affixes, *Sterb-* (stem) + *lich* (derivational suffix) + *keit* (derivational suffix) + *en* (inflectional suffix). This is typical for the vast majority of word structures in German but there are exceptions of the type *Kinderchen*, *Wägelchen*, where the pl. suffix (inflectional) comes before the diminutive (derivational). These exceptions can be explained historically as analogical formations to forms such as *Hämmerchen*, *Vögelchen*, where the *-er*, *-el* is part of the stem (Fleischer and Barz 1992: 180f.). Synchronically they form an interesting minor exception to this criterion. Seventh, derivational forms may be replaced by simple forms, i.e. without the affix, but inflectional forms may not. Thus *Möglichkeit* in the sentence *Ich sehe keine Möglichkeit* can be replaced by *Chance*, but in *Autos sind nicht gerade billig*, *Autos* may not be replaced by *Auto*. **Auto sind nicht gerade billig* is an ungrammatical sentence.

9.3 PRODUCTIVITY IN WORD FORMATION

(Bauer 1988: 57–62; Bergenholtz and Mugdan 1979: 166f. and 174–6; Fleischer and Barz 1992: 71f.)

Only to analyse words into their component morphemes tells us nothing about which affixes are used to produce new words and which only exist in a few fossilized forms. At one extreme there is the suffix *-mäßig*, which is highly productive, giving rise to many new forms; at the other extreme is the suffix *-t*, which occurs in such nouns as *Fahrt*, *Sicht* and which does not give rise to any new forms. Rather than have the two poles of productivity, productive and non-productive, it is useful to have an intermediate type, active (Fleischer and Barz 1992: 60f.). Productive affixes are those which give rise to a large number of new forms, for example *-er*, *-ung*, *-ig*; active affixes are those which give rise to analysable forms, but they are limited in number, for example *-icht*, *-nis*, *-tum*, and unproductive affixes are those which are morphemically segmentable but produce no new forms, for example *-t*. The productive and active suffixes will be dealt with under the appropriate section of derivation (9.4.2.1).

9.4 TYPES OF WORD FORMATION

The main types of word formation which are used to form new words in German are compounding and derivation (prefixation and suffixation). In derivation we can distinguish between explicit derivation, where affixes are used, and implicit derivation, where no overt affix is added. The mere changing of word class, as in *ticken* but *das Ticken der Uhr*, without any overt change is called conversion and will be dealt with under implicit derivation. There are also more minor processes such as clipping, blending, reduplication and forming acronyms.

9.4.1 Compounding

(Bergenholtz and Mugdan 1979: 168–74; Erben 1983: 57–66; Fleischer and Barz 1992: 87–145; Fox 1990: 134–43; Naumann 1986: 61–7; L. Ortner *et al*. 1991; Pümpel-Mäder *et al*. 1992; Wellmann 1984: 439–58)

Compounding is the combination of two stems to form another word, *Schlaf* + *Sack* = *Schlafsack*. This process can occur with nouns, adjectives, adverbs and verbs but it is most productive in the case of nouns. Our main discussion will concern nouns but a short account of compounding with other parts of speech will be given. Most compounds consist of a basic component or head (*Grundwort* or *Determinatum*), which gives noun compounds their grammatical gender and a determining first component or modifier (*Bestimmungswort* or *Determinans*), for example *Haustür*, where *Haus* is the modifier and -*tür* the head. This type can be called a subordinating compound (*Determinativkompositum*). Since the compound can be replaced in a sentence by a simple word of the same word class it is also called an endocentric compound, for example *Tür* can replace *Haustür* in *Die Haustür stand offen*. The modifier restricts the meaning of the head in the compound. The simple word *Tür* can cover an opening/closing means of access to many things, whereas a compound restricts its meaning to one item, to one type of opening or a certain type of door: *Autotür*, *Garagentür*, *Kellertür*, *Toilettentür*; *Doppeltür*, *Drehtür*, *Klapptür*, *Pendeltür*; *Außentür*, *Innentür*, *Seitentür*, *Vordertür*; *Gittertür*, *Glastür*, *Stahltür*. Nominal compounds consist of at least two stems, *Zimmerpflanze*, but they can be increased to give such forms as the legendary *Donaudampfschifffahrtsgesellschaftskapitäns-kajütenschlüssel*. Jacob Grimm records *Rheinschifffahrtszentral-kommission* (quoted in Naumann 1986: 65). Our remarks on compounds will assume just two components.

In most cases the modifier appears uninflected, for example *Haustür*, *Schlafsack*, *Zimmerpflanze*, but in some instances different word forms appear, for example *Landbau*, *Landsmann*, *Landesbank*, *Länderkampf*; *Tagdienst*, *Tageskarte*, *Tagereise*; *Sprachkenner*, *Sprachenfrage*. The elements -*(e)s*, -*er*, -*e*, -*en* look like inflectional endings and historically this is the case. From *des Meeres Grund* (noun phrase in the gen. + noun) there evolved *Meeresgrund* (compound noun). Synchronically, however, they are merely linking morphemes (*Fugenelemente*) with no inflectional meaning. We find, for instance, semantic anomalies such as *Bischofskonferenz*, with a sg. -*s* but where there are a number of bishops, and *Tagereise*, with a pl. -*e* but where the reference is to only one day's journey. There are also morphological anomalies with -*s* occurring with feminine nouns, for example *Liebesbrief* and always after -*ung*, as in *Bevölkerungszunahme*, *Einbildungskraft*. Although in some words these linking elements may correspond to pl. or gen. meaning, for example *Wörterbuch*, *Pferdemarkt*, *Urlaubsort*, they are best regarded as empty morphemes. Thus *Urlaubsort* could be divided mophemic-ally into *Urlaub+s+ort*. According to Wellmann (1984: 452) two-thirds of all modifiers in noun + noun compounds occur without linking elements, -(*e*)*s*, -(*e*)*n* occur in 10–20 per cent while -*er* and -*e* are much rarer, occurring in only 1–2 per cent of examples.

Nominal compounds can be classified in different ways: first, according to the part of speech of the modifier. All the major parts of speech occur in this function: *Autoschlüssel* (noun + noun), *Großstadt* (adj. + noun), *Dreirad* (numeral + noun), *Innenkurve* (adverb + noun), *Ichform* (pronoun + noun) and *Bratpfanne* (verb + noun). This classification only deals with the surface structure and tells us little about the syntactic or semantic relationship between the head and the modifier.

Second, compounds can be described in terms of the syntactic relationship between the components. The following types occur: (1) subordinating compounds; (2) co-ordinating (or appositional) compounds; (3) exocentric compounds; and (4) copulative compounds. Subordinating compounds show a great freedom, combining noun-last components with modifiers from most other major parts of speech: nouns *Schlüsselloch*, adjectives *Großeinkauf*, numerals *Viereck*, adverbs *Außentür*, pronouns *Ichsucht*, verbs *Auslegeware*. A sub-type of subordinating compounds is represented by forms such as *Dickkopf*, *Lästermaul* which refer to people with certain traits or who do certain things. Although they refer to a head which is not contained in the compound, their use is usually figurative. They have the same structure as the other subordinating compounds. Second, there are co-ordinating (or appositional) compounds, where the two components are of equal weight: a *Stadtstaat* 'city–state' is both a *Stadt* and a *Staat*. This type is not nearly so frequent and comprises: (1) designations for clothing, *Strumpfhose*, *Schürzenkleid*; (2) people, *Fürstbischof*, *Dichterkomponist*, *Waisenkind*. Another example which does not fit into either of the two categories is *Strichpunkt* 'semi-colon'. This type of compound is also endocentric.

The third type of nominal compound is represented by words like *Taugenichts* where the head of the compound lies outside its components. It refers to a person by paraphasing what the person does or is. The components of the compound are different parts of speech from the compound itself. Thus *Tauge-* is a verbal stem and *nichts* a negative pronoun. This is known as an exocentric compound. Other examples are: *Störenfried*, *Nimmersatt*, *Dreikäsehoch* and *Wendehals* 'turncoat' (even though its original use was for a bird 'wryneck').

The fourth type of compound is the copulative compound, mostly represented by names, for example *Schleswig-Holstein*, *Rheinland-*

Pfalz. Both parts are of equal rank, designating separate entities which together produce a new entity.

Third, compounds can be described in terms of the meaning relationship between the two components. In this instance the following types have been suggested: (1) the head represents the subject of an underlying sentence, *Lebewesen = Wesen, das lebt, Kletterrose = Rose, die klettert*; (2) the head is the object, *Mischfutter = Futter, das man mischt, Schlagsahne = Sahne, die man schlägt*; (3) the head is in an instrumental relationship to the modifier, *Gießkanne = Kanne, mit der man gießt, Rasierapparat = Apparat, mit dem man sich rasiert*; (4) the head is modified by a relative clause denoting locality, direction or time, *Spielplatz = Platz, auf dem man spielt, Sendebereich = Bereich, in dem man etw. sendet, Waschtag = Tag, an dem man wäscht*; (5) the modifier produces or causes some action or reaction, *Juckpulver = Pulver, das Jucken bewirkt, Schleuderunfall = Unfall, der durch Schleudern entsteht*; (6) the head is modified by a relative clause explaining its meaning in more detail, *Erzähltalent = Talent, das das Erzählen betrifft, Bastelarbeit = Arbeit, die darin besteht, daß jmd. bastelt*. In this section we will treat them according to the relationship between their parts.

Adjective compounds can also be formed in German. The head is an adjective and the modifier usually a noun, *lebensnah*, or another adjective, *hellblau*. Exceptionally a verb stem occurs, *röstfrisch, tropfnaß*. As with nouns, subordinating compounds are the main type. They have the following functions: (1) they represent compulsory prepositional, gen., dat. or acc. constructions: *reformbedürftig = bedarf der Reform, fachfremd = dem Fach fremd, kilometerbreit = mehrere Kilometer breit, kompromißbereit = bereit zum Kompromiß*; (2) they represent optional prepositional constructions which modify the head: *diensteifrig = eifrig beim (im) Dienst, weltbekannt = in der Welt bekannt, morgenmüde = müde am Morgen*; (3) they represent comparisons: *grasgrün = grün wie gras, daunenweich = weich wie Daunen*. Co-ordinating adjective compounds also occur, *taubstumm*. They are less frequent than the subordinating type among the adjectives but more frequent than the nominal co-ordinating compounds. Other examples are *naßkalt, süßsauer, feuchtwarm* and the national colours such as *blauweiß, schwarzrotgold*. The colloquial formation *feuchtfröhlich* 'merry (through drink)' also fits in here. Derived adjectives are often divided by a hyphen, *deutsch-französisch, wissenschaftlich-technisch*.

Compounds among verbs are even more restricted. The use of verbal stems, nouns and adjectives as modifiers, for example *trennschleifen* from *trennen* + *schleifen* 'to cut off', *kupferkaschieren* 'to copper-bond' and *buntweben* 'to colour weave' are typical of technical language (see 9.7) and individual literary language, for example Arno Holz (1863–1929): *grinskeuchen = grinsen + keuchen*, *schnaufwittern = schnaufen + wittern*. There are, however, some genuine verbal compounds with a noun or adjective modifier: as a direct object of a verb, *achtgeben, danksagen, stattfinden, teilnehmen*; representing a state, *stillsitzen, übrigbleiben*; functioning as an adverb, *blindschreiben, falschspielen, schieflaufen*. The most frequent type represents the achieving of a result: *fertigstellen, freischaufeln, schönfärben, trockenlegen, volltanken*. The most productive process of forming compound verbs, however, is with adverbial particles. These comprise formations with *da(r)-, her-, hin-, empor-, hoch-, fort-, weg-, weiter-, heim-, zurück-, zusammen-* and combinations with *einander, auseinander-, durcheinander-*, etc. The separable verbal prefixes *ab-, an-, auf-, aus-, bei-, durch-, hinter-, los-, nach-, über, um-, unter-, vor-, wider-, zu-* all occur as free morphemes; however, in view of the difference in function and meaning they are reckoned not as parts of compounds but as semi-prefixes or prefixoids (see 9.4.3).

9.4.2 Derivation

(Bergenholtz and Mugdan 1979: 155–67; Erben 1983: 66–116; Fleischer and Barz 1992: 146–209; Fox 1990: 124–34; Naumann 1986: 61–7; Wellmann 1984: 458–81 and 489–500)

Derivational constructions typically comprise stems and affixes, for example to the stem *bind-* the nominal suffix *-ung* can be added to give *Bindung*, and the prefix *Ver-, Verbindung*. This main type of derivation is called explicit derivation. In opposition to that are forms such as the verb *essen* and the noun *das Essen*, or the verbs *fallen, rufen* and the nouns *der Fall, der Ruf*. In these cases no affixes are added. This type of formation with a 'zero affix' is known as conversion. A further part of the process is when the nominal stem contains a different vowel from the verb, for example *beißen, der Biß, ziehen, der Zug*. This type of derivation without any overt affix is called implicit derivation.

9.4.2.1　Explicit derivation

We will deal with the productive and active affixes only. Kühnhold and Wellmann (1973), Wellmann (1975) and Kühnhold *et al*. (1978) are corpus-based studies which enable us to get a picture of the numerical strengths and weaknesses of the different nominal affixes, even if it is difficult to draw an exact line between productive and active affixes. The figures represent an oversimplification since they do not reveal the productivity of particular meanings of an individual affix: for instance, although the adjectival suffix *-bar* is productive with regard to deverbal formations it is not so with denominal formations. However, the figures do give some idea of how productive affixes are relative to each other. The examples are given in the order 'form from which the affixed form is derived' followed by 'affixed form'. The figures for the nominal suffixes appear below:

-ung, dichten, Dichtung, vergeben, Vergebung, Holz, Holzung (2,515);

-keit/-heit, sauber, Sauberkeit, frei, Freiheit, dunkel, Dunkelheit, vergangen, Vergangenheit (1,549);

-er, Fußball, Fußballer, Handwerk, Handwerker, prüfen, Prüfer, malen, Maler (1,270);

-(er)ei, Tyrann, Tyrannei, Bäcker, Bäckerei; sticken, Stickerei, fragen, Fragerei (498);

-in, Arzt, Ärtzin, König, Königin (466);

-e, pflegen, Pflege, ausleihen, Ausleihe; eng, Enge, glatt, Glätte (389);

-chen, Auto, Autochen, Spiegel, Spiegelchen (359);

-(at)ion, Institut, Institution, diskret, Diskretion, demonstrieren, Demonstration (279);

-ismus, ideal, Idealismus, Marx, Marxismus (228);

-ität, anonym, Anonymität, Lokal, Lokalität (173);

-ik, kritisch, Kritik, Drama, Dramatik (172);

-schaft, Freund, Freundschaft, bereit, Bereitschaft (166);

-ist, Humor, Humorist, komponieren, Komponist (159);

-ie, melancholisch, Melancholie, Aristokrat, Aristokratie (132);

-tum, Fürst, Fürstentum, reich, Reichtum, irren, Irrtum (132);

-ler, Sport, Sportler, abweichen, Abweichler (109);

-ling, Haft, Häftling, weich, Weichling, ankommen, Ankömmling (106);

-lein, Vogel, Vöglein, Kind, Kindlein (85);

-ator, organisieren, Organisator, Aggression, Aggressor (73);

-nis, Bund, Bündnis, finster, Finsternis, erleben, Erlebnis (69);

-entl-ant, *-enzl-anz*, *emigrieren*, *Emigrant*, *Abitur*, *Abiturient*, *arro-gant*, *Arroganz*, *tendieren*, *Tendenz* (68);
-iker, *skeptisch*, *Skeptiker* (65);
-eur, *kommandieren*, *Kommandeur*, *Inspektion*, *Inspekteur* (62).

The suffixes *-är*, *-(i)at*, *-bold*, *-el*, *-erie*, *-euse*, *-icht*, *-ner*, *-sche* had under thirty occurrences each. Nominal prefixes form a much smaller group. The most productive is *Ge-* followed by a final *-e* or no ending: *fragen*, *Gefrage*, *bellen*, *Gebell*, *Wolke*, *Gewölk* (375). Wellmann (1975: 50f.) subsumes the collective meaning of this prefix. Since in words like *Gebirge* the meaning is expressed by discontinuous elements, *Ge-* . . . *-e*, it would be more accurate to talk here of a circumfix rather than a prefix. None of the other prefixes comes anywhere near the high score for this morpheme. The negative prefixes scored as follows: *Miß-* (26) and *Un-* (49) (Wellmann 1975: 52f.).

The following list shows the productivity of adjectival suffixes:

-ig, *Schlamm*, *schlammig*, *finden*, *findig*, *faul*, *faulig*, *dort*, *dortig* (2,008);
-isch, *Student*, *studentisch*, *necken*, *neckisch*, *genial*, *genialisch* (1,387);
-lich, *Kirche*, *kirchlich*, *entbehren*, *entbehrlich*, *klein*, *kleinlich* (940);
-haft, *Ekel*, *ekelhaft*, *schmeicheln*, *schmeichelhaft*, *böse*, *boshaft* (429);
-all-ell, *Form*, *formal*, *formell* (403);
-bar, *heilen*, *heilbar*, *Frucht*, *fruchtbar* (389);
-(at)iv, *Qualität*, *qualitativ*, *generieren*, *generativ* (251);
-mäßig, *Beruf*, *berufsmäßig* (206);
-ern, *Stein*, *steinern* (159);
-osl-ös, *Religion*, *religiös* (131);
-arl-är, *Illusion*, *illusionär* (124);
-antl-ent, *Arroganz*, *arrogant*, *brillieren*, *brillant* (96);
-abell-ibel, *akzeptieren*, *akzeptabel*, *Komfort*, *komfortabel* (73);
-sam, *streben*, *strebsam*, *Furcht*, *furchtsam*, *beredt*, *beredsam* (64).

The suffixes *-oid* and *-esk* had only forty and twenty-eight forms respectively. The most productive adjective prefix was *un-* with 1,116 forms (Kühnhold *et al.* 1978: 96).

Verbs show the least number of derivational suffixes. The inflectional ending of the infinitive is *-en* and any derivational suffix is inserted before this, for example *reinigen*, *radeln*. The following types appear: *blöde*, *blödeln*, *Rad*, *radeln*, *mild*, *mildern*, *Loch*, *löchern, rein, reinigen, Angst, ängstigen.* The largest group, about 1,700, is represented by the originally foreign suffix *-ieren*, as in *proben, probieren, Student, studieren.* This suffix has no meaning of its own but serves to form verbs from foreign words. In the course of time it has been reinforced by extended forms such as *-isieren*, *-ifizieren*: *Signal, signalisieren, Person, personifizieren.*

9.4.2.2 Conversion and implicit derivation

The formation of nouns from verbal infinitive forms, for example *schreiben, das Schreiben,* is very productive. The only changes are to capitalize the word and use the appropriate form of the definite article. Once formed, these nouns can be inflected, *ich bin des Wartens müde.* This forming of new words by changing their part of speech without any overt ending is known as conversion (*Konversion*). Not only can verbs be nominalized but also other parts of speech as well. The resulting noun is always neuter, for example pronouns, *das Ich*, numerals, *die Vier*, particles, *das Für und Wider, das Diesseits, mein Gegenüber.* The nominalization of adjectival forms has a slightly different outcome in that the resultant forms are still inflected like adjectives and may also take any of the three genders, depending on the context. These adjective–nouns comprise past participles, *der Gefangene*, present participles, *der Studierende*, and simple and derived adjectives, *der Alte, der Fremde, der Jugendliche, der Industrielle*.

The implicit derivation of nouns from verbs is numerically very strong but not productive, since no new nouns are formed in this way: *setzen, der Sitz; ziehen, der Zug; arbeiten, die Arbeit, anworten, die Antwort; baden, das Bad.* Of the 678 nouns noted by Wellmann (1975: 96f.) 618 are masculine, 43 are feminine and 17 are neutral. In those cases where there is also a change of vowel the following alternations occur: verb *ei*, noun *i* (either short or long), *reißen, Riß; treiben, Trieb*; verb *ie*, noun *u* (either short or long), *fließen, Fluß, ziehen, Zug*; verb *i*, noun *a* as in *fingen, Fang*; verb *i*, noun *a* and *u*, as in *binden, Band, Bund, trinken, Trank, Trunk*; verb *e*, noun *u*, as in *sprechen, Spruch, werfen, Wurf*; and other alternations, *wachsen, Wuchs, tragen, Trug, fließen, Floß, schwören, Schwur*. This process bears a great similarity to the alternations among the irregular, or strong, verbs, cf. *beißen, biß, gebissen; trinken, trank, getrunken*. This process is called vowel gradation (*Ablaut*). Some of the forms which have no corresponding verbal stem vowel in modern German can be found in earlier periods of the language: for instance, *u* in

Zug, Fluß, can be found in MHG in the past tense pl. forms *wir zugen, ir zuget, sie zugen.*

9.4.3 Compound or derived form?

(Erben 1983: 81f.; Fleischer and Barz 1992: 177f., 316–48 and 227–34; Naumann 1986: 92–6; Wellmann 1984: 279–81 and 291–4)

We have assumed up to now that the components of a compound are usually free morphemes, *Autoschlüssel, Haustür*, whereas in a derived form there is a free or bound stem plus a bound prefix or suffix, *verkaufen, käuflich*. The derivational affixes which we have dealt with usually contain one or two syllables, *be-, ent-, anti-, ultra-, -bar, -sam, -iker, -ismus.*

Problems can arise when a formal identity seems to exist between part of a complex word and a free morpheme. If we contrast the words *Pumpwerk, Porzellanwerk* and *Laubwerk, Schuhwerk*, the free form *Werk* exists meaning 'work; works, factory'. Thus *Pumpwerk* is 'pumping plant' and *Porzellanwerk* 'porcelain factory'. In these cases the meaning of the second component is the same or similar to the meaning of the free form *Werk*. In addition the relationship between the two parts is that of subordination. Both the words are some kind of *Werk*. Also, the first component could be omitted and the context would tell us what *Werk* was being talked about. These criteria confirm that *Pumpwerk, Porzellanwerk* are compounds. In the case of *Laubwerk* 'foliage' and *Schuhwerk* 'footwear' these criteria are not fulfilled. The meaning of the second component *-werk* is not 'work; works, factory', but simply shows that these nouns are collective nouns. The similarity in form is not paralleled by a similarity in meaning. The relationship between the two parts of these words is also different from the previous examples. No paraphrase can illustrate their meaning, the two components must remain together and their meaning is that of the word as a whole. The semantic head of the word is the first component, *Laub-* and *Schuh-*. From this it follows that the second component cannot occur on its own and its meaning would be derived from the context. In addition, the second component, *-werk*, behaves like a suffix, occurring in many other forms, derived from nouns, with the same meaning of collectivity, *Astwerk, Blattwerk, Fachwerk, Regelwerk*. The second element *-werk* also has the meaning of 'what is produced' when used with formations from verbs, *Backwerk, Flechtwerk*. The term for these morphemes which have a formally identical homonymic form and seem to be halfway between compound elements and affixes is semi-affix or affixoid. They can be divided into semi-prefixes, prefixoids, and semi-suffixes, suffixoids *Halb(präfix/suffix)*, *Präfix/ Suffix(oid)*. Their main characteristics are: (1) they are the basis for new formations; (2) their meaning is more generalized and abstract than the formally identical free morpheme; (3) there has been a shift of meaning in the relationship between the two parts of the word so that the first component determines the basic meaning; and (4) the use of the free homonymic form becomes more limited. This is part of the historical development of the word-formation system. In the distant past such suffixes as *-heit*, *-lich* came from independent words.

Suffixoids appear in nominal and adjectival forms. *Duden 10: Das Bedeutungswörterbuch* (1985) has entries for affixoids with examples from the Duden archives. Noun suffixoids (see the list below) very often designate people. Some of the meanings, particularly the metaphorical extensions, for example *-welle* 'wave', are also to be found in English.

-fabrik, *Ferienfabrik*, *Medienfabrik*, *Traumfabrik*,

-fritze 'designates a person' (slightly pejorative), *Bummelfritze*, *Immobilienfritze*, *Psychofritze*,

-gut, 'totality of things or people', *Gedankengut*, *Saatgut*, *Krankengut*, *Schülergut*,

-hai 'shark', *Abschreibungshai*, *Miethai*, *Versicherungshai*,

-heini 'denotes a person' (slightly derogatory), *Couchheini*, *Plattenheini*, *Wackelheini*,

-huber 'denotes a person' (slightly derogatory), *Stoffhuber*, *Zipfelhuber*,

-imperium 'empire', *Bierimperium*, *Ölimperium*, *Playboyimperium*,

-mafia, *Bayernmafia*, *Büromafia*, *Spielbankmafia*,

-marathon, *Abstimmungsmarathon*, *Lesemarathon*, *Sitzungsmarathon*,

-muffel 'designates a person' (pejorative), *Fernsehmuffel*, *Gurtmuffel*, *Modemuffel*,

-nudel 'designates a person' , *Betriebsnudel*, *Giftnudel*, *Skandalnudel*,

-papst, *Diätpapst*, *Literaturpapst*, *Sexpapst*,

-salat, *Beinsalat*, *Bildsalat*, *Soundsalat*,

-schwemme 'flood', *Akademikerschwemme*, *Geldschwemme*, *Obstschwemme*,

-silo, *Autosilo*, *Hotelsilo*, *Wohnsilo*,

-welle, *Ausreisewelle*, *Freßwelle*,

-werk, *Fahrwerk*, *Kartenwerk*, *Wurzelwerk*,

-wesen, Beamtenwesen, Gesundheitswesen, Vereinswesen,
-zar, Fernsehzar, Popzar, Zeitungszar,
-zeug 'totality of material', *Badezeug, Nachtzeug, Schulzeug.*

Adjectives have developed many suffixoids. The following list gives statistics for the productivity of the individual forms for those occurring over fifty times (based on Kühnhold *et al.* 1978: 120–73):

-artig (223),
-reich (171),
-fähig (156),
-voll (150),
-frei (129),
-förmig (102),
-farben/-farbig (93),
-freudig (87),
-arm (64),
-gerecht (55),
-bereit (53).

The following were recorded fewer than fifty times: *-ähnlich* (22), *-bedürftig* (26), *-eigen* (29), *-feindlich* (33), *-fertig* (48), *-fest* (48), *-fremd* (23), *-freundlich* (35), *-froh* (22), *-gemäß* (26), *-getreu* (13), *-(be)gierig* (27), *-haltig* (54), *-kundig* (22), *-leer* (24), *-los* (413), *-lustig* (31), *-orientiert* (34), *-pflichtig* (39), *-reif* (41), *-schwach* (24), *-schwer* (25), *-sicher* (40), *-stark* (48), *-süchtig* (47), *-technisch* (35), *-trächtig* (37), *-wert* (54), *-widrig* (28), *-willig* (31), *-würdig* (47). The following were the least frequent, being recorded fewer than twenty times: *-aktiv, -beständig, -betont, -dicht, -durstig, -echt, -eifrig, -empfindlich, -faul, -fern, -geil, -gleich, -hungrig, -intensiv, -intern, -kräftig, -lüstern, -müde, -nah, -schwanger, -selig, -tauglich, -tüchtig, -verdächtig, -weit, wütig. Duden 10: Das Bedeutungswörterbuch* (1985) has further examples, albeit without any statistical information: *-abhängig, -anfällig, -bedingt, -bewußt, -bewegt, -bezogen, -frisch, -günstig, -lastig, -leicht, -neutral, -politisch, -seitig, -sicher, -spezifisch, -wirksam, -zentriert.*

Verbs do not have any suffixoids but they do have prefixes or prefixoids. These fall into three classes: (1) the unstressed inseparable prefixes, for example *be-, ent-, ver-,* etc.; (2) those that are always stressed and separable, *ab-, an-, auf-, aus-, bei-, da(r)-, ein-, zu-,* etc.; and (3) those that are sometimes stressed and separable and sometimes unstressed and inseparable, differentiating the meaning of the verb, *durch-, hinter-, über-, um-, unter-, wider-*. The prefixes in groups 2 and 3 have formally identical free morphemes, for example prepositions *ab*, *an*, *auf*, *aus*, *bei*, *durch*, etc. Since the meaning of the prepositions and verbal prefixes are sometimes similar, for example *aus*, *ausgehen*, they could be regarded as compound verbs. However, since the prefixes often bear little relation to the meaning of the preposition, it might be just as appropriate to call them prefixoids. This is the solution adopted by Wellmann (1984: 425–32).

9.4.4   Minor processes

(Fleischer and Barz 1992: 218–23; Naumann 1986: 225–7; Wellmann 1984: 392–7)

New, shortened, words (*Kurzwörter*) can be formed from compounds by clipping the first or last component (in parentheses): *Akku*-(*mulator*), *Demo*(*nstration*), *Dino*(*saurier*), *Disco*(*thek*), *Hasch*-(*isch*), *Klo*(*sett*), *Labor*(*atorium*), *Limo*(*nade*), *Krimi*(*nalroman*), *Po*(*dex*), *Uni*(*versität*); *Omni*(*bus*). The former, which are more numerous, are called 'headwords' (*Kopfwörter*) and the latter 'tail words' (*Schwanzwörter*). Most of these occur in both their short and long form, but others are only discernible historically, for example *fesch* (an Austrian form from Engl. *fashionable*). Some are loans from English, for example *Disco*, where the same process is at work. Tail words such as *Bahn* for *Eisenbahn* result from the lexicalization of the compound. In some cases the middle section of a word is omitted: *Ansichts*(*post*)*karte*, *Bier*(*glas*)*deckel*, *Fern*(*sprech*)*amt*, *Kr*(*aftfahrr*)*ad*, *Zell*(*wand*)*stoff*. These are known in German as *Klammerformen* ('bracketed forms').

In blending or contamination parts of two words are combined, cf. Engl. *smog* from *smoke* and *fog*. In German there are very few of these in the standard language: *Kurlaub*, *Klamotte* (from Czech *klamol* 'fragment' and *Schamotte* 'fire-clay; rubbish'), *Postkarte* (from *Postblatt* and *Korrespondenzkarte*), *Gebäulichkeit* (from *Gebäude* and *Baulichkeit*) and *Schlamassel* (from *schlimm* and Yiddish *masol* 'good fortune'). There are more in dialect speech, for example *Erdtoffel* 'potato' in a transitional area between an area with *Erdapfel* and one with *Kartoffel*.

Acronyms, words formed with the first letters of phrases, are a productive source of new words. The designations for vehicles, *Kfz*, *LKW*, *PKW*, are perhaps the most familiar and they have been joined by *PC*, *LP*, *CFC* and *CD*, borrowings from English. German examples are *ABM*, *Arbeitsbeschaffungsmaßnahme*, *EDV*, *Elektron*-

ische Datenverarbeitung, UKW, Ultrakurzwelle, uk, unabkömmlich 'unfit for military duty', *WG, Wohngemeinschaft* and *HO, Handelsorganisation* and *LPG, landwirtschaftliche Produktionsgenossenschaft* (used in former East Germany). The words are pronounced by giving each letter its pronunciation as a letter of the German alphabet, for example [ɛlkaveː], [eːdeːfau] with the stress on the last syllable. Exceptions to this are the word *Aids*, which is pronounced as it is in English, [eːds], and other acronyms which are pronounced as words: *Bafög, GAU, größter anzunehmender Unfall, UNO.* Many acronyms refer to organizations, firms or are only in use in specialist language. Some examples under *L* in *Duden Rechtschreibung* are listed below:

LA, Lastenausgleich;
LG, Landgericht;
LRS, Lese-Rechtschreib-Schwäche;
LSG, Landschaftsschutzgebiet/Landessozialgericht;
LVA, Landesversicherungsanstalt;
LZB, Landeszentralbank.

A similar process involves using the first syllables of words instead of merely first letters. The word *Azubi* (from *Auszubildende*) probably belongs here. Older examples of this are *Gestapo = Geheimestaatspolizei, Schupo = Schutzpolizist* and examples from the former GDR, *Stasi = Staatssicherheitsdienst* and *Vopo = Volkspolizist.*

Another minor type of word formation consists in the repetition of the whole or part of a morpheme. There are: (1) complete reduplications, *die Pinkepinke* 'money', *das Tamtam* 'noise, fuss'; (2) rhyming forms, differing only in the initial consonant(s), *der Klimbim* 'odds and ends; fuss', *der/das Kuddelmuddel* 'mess, muddle', *das Larifari* 'nonsense', *das Schorlemorle* 'white wine mixed with mineral water', *das Techtelmechtel* 'affair, flirtation'; (3) ablaut formations, differing only in the stem vowel, *der/das Hickhack* 'squabbling', *der Krimskrams* 'odds and ends', *der Schnickschnack* 'poppycock; paraphernalia', *das/der Tingeltangel* 'dance, hop'.

9.5 SEMANTICS IN WORD FORMATION

The approach to word formation that has mostly been adopted here has started with the form of the affixes and compounds. Meaning or function, where it has been discussed, has been of individual affixes. A complementary approach is to start with certain areas of meaning and see which affixes are used to express them. This approach is taken by Kühnhold and Wellmann (1973) on the verb, Wellmann (1975) on the noun and Kühnhold *et al.* (1978) on the adjective. If we take as an example the expression of the diminutive, we find that several different affixes are involved: *-chen, Bein, Beinchen, -lein, Brief, Brieflein, -el, Knochen, Knöchel, -ling, Tanne, Tännling, -ette, Sandale, Sandelette* and the prefix *Mini-, Minirock, Miniausgabe*. Other semantic areas among nouns include feminine formations, *-in, Lehrerin, -euse, Friseuse*, abstract nouns, *-heit/-keit, Schönheit, Fröhlichkeit, -ung, Vergebung, -schaft, Freundschaft, -e, Größe, -nis, Erlebnis*. The meaning of some nouns can be strengthened by adding augmentative morphemes, mostly prefixoids, for example, *Affen-, Affenhitze, Bomben-, Bombenerfolg, Erz-, Erzschelm, Heiden-, Heidenlärm, Riesen-, Riesenspaß*. These are mostly used in colloquial speech. Adjectives have forms to express opposites, *un-, unwichtig, in-, intolerant, a-, anormal*, or belonging *-isch, heidnisch, -lich, väter- lich, -al, klerikal, -är, familiär*. The formation of adjectives meaning 'can be + verbal stem' is usually derived by the passivization suffix *-bar*, as in *machbar = kann gemacht werden*, but there are also competing suffixes, *-lich, käuflich, -abel, akzeptabel, -ig, zulässig, -ativ, koordinativ*.

9.6 BORROWED AFFIXES

Suffixes have been borrowed from French, *-ei, Bäckerei* and also Latin *-al, horizontal* in the development of German (Russ 1984, 1986). In more recent times suffixes and prefixes have also been borrowed from English and new ones created by a reanalysis of English loans. A very widespread English prefix is *super-/Super-*, which combines with adjectives or nouns, *superklug, superwasser- dicht, Superbreitwand, Superspion*. Examples and a description of the meaning and distribution of this and the following affixes can be found in *Duden 10: Das Bedeutungswörterbuch*, which lists forty adjective and thirty noun forms. *Schulz/Basler* (1977–8) shows a steady increase of *super-/Super-* forms after 1945. There have been attempts to use a loan translation, *über-/Über-*, for example *Überspieler Pele*, but this has not caught on. The prefix *Ex-*, which is only added to nouns, is also very frequent and is added to both German and English nouns, *Ex-Minister, Ex-Gatte, Ex-Kolonie, Ex- Zuchthäusler* and now *Ex-DDR*. Thirty-two such noun forms are listed in *Duden 10*. The semi-suffixes *-bewußt* and *-weit* are con- sidered loan translations of English '-conscious, -wide', *selbstbewußt* 'self-conscious', *weltweit*, 'world wide'. The semi-suffix *-bewußt* has also been productive in forming new words, *marketingbewußt, vertei-digungsbewußt* (*Duden 10* lists thirty-four forms), whereas *-weit* has been restricted to a few forms such as *bundesweit, DDR-weit, welt-weit* which themselves are very frequently used. From the noun *das Musical* a morpheme *-ical* has been abstracted, although only pro-ductive for a limited length of time, and is used for new formations such as *Grusical* 'horror show', *Logical* 'puzzle (based on the rules of logic)', although some are often jocular nonce-forms like *Absurdical* 'absurd play', *Frostical* 'show on ice' (Carstensen 1985). The English agentive suffix *-er*, although present in German, has become used more frequently under English influence both for people, *Geldmacher, Discounter, Abrüster, Platzhalter*, and also for instru-ments, *Senkrechtstarter, Viertürer* (Carstensen 1965: 55–8).

The extent to which English loans have penetrated the vocabulary of German can be gauged by the large number of hybrid words that have been formed, i.e. words containing both an English and a German morpheme, for example *Jetflug, Bluttest*. In most cases these can be regarded as semi-loan translations where only one member, instead of both members, of a compound is translated. Some examples of these are: *Babyalter, Babyausstattung, Babyjahr, Babyrassel, Babywäsche, Diskountpreis, Nonstopflug, Supermarkt, Haarspray, Flugticket*. These forms are regarded as sufficiently German not to be found in *Fremdwörter* dictionaries but only in German dictionaries. Further evidence for the integration of English words into the German system of word formation is given by the fact that even a derivational German suffix such as *-in* for forming feminine nouns can be added to English words: *Layouterin, Bodybuilderin, Cutterin*. The English verbal particle *on* is rendered *an*, for example *anturnen* 'to be turned on (usually to drugs)'.

9.7 WORD FORMATION IN TECHNICAL LANGUAGES

(Feinäugle 1974: 14–17; Fluck 1976: 47–55; 1984: 16–19 and 50–66)

Compounding, which as we have seen (9.4.1), is an important means of creating new words, is very productive in technical languages and characteristic of them. Compounds help to differentiate between several words all containing the same basic component or head. Thus the carpenter can distinguish between different types of 'plane' by forming nominal compounds with *Hobel* as the head, and other words as the first components or modifiers: *Schlichthobel* 'smoothing plane', *Schrupphobel* 'jack plane', *Zahnhobel* 'toothing plane' *Simshobel* 'rebate plane', *Grundhobel* 'router plane', *Schabhobel* 'spokeshave' and *Schiffshobel* 'compass plane'. The shoe-making industry, for instance, makes use of a large number of compounds with *-maschine* as the base form to designate different tasks to be performed: *Oberleder-Stanz-Maschine*, *Futterschneidemaschine*, *Oberleder-Spalt-Maschine*, *Oberleder-Schärf-Maschine*, *Knopfannäh-Maschine*, *Sohleauflege-Maschine*, *Sohlenbeschneid- und Rißmaschine*. Sometimes such compounding can result in very long words whose structure is not always immediately clear: *Kraftfahrzeughaftpflichtversicherung*, *Ultrakurzwellenüberreichweitenfernsehrichtfunkverbindung*. One way of making these massive compounds clearer is by using hyphens, for example *Fahrzeug-Leergewicht*, *Kurbel-Versenkfenster*. This is usual for compounds which consist of four or more elements, but a hyphen may be necessary for smaller compounds if there is danger of ambiguity; *Druckerzeugnis* can be divided *Druck-Erzeugnis* 'printed product' or *Drucker-Zeugnis* 'printer's report'. This is particularly the case where it is not clear whether the middle elements are part of the determiner, for instance *Schmalkeilriemen-Getriebe* 'gear with a narrow fan-belt' or of the determinatum *Schmal-Keilriemengetriebe* 'a narrow gear with a fan-belt'. Compounds are useful in that they can be used instead of sentences, for example *Ableselineal = Lineal, an dem man etwas abliest*, or *Schneidschraube = Schraube, die sich das Gewinde, in das sie hineingedreht werden soll, selbst schneidet*.

Compound verbs formed by prefixing another verbal stem to a verbal stem, for example *trennschleifen* from *trenn(en)* + *schleifen* 'to cut off' occur very frequently in specialist language. These verbal compounds are known as 'twin verbs' (*Zwillingsverben*). Other verbal compounds are formed by prefixing nouns and adjectives/adverbs to simple verbs, for example *kupferkaschieren* 'to copper-bond', *buntweben* 'to colour weave'. There is considerable uncertainty as to whether such verbs are separable or inseparable. Since the prefix is stressed the verbs should theoretically be separable and this is usually the case with adjectival prefixes, for example *ich beize blank, tiefgekühlt*. However, when the prefix is a noun the non-finite forms of these verbs render the prefix, or semi-prefix by a phrase or other word, for example *gesenkschmieden* 'to drop forge': *ich schmiede im Gesenk*; *punktschweißen* 'to spot weld': *ich schweiße punktweise*. A more frequent tendency is to conjugate the verb inseparably: *flammhärten* 'to flame-harden', *ich flammhärte*; *sandstrahlen* 'to sand blast', *ich sandstrahle*. Many of these verbs are defective, occurring only in one or two forms, for example *geräuschdämpfend* 'noise-deadening', *farbabweisend*, *lichtbrechend* 'refracting' only occur in the present participle, while *faserverstärkt*, *kugelgelagert* 'ball-bearing mounted', *stückgefärbt* 'dyed *in toto*' only occur in the past participle. The twin verbs, for example *gefriertrocknen* 'to freeze-dry', *glühfrischen* 'to mould by injection', *spritzgießen* 'to injection mould', are usually only used in the present, past participle and infinitive. Finite forms do occur but mostly only in subordinate clauses.

The most frequent derivational suffix is the agentive *-er* added to verbal stems to designate things as well as people. Thus *der Bohrer* avoids the tedious repetition of words such as *-gerät*, *-apparat*, *-maschine*. Thus *Elektrorasierer* is used for *elektrischer Rasierapparat*, *Rasenmäher* for *Rasenmähmaschine* and *Gabelstapler* for *Gabelstapelgerät* 'fork-lift truck'. Sometimes *-er* can replace other elements in a compound, for example *Mischer* from *Mischanlage*. Some nouns with *-er* are derived from compound verbs but not from the corresponding simple verb, for example *Auslöser*, *Aufnehmer*, *Entstauber*. The suffix *-er* frequently occurs in compounds whose base consists of a numeral + noun, for example *Viertürer*, *Zweimaster*. This usage goes back to early NHG but it has only become widely used in modern technical language.

Nominalizations from verbs, either by adding the suffix *-ung* to the verb stem or by simply using the infinitive as a noun, are very frequent in specialist language. The suffix *-ung* can be used for both the process of an action, *Kühlung*, and the product, *Zeichnung*. In the function of designating the process it competes with the nominalized infinitive: *bei der Schweißung* or *beim Schweißen des Stahls*, although the latter is considered 'better'. In the function of designating a process *-ung* also competes with *-verfahren*, *-methode*, for example *Schweißverfahren*, *Schweißmethode*. In designating the result of a process words in *-ung* can add *-produkt* to clarify any ambiguity, for example *Kreuzung*, *Kreuzungsprodukt*. In the language of mathematics words formed with *-ung* only designate the result of a process or a constituent of something and never the process itself, for example *Vereinigung* means 'that which has been joined'. Nominalizations with the suffix *-ung* from verbs in *-ieren* compete with forms in *-ion*, *Automatisierung*, *Automation*.

The suffix *-bar* is mostly used in a passive sense, *waschbar* 'can be washed, washable'. In technical language the semi-suffix *-fähig* competes with *-bar*, especially with verbs which cannot form a passive. The form *explodierfähig* is to be preferred over *explodierbar*. In some cases an opposition has developed between *-bar* and *-fähig*: *tragbar* 'can be carried', *tragfähig* 'capable of carrying (something)'; *lieferbar* 'can be delivered', *lieferfähig* 'capable of delivering'. The prefixes *be-* and *ver-* are used very frequently, *belüften*, *bestreiken*; *Verdampfer*, *verunreinigen*, *Verzahnungsmaschine*, with similar meaning to the standard language.

Another productive process of compounding is by joining an uninflected adjective to a noun: *Buntmetall* 'non-ferrous metal', *Dunkelkammer*, *Edelstein*, *Hochofen*, *Schweröl*. The resultant compounds often have a different meaning from the syntactic construction article + adjective + noun, so that *ein Hochofen* is not simply *ein hoher Ofen* but 'a blast furnace'. Some of the adjectives in these compounds can be used to form classificatory oppositions: *Leichtöl – Schweröl*; *Halbleinenband – Ganzleinenband*. This is particularly true of compound adjectives, whether the adjective is the first component, *vollautomatisch* : *halbautomatisch* : *automatisch*, or the second component, *phosphorreich* : *phosphorarm*. The number of adjectives which enter these oppositions is not numerous: *betriebseigen* : *betriebsfremd*; *seuchenanfällig* : *seuchenfest*; *Kleinbetrieb* : *Mittelbetrieb* : *Großbetrieb*. A distinction between the suffixes *-los* and *-frei* is carefully made in technical language. The suffix *-los* is used for a purely factual statement about the absence of something, for example *drahtlos, fettlos, nietlos, zahnlos*, whereas the suffix *-frei* is used when the absence of something has resulted from a desired effect and is a positive state, for example *chlorfrei, fettfrei, rauchfrei, säurefrei*.

Abbreviation is another method of word-formation used in technical language: *Pkw* (*Personenkraftwagen*), *UKW* (*Ultrakurzwellen*), *HD-Öl*, *DIN* (*Deutsche Industrienorm*), *I-Eisen*. There are also compounds consisting of an abbreviation plus another element, for example *T-Träger*, *U-Profil*, *V-Mann* 'contact, informant', from *Verbindungsmann*.

9.8 TRENDS IN WORD FORMATION

(Braun 1987: 166–79; Glück and Sauer 1990: 75–93; Sommerfeldt *et al*. 1988: 174–92)

The same type of units and processes continue to be used to produce new words. Among nouns there are two seemingly opposing trends. The size of nominal compounds is increasing, *Ferienrückfahrkarte*, *Werkstoffprüfmaschine*, but there is also a tendency to shorten some words or to form acronyms (see 9.4.4). The lengthening serves to specify in more detail and is often found in technical texts (see 9.7), while the shortening and formation of acronyms often results from the need to communicate orally in the workplace. The lengthening of words is expressed in adjectival formations by the derivation from word groups, *sechzehngeschossig, viertürig*. Longer words are also created by phrases becoming words (*Univerbierung*), *Instandsetzung*, *Senkrechtstarter, Verkehrszeichen*. Although these forms represent a morphological lengthening they represent a syntactic shortening. There is one word, *Verkehrszeichen*, instead of the phrase *Zeichen zur Regelung des Verkehrs*. This trend is confirmed by the further tendency to shorten sentences and to use fewer subordinate clauses in favour of noun phrases (see 8.5.2).

As we have seen (9.4.5) the transition from a free component of a compound to a bound affix is often fluid. One of the trends in word formation is for elements of compounds to become affixoids or semi-affixes. There has been a large increase in the productivity of these among nouns and adjectives (see 9.4.3). Another source of new affixes is the analysis of a previously existing word into affix + stem. Then the affix is used to form other words and eventually becomes used as a free form. This has happened with the new prefixes *Bio-* 'natural, organic', and *Öko-* 'ecologically aware'. The new prefixes originally occurred only as part of a few words such as *Biologie, Ökologie*. Now, with their developed meanings, they have become very productive. The following examples have been taken from Strauß *et al.* (1989): *Bio-Äpfel, Bio-Bauer, Bio-Boom, Biobranche, Bio-Forscher, Biogas, Biogefahren, Bio-Hotel, Bio-Kost, Bio-Matratze, Bio-Müll, Biosektor, Biosprit, Biotop*; *Öko-Bauer, Öko-Bewußtsein, Öko-Freak, Öko-Gewissen, Öko-Landbau, Ökopax, Ökotop, Ökozid*. The new independent word *der Öko*, pl. *-s*, 'ecologically minded person' has arisen from the prefix. The shortened free form *Bio* exists, but as an abbreviation for *Biologie*.

Among the existing affixes tendencies can be noted in the increased use of certain morphemes. The verbal prefix *be-*, is particularly frequent in its ornative (formations from nouns), for example *besohlen, beschriften, bestuhlen*, and perfective (formations from verbs) functions, *beliefern, besteigen, begießen*. The suffix *-i* has been used in German for endearment terms among families, for example *Mutti, Vati, Schatzi*, and with names, *Wolfi, Susi*. Forms with *-i* also derive from abbreviated forms, *Chauvi(nist), Dissi(dent)*. Its use has now been extended to refer to people in general, being added to nominal stems (the pl. is *-s*), *Drogi* 'drug-addict', *Fluggi* 'leaflet', *Fundi* 'fundamentalist' (in the Green Party), *Grufti* 'older people', *Knasti* 'prisoner'. These forms are supported by older abbreviations, *Abi*

240 *The German language today*

(*Abitur*), *Pulli* and English loans *Hippy*, *Profi*. The vowel *-o* is also used to form new words. In the shortened forms *Demo*, *Disco*, *Info*, *Majo* (= *Mayonnaise*) it is part of the stem. The ending has, however, been added to stems ending in consonants: (from adjectives) *Brachialo* 'violent person', *Brutalo*, *Normalo*, *Nudo*, *Realo*, *Zentralo*.

SELECT BIBLIOGRAPHY AND FURTHER READING

Althaus, H. P., Henne, H. and Wiegand, H. E. (eds) (1980) *Lexikon der Germanistischen Linguistik*, Tübingen: Niemeyer.

Bauer, L. (1988) *Introducing Linguistic Morphology*, Edinburgh: Edinburgh University Press.

Bergenholtz, H. and Mugdan, J. (1979), *Einführung in die Morphologie*, Stuttgart: Kohlhammer.

Braun, P. (1987) *Tendenzen in der deutschen Gegenwartssprache: Sprachvarietäten*, 2nd edn, Stuttgart: Kohlhammer.

Carstensen, B. (1965) *Englische Einflüsse auf die deutsche Sprache nach 1945*, Heidelberg: Winter.

—— (1985) 'Deutsch -ical', in K. Hyldgaard-Jensen and A. Zettersten (eds), *Symposium on Lexicography II: Proceedings of the Second International Symposium on Lexicography May 16–17, 1984 at the University of Copenhagen* (= *Series Maior*, 5) Tübingen: Niemeyer, pp. 101–19.

Erben, J. (1983) *Einführung in die deutsche Wortbildungslehre*, Berlin: Schmidt.

Feinäugle, N. (1974) *Fach- und Sondersprachen: Arbeitstexte für den Unterricht*, Stuttgart: Reclam.

Fleischer, W. and Barz, I. (1992), *Wortbildung der deutschen Gegenwartssprache*, Tübingen: Niemeyer.

Fluck, H.-R. (1976) *Fachsprachen*, Munich: Franke, Uni-Taschenbücher 483.

—— (1984) *Fachdeutsch in Naturwissenschaft und Technik*, Heidelberg: Groos.

Fox, A. (1990) *The Structure of German*, Oxford: Clarendon Press.

Glück, H. and Sauer, W. W. (1990) *Gegenwartsdeutsch*, Stuttgart: Metzler.

Henzen, W. (1965), *Deutsche Wortbildung*, Tübingen: Niemeyer.

Keller, R. E. (1978) *The German Language*, London: Faber & Faber.

Kühnhold, I. and Wellmann, H. (1973), *Deutsche Wortbildung: Typen und Tendenzen in der Gegenwartssprache 1. Das Verb* (Sprache der Gegenwart, 29), Düsseldorf: Schwann.

Kühnhold, I., Putzer, O. and Wellmann, H. (1978), *Deutsche Wortbildung: Typen und Tendenzen in der Gegenwartssprache 3. Das Adjektiv* (Sprache der Gegenwart, 43), Düsseldorf: Schwann.

Lipka, L. and Günther, H. (eds) (1981) *Wortbildung*, Darmstadt: Wissenschaftliche Buchgesellschaft.

Müller, W. (ed.) (1985) *Duden 10:. Das Bedeutungswörterbuch*, Mannheim: Dudenverlag.

Naumann, B. (1986), *Wortbildung in der Gegenwartssprache*, Tübingen: Niemeyer.

Olsen, S. (1986), *Wortbildung im Deutschen*, Stuttgart: Kröner.

Ortner, L., Müller-Bolshagen, E., Ortner, H.-P., Wellmann, H., Pümpel-Mader, M. and Gärtner, H. (1991) *Substantivkomposita: Deutsche Wortbildung. Typen und Tendenzen in der Gegenwartssprache 4* (Sprache der Gegenwart, 79), Berlin: de Gruyter.

Pümpel-Mader, M., Gassner-Koch, E., Wellmann, H. and Ortner, L. (1992) *Adjektivkomposita und Partizipialbildungen: Deutsche Wortbildung. Typen und Tendenzen in der Gegenwartssprache 5* (Sprache der Gegenwart, 80), Berlin: de Gruyter.

Russ, C. V. J. (1984) 'The Foreign Element in German Derivational Morphology: The Adjectival Suffixes', in C. V. J. Russ (ed.), *Foreign Influences on German*, Dundee: Lochee, pp.27–37.

—— (1986) 'The Integration of Foreign Suffixes into German: A Synchronic and Diachronic Study, Exemplified by the Adjectival Suffixes -abel/-ibel, -al/-ell, ant/-ent, -ar/-är, -iv and -os/-ös', *Quinquereme. New Studies in Modern Languages*, 9: 1–15.

Sommerfeldt, K.-E., Fleischer, W., Huth, H., Langner, H., Meier, H., Michel, G., Porsch, P., Schröder, M., Starke, G. and Wiese, I. (1988) *Entwicklungstendenzen in der deutschen Gegenwartssprache*, Leipzig: Bibliographisches Institut.

Strauß, G., Haß, U. and Harras, G. (1989) *Brisante Wörter von Agitation bis Zeitgeist* (Schriften des Instituts für deutsche Sprache, 2), Berlin: de Gruyter.

Wellmann, H. (1975), *Deutsche Wortbildung: Typen und Tendenzen in der deutschen Gegenwartssprache. 2. Das Substantiv* (Sprache der Gegenwart, 32), Düsseldorf: Schwann.

—— (1984) 'Die Wortbildung', in G. Drosdowski, G. Augst, H. Gelhaus, H. Gipper, M. Mangold, H. Sitta, H. Wellmann and C. Winkler (eds) *Duden 4. Die Grammatik*, Mannheim: Dudenverlag, pp. 386–501.

10 Vocabulary

The vocabulary of a language comprises lexical items and their meaning and use. By lexical items we understand primarily words but there are also idiomatic phrases such as *zwischen Tür und Angel* 'in passing', *jemanden auf die Palme treiben* 'to annoy someone'. The idiomatic phrases (*Phraseologismen*) comprise several words but unlike normal phrases they always occur in the same order and with no changes to their internal structure. The meaning of the whole phrase cannot be derived from the meaning of the parts (Fleischer 1982; Schippan 1992: 47–50). In this chapter we shall concentrate on words and not deal with idiomatic phrases.

The meaning of words has always proved difficult to describe even though most speakers think they know what they mean by a particular word. We shall not attempt to define meaning but refer the reader to Leisi (1971), Lyons (1977), Palmer (1981), Cruse (1986), Rothacker and Saile (1986) and Schippan (1992: 121–87).

Since the vocabulary is the most 'open' level of language, i.e. the one most susceptible to the acceptance of new forms, we shall place a good deal of emphasis on how it is changing, being influenced by English (10.2.1), characterized by new formations (10.2.2), loss of words (10.2.3) and changes in meaning (10.2.4).

10.1 THE STRUCTURE OF THE VOCABULARY

(Gipper 1984; Schippan 1992: 188–227)

In the chapter on word formation (9) we saw how words with a similar stem but different endings formed a word family: *Haus*, *häuslich*, *hausen*, *hausieren*. If, on the other hand, instead of looking for similarities in the form of words we look for similarities in meaning, then we find other groups of words. For instance, the following are all words which designate 'horse' in some way (*Duden 8* 1986: 508): *Pferd, Hengst, Stute, Wallach, Füllen/Fohlen, Schimmel, Rappe, Fuchs, Schecke, Roß, Gaul, Klepper, Mähre, Renner, Vollblüter, Kracke, Pony, Hafermotor.* These words can thus be said to belong to the same semantic, lexical or word field. The members of a semantic field can be separated from each other by the different aspects of the main class feature they emphasize. *Stute* can be characterized by the feature 'female' as opposed to *Hengst*, which is male. Both *Stute* and *Hengst* are fully grown, whereas *Füllen/Fohlen* 'foal' is not fully grown. *Wallach*, 'gelding', can be characterized as unable to procreate, whereas *Zuchthengst* and *Zuchtstute* are used for producing young. The colour of the horse is emphasized by *Schimmel* 'white horse', *Rappe* 'black horse', *Fuchs* 'chestnut' and *Schecke* 'dapple'. The words *Klepper, Mähre, Kracke* are all pejorative designations. *Pony* emphasizes the smallness of the animal; *Renner* emphasizes the good performance of the horse in racing; *Vollblüter* emphasizes the horse's good breeding. *Hafermotor* (lit. 'engine running on oats') is a jocular term. *Roß* is used in elevated styles and in certain expressions, for example *auf seinem hohen Roß* 'to be on one's high horse'. Jost Trier (1894–1971) was one of the main scholars who put forward theories about lexical semantic fields in the 1930s. They were an attempt to give some systematic structure to the vocabulary of a language. Despite many criticisms, such as the difficulty of delimiting them, the fact that they are not as complete as was thought and that different native speakers do not often agree on what items should be included in a particular field, they are nevertheless a useful and practical way of describing systematically at least part of the vocabulary of a language. A selection of articles on lexical fields is provided by Schmidt (1973).

Another approach to the study of the vocabulary is to look for contrasting meaning components between words. For instance, *Mann, Vater* and *Frau, Mutter* are differentiated by the component feature 'sex'. The words *Junge* and *Mädchen, Vater* and *Mutter* are not only distinguished by the feature 'sex' but the latter are 'grown up', whereas the former are 'not grown up'. These meaning components can be called features and, as in phonology, they can function with + or − values as binary features. Thus *Mutter* and *Vater* are [+ grown up], while *Junge* and *Mädchen* are [− grown up]. When more than a simple twofold contrast is involved it is more appropriate to use the names of the features themselves and not simply plus and minus values (Hundsnurscher 1971: 29–37). If we take a list of words belonging to a semantic field and a list of features which characterize

Table 10.1   Kinship terms in German

	Vater	Mutter	Bruder	Schwester	Neffe	Nichte	Vetter	Cousine
Direct	+	+						
Colineal			+	+				
Ablineal					+	+	+	+
Affinal								
Sex	m	f	m	f	m	f	m	f
Generation	1	1	0	0	−1	−1	0	0

	Onkel	Tante	Groß-vater	Groß-mutter	Schwager	Schwieger-mutter
Direct			+	+		
Colineal						
Ablineal	+	+				
Affinal					+	
Sex	m	f	m	f	m	f
Generation	1	1	2	2	0	1

Table 10.2   Semantic features of types of water

	Fluß	Bach	Kanal	Graben	See	Tümpel	Teich	Becken
Flowing	+	+	+	+	−	−	−	−
Standing	−	−	−	−	+	+	+	+
Natural	+	+	−	−	+	+	−	−
Artificial	−	−	+	+	−	−	+	+
Large	+	−	+	−	+	−	+	−
Small	−	+	−	+	−	+	−	+

them, we can produce a diagram showing the contrasting features for each item of a semantic field. The semantic field of 'kinship' in German is represented by features in Table 10.1. The degrees of kinship involve the feature 'lineality' which is direct for *Vater*, *Großvater*, colineal for *Bruder*, *Onkel* and ablineal for *Vetter*, *Cousine*. The generations are not shown by binary features but by numerical values, taking the generation of ego as 0. The feature 'affinal' means related 'by marriage'. The feature 'sex' is realized as male or female. Hundsnurscher (1971: 42) illustrates this approach to inanimate nouns signifying types of water as can be seen from Table 10.2.

Not only nouns can be dealt with in this way but also adjectives and verbs. The verbs of movement in German form a semantic field which can be differentiated by means of semantic features (Diersch 1972: 201f.; Wotjak 1971: 180–99) as is exemplified in the following list:

walking (in different ways)	gehen, trippeln, watscheln
with haste	eilen, hetzen
with an impediment	hinken, humpeln, lahmen
with a purpose	spazieren, wandern
in definite formation	marschieren, paradieren
running	laufen, rennen, rasen
jumping	springen, hüpfen
sliding	gleiten
climbing	schleifen
riding	reiten, traben, galoppieren

Semantic fields also exist among adjectives. The most frequently cited one is that of the colour terms: *rot, gelb, blau, rosa, braun, orange, grün, violett, schwarz, grau, weiß*. Some adjectives do not occur as a part of a continuum with others but can be paired with another adjective whose meaning is the exact opposite, for example *alt : jung; ledig : verheiratet*. These words form pairs of lexical opposites, or antonyms. The antonyms can be divided further into gradable and ungradable opposites. Our example *ledig : verheiratet* is ungradable. Normally one cannot say *X ist lediger als Y* or *X ist nicht so ledig wie Y*. They are mutually exclusive. The sentence *X ist verheiratet* excludes the sentence *X ist ledig*. Pairs such as *groß : klein; kurz : lang; hart : weich*, on the other hand, are gradable. We can say *X ist so groß (kurz, hart) wie Y*, or *X ist größer (kürzer, harter) als Y*. It must be emphasized, however, that the norm against which these adjectives are graded is a relative one. The phrase *ein kleiner Elephant* implies smallness in relation to the size of other elephants while *eine große Maus* implies bigness in relation to the size of other mice. A small elephant is still larger than a big mouse!

Most morphological complex adjectives are ungradable, for example *nahtlos, zusammenklappbar, gläsern*.

Other adjectives do not occur as simple opposites but contrast with several different words. The set of words denoting differences in temperature from 'cold' to 'hot', for example *kalt, kühl, lauwarm, warm, heiß*, can be viewed as a scale bounded by the two outermost members, *kalt* and *heiß*. Again, the qualities expressed by these adjectives are relative to what is being described. Other groups of words such as the designations for the seasons of the year, the days of the week, months of the year, have no obvious beginning or ending term. To begin the New Year with January is arbitrary. Such groups with no obvious beginnings or endings can be called cycles. Sometimes the same semantic field contains both a scale and a cycle. In the field of colours, for instance, the terms *schwarz*, *grau* and *weiß* form a scale, whereas *rot*, *gelb*, *grün*, *blau*, *purpur* form a cycle.

The words *Blume*, *Rose*, *Veilchen*, *Schneeglöckchen*, etc., form part of the lexical semantic fields 'garden flowers'. The relationship between the members of the field is hierarchical. The term *Blume* subsumes all the other members of the field. This can be expressed by the paraphrases *Eine Rose ist eine Blume* or *Ein Beispiel einer Blume ist eine Rose*. *Blume* is thus a superordinate term, while the words for specific flowers are subordinate terms and called hyponyms or co-hyponyms. This relationship of hyponymy is seen below:

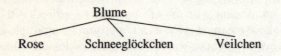

Another example of hyponymy is that between *Medikamente* or *Arnzeimittel* as the superordinate term and *Tropfen*, *Tabletten*, *Pillen*, *Saft*, *Dragees* and *Zäpfchen* as hyponyms. In some cases the relationship of the superordinate term to its subordinate terms is one of possession or inclusion, for example, in the case of the parts of physical objects, plants or parts of the body. Thus the parts of the hand could be portrayed as on p. 247.

The relationship of hyponymy shows the hierarchical ordering of elements in parts of the vocabulary. The semantic fields that we have discussed so far have contained words of the same part of speech. Also the individual members have been mutually exclusive. These fields can be termed paradigmatic fields.

There are, however, other cases where words, this time of different parts of speech, occur together frequently. The term collocation is sometimes used to describe the combinations and restrictions between nouns and adjectives and verbs and their subjects. For instance, there are many adjectives that can modify the noun *Haar*: *schwarz*, *grau*, *weiß*; *rot*, *braun*, *golden*, *silbern*, etc. However, in

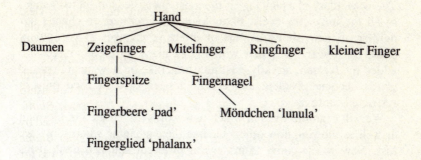

addition the adjective *blond* is usually only applied to hair (apart from its colloquial application to beer). The verbs *essen* and *fressen* have as their objects food of different kinds and not metals or people. Their choice of subject is even more limited. The verb *essen* only has human subjects, whereas *fressen* only has animal subjects, except when a person's behaviour is being likened to that of an animal. Words that show this close determination by another one are part of a syntagmatic word field. This method of classification was first suggested by Walter Porzig (1895–1961). Describing types of subjects and objects is also part of syntax. Valency grammar uses information on types of subject and object a verb chooses (for a full description of a verb see 8.6).

What we hope to have shown in this section is that the vocabulary of a language is not simply an unordered list of individual words. In fact most words are not isolated but are interconnected with other words through various relationships, semantic fields, antonymy, hyponymy, etc. An alphabetical dictionary does not show these relationships, except in some cases for antonymy. So-called synonym dictionaries, for example *Duden 8* (1986), help us in the search for words which belong to the same semantic field, but the main entries for the fields appear in alphabetical order with the subsidiary members entered at their appropriate alphabetical place with an arrow referring the reader to the main entry. For instance, in the case of *Gaul* and *Roß* one is referred to *Pferd*. Non-alphabetical dictionaries arranged according to concepts and areas of meaning for German on the model of *Roget's Thesaurus* are Dornseiff (1970) and Wehrle and Eggers (1961). *Duden 3: Bildwörterbuch* deals with that section of the vocabulary which can be portrayed in picture form.

10.2   DEVELOPMENT OF GERMAN VOCABULARY

The vocabulary of a language is the most open, i.e. subject to change, of all the linguistic levels. Phonology and grammar do change but neither of them shows as vast or intensive changes as vocabulary does. Each year many new words from many different sources are added to German, already existing words take on new meanings and words become obsolete and are no longer used or used only in restricted contexts.

We will examine ways in which new words are created in German as well as showing how others change their meaning while some are lost. New words come from several different sources: neologisms (*Neuwörter*), for example *Laptop*, *Leggings*, which are mostly borrowings; new formations (*Neubildungen*), formed from already existing words and morphemes, *entsorgen* 'to dispose of refuse', *Nulltariff* 'free of charge'; and new meanings (*Neubedeutungen*), for example *Wanze* 'bug', *realisieren* 'to realize'. A study of the East German *Wörterbuch der deutschen Gegenwartssprache* (*WDG*) (Ising *et al.*, 1988: 146f.) showed that of 3,484 new words there were 180 neologisms (5.2 per cent), 426 new meanings (12.2 per cent) but a massive 2,878 new formations (82.6 per cent).

10.2.1   English loans in German

The most common source of new words is borrowing. German, like many other languages, has absorbed words from different languages during its history. French and Latin have continually contributed to the lexical stock of German but in the twentieth century, particularly since 1945, it has been English, especially American English, which has been the main source of borrowing. Siegl (1989: 334–87) registers an increase in the amount of borrowed words listed in both the Mannheim and Leipzig *Duden Rechtschreibung* volumes from the fourteenth to the eighteenth editions only in the case of English. The number of English loans, or Anglicisms, rose from 868 (2.9 per cent) to 1,404 (3.89 per cent). Surveys of English influence are provided by Stanforth (1968, 1991), Carstensen (1984a) and W. Viereck (1984, 1986). It is the purpose of this section to review the phenomenon of borrowing of English loans, outlining the sociolinguistic and linguistic factors that are involved, to examine the changes that English loans have undergone in their adoption by German, to give examples of the main areas where borrowing has taken place and to show the channels through which borrowing is said to have occurred.

10.2.1.1 Motives for borrowing

The most easily understood motive for the borrowing of a word from a foreign language is when the actual object or concept is also imported. This is the case in such English loans as *Airbag*, *Computer*, *Laser*, *Landrover*, *Lumberjack* (all m.), *Milkshake*, *Marketing* (both nt.) and *Public Relations* (pl.). This is particularly true of certain areas of the vocabulary, for example pop and rock music, with *LP*, *Band*, *Hit*, *Song*, *Rock*, *Pop*, *Fan*, *Album*, *Single*, *Star* being the ten most frequent English words (L. Ortner 1982: 264), and fashion, where out of sixty-nine frequent loan words, forty were English, for example *Bermudas*, *Body-Stocking*, *Coat*, *Jumpsuit*, *Lambswool*, *Patchwork*, *Separates*, *Sweatshirt*, *T-Shirt*, *wash and wear* (H. Ortner 1981: 236–44). Often, however, the motive for borrowing is the desire on the part of certain speakers to show that they know a certain language by lacing their own speech with borrowings. Foreign words have a greater prestige than native ones in certain areas, for example in fashion, when *Accessoires* is used instead of *Zubehör*, *Line* instead *Linie*, *Sailor* instead of *Matrose* and *navyblau* instead *marineblau* (H. Ortner 1981: 231–6). When crazes start in the English-speaking world and spread to other countries the English designation usually spreads as well, for example *Skateboarding*, *Aquaplaning*, *Aerobics*.

10.2.1.2 *Loan words and* Fremdwörter

The post-1945 English loans fall generally into the pattern of being unassimilated or partially assimilated loans (*Fremdwörter*), whereas older assimilated loans (*Lehnwörter*), for example *Mauer*, *Pfeil*, (from Latin, *mūrus*, *pīlum*) are only recognizable as loans by historical evidence and etymology. Unassimilated and partially assimilated loans very often show features which are not present in German. These can be: (1) pronunciation, for example some English sounds, for instance [dʒ] and initial [s] do not occur in standard German; (2) spelling, many letters and combinations of letters do not occur in German, *clever*, *Camping*, *Leasing*, *Toast*; (3) inflection, many English loans have a pl. ending *-s*, such as *Party*, *Parties*. These criteria are not always a clear guide and are modified in several ways to integrate the loans into German (see sections 10.2.1.5–7). In the case of pronunciation, approximate sounds in German are used to substitute for English sounds not available in German, for example [tʃ] for [dʒ], [z] for initial [s], although South German has initial [s-], and [ε] for [æ], (see 10.2.1.6). Spelling becomes altered to conform to German rules, *cl-* is replaced by *kl-*, *Clown* by *Klown* (although the form *Clown* is also used), English *strike* was already altered to *Streik* in 1884. Some English nouns when they are borrowed do not take the ending *-s* but conform to the German inflectional pattern, those in *-er* take no ending in the pl., for example *Gangster*. Form is not always a guide to whether a word is a loan or not, for instance *killen*, *Lift* conform in pronunciation, orthography and inflection to German patterns but it is only the knowledge that these words are similar in form and meaning to Engl. *to kill* and *lift* that tells us they were probably borrowed. Often native speakers of German are uncertain as to which words are unassimilated loans when given an arbitrary list of loans and native words. For instance in one such test 97 per cent of those asked considered *Eventualität* an unassimilated loan, 86 per cent *Impression*, *Mannequin*, 73 per cent *Interview*, 68 per cent *killen*, *Streß*, 52 per cent *Gangster*, 45 per cent *mixen*, 37 per cent *Pullover*, 30 per cent *Test* and 22 per cent *Start* (Augst 1977: 66f.).

English loans are also to be expected in the speech of some speakers, for example those who are educated, for instance politicians, academics, and in talking about certain topics, for instance politics, economics, rather than by other speakers and in other topics. Since they are more used by educated speakers with a good knowledge of English, their proper use tends to be a shibboleth identifying members of different groups. W. Viereck (1980b: 272ff.) found that of a list of forty-two English loans, or compounds containing English components, the five most easily understood were *Testfahrzeug*, *Tip*, *Fitneßraum*, *Live-Übertragung*, *Callgirl*, and the five least understood were *Ghostwriter*, *Disengagement*, *Lobby*, *Impeachment*, *Split-Level-Bauweise*. In a survey of what various loans might mean some speakers of German confused the *set* in *Jetset* with the *set* in *Twinset* and regarded the former as 'combination of clothes'. Some thought that *Ghostwriter* was a 'writer of ghost stories'. *Streß* was confused with *Dreß* by some speakers, and *Dressman* was regarded as 'someone who trains (*dressiert*) dogs' (W. Viereck 1980b: 315f.). Carstensen and Hengstenberg (1983) in a study of fifty English words found that thirty were understood correctly by 60 per cent of their informants. The words that were understood correctly by over 90 per cent of informants were *Surfing*, *Skateboard*, *Tramper*, *Discoroller*, *Lunch*, and by over 80 per cent *Boom*, *Mixed Pickles*, *Jogging*, *Know-how*, *Top Ten*, *Pumps*, *Sideboard*. At the other end of the scale the following were understood correctly by under 30 per cent of the informants: *Deadline*, *Brain Drain*, *Underdog*. The criterion of topicality is important in the understanding of English words. As we shall see, however, some deviations from English practice in the usage of some English loans have become standard in German.

10.2.1.3 *Attitudes to loans*

Reactions to loans in general in German have always varied over the centuries. After the establishing of the united German Empire in 1871 nationalistic feeling ran high and there was a reaction against accepting loans. In 1874 the Postmaster-General Heinrich von Stephan (1831–97) replaced 760 official postal and transport terms by German equivalents, for instance *Eilbrief* for *Expressbrief*, *einschreiben* for *rekommandieren*, and *Postkarte* for *Korrespondenzkarte*. Then in 1885 Hermann Riegel (1834–1900) formed the Allgemeiner Deutscher Sprachverein ('General German Language Society'), one of whose tasks from then on was to stem the tide of loans and suggest German words to substitute for foreign ones. This resulted in a large number of 'Germanicizing dictionaries' (*Verdeutschungswörterbücher*) being produced. One of the more successful coiners was Otto Sarrazin (1842–1921), who was responsible for introducing *Abteil* for *Coupé*, *Bahnsteig* for *Perron* and *Fahrkarte* for *Billett*. This tradition of purism continued into the twentieth century. During the Nazi period, in fact, there were many cries to reject borrowing but Hitler himself eventually forbade the witch-hunt for foreign words. He himself used many loans for specific propaganda purposes. They lent his statements and speeches a pseudo-scientific air, very often clouding the listeners' reason since they did not know exactly what he meant when he talked about *Emanzipation*, *Germanisation*, *Inflation*, *Intelligenz*, *Propaganda*, *Sterilisation*, *Zentralisation* (von Polenz 1967b). After 1945 more moderate views are to be found among lexicographers and societies such as the Gesellschaft für deutsche Sprache, founded on 10 January 1947 in Lüneburg by Max Wachler (its headquarters were moved to Wiesbaden in 1965), which expressly forbade any 'witch-hunt' of foreign words. The Duden volumes are happy to accept assimilated loans, especially, as technical terms, if they are part of a specialist jargon. They can sometimes be more neutral than native words and provide a source of stylistic variation. Some lay opinions, however, against the use of Anglicisms do still exist and represent a wide spectrum of reasons, ranging from revealing a 'laziness of thinking', 'besmirching of the language', through 'kow-towing to the Americans', 'separating groups in society' to 'endangering national identity' (Stickel 1984: 43–7). In the answers to a questionnaire published in two regional papers about modern German 77.7 per cent of those who replied agreed with the statement 'Es werden insgesamt zu viele Fremdwörter gebraucht' ('Too many foreign words are used'), with only 18.7 per cent disagreeing and 3.6 per cent abstaining. In some quarters the opposition to foreign words dies hard, although speakers do not distinguish between foreign words and technical vocabulary which is in general only known to those interested in a specific vocabulary area.

10.2.1.4 Types of borrowing

Before we deal with integration of English loans in German we will outline a typology of borrowing which we will use in our discussion of loans. The basic scheme goes back to Betz (1974), but was developed between 1936 and 1949. A good discussion is given in Seebold (1981: 194–217). The English terminology is derived from Haugen (1950) and Weinreich (1953). Most of the examples are taken from Carstensen (1965).

Simple loans may be unassimilated, for example *smart*, or else assimilated, for example *Streik*. We have already shown how it is difficult to draw the line between these two types. In both cases, however, the original form of the loan is easily discernible. Loan formations, on the other hand, attempt in varying degrees to represent the English words and affixes by German ones. In these cases the English words are mostly compounds, *floodlight*, or derived forms comprising a base plus an affix. If each part of the English word is rendered literally by its German counterpart we may speak of a loan translation (*Lehnübersetzung*), for example *Flutlicht* from *floodlight*, *Gehirnwäsche* from *brain washing*, *Geschmacksknospen* from *taste buds*, *brandneu* from *brand new*, *Eierkopf* from *egg-head*, and *Spätentwickler* from *late developer*. If the rendering of the English word is only partially literal, for example *Wolkenkratzer*, literally *cloud-scraper*, for *sky-scraper*, then we speak of loan rendition (*Lehnübertragung*). Other examples of this type are: *Marschflugkörper* 'cruise missile', *Schlafstadt* 'dormitory town', *Urknalltheorie* 'Big Bang theory'. According to W. Viereck (1986: 118) *Untertreibung* for 'understatement', which is often used to illustrate this type, is not post-1945 but dates from 1910. If, on the other hand, nothing of the English word is literally translated but an attempt is made at an interpretation of its meaning by an approximate translation, then we speak of loan creation (*Lehnschöpfung*), for instance, *Luftkissenfahrzeug* for *hovercraft*, *Nietenhose* for *jeans*, *Klimaanlage* for *air-*

conditioning, and *Holzkohlengrill* for *barbecue*. W. Viereck (1986: 118) feels dubious about loan creations and wonders if they can really be described as borrowing at all since all their components come from the native language. Carstensen (1983: 22) rejects this latter category as well, preferring to say that, for instance, German *Luftkissenfahrzeug* merely 'renders' Engl. *hovercraft*. Kirkness (1984: 22f.) also rejects the category of loan creation from borrowing.

Another frequent type of borrowing is semantic borrowing (*Lehnbedeutung*). A German word which already has one or more meanings is given a new meaning on the model of an English meaning of the cognate word. For instance *feuern* and *to fire* both mean 'to shoot (at)' but the extension of meaning in English to 'to dismiss from a job' has now also been taken on by the German word. *Realisieren*, which in German was for a long time only used for 'to make possible', is now often used in its English sense of 'to understand clearly, become aware of, to realize'; *kontrollieren* in the sense of 'to control' is used alongside its other meaning of 'to check', *buchen* in the sense of 'to book (a room etc.)', although originally borrowed in the eighteenth century, has vastly increased in use since 1945; *herumhängen* can be used of people who are 'hanging around', as in English, and not merely of things; *das Paket* is used for a '(political) package', for example *Steuerpaket*, *Sozialpaket*, on the model of English.

The last category of borrowing is one which, as yet, seems mainly illustrated by examples of English loans in German after 1945. This is the pseudo-loan (*Scheinentlehnung*, *Sekundärentlehnung*), where English morphemes are used to produce words which look English but which do not occur in English. Some of these are the products of the advertising industry. The most famous of these is *Twen*, from Engl. *twenty* meaning 'someone in his or her twenties'. Others are *Dressman* 'male counterpart to mannequin' (male model)', *Showmaster* 'compere', possibly formed by analogy with *Quizmaster*, *Pullunder* 'a sleeveless pullover', *Trench* 'trench-coat' and *Mokick* 'a small (50cc) motor bike with a kickstarter', which is a blend of *Moped* and *Kickstarter* (Hannah 1988). This category is rejected by Kirkness (1984: 23) and others on the grounds that although the elements may be borrowed, and thus 'foreign', the patterning is not but occurs in the native language. Of these four types, loan translation and loan meaning seem the most frequent. Contemporary dictionaries tend not to mark words according to these types. The only exceptions are *Duden Universalwörterbuch* and *Duden: Das Große Wörterbuch* which mark words as being loan translations. Using historical dictionaries can show which of the three types (loan translation, loan rendition, loan meaning) are most frequent. An examination of the seventh edition of Paul's *Deutsches Wörterbuch* (although it covers the whole of the historical development of German) yielded 275 loan translations, 66 loan renditions and 44 loan meanings.

10.2.1.5   *Orthography and English loans*

Although English and German both belong to the German language family, sharing many common words and constructions, their sound systems, orthographies and grammars are sufficiently different for English loans to have to undergo basic changes in order to be integrated into German. In the following sections we will show how English loans are changed as they become integrated into German.

The most obvious way in which English loans stand out in German texts is in how they are written. In a few cases English loans happen to be spelt in a manner conforming to German orthography, *killen*, *Lift*. English vowel sounds usually remain unaltered, *Toast*, *Leasing*, *Soul*. The most obvious sign of orthographic integration is the use of capital letters for nouns, *vom Streß in der City zu shoppen*. The initial clusters *cl-*, *cr-* in English correspond to *kl-*, *kr-* in German, and English initial *k-* before a back vowel corresponds to *k-* in German. Examples can be found of fluctuation between the two spellings, *Klub*, *Club*; *kracken*, *cracken*; *Katgut*, *Catgut*; *Kode*, *Code*, but most loans retain *c*. In English the letter *c* is also used for [s] before front vowels, *cigarette*, *certificate* and these two words, originally from French, are written with both *c* and *z* in German, *Cigarette*, *Zigarette*; *Certifikat*, *Zertifikat*, probably in imitation of English. The voiceless post-alveolar fricative [ʃ] is spelt *sh* in English but *sch* in German with the result that a few English loans have alternative forms with *sch*, such as *Schock*, *schocking*, *Sketsch*, but the majority retain *sh*, as in *Show*, *Shaker*, *Shorts*. In *schrinken*, *Schrapnell*, both older loans, only *sch* occurs. English word-final *-ss* is usually written *ß*, *Streß*, *Boß*, *Stewardeß*. English loans have introduced the use of final *-y* into German, *Boy*, *Baby*, *Party*, *Rowdy*. The English spelling rule of changing the *y* to *i* before adding the pl. ending *-es*, *Party*, *Parties*, is usually adhered to but very often one finds pl. forms such as *Partys*, *Rowdys*, where the rule has not been applied.

Not only letters play a role in orthography but also the hyphen and apostrophe. Many English loans which are hyphenated compounds still retain the hyphen in German, *Make-up*, or are written as two words *Public Relations*, but most are written as a single orthographic word, *Comeback*, *Babysitter*, *Diskjockey* (cf. Engl. *comeback*, *baby-*

sitter, *disc-jockey*). The genitive apostrophe in English, *Tom's hat*, is also, under English influence, to be found with the genitive of proper names in German *Faden's Tannen* (street name) and especially in advertisements, *Beck's Bier*. This usage probably goes back to at least the nineteenth century. The apostrophe is strictly only allowed when the name ends in *s*, *ß*, *tz*, *x* or *z*, for example *Sokrates' Finger*.

10.2.1.6   *Pronunciation and English loans*

If an English word contains a sound which is not to be found in German then usually the phonetically nearest sound to it is used by a German speaker. The skill in reproducing English sounds will of course depend on the amount of linguistic training of the speaker concerned. Fink (1980) investigated the pronunciation of forty-four English words and phrases and found a great variety of pronunciations for each word. Students, academics and pupils were, not surprisingly, the groups whose pronunciation and understanding of Anglicisms was the best. Younger speakers were also better than older ones. Here we shall discuss some sound substitutions which can be commonly heard among German speakers. In many cases information in dictionaries confirms these observations. For the English diphthongs [ei] and [əu] German speakers substitute either [eː] or [ɛː], for example *Trainer*, *Spray*, and [oː], *Soul*, *Toast*. English [ɜ] as in *girl*, *shirt* does not exist in German and often [øː] is substituted for it. Similarly the short English [ʌ] does not exist in German and [a] is used instead by German speakers in words like *Curry*, *Cutter*, and in a few cases the spelling *a* may be found, for example *Bags Banny* (*Bugs Bunny*). The English [æ] sound is perceived by German speakers to be closer to [ɛ] than [a] and is consequently pronounced [ɛ]. It is sometimes written *ä* in brand names, *Das Big-Mäc* (hamburger), or to Germanicize foreign words, for example *Cräcker*, 'cream cracker', *Täcks* 'tack'. In other cases words containing English [æ] are pronounced [ɛ] but the vowel is spelt *a* as in English, for example the older loan *Tram* (1875) and also modern *trampen* 'to hitch-hike', *Gag*.

The following substitutions are made among the consonants. English [dʒ] does not exist in German and [tʃ] is often used instead, *Job*, *Jeans*, *Jet*. The German uvular *-r* [ʀ] is substituted for the English prevocalic or intervocalic flapped [ɾ], *Trainer*, *Sherry*. Other differences do not result from the absence of the sound in German but from its different distribution. Intervocalic voiceless [s] occurs in German, *reißen*, *wissen*, but in initial position before vowels a voiced

[z] is used in standard German (southern colloquial speech does have initial [s], however). In general most German speakers use initial [s] without difficulty in English loans, *Safe, Set, Single, Software, Surfing*; however, some words do occur with [z], which is an indication of their integration into German. The prefix *Super-/super-* which is added to adjectives or nouns, *supermodern, Supershow* is also pronounced with [z], as is the less common prefix *Sub-/sub-*. The English initial consonant cluster *tw-* does not occur in German but with the borrowing of a number of words, *Tweed, Twill, Twinset, twisten*, it has been re-introduced into German (MHG *tw-* became *zw-* or *qu-* in modern German). Due to a sound change of [s] [→] [ʃ] before initial consonants modern German has no clusters of *s* + consonant in native words. English, on the other hand, has only one cluster of [ʃ] + consonant, *shrimp*. Consequently any words borrowed from English with initial [s] + consonant are either felt to be unassimilated loans and pronounced [sp-, st-] etc., for example *Spike, Star*, or else they become integrated and are pronounced [ʃp-, ʃt-] etc., for example *Sport, Stop(p)*. The fluctuation of pronunciation can be seen easily by consulting any monolingual or pronouncing dictionary. A general rule of German phonology is that all consonants in word- or morpheme-final position are voiceless, which is not the case in English, where both voiced and voiceless consonants occur, *cab, cap*. This means that final voiced consonants in English loans become devoiced in German speech, *Job* [tʃɔp], *live* [laif], cf. *Live-Sendung* [laifzɛnduŋ] 'live-broadcast'.

10.2.1.7   Inflection and English loans

English has lost most of the inflectional endings and grammatical categories it originally had, which German has retained, for example inflection of adjectives, several different pl. endings, personal endings in verbs and gender in nouns. English loans thus have to be adapted to fit in with this system. Nouns form by far the largest word class of Anglicisms, followed a long way behind by verbs and adjectives. In Oeldorf's list (1990: 49–52) there were 120 nouns, four verbs and four adjectives. A sample from *Der Spiegel* of 10 December 1990 brought a similar result: 101 nouns, six adjectives and five verbs. The majority of English loans are nouns, which presents a great problem of integration. English has no grammatical gender whereas German has three genders. English has mainly the one pl. ending *-s* whereas German has five: *-e*, *-e* accompanied by mutation of the stem vowel, *-er* accompanied by mutation of the stem vowel, *-en* and *-s*.

English loans must, therefore, be assigned to one of the three grammatical genders in German. In many cases this is done by assigning it to the grammatical gender of its nearest German equivalent, for example *der Cowboy* (*der Junge*), *die Lady* (*die Dame*), *das Girl* (*das Mädchen*), *der Lift* (*der Aufzug*), *die Show* (*die Schau*), with natural gender also being a major influence where applicable. An exception is *Vamp*, which, although it refers to a female person, is grammatically masculine. However, an additional important factor is the influence of the phonological shape of the word on the gender to which it is assigned. Nouns ending in *-ion* and *-eß* are feminine, *die Lotion*, *die Hosteß*, (but *das Business*), those ending in *-ing*, *-ent* and the suffix *-in* are neuter, *das Doping*, *das Hearing*, *das Treatment*, *das Management*, *das Sit-in*, and those in *-er* are masculine, *der Layouter*, *der Computer*. With monosyllabic inanimate nouns there is a great deal of arbitrary gender assignment since natural gender and phonological shape do not help us. The following examples illustrate this: *das Layout*, *das Limit*, *der Liquor*, *die Lobby*, *der Look*, *der Lunch*, *der Lag*, *der Lob* (in tennis), *die Lounge*, *das Lullaby*. Since the criteria for assigning gender are not clear, nouns may fluctuate in grammatical gender: *der/das Lasso*, *das/der Lockout*, *der/das Looping*. Carstensen (1980) shows how unreliable dictionary information on gender assignment may be. Also there is no information in dictionaries about the frequency of the use of the different genders. Carstensen tested gender assignment with informants and found that the certainty of the gender of a noun depended on the degree of understanding of its meaning. This is an area where research can usefully be done.

Most English nouns form their pl. by adding *-s*, *Layouts*, *Looks*, *Lobs*, *Loopings*, but those ending in *-er* take no ending, as in German, *die Teenager*, *die Layouter*, *die Bestseller*. Some nouns such as *Sketsch*, *Lift*, have alternative pl. forms in *-e*, and in the case of *Toast* the two forms have, for some speakers at least, become separated in meaning, *Toaste* 'the slices of toasted bread' and *Toasts* 'the speeches and calls to drink at functions'. The pl. of *Boß* is *Bosse*. The feminine nouns in *-eß* add *-en* in the pl., *Stewardessen*, *Hostessen*. One of the effects of the English loans has been to increase the incidence of *-s* pl. nouns in German.

English verbs are more easily integrated and simply add *-en*, *kill* → *killen*, *test* → *testen*, *dope* → *dopen* and are always conjugated like weak (regular) verbs, *killte*, *gekillt*. The verb *babysitten*, however, is only used in the infinitive. The verb *recyclen* retains its English spelling when used in the past participle, *recycelt* and other forms *er*, *sie*, *es*; *ihr recycelt*. The competing form *recyclet* is less frequent. Participle forms are used adjectivally, for example *pushende*, *gecharterten*. Most adjectives such as *smart*, *clever*, *cool*, *fair*, *postmodern* also present no problem since they simply take the appropriate endings, for example *ein faires Angebot* 'a fair offer'. Some adjectives do not inflect since they mostly occur in predicative position, for example *down*, *groggy*, *sexy*, *lady-like*, *live*.

10.2.1.8   *Entrance and distribution of English loans*

English loans were able to spread quickly in German because of the influence of the mass media, particularly through magazines like *Der Spiegel*, which has been shown to have a special role (Carstensen 1965: 22–5; 1971). However, although English loans are widely used in the mass media it is difficult to ascertain exactly how widespread their use is among the general population.

Advertising, in the press, on television and on hoardings, is another channel through which English loans have slipped into German. The motivation behind advertising is often to appeal to people's snobbish tendencies either so that they will buy a certain product or so that they will apply for certain jobs. It is significant that the pseudo-loans *Dressman*, *Twen*, are inventions of the advertising industry. Most cosmetic terms are English: *Vanishing Cream*, *Deep Cleanser*, *Fluid Make-up*. Aviation is particularly strongly influenced by English. The international language of aviation is English and many of the jobs offered have English designations: *Ticketagent*, *Groundhosteß*. The younger generation are influenced by the predominant use of English as the language of pop and rock music: *Beatband*, *Rockmusik*, *Popmusik* (now accepted in German), *die LP*, *die Single*, *die CD*, *Slide-Gitarre*, *Instrumental-Vokal-Arrangements*. Since English is the first foreign language in schools young people are obviously very open to the importation of English words into their speech.

Many English loans belong to specialist languages and have found their way from there into the mainstream of the vocabulary: *Splitting* 'separate assessment of half of the joint income of a husband and wife for taxation purposes', *Countdown*, *Fallout*, *Software*, *Hardware*. The loans have permeated many fields of vocabulary in German and we will give a list with a few illustrations (some of these words were borrowed before 1945):

1 political and public life: *Appeasement, Disengagement, Hearing, Image*;
2 business and commerce: *Boom, Clearing, Designer, Dumping, Leasing, Marketing, Safe, Trust*;
3 technology and science: *Computer, Fading, Laser, Mikroprozessor Test*;
4 sport: *Doping, fair, Foul, kicken, Trainer, Fan, Champion, Team, Looping*;
5 fashion and clothes: *Deodorant, Jumper, Look, Lotion, Make-up, Nylon, Pullover, Slip, Spray, Tweed*;
6 food and drink: *Chips, Long-, Shortdrink, Cocktail, Grapefruit, mixen, Sherry, Toast, Soft-Eis*;
7 entertainment and leisure: *Bar, Comics, Festival, Gag, Happening, Musical, Party, Quiz, Show, Western*.

10.2.1.9 *Borrowing in other German-speaking countries*

Not only West Germany but all the German-speaking countries have been affected by English loans, even former East Germany, although not to the same extent. Pop music, sport and entertainment are the areas through which many English loans like *Feature, Sound, Evergreen, Poster, Single* penetrated into former East Germany. Lehnert (1986) points out that English influence is not to be underestimated. Peculiar to former East German were some borrowings that came via Russian, for example *Dispatcher, Kombine, Meeting, Pressebriefing* and *Plattform* (for political views). Siegl (1989: 345 and 357) shows how the eighteenth Mannheim Duden has 603 English words (3.89 per cent) and the seventeenth Leipzig Duden has 377 English words, which do, however, make up 3.74 per cent of all the words. The absolute figures may differ but the percentages show that the influence of English on both West and former East Germany was considerable. Lehnert (1986: 147) points to some specifically East German coinings such as *Intershop, Interhotel, Plaste*. More understandably Austria and Switzerland have also been heavily affected by English borrowings (Dalcher 1986; K. Viereck 1986). In fact the language of sport in these two countries retains more English sporting terms such as *Penalty, Corner*, which in West Germany have become *Elfmeter* and *Eckball*. In Austria K. Viereck found that the number of Anglicisms had increased greatly, both in a local Graz paper and *Die Presse* in a ten-year period (1986: 163–8), particularly 'partial substitutions', i.e. loan translations, hybrid compounds. In the local Graz paper sport was the area most affected whereas in *Die Presse* it was advertisements and announcements which contained most Anglicisms. Dalcher (1986) found that in Switzerland the greater degree of education influenced the use and understanding of Anglicisms. The older loans tended to be those that were used more. The basic mechanisms of borrowing, types of integration of Anglicisms into German, the areas of the vocabulary which are affected tend to be similar in all German-speaking countries. A temporary difference was that the quantity of Anglicisms was perhaps not so great in absolute terms in former East Germany.

10.2.2   New formations

(Braun 1987: 166–83; Glück and Sauer 1990: 75–93; Sommerfeldt 1988: 174–92)

Although some new formations are introduced by the borrowing of foreign affixes, the bulk are the result of the extension and combination of native stems and affixes in derived forms and compounds. In 1992 four of the most widespread new formations were *Ausländerfeindlichkeit, Blauhelmeinsatz, Fremdenhaß* and *Lichterkette*. All the components of these words existed previously but were never combined before. Dictionaries give some idea when a new word has become part of the language but the words are of course current before the dictionaries record them. The archives of the Dudenredaktion in Mannheim have been recording the lexical comings and goings in German for many years. Müller (1980) records some of the topical words which came into being between 1965 and 1980: *Auslegeware, Bezugsperson, Bioladen, Blutwäsche, Chaote, Chefetage* 'management floor', *Chefideologe, Datenschutz, Dunkelziffer* 'number of unrecorded cases', *Emanze, Erfolgserlebnis* 'feeling of achievement', *Erfolgszwang, Farbbeutel* 'paint bomb', *Feindbild, Fernwärme, Flugzeugentführer, Fotosatz, Freigänger* 'day-release prisoner', *Freizeitwert* 'leisure amenities', *Friedensforschung, Fußgängerzone, Gleitzeit* 'flexi-time', *Hausbesetzer, Hausmann, Herzschrittmacher, Kinderladen, Lebensqualität, Mondscheintarif, Pillenknick, Rasterfahndung* 'computer-aided police search', *Scheidungswaise, Schulstreß, Schulterschluß* 'solidarity', *Schwellenangst, Tagesmutter, Tastentelefon, Umweltschutz*.

Another source of information on new words are annual reports, for example Müller (1982, 1983), Carstensen (1984b, 1985). Some of the new formations of the 1980s were: *Beschäftigungsprogramm, Beziehungskiste, Bindestrichfrau, Düsenrucksack, Ellbogengesell-*

schaft, Entsorger, Ersatzmutter 'surrogate mother', *flächendeckend, Geldautomat, grünrote (Koalition)* 'green–red coalition', *Handlungs-bedarf, Leihschwangerschaft, Nullösung, Rückkehrhilfe, Scheinehe, Schiedsfrau, Sterbehilfe, Versorger, Zwangsanleihe.*

Another method of ascertaining new words is to compare different editions of *Duden 1: Rechtschreibung.* This is not entirely reliable since words may have been held up before being entered in the new edition but it is a good pointer. A sample obtained from comparing the nineteenth (1986) and twentieth editions (1991, the new united Duden) of the *Duden 1: Rechtschreibung,* gave a total of 139 new words, of which 130 were nouns, seven adjectives and two verbs. Twenty-seven of the nouns were new feminine forms, for example *Landfahrerin, Landstreicherin, Langschläferin, Lebensretterin, Leichtathletin, Lieblingsdichterin, Linkshänderin, Lokalreporterin.* Of the rest ninety-eight were new formations, eighty-nine of which were nouns, for example *Lagerinsasse, Landschaftpflege, Langzeit-wirkung, Laola-Welle* 'Mexican wave', *Laserdrucker, Laufrad, Lawinenhund, Leberwert, Leerwohnung, Legebatterie, Leihstimme, Leitzins, Leselupe, Lesewut, Lichterfest, Linienbus, Linkskurs, Lockenstab, Lokalpresse, Lötgerät, Lüsterklemme, Lustfeidlichkeit.* The adjectives were *lärmarm, lebensbedrohlich, lebensbedrohend, leitmotivisch, lohnenswert, lustfeindlich* and the verbs were *lichteln, lobben.*

The gradual productive increase in new formations over time can be seen by taking one part of a compound and plotting the first recording of new compounds. For instance, using the revised edition of the *Deutsches Wörterbuch (DWB^2),* we find the following result for compounds beginning with *Einkaufs-: Einkaufsreise* (1947), *Einkaufstermin* (1952), *Einkaufsberatung, -plan, -straße, -tag* (1958), *Einkaufsberater* (1959), *Einkaufsliste* (1961), *Einkaufsbedingung, -bummel, -gang, -zentrum* (1961), *Einkaufsabteilung* (1964), *Einkauf-serfahrung, -experte, gruppe, -leiter, -schlacht, -stätte, -trubel, -vorteil, einkaufsgünstig, -willig* (1965); *Einkaufshelfer* (1966), *Einkaufswagen* (1968); *Einkaufsplanung* (1971), *Einkaufstip* (1974).

Another approach is to take an area of the vocabulary and examine the new formations within it. This can be done by looking at Strauß *et al.* (1989), which treats three areas: (1) politics and ideology; (2) the environment; and (3) culture and education. The environment section (1992: 397–557) covers everything from *alternativ,* through formations with *Bio-/bio-* and *Öko-/öko-* to *Recycling, Störfall* and the compounds with *Umwelt-/umwelt-.* The description is in the form of a dictionary with quotations so that the reader can see the different interpretations given to words by different groups of speakers, for example *Kern-* and *Atom-*.

10.2.2.1   *The influence of specialist languages*

(Fluck 1976: 160–5 and 1984: 32–48; Mackensen 1971: 49–79; Sommerfeldt 1988: 145–57)

There is a mutual dependence between the specialist languages and the standard language. The former use the linguistic resources common to all the varieties of German and the latter has been enriched and is still being enriched by the use of terms and phrases from specialist languages which have become part of the general vocabulary. It has been found in an investigation of leading articles in present-day newspapers that there were twelve areas of specialist languages from which more than ten words and phrases were taken among which military matters were top with 104 items, then religion with 30 items, sport 27, commerce and economics 27 and medicine 26. In the past other areas have provided the standard with words and phrases, for example mining terminology, *Ausbeute*, *Fundgrube*, *Schicht*, *Stichprobe*, hunting, *Fallstrick*, *naseweis*, *nachspüren*, *unbändig*, and seamanship, *Abstecher*, *Ballast*, *flott*, *scheitern*. Specialist languages are thus far from being peripheral systems but how do they feed vocabulary into the standard? Specialist knowledge is not only communicated between experts in the same field but also by them to lay people. The doctor does not only deal with colleagues but also with patients: for instance, he or she will speak to patients about *Leberschaden* or *Lebergeschichte* rather than use the technical term *Leberzirrhose*. The lexical differentiation according to context can be illustrated by the use of different terms for 'diabetes' and 'being a diabetic'. This can be seen from Table 10.3 (Fluck 1976: 95). The clinical diagnoses are typically more precise. *Diabetes mellitus* has to be distinguished from *diabetes insipidus* and *diabetes renalis*. It is also seen explicitly in connection with lack of insulin, *insulinrefraktär*. It is through the oral communications of general practice and through information on prescribed medicines that many specialist terms become communicated to lay people. The more exciting and controversial scientific and technological discoveries are also popularized through programmes on television, articles in magazines and popular books and encyclopedias.

The standard language has been enriched by the metaphoric use of words and phrases from specialist languages. Particularly since the

Table 10.3 Differentiation of vocabulary in medical terms

Self-diagnosis by patient	Diagnosis in general practice	Clinical diagnoses
Diabetes	Diabetes	
Diabetiker		
Diabetes mellitus	Diabetes mellitus	Diabetes mellitus
Zuckerkrankheit		Zuckerkrankheit
Zucker		Zuckerharnuhr
Es hat sich Zucker eingestellt		Altersdiabetes insulinrefraktär

nineteeenth century many technical advances and many metaphors from specialist languages have become part of everyday language. From the language of railways come *abdampfen* 'to clear off', *abfahren* 'to die (vulg.)', *Anschluß finden*, *suchen* 'to make friends; to try to make contact with people', *eine Fahne haben* 'one's breath smells (from alcohol)', *Puffer* 'buffer', *Weichen richtig (falsch) stellen* 'to follow the right (wrong) way of life'. The verbal compounds of *steigen* can all be used metaphorically: *aussteigen* 'to disengage from something', *Er will aus dem Geschäft aussteigen*; *einsteigen* 'to get in on something', *Er will in das Geschäft einsteigen*; *umsteigen* 'to change to something else', *Er ist vom Autofahren aufs Radfahren umgestiegen*. Other areas have supplied words which are used metaphorically: electricity, *einschalten* 'to step in, join in', *Kontakt finden* 'to find contact with people'; motoring, *anlaufen* 'to start' (orginally used of motors); photography, *auslösen* 'to cause', which was originally used of the camera shutter, *im Bilde sein* 'to be informed'; sport, *sich durchboxen* 'to push through', *sattelfest* 'well up in a subject', *in Form sein* 'to be in form'; technology, *aufziehen* 'to carry out', which was originally only used of winding up clocks, *am laufenden Band* 'continuously', originally applied to a conveyor belt, *der Groschen ist gefallen* 'something has been understood', which comes from slot machines which worked when a coin which was inserted to start the mechanism. The original technical use of these metaphors is still perceived by the majority of speakers and their literal meanings are still in use. In many cases, however, word and phrase metaphors from technical language are no longer perceived as such since their literal meaning has died out. They have consequently become idioms. For instance, *durch die Lappen gehen* 'to escape' was originally a hunting term. Quarry that escaped were those that got past the sheets of cloth (*Lappen*) held by the hunters. The phrase *außer Rand und Band sein* 'out of hand' is a cooper's term referring to a barrel that could not be fitted with hoops. *Verzwickt* 'difficult' contains the obsolete verb *zwicken* 'to fit with nails', cf. *Reißzweck* 'drawing-pin'. The phrase *auf Anhieb* 'at the first attempt' referred originally either to the first blow in cutting down a tree or the first stroke in fencing. The idiomatization of metaphors drawn from specialist language has thus played an important role in the formation of the vocabulary of German. Although old metaphors are becoming idiomatized, modern specialist languages are using metaphors to create new terms: steel can be *beruhigt* ('killed'), or *unberuhigt*; materials can have *Grübchen* 'pittings, stain', (lit. 'dimples'), they can become 'tired', *ermüden* or 'old', *altern*; some cranes are known as *Katzen*.

Since many scientific discoveries or inventions were made by individuals, often in different countries, many originally proper names have come to be used as common nouns: *Volt* after Count Volta (1745–1827), *Röntgen-Strahlen* after W. G. Röntgen (1854–1923), *Dieselmotor* after R. Diesel (1858–1913), *Hertz* after H. Hertz (1857–94), *Brucelose* after D. Bruce (1855–1931). Verbs can be formed from such nouns by adding -(*e*)*n*, as *dieseln*, *verdieseln* 'to change to diesel', *lumbecken* 'to bind (a book)', after E. Lumbeck (1886–1979), *morsen* 'to transmit by morse code' after S. Morse (1791–1872), or in some cases in -*isieren*, as in *pasteurisieren* after L. Pasteur (1822–95), *galvanisieren* after L. Galvani (1737–98). Adjectives can be formed from names by adding -(*i*)*sch*, as in *galvanische Abscheidung*, *Plancksches Wirkungsquantum* 'Planck's constant'.

10.2.3   Loss of words

(Braun 1987: 183–90; Osman 1971)

Linguistic change not only expresses itself in the creation of new lexical items but also in the loss of others. Many French loan words, such as *Chaussée*, *Salon* and *Perron*, which were in common use at the beginning of the century, are no longer used. They have been replaced by other words, *Bürgersteig*, *Landstraße*, *Wohnzimmer* and *Bahnsteig*. *Backfisch* has been replaced by *Teenager* and *Lehrling* is in the process of being replaced in official circles by *der/die Azubi* (*Auszubildende*). The loss of a word takes place over a considerable length of time. In a speech community a word may slip from current use by the majority of speakers but may well still be known, if not actually used, by older generations or in certain styles. *Duden: Großes Wörterbuch* (Drosdowski *et al.* 1976–81, 1: 16) distinguishes between obsolescent (*veraltend*), a word 'being only seldom used, mostly by the older generation' and obsolete (*veraltet*), a word that is 'no longer part of the vocabulary of the modern language'. Thus *Absud*, *Boudoir*, *Backfisch*, *Gendarm* are obsolescent, while *Binokel*, *Eidam*, *fürbaß* are obsolete.

Words may be lost for various reasons. The thing or concept that they signify goes out of use, an institution is changed, and hence the word denoting it is also lost, for example *Armenhaus*, *Droschke*, *Glühstrumpf*, *Raspelhaus*, *Senkler*. The most obvious examples of these are old coins and measures, *Batzen*, *Gulden*, *Kreuzer*.

There may also be linguistic reasons for the loss of words. If through sound change two words with different meaning come to have the same form then, to avoid confusion, one may be lost or changed: *englisch* 'angelic' has been replaced by *engelhaft* but retained in the meaning 'English'. The word *Maus* 'muscle' has been replaced by *Muskel* but *Maus* in the meaning 'mouse' remains. It must be stressed that this does not always happen since modern German still contains many homonyms, words that are pronounced the same but have different meanings: *Gericht*; *Stil*, *Stiel*. The use of a word with a tabu meaning can lead to its loss and replacement with a euphemism. The use of the word *After* in the meaning 'anus' has led to the loss of many compounds with *After*, *Aftermiete* 'sub-tenancy', *Afterrede* 'slander', *Afterkind* 'illegitimate child', *Afterwelt* 'after life'.

10.2.4 Changes in meaning

(Oksaar 1971; Paul 1920: 84–105; Seebold 1981: 278–82; Ullmann 1962: Chapter 8)

So far we have considered changes in vocabulary which have shown additions or losses to the number of words present. In addition there are changes in the meaning of words. The types of changes can be described by the result they have on the range of meaning of the word concerned. Changes of meaning which are taking place at the present are often difficult to describe since there are speakers who know the old meanings of the word and others who only know the new meaning.

Changes in meaning can be classified according to the result of the change. How has the range of meaning changed? The meaning of a word may be narrowed or more restricted than before. Thus MHG *hôchgezîte* referred to any kind of festivity whereas modern German *Hochzeit* is restricted to wedding festivities. This development was also influenced by the borrowing of *Fest* (Lat. *festus*). A more modern example would be the noun *Rock* in the sense 'coat', which is still used by older speakers and also occurs in the compound forms *Morgenrock*, *Schlafrock*. Otherwise it has become restricted to a 'skirt'. *Flieger* was originally anything that flies but is now usually restricted to someone who flies an aeroplane. Many loan words undergo a narrowing of meaning when they enter another language, for example Engl. *city* 'a large town' has come to mean 'city centre' in German. Sometimes the narrowing in meaning concerns the connotations or ideas suggested by a word. Such changes have either a positive or a negative effect. A word with originally neutral connotations may develop pejorative connotations and be used only in a disparaging sense. In MHG *wîp* was the normal term for 'person of the female sex', but now it is used in a pejorative sense, especially in compounds such as *Fischweib*, *Waschweib*. It does still exist as a neutral term in some dialects in the south of Switzerland. The normal word in NHG for 'person of the female sex' is *Frau*, which was originally only used of ladies of noble birth. For a more polite term the word *Dame* was borrowed from French.

In other cases words gain positive connotations. In MHG *Mut* was used for 'mind, disposition', but now it is used for 'courage'. The adjective *artig* originally meant belonging to a particular type or kind (*Art*), whereas now it means 'well behaved'. The most frequently quoted example of a positive change is that of *Marschall* which comes originally from *Mähre* 'horse' and *Schalk* 'servant'. This lowly position eventually became one of the main offices at the court of Charlemagne. In modern German there is a full scale shift underway in the names for various jobs and professions. Ordinary terms such as *Bauer*, *Putzfrau*, *Postbote* are felt to be not fine enough. The status of the job and the standing of the person are deemed to be upgraded by replacing the word by *Landwirt*, *Raumpflegerin*, *Briefzusteller*.

A more frequent change is the widening of the meaning of a word. The original meaning is still present so the result is polysemy, one word used with several different meanings. Thus *Strom*, originally used to refer to water, was extended after the invention and harnassing of electric power to refer to the flow of electricity. Likewise *Birne* or *Glühbirne* was extended from its original meaning of 'pear' to refer to an electric light bulb which had a pear-like shape. The word *Körper* was originally restricted to the body of people and animals but it can now be used for inanimate objects as well, *Flugkörper*, *Heizungskörper*, *Feuerwerkkörper*, and to collections of people, *Verwaltungskörper*, *Wirtschaftskörper*. The word *bißchen* probably still maintains a connection with the verb *beißen* for most speakers but its meaning has been extended beyond its original one. It can be used to modify most nouns, *ein bißchen Frieden*, *ein bißchen Zeit*, or adjectives, *ein bißchen müde*, or on its own, *ich nehme doch ein bißchen*. In its meaning 'a bite' it has been replaced by *Bissen* or *Happen*.

Only when the older meanings of the word die out leaving only the new meaning of a word in all its occurrences can we say that a semantic change has taken place. This has happened in the following cases. Orginally *fertig* meant 'ready to go on a journey' (it is morphologically related by umlaut to *Fahrt*), but now it means simply 'ready, finished'. The verb *schenken* originally meant 'to offer or pour (a drink)' which is maintained by the words *einschenken*, *Mundschenk* 'wine-waiter'. Its range of meaning has, however, been widened to mean 'to give something as a present'. *Trinkgeld* was originally something given to buy a drink as a reward for a service but now it is used simply as a monetary reward for a small service. *Nachricht* was originally a message which one acted upon (*wonach man sich richtete*), but today it is a more general communication.

10.2.4.1 Changes in meaning in loan words

While many English loans retain their English meaning after being borrowed into German, for example *Baby*, *Computer*, some have their meaning altered to a greater or lesser degree. The same categories of widening or narrowing of meaning as well as changes in connotation can be seen at work. The following examples are mainly drawn from Buck (1974) and Carstensen (1965). The meaning of some words has been extended in German: for instance, *Bestseller* can be applied to anything that sells well and not only to books; the word *Boy* has been extended from referring to a person, for example *Liftboy*, *Hotelboy*, to apply to things that can help the housewife, *Blumenboy*, *Schuhboy* (containers for flowers or shoes). In many cases these are brand names. On the other hand, the meaning of some words has been narrowed: *Ticket*, for instance, applies mostly to air-tickets, although it can be used for entrance tickets. A narrowing in meaning normally takes place where there are other native words available in the same semantic area. The importation of English words helps to provide separate lexical items for specialized meanings, for instance *Song* 'a satirical song', *Hit* 'a successful piece of music', *Schlager* 'something popular at the moment, a song, film or play'. Coers (1979) investigated this word field and found a tendency for *Song* to be used not only for songs dealing with themes of politics and social critique but also for popular or sentimental songs. *Job* in German has come to mean 'temporary, short-term employment' and stands in opposition to *Beruf* and *Stelle*. The connotations of English loans in German may be different from in English. The adjective *clever* usually has a pejorative sense of being 'cunning'. Sometimes the change in meaning does not seem to fit into any category, for example *der Flirt* in German is the action of 'flirting' and does not refer to a person. The term *in sein* means not simply 'to be fashionable', for example *Auslandsreisen sind jetzt in* 'Foreign trips are now "in"', but also 'to know about what is fashionable and "in"', for example *Ihr seid in, wenn* . . . 'You are "in", if . . .'.

10.2.4.2   Changes in meaning in specialist languages

One method of providing different vocabulary for specialist languages is not to introduce new word forms but to give new meanings to already existing words. This can take the form of polysemy, one word developing several different meanings, or the metaphorical use of words: for instance, *Wurzel* 'root (of a plant or vegetable)' is also applied in mathematics to the root of a number and in linguistics to the root of a word: *der Stollen* is applied to a mining gallery, a special Christmas cake with layers, the calkin of a horse-shoe, the beginning of a stanza, the bar on a football boot to prevent slipping and a tanning tool. Transference of meaning can be well illustrated from the traditional art of tanning with natural agents in which the words *Satz*, *Hut*, *sauer*, *Speckstreifen* and *erschrecken* have their own special meaning. *Satz* is the complete load or filling of the tanner's wooden vat. *Hut* is the thick layer of fermented tanning-bark. After water has been poured on to this the resultant mixture ferments and becomes *sauer*. If a hide were put in a mixture of tanning-bark too soon the outer edges would become full of tan which would not penetrate to the inside whereas in the middle raw hide would remain, the so-called *Speckstreifen*, stopping penetration into the centre of the hide, this last process being known as *erschrecken*. Sometimes transferences of meaning show a sense of humour at work. In printing an omitted word is called *eine Leiche*, whereas one that is set twice is called *eine Hochzeit*. Of two curved pan-tiles whose ends overlap the top one is *der Mönch* and the underneath one *die Nonne*. *Der Mönch* is also used for a young stag without antlers and for an apparatus to regulate the flow of water that has been treated for sewage while *die Nonne* is used for a night moth (*Lymantria monacha*). Transference of meaning is mostly found among older crafts. Any ambiguity which might arise from the several meanings taken on by one word is nearly always resolved by the context.

A more intentional development is the coining of new words with specific meanings for specialist languages. This can take the form of the use of native words and stems, for example in geology *auskolken* 'to erode, undermine', *Fernling* 'residual hill in a remote unreduced watershed area', *Härtling* 'residual protuberance (of resistant rock)' and *Kolk* 'pothole (in a river or glacier)'.

Specialist languages, especially those dealing with technology, have to be very precise about the use and meaning of a word which becomes a technical term in a particular field. This means that a difference develops between the more vague sense of a word in everyday language and its precise use as a technical term. This shift in meaning is known in German as *Terminologisierung*, for which we propose 'terminological specialization'. Examples of this would be *abseits*, which is used for 'remote, far from' but which in football is 'offside, i.e. if a player has less than two opposing players between himself and the goal'; *Teilchen* in physics, which means 'particle' as against 'small piece (of something)' in everyday usage; also in physics *Rauschen* means 'noise' and can be accompanied by adjectives such as *weißes* or *thermisches* to designate a specific kind of noise, whereas in everyday usage it can mean 'roar, rustle, etc.'; and *Engländer* as a technical term means 'adjustable spanner, monkey wrench' but 'Englishman' in ordinary usage.

Many specialist languages make extensive use of loan words. Which language words are borrowed from depends on the specialism concerned. For instance, the craft of glove-making uses primarily French loans: *depsieren* 'to measure out', *ridellieren* 'to measure', *etabieren* 'to test against', *debordieren* 'to stretch, pull out', *die Ridelle* 'unit of measurement', *fantieren* 'to stamp out the pattern form', *Ampon, Pli, Fente, Rebra* 'pieces of cut-out leather'. The world of pop-music, on the other hand, uses English loans: *Dance-Charts, Reggae-Liveband, Dance-floor-Experiment, Top-Single, gerappt und gescratcht, Hardcore-Sound, auf dem Cover des Onyx-Albums, Rock-Fans, Soundsamples, Groove, Song* (from the magazine *Bravo*, 19 August 1993, 63f.). The language of fashion uses both French, *Prêt-à-porter, Kollektionen, Haute Couture*, and English loans, *Cape, Cardiganjacken, Outfits, Trenchcoats, Dior-Look Tweed, Jersey*. Many of these imported words are used to designate new objects, processes and concepts.

Linked with the borrowing of words is the adoption or common development of internationalisms, words which have a similar form and meaning in several European languages. Many of these are formed from Greek and Latin stems, for example *Allophon*, *Appendizitis*, *Äquinoktium*, *digital*, *Dinosaurier*, *erodieren*, *Fauna*, *Morphem*, *Phonem*.

SELECT BIBLIOGRAPHY AND FURTHER READING

Augst, G. (1977) 'Fremdwort – fremdes Wort', in *Sprachnorm und Sprachwandel*, Wiesbaden: Athenaion, pp. 61–123.

Betz, W. (1974) 'Lehnwörter und Lehnprägungen im Vor- und Frühdeutschen', in F. Maurer, and H. Rupp (eds) *Deutsche Wortgeschichte*, vol. 1, Berlin: de Gruyter, pp. 135–63.

Braun, P. (ed.) (1979) *Fremdwort-Diskussion*, Heidelberg: Francke.

—— (1987) *Tendenzen in der deutschen Gegenwartssprache. Sprachvarietäten*, 2nd edn, Stuttgart: Kohlhammer.

Buck, T. (1974) ' "Selfmade-English": Semantic Peculiarities of English Loan Material in Contemporary German', *Forum for Modern Language Studies*, 10: 130–46.

Carstensen, B. (1965) *Englische Einflüsse auf die deutsche Sprache nach 1945*, Heidelberg: Winter.

—— (1971) *Spiegel/Wörter: Spiegelworte*, Munich: Hueber.

—— (1980) 'Das Genus englischer Fremd- und Lehnwörter im Deutschen', in W. Viereck (ed.) *Studien zum Einfluß der englischen Sprache auf das Deutsche/Studies on the Influence of the English Language on German* (Tübinger Beiträge zur Linguistik, 132), Tübingen: Narr, pp. 37–75.

—— (1983) 'English Elements in the German Language: Their Treatment and Compilation a Dictionary of Anglicisms', in *Symposium zur Lexikographie, Kopenhagen 1982 = Germanistische Linguistik* 5–6/83, pp. 13–34.

—— (1984a) 'Wieder: die Engländerei in der deutschen Sprache', in B. Carstensen, F. Debus, H. Henne, P. von Polenz, D. Stellmacher and H. Weinrich (eds) *Die deutsche Sprache der Gegenwart. Vorträge gehalten auf der Tagung der Joachim Jungius-Gesellschaft der Wissenschaften Hamburg am 4. und 5. November 1983* (Veröffentlichung der Joachim-Jungius Gesellschaft der Wissenschaften, 51), Göttingen: Vandenhoeck & Ruprecht, pp. 43–57.

—— (1984b) 'Wörter des Jahres 1984', *Sprache und Literatur in Wissenschaft und Unterricht*, 55: 3–12.

—— (1985) 'Wörter des Jahres 1985', *Sprache und Literatur in Wissenschaft und Unterricht*, 56: 110–18.

Carstensen, B. and Hengstenberg, P. (1983) 'Zur Rezeption von Anglizismen im Deutschen', in H. E. Wiegand (ed.) *Germanistische Linguistik* 1–4/82 (*Studien zur neuhochdeutschen Lexikographie III*), Hildesheim: Olms, pp. 67–118.

Coers, A. (1979) 'Song – Lied – Schlager – Chanson: semantische Probleme', *Muttersprache*, 89. 208–26.

Cruse, D. A. (1986) *Lexical Semantics*, Cambridge: Cambridge University Press.

Dalcher, P. (1986) 'Anglicisms in Swiss German: The Evaluation by Computer of a Survey Conducted in 1964/5', in W. Viereck, and W.-D. Bald (eds) *English in Contact with Other Languages*, Budapest: Akademiai Kiado, pp. 179–206.

*DWB*² (1965ff.) *Deutsches Wörterbuch von Jacob und Wilhelm Grimm*, revised by Akademie der Wissenschaften in Berlin and Göttingen, Leipzig: Hirzel.

Diersch, H. (1972) *Verben der Fortbewegung in der deutschen Sprache der Gegenwart* (Abhandlungen der sächsischen Akademie der Wissenschaften zu Leipzig, Philologisch-historische Klasse, 62, 3), Berlin: Akademie.

Dornseiff, F. (1970) *Der deutsche Wortschatz nach Sachgruppen*, 7th edn, Berlin: de Gruyter.

Drosdowski, G., Köster, R., Müller, W. and Schrupp, C. (1976–81) *Duden: Das große Wörterbuch der deutschen Sprache*, 6 vols, Mannheim: Bibliographisches Institut.

Duden 8 (1986) *Sinn- und sachverwandte Wörter. Wörterbuch für den treffenden Ausdruck*, 2nd edn, ed. W. Müller, Mannheim: Dudenverlag.

Duden 10 (1985) *Das Bedeutungswörterbuch. Wortbildung und Wortschatz*, 2nd edn, ed. W. Müller, Mannheim: Dudenverlag.

Fink, H. (1980) 'Zur Aussprache von Angloamerikanischem im Deutschen', in W. Viereck (ed.) (1980) *Studien zum Einfluß der englischen Sprache auf das Deutsche/Studies on the Influence of the English Language on German* (Tübinger Beiträge zur Linguistik, 132), Tübingen: Narr, pp. 109–83.

Fleischer, W. (1982) *Phraseologie der deutschen Gegenwartssprache*, Leipzig: Bibliographisches Institut.

Fluck, H.-R. (1976) *Fachsprachen*, Munich: Franke, Uni-Taschenbücher 483.

—— (1984) *Fachdeutsch in Naturwissenschaft und Technik*, Heidelberg: Groos.

Gipper, H. (1984) 'Der Inhalt des Wortes und die Gliederung der Sprache', in *Duden 4. Grammatik*, Mannheim: Dudenverlag pp. 502–58.

Glück, H. and Sauer, W. W. (1990) *Gegenwartsdeutsch*, Stuttgart: Metzler.

Hannah, J. A. (1988) ' "Trench", "Dressmann", and "Pullunder": Some Analogy Processes in the Coining of Pseudo-Anglicisms', *German Life and Letters*, 42 :60–71.

Haugen, E. (1950) 'The Analysis of Linguistic Borrowing', *Language*, 26: 210–31.

Hundsnurscher, F. (1971) *Neuere Methoden der Semantik. Eine Einführung anhand deutscher Beispiele* (Germanistische Arbeitshefte, 2), Tübingen: Niemeyer.

Ising, E., Kraus, J., Ludwig, K.-D., and Schnerrer, R. (1988) *Die Sprache in unserem Leben*, Leipzig: Bibliographisches Institut.

Kirkness, A. (1984) 'Aliens, Denizens, Hybrids and Natives: Foreign Influence on the Etymological Structure of German Vocabulary', in C. V. J. Russ (ed.) *Foreign Influences on German*, Dundee: Lochee, pp. 1–26.

Lehnert, M. (1986) 'The Anglo-American Influence on the Language of the German Democratic Republic', in W. Viereck, and W.-D. Bald (eds) *English in Contact with Other Languages*, Budapest: Akademiai Kiado. 129–57.

Leisi, E. (1971) *Der Wortinhalt: Seine Struktur im Deutschen und Englischen*,

Heidelberg: Quelle & Meyer.

Lyons, J. (1977) *Semantics*, 2 vols, Cambridge: Cambridge University Press.

Mackensen, L. (1971) *Die deutsche Sprache in unserer Zeit*, Heidelberg: Quelle & Meyer.

Müller, W. (1980) 'Wörter im Wandel oder Goethe noch ohne "Erlebnis" ', *Bücherkommentare*, 3, 4, 50–4.

—— (1982) 'Neue Wörter und Wortbedeutungen', in *Meyers Neues Lexikon, Jahrbuch 1982*, Wuppertal: Brockhaus, pp. 281–3.

—— (1983) 'Neue Wörter und Wortbedeutungen', in *Meyers Neues Lexikon, Jahrbuch 1983*, Wuppertal: Brockhaus, pp. 282–4.

Oeldorf, H. (1990) 'Von "Aids" bis "Yuppification" – Englische Lehnwörter in der Wochenzeitung "Die Zeit" ', *Muttersprache*, 100: 38–52.

Oksaar, E. (1971) 'Das heutige Deutsch – ein Spiegel sozialer Wandlungen', in H. Eggers, J. Erken, H. Newmann, H. Steger and Hugo Moser (eds) *Sprache und Gesellschaft* (Sprache und Gegenwart, 13), Düsseldorf: Schwann, pp. 279–94.

Ortner, H. (1981) *Wortschatz der Mode* (Sprache der Gegenwart, 52), Düsseldorf: Schwann.

Ortner, L. (1982) *Wortschatz der Pop-/Rockmusik* (Sprache der Gegenwart, 53), Düsseldorf: Schwann.

Osman, N. (1971) *Kleines Lexikon untergegangener Wörter*, Munich: Beck.

Palmer, F. (1981) *Semantics: a New Outline*, 2nd edn, Cambridge: Cambridge University Press.

Paul, H. (1920) *Prinzipien der Sprachgeschichte*, repr. 1968, Tübingen: Niemeyer.

—— (1981) *Deutsches Wörterbuch*, 7th edn, revised by W. Betz, Tübingen: Niemeyer.

Polenz, P. von (1967a) 'Fremdwort und Lehnwort sprachwissenschaftlich betrachtet', *Muttersprache* 77: 65–80; repr. in P. Braun (ed.) *Fremdwort-Diskussion*. Heidelberg: Francke, 1979, pp. 9–31.

Polenz, P. von (1967b) 'Sprachpurismus und Nationalsozialismus', in P. Braun (ed.) *Germanistik – eine deutsche Wissenschaft*, Frankfurt-on-Main: Suhrkamp, pp. 111–65.

Porzig, W. (1950) *Das Wunder der Sprache*, 5th edn, Berne: Francke.

Rothacker, E. and Saile, G. (1986) *Ich weiß nicht was soll es bedeuten. Grundfragen der Semantik*, Opladen: Westdeutscher Verlag.

Schippan, T. (1992) *Lexikologie der deutschen Gegenwartssprache*, Tübingen: Niemeyer.

Schmidt, L. (ed.) (1973) *Wortfeldforschung*, Darmstadt: Wissenschafliche Buchgesellschaft.

Schulz/Basler (1977–78) eds A. Kirkness, E. Link, I. Nortmeyer, G. Strauß, assisted by P. Grebe, *Deutsches Fremdwörterbuch*, vol. 4, Berlin; vol. 1, A–K, ed. H. Schulz, 1913; vol. 2, L–P, ed. O. Basler, 1942; vols 3–6, ed. A. Kirkness *et al.*; Q–R, 1977; S, 1977–8; T, 1979–80; U–Z, 1981.

Seebold, E. (1981) *Etymologie: eine Einführung am Beispiel der deutschen Sprache*, Munich: Beck.

Siegl, E. (1989) *Duden Ost-Duden West: zur Sprache in Deutschland seit 1945* (Sprache der Gegenwart, 76), Düsseldorf: Schwann.

Sommerfeldt, K.-E. (1988) *Entwicklungstendenzen in der deutschen Gegenwartssprache*, Leipzig: Bibliographisches Institut.

Stanforth, A. W. (1968) 'Deutsch-englischer Lehnwortaustausch', in W. Mitzka (ed.) *Wortgeographie und Gesellschaft: festgabe für L. E. Schmitt zum 60. Geburtstag am 10. Februar 1968*, Berlin: de Gruyter, pp. 526–60.
—— (1991) 'English Linguistic Influences on Post-war German', in E. Kolinsky (ed.) *The Federal Republic of Germany: The End of an Era*, Oxford: Berg, pp. 333–40.
Stickel, G. (1984) 'Anmerkungen zur Anglizismusforschung', in C. V. J. Russ (ed.) *Foreign Influences on German*, Dundee: Lochee, pp. 38–57.
Strauß, G., Haß, U. and Harras, G. (1989) *Brisante Wörter von Agitation bis Zeitgeist: ein Lexikon zum öffentlichen Sprachgebrauch* (Schriften des Instituts für deutsche Sprache, 2), Berlin: de Gruyter.
Ullmann, S. (1962) *An Introduction to the Science of Meaning*, Oxford: Basil Blackwell.
Viereck, K. (1986) 'The Influence of English on Austrian German', in W. Viereck and W.-D. Bald (eds.) *English in Contact with Other Languages*, Budapest: Akademiai Kiado, pp. 159–77.
Viereck, W. (ed.) (1980a) *Studien zum Einfluß der englischen Sprache auf das Deutsche/Studies on the Influence of the English Language on German* (Tübinger Beiträge zur Linguistik, 132), Tübingen: Narr.
—— (1980b) 'Empirische Untersuchungen insbesondere zum Verständnis und Gebrauch von Anglizismen im Deutschen', in W. Viereck (ed.) *Studien zum Einfluß der englischen Sprache auf das Deutsche/ Studies on the Influence of the English Language on German* (Tübinger Beiträge zur Linguistik, 132), Tübingen: Narr, pp. 237–321.
—— (1984) 'Britisches Englisch und Amerikanisches Englisch/Deutsch', in W. Besch, O. Reichmann and S. Sonderegger (eds) *Sprachgeschichte: ein Handbuch zur Geschichte der deutschen Sprache und ihrer Erforschung*, vol. 1, Berlin: de Gruyter, pp. 938–48.
—— (1986) 'The Influence of English on German in the Past and in the Federal Republic of Germany', in W. Viereck and W.-D. Bald (eds) *English in Contact with Other Languages*, Budapest: Akademiai Kiado, pp. 107–28.
Viereck, W. and Bald, W.-D. (eds.) (1986) *English in Contact with Other Languages*, Budapest: Akademiai Kiado.
Wehrle, M. and Eggers, H. (1961) *Deutscher Wortschatz*, Stuttgart: Klett.
Weinreich, U. (1953) *Languages in Contact*, The Hague: Mouton.
Wotjak, G. (1971) *Untersuchung zur Struktur der Bedeutung*, Munich: Hueber.

Index